The Agrarian Sociology of Ancient Civilizations represents a sustained historical synthesis of a type unlike anything else in Weber's writings. The work began as an essay on agrarian relations in the ancient world published in 1897, which Weber rewrote in a massively expanded form over four months of intensive creative work during 1908 and which was finally published in 1909. This work was one of the first examples of the conscious use of Weber's new methodology – including the notion of the 'ideal type' – in relation to historical research.

Weber starts with a general introduction that explores the necessary concepts for relating 'economic theory' and 'ancient society'. He then proceeds to a chronologically ordered study of the agrarian character of the socio-economic structures of Mesopotamia and Egypt – the two great riverine civilizations of High Antiquity; of Hebrew society in Israel, from its tribal to its royal forms; of the classical city-states of Greece; of the imperial Hellenistic realms which succeeded them in the Near East; and, finally, of the evolution of Roman society, from the Republic to the Empire. The volume concludes with a groundbreaking panoramic essay, first published in 1896, where Weber rooted the decline of Rome in the agrarian situation and the 'deurbanisation' of the Empire.

MAX WEBER was born in 1864 in Erfurt and was educated at Heidelberg, Strasbourg, Göttingen, and Berlin where he studied law, economics, history and philosophy. He held chairs in Political Economy at Freiburg and Heidelberg. From 1904 he edited the *Archiv für Sozialwissenschaft und Sozialpolitik*. He died in Munich in 1920. His many publications include *The Methodology of the Social Sciences* (1904), *The Protestant Ethic and the Spirit of Capitalism* (1904–5), *Economy and Society* (1921), and *General Economic History* (1923).

VERSO
CLASSICS

The last few decades have seen an immense outpouring of works of theory and criticism, but, as the number of titles has increased dramatically, it has become more and more difficult to find one's way around this vast body of literature and to distinguish between those works of real and enduring value and those of a more ephemeral nature. The Verso Classics series will rise to the challenge by taking stock of the last few decades of contemporary critical thought and reissuing, in an elegant paperback format and at affordable prices, those books which genuinely constitute original and important intellectual contributions.

Many of these works are currently out of print or difficult to obtain: Verso Classics will bring them back into the public domain, building a collection which will become the 'essential left library'.

The Agrarian Sociology
of Ancient Civilizations

MAX WEBER

Translated by R.I. Frank

VERSO

London · New York

901. 91
W384a

First published as 'Agrarverhältnisse im Altertum,' in *Handwörterbuch der Staatwissenschaften*, 1909; and 'Die sozialen Gründe des Untergangs der antiken Kultur', in *Die Wahrheit* May 1896. Republished in Max Weber, *Gesammelte Aufsätze zur Sozial- und Wirtschaftsgeschichte*, Tübingen 1924.

First English edition published by NLB, 1976
This edition published by Verso 1998

© Verso: 1998
All rights reserved

Verso
UK: 6 Meard Street, London W1V 3HR
USA: 29 West 35th Street, New York, NY 10001–2291

Verso is the imprint of New Left Books

British Library Cataloguing in Publication Data

Weber, Max, *1864–1920*
    The agrarian sociology of ancient civilizations.
    1. Ancient world. Economic conditions
    I. Title
    330.93

ISBN 1–85984–275–5

US Library of Congress Cataloging-in-Publication Data

Weber, Max, 1864–1920.
    [Selections, English. 1988]
    The agrarian sociology of ancient civilizations / Max Weber: translated by R.I. Frank.
        p.   cm.
    "First published as 'Agrarverhältnisse im Altertum,' in Handwörterbuch der Staatwissenschaften, 1909; and 'Die sozialen Gründe des Untergangs der antiken Kultur,' in 'Die Wahrheit, May 1896' – T.p. verso.
    Reprint. Originally published: London: NLB; Atlantic Highlands: Humanities Press, 1976.
    Contents: Translator's introduction — Economic theory and ancient society — The agrarian history of the major centres of ancient civilization — The social causes of the decline of ancient civilization.
    Includes bibliographies and indexes.
    ISBN 0–86091–938–2 (pbk.): $23.95
    1. Economic history — To 500.   2. Agriculture — History.   3. Social history — To 500.   4. Civilization, Ancient.   5. Middle East — Economic conditions.   I. Title.
HC31.W42213   1988

Typeset in Intertype Caledonia
Printed in Great Britain by Biddles Ltd, Guildford

Contents

Translator's Introduction

'In science, each of us knows that what he has accomplished will be antiquated in ten, twenty, fifty years'.[1] Such was Max Weber's somewhat poignant view of a scholar's work, but in fact the fate of his own writings shows that he was too optimistic about the advance of scholarship. The present book, in particular, was not studied or used for over fifty years. As late as 1965 a distinguished ancient historian could call it 'still the most original and penetrating account ever written of Antiquity's social and economic development'.[2] Analysis had till then largely held the field. Now, however, there is a renewed interest in theory and synthesis, and this work should at last gain the audience it deserves. Readers will find here a remarkable survey of 3,000 years, one which traces the institutional framework within which political and intellectual developments took place. They will find more if they know something about the author and his premises, methods, and purpose. What follows aims to give the essential information on these matters together with references for further study.

1. Author

Max Weber was born in 1864. His father was a wealthy lawyer and a leading member of the Imperial Parliament, so he grew up in Berlin and as a young man met many of the leading figures in German politics and scholarship. At the University of Berlin he studied law, writing his first dissertation on the mediaeval trading

1. H. Gerth and C. Mills (eds), *From Max Weber* (New York, 1946), p. 138.
2. A. Heuss, 'Max Weber's Bedeutung für die Geschichte des griechisch-romischen Altertums', *Historische Zeitschrift*, 201 (1965), pp. 529–56, at p. 538.

companies (1889)[3] and his second on Rome's land use system (1891).[4] Thus Weber qualified himself in both German and Roman law, an unusual feat in those days and an early indication of his independence of traditional disciplinary boundaries. The second dissertation is in many ways a key to Weber's studies. It is based on complete mastery of the primary sources, in this case mainly a collection of abstruse Latin documents on surveying; here we see Weber's link with the German school of legal historians who used philological methods to interpret legal sources and to trace the development of institutions. Weber in fact had close ties with the greatest member of this school, Theodor Mommsen, 'prince of philologists'. At Weber's first doctoral examination Mommsen questioned him closely on one of his theses, then concluded by saying that although still unconvinced he would offer no further objections. 'Younger men often have ideas which at first seem unacceptable. . . But when the time comes for me to go, there is no one to whom I would rather entrust my work than the much esteemed Max Weber.'[5]

Now the historical school was characterized by Savigny's famous argument against legal reform, and by his view of social change as 'organic', rooted in national character. Hence its members tended to ignore classes and conflicts of interest.[6] Even Mommsen's legal works show this trait, the more noteworthy since his personal views in politics were quite dissimilar.

But Weber's 1891 work shows the influence of a very different approach. After registering his great debt to Mommsen he goes on to say that he had studied Roman agrarian institutions by first looking at their practical importance for particular interest groups, a method he had learned from his teacher, August Meitzen.[7] The latter, to whom in fact the work was dedicated, had written a

3. *Zur Geschichte der Handelgesellschaften im Mittelalter* (Stuttgart, 1889), reprinted in *Gesammelte Aufsatze zur Sozial- und Wirtschaftsgeschichte* (Tübingen, 1924), pp. 312–443.
4. *Die römische Agrargeschichte in ihrer Bedeutung für das Staats- und Privatrecht* (Stuttgart, 1891; rptd. Amsterdam, 1966).
5. Marianne Weber, *Max Weber: Ein Lebensbild* (Tübingen, 1926), p. 121; cf. P. Honigsheim, *On Max Weber* (New York, 1968), p. 45; 'Mommsen was said to have tried to get him a chair in ancient history or Roman law.'
6. G. Gooch, *History and Historians in the Nineteenth Century*, 2nd ed. (London, 1952), pp. 39–49.
7. *Die römische* . . . (above, n. 4), p. 5; cf. Honigsheim (above, n. 5), pp. 53, 144.

major work on the land use systems of Celts, Slavs, and Germans. Again and again he explained the appearance and character of agricultural – i.e. economic – institutions by the interplay of political and social factors. For example, he argued that among the Celts the influence of Christian monasticism caused sedentary agriculture to become predominant, and as a result of this Celtic chiefs became manorial lords. Again: he traced the origin of the Russian mir from the taxation system introduced by the Mongols. In such analyses the political factor tended to dominate the economic and intellectual.[8]

During the next few years this tendency to emphasize political factors grew more pronounced. Weber's thinking centred on the struggle for power. He made this plain in the inaugural lecture he delivered in 1895 at Freiburg University on assuming the chair of economics: 'Even behind the processes of economic development we find the struggle for power, and when the nation's power is at stake this immediately becomes the determining factor in shaping our economic policies. The study of economics is a political study, and it serves in the formation of policy – not the policy of whatever class or clique holds power, but rather the policy which serves the permanent power interests of the nation.'[9] Soon after Weber told delegates to a political convention that 'everyone in politics must be free of illusions and must keep in mind one fundamental reality – the inescapable, unending struggle on earth of group against group'.[10]

Such statements have been interpreted as reflections of Weber's oedipal hostility to his father and everything he stood for. This psychological explanation can be supported by a good deal of biographic data, and indeed the harshness of his views may have been connected with the severe inner conflicts he experienced during these years.[11] The aspect which I should prefer to emphasize here is Weber's self-consciousness as a member of a particular class. His inaugural lecture makes this explicit – and rather unconventional – confession: 'I am a member of the bourgeoisie,

8. P. Honigsheim, 'Max Weber as Historian of Agriculture and Rural Life', *Agricultural History*, 23 (1949), pp. 179–213, esp. pp. 201–4.

9. M. Weber, *Gesammelte politische Schriften*, 3rd ed. by J. Winckelmann (Tübingen, 1971), p. 14.

10. *Ibid.*, p. 29 (from speech of 1896 at the founding convention of the National Social Party).

11. A. Mitzman, *The Iron Cage* (New York, 1970), pp. 82–4, 136–43.

I was reared in its values and ideals, and I identify myself with it.'[12]

This aspect is crucial because it is a link with the two concerns which soon came to dominate Weber's thought on politics and history, concerns which are of central importance in the present work: capitalism and rationalism.

The connection between capitalism and the modern bourgeoisie is well understood today by all. However in Imperial Germany the matter was more problematic because the issue between feudalism and industrialism had not yet been settled. The Junkers had gained a new lease of rule with Bismarck, and remained a dominant force until the fall of the monarchy. Because of Weber's commitment to national power and his own political feelings he was necessarily strongly in favour of new leadership and new policies. Hence the great political struggles of the period forced him to think constantly of the relation between capitalism and his values as a member of the bourgeoisie and as a German.[13]

At this point, however, Weber added a highly personal contribution: he insisted on the intimate connection between bourgeoisie, capitalism, and *rationalism*. In 1904 he published the first part of his famous study on the relation between Calvinism and capitalism, 'one of the few great historical interpretations that have posed a problem where once was universal agreement or a void', in which he argued that the drive for profit had sprung from Puritan morality, the heir of monastic asceticism.[14] In the same year Weber assumed joint responsibility for a leading journal of the social sciences and as a statement of editorial policy he published an extended essay on method, in which he argued for objectivity in scholarly work and for the exclusion of value judgements. In his own work during the remaining years of his life he sought to maintain this ideal, devising concepts and models bereft of all metaphysical associations. A famous example is his definition of the state as a political institution which claims for itself a monopoly of physical coercion for the enforcement of its orders. The aim of Weber's work was to develop a whole set of value-free,

12. *Ibid.*, p. 20.
13. W. Mommsen, *Max Weber und die deutsche Politik 1890–1920* (Tübingen, 1950), pp. 103–52.
14. C. Antoni, *From History to Sociology*, tr. H. White (Detroit, 1959), p. 147; but cf. (*contra*) R. Bendix and G. Roth, *Scholarship and Partisanship* (Berkeley and Los Angeles, 1971), pp. 305–6.

rationally conceived concepts for the study of society to take the place of the traditional ones.[15] Along with this went a series of studies on the development of law, religion, and society – together constituting 'a history of rationalization in the political, religious, economic, and legal institutions of man'.[16]

Here it is appropriate to note that this emphasis on rationalism began in 1904, just after Weber had recovered from a severe mental illness which afflicted him for six years.[17] It seems a plausible inference that his struggle to regain sanity led him to centre his values about rationalism and also made him unusually sensitive to irrational tendencies in himself and his society.

This emphasis on rationalism helps us place Weber in the context of his times. The German academic community during 1890–1920 was divided sharply between supporters of traditionalism and modernity, and Weber became the leading modernist.[18] From this came many distinctive features of the present work – its attention to the struggle between secularism and theocracy, and its emphasis on bureaucracy (which Weber regarded as the inevitable – though personally distasteful – corollary of rational government). It also explains such particulars as the fact that he stops to condemn vigorously anti-Semitism, which was already an important element of irrational, anti-modernist thought.[19]

Weber seems to have seen the historical tendency towards rationalism and rational organization as inevitable, and in some way he identified himself with studying this tendency and its progress. One consequence was that in 1905 the outbreak of the first revolution in Russia evoked passionate interest in him. He taught himself the Russian language in order to follow events in Russian newspapers. For months he read, discussed, and wrote about the struggle for constitutional government there.[20]

To this period, too, belongs a series of fundamental articles on the character and methods of the cultural sciences. Again and again, Weber returns to the criteria which are crucial for him:

15. Marianne Weber (above, n. 5), pp. 690–4.
16. Mitzman (above, n. 11), p. 180.
17. *Ibid.*, pp. 167–80.
18. F. Ringer, *The Decline of the German Mandarins* (Cambridge, Mass., 1969), pp. 128–99.
19. *Ibid.*, pp. 135–9; cf. F. Stern, *The Politics of Cultural Despair* (Berkeley and Los Angeles, 1961), pp. 61–4, 139–43.
20. Marianne Weber (above, n. 5), pp. 342–3.

rationalism and objectivity. His basic conclusion was that the methods and conclusions of the cultural sciences must be subjected to the most exacting tests of objectivity, but the problems studied and even the material exploited must inevitably be defined by the student's own values. 'Empirical reality becomes "culture" to us because and insofar as we relate it to value ideas. It includes those segments and only those segments of reality which have become significant to us because of this value relevance. Only a small portion of existing concrete reality is coloured by our value-conditioned interest and it alone is significant to us.'[21]

This is an important aspect of Weber's thinking. He took it as axiomatic that the historian studies *what interests him*, and his own researches exemplify this. That is why the present work gives so much attention to transfer of land, various forms of contract, and other phenomena which interested Weber – for the light they shed on different economic systems. Likewise this explains the frequent analogies with Russian institutions – which Weber had just been studying. At the same time, however, Weber insisted that the historian must pursue the answers to his questions with every resource available and must, above all, define clearly the basic concepts he uses. Just because he accepted the subjective character of the scholar's questions he insisted that the answers given must be based on objective and critical use of all available evidence.

In 1908 Weber gave concrete proof of his interest in objective research. The Association for the Study of Social Policy, of which he was a leading member, had decided to conduct an extensive survey of the effects of factory labour on industrial workers. Weber took over the project and made it a model of its kind. Instead of aiming to produce a descriptive study he focused on basic problems and their causes. Even more important, he devised a much improved type of questionnaire and then – for the first time in Germany – insisted that it be answered by the subjects themselves, the workers. Weber himself published a series of articles on the interrelations between the psychological and phy-

21. From ' "Objectivity" in Social Science and Social Policy' (1904), translated in E. Shils and H. Finch, translators, *Max Weber: The Methodology of the Social Sciences* (Glencoe, 1949), pp. 50–112, at p. 76; cf. H. Hughes, *Consciousness and Society* (New York, 1958), pp. 300–10.

siological aspects of factory work, based on his own synthesis of relevant work in the fields of psychology, medicine, and psychiatry. Then he himself spent several months analysing the accounts and production figures of a textile mill for the project. The result was a pathbreaking study, in many ways a remarkable forerunner of modern social surveys.[22]

This study of modern factory work engrossed Weber's energies during the summer and autumn of 1908. No sooner was it completed than he plunged into intensive work on an entirely different subject, agricultural conditions in Antiquity. The editors of an encyclopedia had asked Weber for an article on this subject because of his 1891 dissertation on Roman agriculture, but in fact Weber gave them something very different, a book-length study of the social and economic system of the ancient world.[23] That work, translated for the first time, is the substance of the present volume.

Weber was then at the height of his creative powers. There is no surer proof of this than that he wrote the work in four months.[24] It was published in 1909, and internal evidence indicates that Weber neither revised nor even corrected it, despite his mention of seeing proofs. As a result there are certain faults of style and organization, due to haste; for example, his remarks on the comparative method – a crucial matter! – come as an afterthought at the end of the bibliography.

On the other hand the work gains greatly in unity. From first to last Weber concentrates his focus on a few basic themes, and throughout he keeps his main purpose clearly in view. These aspects will be discussed below.

1909 marks the beginning of the third and final phase of Weber's career, in which he devoted himself fully to sociology. Weber had originally been trained in law and was then called to Freiburg and Heidelberg as an economist. His work was in the tradition of the historical school of economics, and in fact in 1909, when

22. A. Obershall, *Empirical Social Research in Germany, 1848–1914* (Paris and The Hague, 1965), pp. 114–31.
23. 'Agrarverhältnisse im Altertum', *Handwörterbuch der Staatswissenshaften* (3rd ed. 1909), vol. 1, pp. 52–188, reprinted in Max Weber, *Gesammelte Aufsatze zur Sozial- und Wirtschaftsgeschichte* (Tübingen, 1924), pp. 1–288; cf. Marianne Weber (above, n. 5), pp. 343–4, and G. Roth, 'Introduction to Max Weber', *Economy and Society*, ed. G. Roth and C. Wittich, 3 vols. (New York, 1968), vol. 1, xliv–li.
24. Marianne Weber, foreword to *Gesammelte Aufsatze . . .* (above, n. 23), p. iii.

the Heidelberg Academy was founded, he was elected as an historian. Sociology was then unacknowledged as an academic discipline: 'Although in Heidelberg at that time many things were considered from the standpoint of sociology, the science of society as such did not appear in the college catalogue.'[25]

From 1909, however, Weber was actively engaged in a series of projects designed to establish sociology as an autonomous discipline. In that year he accepted direction of the *Handbook of Social Economy*, a series of monographs designed to give an outline of the social sciences. Weber himself wrote a general introduction to the series; this is the massive work now called *Economy and Society*. At the same time he supervised two team projects and also led in founding the German Sociological Society, of which he became organizing secretary. Until his death in 1920 these responsibilities, along with political commitments, occupied Weber entirely.[26]

For our purposes, therefore, we need not concern ourselves with this final, sociological phase of Weber's career. The present work is historical in scope, and in what follows Weber's premises, methods, and aims as an historian will be our concern.

2. *Premises and Methods*

Three intellectual traditions shaped Weber's thinking: historicism, hermeneutics, realpolitik. Let us consider each.

(a) Towards the end of his long life Friedrich Meinecke recalled how he first came to grasp the central doctrine of historicism, individuality. As a university student he attended the lectures on historical method by Johann Droysen, and on one occasion heard this: 'If we call everything that a single person is and has and produces A, this consists of a+x, where a includes all that comes to him from outward circumstances (his country, his race, his period and so on), and the minute x his own contribution, the work of his own free will. But however small (nearly to vanishing point) this x may be, it is of infinite value, and from the moral

25. Honigsheim (above, n, 5), p. 58; cf. pp. 46, 61–8 (economist), and Marianne Weber (above, n. 5), p. 430.
26. Marianne Weber (above, n. 5), pp. 423–9; cf. G. Roth (above, n. 23), pp. lvi-lx.

and human point of view, the only thing of value. The colours, brush and canvas used by Raphael were made of materials that he had not created, and he had learnt how to use them for drawing and painting from such and such masters; the idea of the Virgin, saints and angels had been taken over from the Church's tradition; and such and such a convent engaged him to paint a picture for a particular sum of money. But the fact that such an occasion, such materials and technical conditions, such traditional models were used to create the marvels of the Sistine Chapel, shows the infinite worth of the infinitesimal x in the formula $A = a + x$.'

For Meinecke this was the key, 'this secret of personality, which forms the basis of all historical achievement'.[27] Many years later, when describing the origins of historicism, he remained true to this conception: 'The essence of historicism is the substitution of a process of *individualising* observation for a *generalising* view of human forces in history.'[28]

Note the opposition made explicit by 'substitution'. Historicism arose as an alternative to philosophic and positivistic systems. In this respect Weber was thoroughly historicist, for he rejected any theory based on evolutionary stages or metaphysical connections. Thus his friend Honigsheim noted that in matters relating to philosophy and epistemology 'the man whom Weber thought of as having a position at odds with his own was Hegel'.[29]

However this emphasis on individuality had led to an impasse by Weber's time: the mass of information made available by organized collection and analysis of sources had become so great that the need for guide lines in selection was ever more apparent. Many could find no rational solution, among them even Theodor Mommsen. In an address of 1874 he distinguished between the critical study of sources and the 'pragmatic writing' of history: the former proceeded on the basis of reason and science, but the latter was a matter of intuition and inborn talent. 'The stroke which forges a thousand links, the insight into the uniqueness of men and peoples, evinces such high genius as defies all teaching

27. Quoted by C. Hinrichs in his 'Introduction' to F. Meinecke, tr. J. Reynolds (London, 1972), pp. xxi-xxii. (I use the more usual form, historicism, despite the title given this work.)

28. *Ibid.*, p. lv.

29. Honigsheim (above, n. 5), p. 14.

and all learning. The historian has perhaps greater affinity with the artist than with the scholar.'[30]

Such a conclusion, however, could not satisfy historicists, if for no other reason than that their positivist critics claimed the authority of science. In fact during 1880–1910 there was a remarkably productive debate on the autonomous aims and character of the cultural – as opposed to natural – sciences, history in particular.[31] That debate need not be reviewed here. It will suffice to consider the arguments of Eduard Meyer, partly because in a long essay he summed up the essence of historicist thought as of 1902, but mainly because Weber wrote a long critique of this essay in which he indicated clearly his own relationship to historicism.

Meyer begins in orthodox fashion by distinguishing sharply between the general and the particular: laws and concepts are the province of anthropology and sociology, whereas history deals with individual and unique events.[32] Each event, furthermore, is caused in the first instance by a decision, an act of will by an individual: 'The Second Punic War began because of a decision made by Hannibal.'[33] Finally, the result of such a decision is unpredictable and even in retrospect cannot be explained in terms of cause and effect; at any moment in history innumerable factors interact, and the ultimate resultant of this interaction is determined by chance. Enlargement of the scope of history to include a greater diversity of factors leads to descriptions which are more inclusive but still not really explanatory: 'A causal connection between the various causal chains which interact in the historical process can never be established; . . . in the real world chance determines everything.'[34] Thus, chance determined that Philip II and Mary would not have a child, as a result of which Elizabeth I became queen and England was led to oppose the papacy and embrace Protestantism. Again, chance alone made possible Bismarck's entire political career, for he entered the Prussian legislature as substitute for a deputy who happened to fall ill.[35]

30. Th. Mommsen, 'Rectorial Address', in *The Varieties of History*, ed. F. Stern (Cleveland, 1956), p. 193.
31. Ringer (above, n. 18), pp. 315–34.
32. E. Meyer, 'Zur Theorie und Methodik der Geschichte' (1902), cited here from his *Kleine Schriften* (Halle, 1910), pp. 3–67, at pp. 5–6.
33. *Ibid.*, p. 22   34. *Ibid.*, pp. 24–5.
35. *Ibid.*, pp. 56–7 (Elizabeth I), 60 (Bismarck).

The historian's task, therefore, is to focus on the unique and characteristic, to describe events rather than propound theories. But this leads to 'the fundamental question': of the innumerable facts and events recorded in our sources, which are historical? Which, that is, deserve historical study? Meyer's answer is two-fold: (a) those are historical which have consequences (*was wirksam ist*), (b) among these – still a large mass – the historian will select according as the interest of his time centres on political or economic or religious or artistic matters. The cause of this interest need not be examined; it suffices that it exists.[36]

Now all these notions proceed from a fundamental premise about human personality and human society: that they are auto-nomous entities, motivated by ideas, and entirely free in their choice of means and ends. It is worth noting here that Meyer's discussion of free will begins with consideration of the decision 'whether I shall go out for a walk now', and then actually equates this with historical policies of Alexander, Frederick II, and Bismarck.[37] From this necessarily followed his emphasis on the individual, unique, and characteristic.

It is Meyer's fundamental premise which Weber, somewhat circuitously, carefully analyses and refutes. First he dismisses the idea that the historian's task is to focus on the unique: if so, then the study of Bismarck should begin with his thumbprint.[38]

Then he goes on to Meyer's definition of the historically signifi-cant: that which has had consequences. Not so, says Weber: many facts and events which have had no consequences are none the less important because they can be used to elaborate category concepts, 'heuristic instruments for the establishment of the generic "character" of certain artistic epochs or for the causal interpretation of concrete historical interconnections'. Particular facts must be integrated into concrete contexts shaped by these concepts. Only in this way does history become a 'science of reality'; the idea that the historian's task is simply to describe a pre-existent reality, to report the facts, is naïve and inaccurate.[39]

Weber's argument is based on a fundamental premise com-pletely opposed to Meyer's. Individuals, societies, and events are not regarded as unique entities, but rather representative of one or another general category, and each can be understood only by

36. *Ibid.*, pp. 43–5. 37. *Ibid.*, pp. 20–2.
38. Shils and Finch (above, n. 21), p. 129. 39. *Ibid.*, pp. 131–5.

reference to this category. Furthermore, an historical development ('interconnection') is not a fortuitous accident, but rather an example of a general type of process, and this development can only be explained ('causally interpreted') by reference to that general type.

Meyer had already dismissed any such concern with generalization by deriding the various laws and stages propounded by positivist historians striving to emulate natural science. Weber carefully distances himself from the positivists, basing his theory instead on the concept of 'objective possibility'; this had been first proposed in 1888 by a physiologist and was subsequently adopted by statisticians and criminologists. In an important passage Weber notes an affinity of history with criminology in that they are both basically concerned with human actions and social relationships.[40] To compare this with Meyer's grave analysis of the decision whether or not to go out for a walk, is to see in a flash Weber's greater depth and powers of synthesis.

As to objective possibility, its use solved the dilemma posed by Meyer and like-minded historicists: either determinism or indeterminism, either the rule of laws or the rule of chance. Instead, category concepts could be framed to correlate concrete effects with concrete causes, and do this without necessarily postulating the existence of uniformities. Anyone who has seen recent discussions of such problems as the relation between inequalities in income and cognitive skills will be aware of the scope of this type of analysis.[41] The essence of the matter is that the opposite of chance is not necessity but adequate causation, a relationship established as probable between certain conditions present in a category concept.[42]

This brings us to the crucial element in Weber's argument, the category concept (*Gattungsbegriff*) or, as he later preferred to call it, the ideal type. This tool became the basis of Weber's method, but it was also the key to that important element of his thinking which was derived from hermeneutics.

(b) From the Reformation onwards, hermeneutics – the interpretation of texts – was especially cultivated in Germany, since Protestant doctrine there depended on interpretation of the

40. *Ibid.*, pp. 166-9.
41. E.g., C. Jencks, *Inequality* (New York, 1972), ch. 7.
42. Shils and Finch (above, n. 21), pp. 184–5.

Scriptures. Rules and doctrines developed, and by 1829 they had been given authoritative systematization by the theologian Friedrich Schleiermacher. He defined the task of hermeneutics as the reconstruction of the thought of a text as its author meant it to be understood. The basic step towards this aim was to identify the leading ideas of a text; its subordinate elements would then fall into place.[43]

This method of interpretation was applied to classical texts by August Boeckh. The philologist, he argued, must re-think and so 're-know' a text. He must grasp its individuality, which comes from the creative spirit of the author, but also its structure, which comes from the genre in which it is written, for from this structure comes a text's 'subjective connections'. This is the central (and most original) element in Boeckh's formulation.[44]

These two ideas – re-thinking and structure – were developed into a general method of the cultural sciences by Wilhelm Dilthey. In studying the works and actions of men – 'objectifications of spirit' – the aim, he argued, should not be to subsume them under general laws and so explain them, as in natural science, but rather to grasp each object's structure and individuality, and so interpret it (*verstehen*), as in hermeneutics. To do this one must posit a general concept – an 'ideal type' – of the phenomenon of which the object is a representative, then compare the type with the object to understand the meaningful relationship between its elements and to see its individual characteristics.[45]

Dilthey's work on the cultural sciences started to appear in 1883, and Weber seems to have adopted his basic ideas by the time of his own 1904 essay on method, in which he insists that the cultural scientist must 'not only observe human conduct but also interpret it'.[46] This emphasis on *verstehen* is very reminiscent of

43. J. Wach, *Das Verstehen*, vol. 1 (Tübingen, 1926), pp. 121–8.
44. A. Boeckh, *On Interpretation and Criticism*, tr. .J. Pritchard (Norman, 1968: from the Berlin, 1886, edition), pp. vii, 13, 105; cf. Wach (above, n. 43), pp. 215–22.
45. H. Tuttle, *Wilhelm Dilthey's Philosophy of Historical Understanding* (Leiden, 1969), pp. 8–9 (verstehen), 80 (ideal type); cf. H. Hodges, *The Philosophy of Wilhelm Dilthey* (London, 1952), pp. 236–8, on hermeneutics.
46. M. Weber, *Gesammelte Aufsätze zur Wissenschaftslehre*, 3rd ed., by J. Winckelmann (Tübingen, 1968), p. 183: *nicht nur konstatieren sondern verstehen*: cf. pp. 43 and 93 (first published 1905), with references to Dilthey and his followers. On Weber's debt to hermeneutics in general see L. Lachmann, *The Legacy of Max Weber* (London, 1970), pp. 17–48.

Dilthey, as is the following discussion of ideal types. Then in 1913 Weber published an article on 'interpretative (*verstehende*) sociology', and this along with a reference to Jaspers makes his debt clear. Weber's exact relationship to Dilthey need not be explored here. What is important is that Weber and other scholars used Dilthey's ideas to integrate all the varied aspects of cultural life – not the least of their aims being 'to break the Marxist schema' – and so developed what has been called 'historical hermeneutics'.[47]

Weber's indebtedness to hermeneutics is important because it helps us to 'interpret' his own links with historicism. Weber was historicist in his opposition to all general schemes and in his refusal to explain in causal terms. His use of the ideal type exemplified this orientation.

It must be emphasized here that Weber's historicism separates him from the many other scholars of different tendencies who freely used types, concepts, and comparisons. A glance at a survey of German constitutional theory, for example, shows that as early as 1820 von Haller distinguished three basic types of state: patrimonial, military, and theocratic; and in 1859 von Mohl described six types: patriarchal, patrimonial, theocratic, classical, legal, and despotic.[48] Weber, a graduate of the Berlin law faculty, was undoubtedly familiar with these works and in fact used some of the terms just listed in his own works. Indeed, it has been recently argued that he owed his use of typology to a work in this tradition, Jellinek's 1900 manual of general political theory.[49] Furthermore, one of the classic typologies of all time, Toennies' distinction between *Gemeinschaft* and *Gesellschaft*, was propounded as early as 1887, and Toennies derived inspiration not from historicism and hermeneutics but rather from Thomas Hobbes and the Scottish political economists.[50]

Weber, however, stands apart from these schools of thought in his insistence on the individual and the unique as the ultimate aim of study. The tenacity of historicist principles in his thought

47. Weber, . . .*Wissenschaftslehre* (above, n. 46), pp. 427–74 (*verstehende* sociology); cf. Antoni (above, n. 14), pp. 147–84, esp. p. 149 (historical hermeneutic) and p. 152 (Marxist schema).

48. G. v. Below, *Der deutsche Staat aes Mittelalters* (Leipzig, 1914), pp. 2 (v. Haller), 28 (v. Mohl).

49. G. Roth, 'The Genesis of the Typological Approach', pp. 253–5 in Bendix and Roth (above, n. 14).

50. F. Toennies, *On Sociology*, eds. W. Cahnmann and R. Heberle (Chicago, 1971), pp. 3, 37.

is remarkable. The whole of his 1904 essay on method is permeated by them: 'Where the individuality of a phenomenon is concerned, the question of causality is not a question of laws but of concrete causal *relationships*: it is not a question of the subsumption of the event under some general rubric as a representative case but of its imputation as a consequence of some constellation. *It is in brief a question of imputation.* Wherever the causal explanation of a "cultural phenomenon" – an "historical individual" – is under consideration, the knowledge of causal *laws* is not the *end* of the investigation but only a *means* ... In the cultural sciences, the knowledge of the universal or general is never valuable in itself.'[51]

This close link with historicism may have been a corollary of a Kantian epistemology. There is no need to discuss the latter here. What is important is that these two lines of thought seem to have drawn Weber towards Dilthey's interpretative (*verstehende*) method, and in concrete terms this meant that he regarded his ideal types as nominalist constructs to be used solely for heuristic purposes in defining as clearly as possible the individuality of each development in history. That is stated clearly in the concluding note on method at the end of the present work, and it is set out at greater length in a letter to the conservative historian Georg von Below. This letter is the more interesting in that it contains a direct reference to the present work. The relevant passage is as follows: 'This winter I intend to publish a rather extensive contribution to the *Outline of the Social Sciences* series on the forms of political associations. It will deal with the subject in a comparative and normative manner, even though some may well sneer "Dilettantes compare". For I think that one can only define the specific characteristics of, for example, the mediaeval city – and that is precisely the sort of thing which is the historian's task (in that we are absolutely in agreement!) – after one has established which of these characteristics were lacking in other cities (classical Chinese, Islamic). That is a general rule. The next task of historians is to give a causal explanation of those specific characteristics. I cannot think that you really disagree with this, and in fact many of your comments seem to support rather than to contradict my idea.

'Now the preliminary, quite modest task [of establishing the

51. Shils and Finch (above, n. 21), pp. 78–80.

common characteristics of a class of phenomena such as the city] can be performed by sociology – at least as I conceive it. Of course it is inevitable in doing this that the sociologist will give offence to the scholar who has mastered a particular field, since after all nobody can be a specialist in all fields. Even so I think such [comparative] works are valuable for science. For example my own article on ancient agrarian history in the *Handwörterbuch der Staatswissenschaften* has proved useful, even on those points where its conclusions have since been corrected. The Leipzig dissertations of Wilcken's students seem to me to indicate that. This is so despite the fact that the article was written in great haste and is by no means a model of its kind.'[52]

These remarks indicate the curious way in which Weber remained within the tradition of historicist and hermeneutic traditions. His intellectual heritage was also shaped by a third, and more modern, tradition: *Realpolitik*.

(c) German history destroyed German idealism. In 1848 rifles and bayonets easily smashed the liberal movement for reform and unification. This seemed proof to many Germans that politics was a matter of power rather than programmes. In 1853 August von Rochau developed the 'realistic' view in a book which added a word to European languages: *Realpolitik*. After 1860 this tendency was strengthened by a new set of ideas deriving from Darwinism. Finally, Bismarck's series of victories during 1862–71 had a tremendous influence on domestic politics, for he achieved great national goals without recourse to the one thing which both liberals and conservatives had considered necessary for them: ideology. The result was a sharp shift in values and outlook. The German middle classes in general became thoroughly militarized, and German historians increasingly tended to glorify the state and its power as ends in themselves.[53]

Two examples of this tendency are relevant to Weber's thinking. Theodor Mommsen entered politics as a passionate liberal

52. Letter of June 1914, printed in the introduction to G. v. Below, *Der deutsche Staat des Mittelalters*, 2nd ed. (Leipzig, 1925), pp. xxiv–xxv.
53. K. Faber, 'Realpolitik als Ideologie', *Historische Zeitschrift*, 203 (1906), pp. 1–45; G. Ritter, *The Sword and the Scepter*, tr. H. Norden, vol. 2. (Coral Gables, 1970), pp. 93–104: 'The Militarization of the German Middle Class'; J. von Rantzau, 'The Glorification of the State in German Historical Writing', pp. 157–74 of *German History: Some New German Views*, ed. H. Kohn (London, 1954).

nationalist, and took an active role in the 1848 revolution. However, the ignominious collapse of the liberal movement convinced him that words alone could accomplish nothing, and he bitterly criticized the dreams of idealists. In the 1862–5 Schleswig-Holstein crisis he supported Bismarck despite the authoritarian character of his regime; in other words, for the sake of unity and strength he was willing to postpone political reform. Mommsen's case is especially significant, since his democratic convictions were never in doubt, and indeed he later became a vigorous opponent of the Bismarck regime. Still, his desire for unity and power was so great that in 1862 even he was willing to compromise.[54] His historical work had a similar emphasis. Eduard Meyer flatly stated that for Mommsen 'the great ideals of human life and culture ... were historically embodied for him in the national idea and its realization by a strong state'. In the same essay, an obituary – written a few days after Mommsen's death – Meyer makes a regretful comment which reveals much about Meyer himself and his 'realistic' colleagues in 1903: Mommsen's unyielding liberalism caused him to break with Bismarck, 'which made many regret that this revered scholar identified himself so entirely with principles which seemed to them outdated and unsuited for the great tasks facing the present age'.[55] Yet by non-German standards even Mommsen's liberalism was somewhat weak. At Oxford he astounded his liberal hosts by sharply condemning Gladstone, Home Rule, and the Irish land law.[56]

Even more significant is the case of Hermann Baumgarten, for he was Weber's uncle and his friend and mentor during 1883–93.[57] In 1866, in the light of Bismarck's stunning victory over Austria, Baumgarten published a pamphlet with the revealing title: *German Liberalism: A Self Criticism*, in which he argued that bourgeois liberals had shown themselves unsuited for action, and must now acknowledge the superior political abilities of aristocrats and therefore accept their leadership. The last few months had done more for German unity than decades of liberal efforts, and now he urged his fellow liberals to put aside

54. A. Wucher, *Theodor Mommsen: Geschichtschreibung und Politik*, 2nd ed. (Gottingen, 1968), pp. 53–4.

55. E. Meyer, 'Theodor Mommsen', pp. 539–49 of Kleine Shriften (Halle, 1910), at pp. 547–8 (ideals), 549 (liberal principles).

56. W. Fowler, *Roman Essays and Interpretations* (Oxford, 1920), p. 252.

57. Mitzman (above, n. 11), pp. 19, 24–5.

'secondary considerations' and work for a powerful German state.[58]

Power, of course, was prized because it was felt that the world –the 'real' world! – was shaped by national conflict and struggle. That was the conclusion of disillusioned liberals after 1848, and became the thesis of *Realpolitik*. Mommsen summed up the essence of the latter with his dictum:

Leben est Wirken
und Wirken ist Kampf.[59]

Now Weber was predisposed to such ideas by his class, family, and education, and in fact they proved fundamental to all his thinking. Politics was for him essentially a relentless struggle among men. When he wrote on economics he insisted on the same model: 'Even under what seems to be the rule of "peace" the economic struggle between national groups (inside Germany) follows its course. . . . No, even in the economic struggle for existence there is no peace.'[60]

This view had its corollaries in Weber's epistemology and even psychology. Scholarship and science, he insisted, could only define appropriate means for a given end, but the end itself must proceed from personal values and individual decision: 'So long as life remains immanent and is interpreted in its own terms, it knows only of an unceasing struggle of these gods with one another. Or, speaking directly, the ultimately possible attitudes toward life are irreconcilable, and hence their struggle can never be brought to a final conclusion.[61] Along with this, on the most profound level, there was Weber's conviction that human personality, including his own, was shaped – and, indeed, enhanced – by the struggle between reason and will, between the rational and the irrational[62] In the individual, as in society, struggle was universal and inescapable.

From these views follow certain conclusions about the nature

58. Faber (above, n. 53), pp. 14–15.
59. Wucher (above, n. 54), p. 61.
60. Weber, . . . *Politische Schriften* (above, n. 9), p. 12
61. Gerth and Mills (above, n. 1), p. 152 (from 'Science as a Vocation', a speech delivered at Munich University in 1918); cf. Honigsheim (above, n. 5), pp. 128–32, and R. Dahrendorf, *Essays in the Theory of Society* (Stanford, 1968), pp. 1–18, and J. Freund, *The Sociology of Max Weber*, tr. M. Ilford (New York, 1968), pp. 17–32.
62. W. Mommsen, 'Universalgeschichtliches und politisches Denken bei Max Weber', *Historische Zeitschrift*, 201 (1965), pp. 557–612, at p. 575.

of society and history – above all, the presumption that conflict, implicit or explicit, is always endemic in them. Since men's differences are irreconcilable, war between societies is inevitable. Within, societies themselves must be held together by force rather than consensus, and those who control this force will use it to further their own interests and values. That was clearly Weber's position, the position of Thrasymachus as against Socrates.[63] Hence, as Franco Ferrarotti has pointed out, Weber was not only generally interested in the nature of power, but particularly concerned himself with the question 'Why do men obey?'.[64] This presumption of struggle is behind the two basic organizing principles of Weber's historical work – contrast and characterization. Contrast is achieved by comparing alternatives, these being sometimes stages or possibilities, sometimes – and here Weber is most challenging – conflicts inherent in an historical structure. Consider, for example, his analysis of archaic Greece in terms of secular versus theocratic forces, or his view of the Gracchan period as a struggle between free and unfree labour. A more general example is the repeated use of the polarity of *oikos* and capitalist forms of economy as an analytic tool.

Even more striking is the manner in which Weber characterizes. He defines a particular society and period in terms of its dominant classes, institutions, and values. The three are inextricably related for Weber and influence each other reciprocally. This gives his approach and his work remarkable focus; Weber does not describe, he 'interprets'. When he deals with a society he imputes a definite direction and character to it, from which necessarily follow certain inherent strengths and weaknesses. In other words, Weber analyses structures. This brings us to the nature of his historical study.

3. *Weber and Historiography*

Historical studies in Weber's time were dominated by Ranke and his successors. The hall-mark of this school was a rigorous criticism of texts, together with a narrow concentration on political and military events and a tendency to focus on heroes and leading

63. Dahrendorf (above, n. 61), pp. 129–50.
64. F. Ferrarotti, *Max Weber* (Milan, 1972), pp. 87–112.

personalities. These characteristics were shared and prized by the men who held the important chairs, edited the leading professional journals, and trained most graduates.

Towards 1880, however, the first signs of impatience with this historical establishment appeared. Rankean methods, it was argued, had reached a dead end, for the professionals were becoming philologists rather than historians, more interested in editing sources than in studying problems. In particular, they showed themselves unable to cope with the new themes and problems connected with industrialism and class conflict.

This opposition to Rankean historiography crystallized in *Kulturgeschichte*, the antecedent of what we know today as social history. One of the earliest general statements of this school was a work on *The Tasks of Cultural History* published in 1889 by Eberhard Gothein, a scholar whom Weber singles out for praise in the present work. In 1891 Karl Lamprecht published the first volume of his *German History*, a landmark in the historical study of society rather than events, and in 1893 this current of historiography reached classical studies with the publication by Robert V. Pöhlmann of the first volume of his *History of Ancient Communism and Socialism*.[65]

Weber, of course, was part of this newer direction of historical studies, and he himself frequently uses the term *Kulturgeschichte* in the present work. He too implicitly rejected the older emphasis on personalities and events, and instead focused on structures and on the interaction of long-term factors.

Where Weber differed, however, was in his general refusal to 'modernize'. He declined to adopt easy analogies between ancient and modern proletariat, industry or capitalism. His rejection of these is, indeed, the origin of most of the polemical asides in the present work, and here again his immediate target was Eduard Meyer.

In 1893 the economist Karl Bücher had published a general outline of economic history, *The Rise of the National Economy*. His thesis was that Antiquity was dominated from first to last by 'house economy', in which production, exchange, and consump-

---

65. G. Oestreich, 'Die Fachhistorie und die Anfänge der sozialgeschichtlichen Forschung in Deutschland', *Historische Zeitschrift*, 208 (1969), pp. 320–63, esp. pp. 326–36; cf. K. Christ, *Vom Gibbon za Rostovtzeff* (Darmstadt, 1972), pp. 212–47, 368–9.

tion all occurred within great households. The next higher stage of economic organization, city economy, did not appear until mediaeval times, and only in the modern age did the highest form of economic organization, the national economy, emerge.[66]

Two years later Eduard Meyer was invited to address the Third Congress of German Historians, and he decided to rebut Bücher's theory. He had little trouble in showing that it was a construct based on the naïve premise that history exhibited a continuous progress which, evidently, culminated in the modern state. Instead, argued Meyer, historians should acknowledge that Antiquity came to a definitive end, that development began anew with the Middle Ages, and that the Mediterranean peoples had therefore experienced 'two parallel periods'.[67]

Meyer used this phrase only in passing, yet it suggests the implicit drift of his analysis. Whereas Bücher stressed the dissimilarity (and primitiveness) of Antiquity, Meyer emphasized its similarity with the present, its modernity. For example: he compared the mass movement of the peasants into Athens in the fifth century as a result of the onset of slavery, to the similar movement into cities in England as a result of the onset of industrialization.[68]

Weber vigorously resisted this tendency to modernize. Many passages in the present work show his insistence on the individual and specific character of the basic institutions of Antiquity, notably ancient capitalism and ancient slavery. Here again he shows his strong ties to historicist tradition, his philological concern with understanding things in their own context and their own terms.

Even more important, Weber was simply too learned and too penetrating a thinker to be satisfied with simple analogies and verbal constructs. Consider, for example, Meyer's views on the fall of the Roman Empire: for him, the fundamental reason for the end of Antiquity was the spread of ancient culture, which led to its extinction. 'Here too the general lesson of experience is confirmed: the more a culture expands, the more shallow it becomes.'[69] Weber's analysis was of another order entirely; it

66. E. Meyer, *Kleine Schriften* (Halle, 1910), pp. 82–5.
67. *Ibid.*, p. 89.
68. *Ibid.*, p. 133.
69. *Ibid.*, p. 147.

was based on a firm grasp of the evolution of ancient political and economic institutions, and proceeded from a close attention to the realities of power. The Roman Empire was finally overrun, after all, because its army became weak, not because its culture became shallow. Weber never forgot fundamental historical realities of this sort, and this was part of his greatness.

Finally, it should be noted that nothing need be said here about the historiography of the time outside Germany. Weber was perfectly ready to use sources edited and published in France, England, Italy, and even America; but he seems to have been totally untouched by historical and sociological thought beyond the borders of his country. This is, perhaps, one of the most important clues to understanding Weber – his strengths and also his weaknesses.

4. Translating Weber

Karl Jaspers, Weber's close friend, has recalled that Weber was remarkably indifferent to his own prestige and status, and attributes to this – among other things – his indifference to the style and polish of his writings: 'Side by side with penetrating thought, exactness of definition, careful organization, we find indifference to the linguistic form, composition, bulk, and proportions of his work... Often we find repetitions, digressions, followed by a leap back to the subject, enumerations that are not absolutely necessary, involved sentences, incidental remarks. Max Weber could not bear to reread even his manuscripts, much less his printed works: he took no pleasure in the published work, but proceeded with the task in which it was only a step.'[70] Guenther Roth has noted particular problems in Weber's style: his excessive use of quotation marks and qualifications, and his 'skilful use of syntax [which] permits more complex construction than is feasible in English'.[71]

These features are present in the text translated here, along with a few others, notably a conspicuous lack of paragraphing and connectives. To make the translation clear and readable the

70. K. Jaspers, *Three Essays*, tr. R. Mannheim (New York, 1964), pp. 265–6.

71. G. Roth, 'Introduction' (above, n. 23), pp. ci–ciii.

translator has consequently taken certain liberties with the text. First, Weber's long sections have been broken up into paragraphs which correspond to the sequence of his reasoning. At times a few words have been transferred from the end of a paragraph to the beginning, in order to supply a connection. Occasionally a word or phrase has been interpolated for the sake of clarification; where this occurs, it is indicated by brackets.

Second, Weber's long sentences have been broken up, and his digressions have been set apart as separate sentences or paragraphs. His few footnotes were evidently afterthoughts, and as they are mostly closer to the logical development of the main work than many digressions actually in it, they have been integrated into the text.

Finally, stylistic features that would seem eccentric and distracting in English have been avoided. Quotation marks have been used sparingly, verbs take the place of abstract nouns, and foreign terms are translated, Where some doubt persists about the precise connotation of a key term it is given in parentheses. Translated foreign terms are also so given.

5. Bibliographic Note

The main work presented here was originally published as an article in an encyclopedia: 'Agrarverhältnisse im Altertum', *Handwörterbuch der Staatswissenschaften*, 3rd ed., vol. 1 (1909), pp. 52–188. After Weber's death his widow reprinted it as part of his *Gesammelte Aufsätze zur Sozial- und Wirtschaftsgeschichte* (Tübingen, 1924). pp. 1–288. Marianne Weber noted on page 1 that the title had been dictated by the encyclopedia, and that in fact the work represented 'much more, namely a social and economic history of Antiquity'.

Weber's account ends with the Early Roman Empire, the later period including the transition to mediaeval conditions having been assigned by the encyclopedia's editors to the article on the colonate by Michael Rostovtzeff. Therefore this volume includes as a continuation an essay by Weber on the decline of the Roman Empire. It was originally presented in 1896 as a popular lecture before the Academic Society (*Akademische Gesellschaft*) of Freiburg in Breisgau, and in the same year was published as an article, 'Die sozialen Gründe des Untergangs der antiken Kultur', in the magazine *Die Wahrheit*, vol. 6 (1896), pp. 57–77. Marianne Weber reprinted it in the above-mentioned book as pp. 289–311.

6. Supplementary Bibliography

Most of the important recent studies of Weber's work are mentioned in the notes. Here let it suffice to comment that any study of the man and his ideas must start with the biography by his widow, Marianne Weber, *Max Weber: Ein Lebensbild* (Tübingen, 1926; 2nd ed., Heidelberg, 1950), a masterpiece of interpretation.

Weber's bibliography of sources and studies is a remarkably full survey of the best works available at the time. For more recent publications the reader should consult the bibliographies of the *Cambridge Ancient History* (12 vols., 1928–39) and Hermann Bengtson, *Introduction to Ancient History*, tr. R. Frank and F. Gilliard (Berkeley, 1970).

The most obvious supplement to this volume is Weber's own *General Economic History*, tr. F. Knight (New York, 1927, rptd. London, 1961); this is based on a course Weber gave in the winter of 1919–20 just before his death, and in it there are extended discussions of feudal and capitalist institutions which illuminate many aspects of Weber's discussions here. It is valuable to compare this with a recently published work of Karl Marx, *Pre-Capitalist Economic Formations*, tr. J. Cohen (London, 1964), since Marx and Weber drew to a great extent on the same tradition of scholarship and both aimed essentially at showing the developments leading to capitalism.

The only formal successor to Weber's work up till now is that of F. M. Heichelheim, *An Ancient Economic History*, tr. J. Stevens, 3 vols. (Leiden, 1958–70). This work has particular features and merits: it shows the great break between bronze and iron age cultures, the rates of development in the Mediterranean world, and the differences between city and imperial policies. Heichelheim used many of Weber's concepts, and shared his 'liberal' dislike of bureaucracy and centralization; nevertheless much of the work is marked by what Weber would have called

'a lack of clear concepts', and in particular the enormous bibliographies are entirely unorganized. See the reviews by R. Blake
and J. Larsen in *Classical Philology* 35 (1940: of the German
edition), pp. 73–6, and 60 (1965), pp. 294–5, respectively.

There are three good short surveys of the economies of Greece
and Rome: J. Toutain, *The Economic Life of the Ancient World*,
tr. M. Dobie (London, 1930), with much information on various
sectors; C. Mossé, *The Ancient World at Work*, tr. J. Lloyd
(London, 1969), mainly about Greece and notable for extended
consideration of 'the idea of work' and other cultural factors;
and J. P. Levy, *The Economic Life of the Ancient World*, tr. J.
Biram (Chicago, 1967), which gives a brief account of Near
Eastern developments as well, is especially valuable for information on monetary policies and problems, and has an excellent
bibliography of recent works.

A more sophisticated work, concerned with basic concepts and
problems in the study of Greco-Roman antiquity, is the latest
volume of the Sather Lectures, *The Ancient Economy* by M. I.
Finley (London, 1973). On many points Finley agrees with Weber,
notably on the character of the ancient city (cf. pp. 138–9); on
some he disagrees, as on the reasons for the decline of slavery.
In general, Finley stresses the importance of cultural rather than
political factors, particularly those which made for 'built-in
inefficiency' (p. 106). Hence his lapidary conclusion: 'the prevailing mentality was acquisitive, but not productive' (p. 144).

General aspects of Antiquity are discussed comparatively in
the following works: K. Polanyi, *Primitive, Archaic, and Modern
Economics* (New York, 1968); K. Polanyi *et al.*, *Trade and Market
in the Early Empires* (Glencoe, 1957); S. Eisenstadt, *The Political
Systems of Empires* (London, 1963) and *The Decline of Empires*
(Englewood Cliffs, 1967), C. Cipolla (ed.), *The Economic Decline
of Empires* (London, 1970, esp. pp. 16–91 on Rome).

Slavery is surveyed by W. Westermann, *The Slave Systems of
Greek and Roman Antiquity* (Philadelphia, 1955); many problems
are touched upon in a reader edited by M. I. Finley, *Slavery in
Classical Antiquity* (Cambridge, 1960). Much monographic work
is now being done in Eastern Europe, and also in Western
Germany under the sponsorship of Joseph Vogt for the Mainz
Academy, so the time for a synthesis is not yet at hand. For com-
parative purposes a valuable work is E. Genovese, *The Political*

Economy of Slavery (New York, 1965); on the other hand its assumptions about slave reproduction in the U.S. South evidently need qualification: see P. Curtin, 'The Slave Trade and the Atlantic Basin', *Key Issues in the Afro-American Experience*, ed. N. Huggins *et al.* (New York, 1971), pp. 74–93.

For particular areas and periods the following studies are valuable:

(a) Egypt: G. Steindorff and K. Seele, *When Egypt Ruled the East*, 2nd ed. (Chicago, 1957); J. Wilson, *The Culture of Ancient Egypt* (Chicago, 1963); W. Hayes, 'Most Ancient Egypt', *Journal of Near Eastern Studies* 23 (1964), pp. 74 ff., 145 ff., 217 ff., 273 ff.

(b) Mesopotamia: L. Delaporte, *Mesopotamia*, tr. V. Childe (London, 1925), esp. part II, 3 on economic organization; C. Kraehling *et al.*, *City Invincible* (Chicago, 1960) on urbanism; A. L. Oppenheim, *Ancient Mesopotamia* (Chicago, 1964).

(c) Israel: Max Weber, *Ancient Judaism*, tr. H. Gerth and D. Martindale (Glencoe, 1952: first published 1917–19); S. Baron, *A Social and Religious History of the Jews*, vols. 1–2 (New York and London, 1937); B. Netanyahu (ed.), *World History of the Jewish People*, series 1, 6 vols. (Ramat-Gan and New Brunswick, 1963–72), esp. vol. 3, ch. 13: 'The Manner of the King', by E. Speiser.

(d) Greece: W. Woodhouse, *Solon the Liberator* (London, 1938); H. Michell, *Economics of Ancient Greece*, 2nd ed. (London, 1957); M. I. Finley, *Studies in Land and Credit in Ancient Athens* (New Brunswick, 1952); J. Fine, *Horoi: Hesperia*, supp. 9 (1951).

(e) Hellenistic Era: M. Rostovtzeff, *Social and Economic History of the Hellenistic World*, 3 vols. (Oxford, 1941); W. Tarn and G. Griffith, *Hellenistic Civilization*, 3rd ed. (London and New York, 1952); H. Bell, *Egypt from Alexander the Great to the Arab Conquest* (Oxford, 1948); M. Rostovtzeff, 'Roman Exploitation of Egypt in the First Century A.D.', *Journal of Economic and Business History* (1929), pp. 337–4.

(f) Rome and Early Empire: T. Frank, *Economic History of Rome* (1926; 2nd ed., New York, 1962); T. Frank (ed.), *Economic Survey of Ancient Rome*, 5 vols. (Baltimore, 1933–40); E. Badian, *Publicans and Sinners* (Ithaca, 1972), on the 'predatory capitalism' of the Late Republic; M. Rostovtzeff, *Social and Economic History of the Roman Empire* (1926; 2nd ed., 2 vols., Oxford, 1957);

S. Wallace, *Taxation in Egypt from Augustus to Diocletian* (Princeton, 1938).

(g) Late Antiquity: M. Chambers (ed.), *The Fall of Rome*, 2nd ed. (New York, 1970); A. Jones, *Later Roman Empire* 3 vols. (Oxford, 1964); R. Latouche, *Birth of Western Economy*, tr. E. Wilkinson (London, 1961); R. Lopez, *Birth of Europe* (New York, 1967).

R. I. FRANK

I. Economic Theory and Ancient Society

Economic Theory and Ancient Society

The pattern of settlement in the European Occident contrasts with that common to the civilizations of East Asia. The differences may be summed up briefly, if somewhat imprecisely, as follows: in Europe the transition to fixed settlement meant a change from the dominance of cattle breeding (especially for milk) to an economy dominated by agriculture, with cattle breeding continuing as a secondary element; in Asia, on the contrary, there was a shift from extensive, and hence nomadic, agriculture to horticulture without milk-cattle breeding. The opposition is a relative one, and may not be true of prehistoric times, but regardless of when it arose, it led to fundamental distinctions. Thus among European peoples private ownership of land is always connected with the division and final assignment of communal grazing lands among smaller groups, whereas among Asians this development did not occur and so the primitive agricultural communal units found in the West – for example, the mark and the commons – were either unknown in Asia or else had a different economic function. For this reason the role of communal property in East Asian village organizations, unless it is of modern origin, for example caused by the tax organization, differs markedly from European parallels. Nor does one find among East Asians the 'individualism' connected with ownership of herds, with all its consequences.

Among Occidentals therefore (mainly, but not only, in Europe) we find everywhere certain characteristics at the start of development. Usually, so far as we can judge, sedentary agriculture arose when the land available for exploitation was reduced through an increasing shift of emphasis from milk-cattle breeding to field crops. This is true not only for North-West Europe but also in essentials for South Europe and the Near East.

However, this development was profoundly modified in pre-historic times in the Near East (Mesopotamia) and in the single major African centre of civilization, Egypt, by the fundamental importance of riverine irrigation systems. Theoretically irrigation agriculture could have evolved directly out of the simple agriculture which existed before the domestication of animals into the later stage of horticulture, but in any case irrigation gave the entire economy of these areas a very specific character in historical times.

In contrast, the Greek and also – despite the ancient sources' emphasis on the use of cattle for work, not milk – the Roman communities had agrarian systems which were fundamentally closer to those of mediaeval Europe. Antiquity took a different course, however, from the time when the masses, having been attached to the land for its intensive development, were no longer available for military service, so that a division of labour arose with a professional military class which then sought to exploit the defenceless masses for its own benefit. The development of military technique into a profession, presupposing permanent training and practice, sometimes accompanied this development and sometimes caused it. In the early Middle Ages of Europe this process, as we know, led to the establishment of 'feudalism'. Only the beginnings of a system similar to mediaeval feudalism can be found in Antiquity; there are no real analogies to the combination of vassalage and benefice or to the development of Roman-Germanic feudal law. Still it appears unnecessary and unwise to limit the use of the concept 'feudalism' to its mediaeval form. Both East Asian and Amerindian civilizations had institutions which, because of their functions, we regard as essentially feudal in character. There is no reason why the concept of feudalism should not be used to characterize all those social institutions whose basis is a ruling class which is dedicated to war or royal service and is supported by privileged land holdings, rents or the labour services of a dependent, unarmed population.

Thus one should call feudal the administrative benefices granted in Egypt and Babylon as well as the constitution of Sparta. The differences between various forms of feudalism arise from variations in the manner in which the warrior class was organized and economically supported. One of various possibilities is the distribution of the ruling class as landlords all over the country, as in that 'individualistic' pattern of feudalism which we find clearly delineated in mediaeval Europe, with origins going back to Late Antiquity.

Another form, however, developed in Mediterranean and in particular Greek Antiquity, where there appeared very early 'feudal cities', fortified centres settled by professional warriors. Not that this 'city feudalism' was the only form of feudalism in Antiquity, but it directly influenced the later centres of 'classical' political civilization in the beginnings of their political development. It was therefore in its way more significant for those centres than was the forcible settlement of the landed nobility in many cities during the Italian Middle Ages.

The import of a foreign and superior military technology took place in Antiquity in South Europe via the sea, and at the same time through the incorporation of conquered coastal areas into a commercial system which was, at least geographically, of considerable extent. The feudal ruling class was at first always that class which derived profit from this trade. Therefore the feudal development characteristic of Antiquity led to the formation of feudal city states. Central Europe, on the other hand, was transformed in the early Middle Ages by a similar development of military technique which came to it via land routes. When Central Europe was ripe for feudalism, it lacked the developed commerce such as had existed in Antiquity, and so feudalism there was based much more on the land; hence arose the manorial system. The tie which held together the dominant military class was therefore essentially that of personal allegiance, whereas in Antiquity it was the much stronger tie of municipal citizenship.

The relation between ancient city feudalism and a trade economy recalls mediaeval developments: the rise of free industry in the cities, the downfall of patrician rule, the latent struggle between 'city economy' and 'manorial economy', and the disintegration of the feudal state due to the money economy of the later Middle Ages and modern epoch. However, such comparisons with mediaeval and modern phenomena, although seemingly quite plausible, are highly unreliable for the most part, indeed are often an obstacle to clarity and understanding. For the similarities are all too easily deceptive. Ancient civilization had specific characteristics which sharply differentiate it from mediaeval and modern civilizations. Its economic focus, until the beginning of the Roman Empire, was the coast in the Occident and the rivers in Egypt and the Near East. Although ancient trade, both interlocal and international, was geographically extensive and highly profitable, it nevertheless, apart from a few important interludes, lagged behind that of the later Middle Ages in the relative volume of goods traded. It is true that ancient trade was varied and included base as well as precious metals, and more numerous raw materials than one would expect. Nevertheless ancient land trade was comparable with that of the later Middle Ages only in particular points and only in particular periods. Even in sea trade most commodities of mass consumption played a really significant role only in few periods of political or economic expansion, above all in cases where monopoly ports ('staples') were established, as at Athens and later at Rhodes, Egypt and Rome.

Thus Beloch estimated that the annual trade of Piraeus in 401–400 B.C. was 2,000 talents (about thirteen million gold francs), basing his estimate on the customs dues collected there in that year. The tariff was one-fifteenth of the value of the goods and 30 or 36 talents were collected: hence the goods were worth about 2,000 talents. Considering that this was in Piraeus alone, that it was so soon after the Peloponnesian War, that no allowance is made for changes in the purchasing power of money, and that even so 2,000 talents is approximately the equivalent of one-tenth of the foreign trade of the present kingdom of Greece (*c*. 130–40 million gold francs), this sum is certainly an impressive figure. It must be accepted if one assumes that in fact customs amounted to only 2 per cent of the value of goods in transit and other taxes were not included. Scholars, however, disagree on these matters.

Even more imposing is the sum of 1 million drachmae (about 140 Attic talents) which the Rhodians *claimed* their island collected in import duties before the establishment of a free port on Delos. Their island, indeed, had extraordinary privileges in virtually all Hellenistic realms, and after the establishment of Delos as a free port they only collected 150,000 drachmae. The problem here is whether we can accept this statement, the accuracy of which is somewhat doubtful owing to its obvious 'official' character. Another documented example is the 5 per cent duty collected on the maritime trade of Athenian allies, but not on the trade of Athens herself and the largest islands. This duty was collected as a substitute for certain levies, and Beloch estimates that the Athenians themselves expected it to raise 1,000 talents. I cannot accept this, however, for the passage in Thucydides on which this is based is surely too compressed to be an adequate source for determining the amount, and the figure is also irreconcilable with the 30–36 talents collected at Piraeus. Furthermore, a tribute which could be discharged by a 5 per cent increase in the price of imports seems to make no sense.

A more important business transaction, in fact probably the largest documented for Antiquity of free private trade without state control or subvention, was the flow of imports to the value of 55 million sesterces (16 million gold francs) from India to Egypt in one year under Vespasian. The evidence for this is apparently reliable.

One must bear in mind that all calculations for trade in Antiquity include not only material goods but also slaves. Because of their portability slaves were a very important part of commerce in times of economic expansion, and in peace they were expensive if of good quality.

In Antiquity dependence on imported grain, wherever it became a constant phenomenon, always led to state intervention and hence institutional and political consequences of fundamental importance, since private commerce was not considered adequate to ensure its provision. Examples include liturgies as in Athens, state purchase with moneys secured by mortgages and then division among citizens as in Samos, and finally the systematic provisioning policy of Rome.

Now of course not only states in the Middle Ages but also the mercantilist monarchies and even Czarist Russia had grain policies similar in purpose to those of Antiquity. However, the 'store-house' policies of absolutist states, even that of Russia (where they were most developed) were hardly comparable in importance with those of the Babylonian and Egyptian grain storage systems, or even the Roman system of the *annona*. Furthermore the absolutist states (even Russia) pursued different aims and used different methods. The element which differentiates the grain policies of ancient from modern states is essentially the contrast between the modern proletariat and the so-called ancient proletariat. The latter was a consumer proletariat, a mass of impoverished petty bourgeois, rather than, as today, a working class engaged in production. The modern proletariat as a class did not exist in Antiquity.

For ancient civilization was either based directly on slavery or else was permeated by slavery to a degree never present in the European Middle Ages. This was partly because of the low cost of human subsistence in the centres where it flourished, partly because of historical and political conditions. Slavery was dominant in some periods, such as the later Roman Republic, and it was still a pervasive influence in other periods, such as the Hellenistic and Roman imperial ages, when legally 'free' labour prevailed. It is of course true that the papyri and ostraca show that in Ptolemaic and Roman Egypt an important role was played by free labour, even outside the skilled crafts, in the Hellenistic East. This is confirmed by the Talmud and by the inscriptions. The distinctly capitalistic concept of the employer (*ergodotos*) seems present in developed form, but it is characteristic that whenever there arose the need for the use of a large and reliable work force during set periods of time, as in the Ptolemaic oil monopoly, it was necessary to impose direct or indirect limitations on freedom of movement. Indeed, slavery flourished especially in those periods and places generally associated with the zenith of 'classical' and 'free' political systems. Although I believe that prevailing views of certain areas and periods of Antiquity overemphasize the number and importance of slaves, especially for Hellenistic Egypt, but also for the earlier Near East and Greece, still the fundamental distinction between Antiquity on the one hand and mediaeval and modern Europe on the other remains valid.

Nevertheless it is still necessary to face the problem whether or not the economic organization of Antiquity had characteristics which rule out the use of the concepts used to analyse the economic history of mediaeval and modern Europe. This question has been debated with vigour, and sometimes with passion, during the last century. The starting point of this controversy was the theory of Rodbertus, according to whom all Antiquity was dominated by what he called an '*oikos* economy', one in which production centred around the household and the household was extended to include unfree workers. He argued that division of labour in Antiquity was essentially only specialization within the great slave households, and that commerce was only an occasional and secondary phenomenon, serving merely to dispose of the excess production of the great households. Hence Rodbertus argued for 'the autarky of the *oikos*'; he regarded the great households of Antiquity as in principle economically self-sufficient.

Karl Bücher accepted Rodbertus' account of the *oikos*, but with a difference. His views may, I think, be interpreted – on the basis of his own statements – in this manner: he considered the *oikos* as an 'ideal type', denoting a kind of economic system which appeared in Antiquity with its basic features and characteristic consequences in a closer approximation to its 'pure concept' than anywhere else, without this *oikos* economy becoming universally dominant in Antiquity, either in time or space. One may add with confidence that even in those periods when the *oikos* was dominant this meant no more than a limitation on commerce and its role in meeting consumer needs. This limitation was, to be sure, strong and effective, and caused a corresponding economic and social degradation of those classes which would have otherwise carried on a more extensive trade.

Despite these reservations Bücher's use of Antiquity as an exemplification of the concept '*oikos* economy' caused him to emphasize certain paradigmatic aspects of ancient economic history to such an extent that a mistaken impression resulted. Historians concluded that Bücher regarded an '*oikos* economy' as characteristic of all Antiquity, at the same time ascribing a 'city economy' (in the ideal-typical sense) to the cities, a formulation of his views which Bücher himself called inaccurate. It was against this formulation that Eduard Meyer argued, going so far as to reject entirely the use of special economic concepts in studying Antiquity. Meyer then made the attempt to operate entirely with modern economic concepts, at least in his analysis of Periclean Athens, and so used such terms as 'factory' and 'factory worker'.[1] He aimed to show that otherwise we cannot

1. The remarkable thing about these ancient 'factories' is that they could be 'confiscated' (*aphobos*) or lost through dissipation (*timerokos*) to such a degree that they disappeared without leaving any physical trace. No modern factory could do that!

understand how 'modern' the economy then was, even with respect to the importance of commerce and banking.

Now in the first place there is no evidence for the existence in Antiquity even of 'cottage industry', such as appeared in Europe as early as the thirteenth century, based on letting out production on contract. This system represents an advance on the simple exploitation of the producer by an experienced merchant, a phenomenon of course known even in Antiquity. [In short: the stage which preceded development of the factory system in modern times has no parallel in Antiquity.]

There is moreover no evidence whatever for the existence in Antiquity of factories even in the purely technical or operational sense of the term, such as would encompass phenomena like Russia's factories manned by serfs rendering corvée labour or state factories producing for state needs. Nor do our sources ever indicate the widespread existence of industrial factories – that is, centres of production deserving the name 'factory' because of their size, continuity of operation, and technological sophistication (involving concentration of production in workshops, division and organization of labour, and use of fixed capital).

For example: the factory was not the normal form of production even in the industries of the Pharaohs, nor in the monopolies of the Ptolemies and of the later Roman Empire – periods where one would most expect to find it (see below). The Hellenistic *ergastērion* was simply the servants' quarters of a wealthy man, usually a merchant – often an importer of costly raw materials such as ivory. There he kept his skilled slaves – they could be of any number, and would have been either purchased or else held as collateral on loans – who worked under the direction of an overseer (*hegemōn tou ergastēriou*) on that part of his raw material which he did not sell to free artisans (Demosthenes XXVII:823.19; see below on Athens). One could divide this *ergastērion* at will by selling a part of the slaves, just as one would divide an ingot of lead; this indicates clearly that we are dealing here with an undifferentiated group of slave labourers, not a differentiated organization of labour.

Here and there 'subsidiary industries' existed to aid the market operations of large agricultural organizations, and there were workshops attached to the monopoly administrations in the Near East and under the Roman Empire. There were also textile enterprises owned by great noblewomen which undoubtedly sometimes grew to large dimensions as in mediaeval times. But all of these concerns were dependent on plantations or tax administrations or an *oikos*; they were not genuine 'factories'. If one does find evidence of first steps towards something like a genuine factory organization – and this of course could occur in Antiquity as it did in Russia during serfdom – it soon becomes apparent that these phenomena, like the Russian factories and for the same reasons (see below), only serve as 'exceptions that prove the rule', for they were never a regular feature of the private sector.

Such an exception is the banking industry, which is supposed to have surpassed in size and character that of the thirteenth century, quantitatively if not qualitatively. In fact, this ancient banking seems to have been in the hands of the tax farmers of a very few centres of political power, Rome in particular as well as Athens and a few others. Furthermore different kinds of business – bottomry loans, merchant partnerships (characteristic of the discontinuity of 'early capitalism'), bank payments and transfers – were transacted with legal instruments essentially similar to those of the early Middle Ages. Thus the bill of exchange, already known in early mediaeval times, existed in a rudimentary form; similarly the rates, terms and legal regulation of interest were all generally comparable to early mediaeval equivalents. There was however an absence of all forms of state debt, something which was already developed in the Middle Ages, and which would have provided a regular source of return for capital. Instead there were typically substitutes for a national debt, such as the colossal hoards of oriental and Persian kings and Greek temples, and their characteristic use. All these phenomena indicate how little the existing stocks of precious metals were used as 'capital'.

Nothing could be more misleading, therefore, than to describe the economic institutions of Antiquity in modern terms. Whoever does this underrates – as often happens – the basic changes effected during the Middle Ages in the legal institutions governing capital, though the mediaeval economy was itself none the less different from ours. As for state and semi-state financial institutions, such as the Ptolemaic bank with its enormous reserves and the companies of Roman tax farmers, even these have striking parallels in corresponding developments in mediaeval city-states (e.g. Genoa). They were moreover surpassed by the commercial techniques of the thirteenth century.

Furthermore one must also emphasize that the *oikos* as defined by Rodbertus did in fact play a very important role in the economy of Antiquity. On the one hand it developed – as I have described elsewhere – in the last stage of Graeco-Roman antiquity (the Empire) as a link to the feudal economy and society of early mediaeval Europe. But the *oikos* also appears in the Near East and also to some extent in Greece at the earliest stage of Antiquity known to us, as the households of kings, princes and priests – sometimes parallel to the modest economy of the masses, sometimes – through corvées – dominant over it.

It is not true, however, that the *oikos* developed out of the autarkic house communities of the masses, as Rodbertus believed. Rather it was partly 'state socialist' in origin, as in Egypt where it arose perhaps mainly as a result of public regulation of the irrigation system. It was also partly shaped in the ancient Near East and in early Greece by the commercial profits reaped by the first promoters of regular trade relations, the chiefs and princes; they enjoyed an effective monopoly of trade through their exchanges of gifts, and also profited from their own ventures (including piracy), collecting treasure to support their prestige and extend their resources.

Naturally in these archaic '*oikos* economies' of the princes and the political ruling class, the bulk of necessities were provided by the natural economy. Requisitions, corvées, and slave raids gave the princes the resources to buy foreign products; but the precious metals of their treasuries did not serve the purpose of a continuous supply of necessities through a money economy, not even in Persia. Instead the treasuries were merely used for rewarding individuals and gaining particular political aims. Similarly at the end of Antiquity (from the third century A.D.), the natural economy increasingly dominated both the manors and the '*oikos* economy' of the state.

However the same is not true for the great slave systems of the classical periods of Antiquity, certainly not to the degree which Rodbertus believed, nor even that which I myself was once inclined to assume. On this matter one must give credit to Eduard Meyer and several of his students (e.g. Gummerus). Likewise I think that it must be admitted that, though justified in themselves, the attempts made to define Antiquity's specific economic characteristics, one of which was undoubtedly slave labour, have usually led to an under-estimation of the quantitative importance of free labour. This error, of which I too have been guilty, has been corrected by the researches of Wilcken on Egypt, even though that country was somewhat atypical.

Antiquity knew not only the unfree and half-free but also the free peasant, as owner or tenant or share-cropper. Likewise there existed, side by side with cottage industry and slave labour shops, production by free artisans – some working on order, some for wages (this was much more common), and some as extra help (this was also common). There were family workshops, one-man shops (much the most frequent), and shops run by a master with one or more slaves and free or (generally) unfree apprentices. There also existed the joint cooperative of artisans (Greek: *synergoi*) similar to the Russian *artel*, as well as the organized crew of skilled craftsmen brought together by a contractor (Greek: *ergolabōn*) for specific purposes, nearly always composed of state workers.

Nevertheless Antiquity had no word corresponding to our 'journeyman', a concept which arose out of the mediaeval struggle against the 'masters', another notion unknown to Antiquity. For throughout Antiquity, despite its wealth of civic associations, the crafts never reached that level of autonomous organization which was attained by the high Middle Ages, nor did they reach mediaeval levels of refined division and organization of labour. Consider the institution of the journeyman!

Where one finds a guild or something similar in Antiquity it is nearly always essentially a state organization for the forced imposition of public tasks. The social position of the artisan was very low, with ephemeral and partial exceptions in the Hellenic democracies, and these exceptions are apparent rather than real. But even the employers evidently never had sufficient political power to secure legal concentration of trade in the cities, such as was achieved in the Middle Ages. (See below on Athens for the causes of this.)

Finally, Antiquity knew the free, unskilled wage earner; this type developed gradually from people sold into temporary slavery by themselves or by others (children, debtors). Wage earners were hired for harvesting, and were used by the state in large numbers for excavation work, construction and other public projects. Otherwise their employment was generally scattered and irregular.

The question to be considered now, therefore, is this: did a capitalist economy exist in Antiquity, to a degree significant for cultural history? To begin with, there is this general factor: the economic surplus of the ancient city – and this applies to the Near East as well as to the archaic *polis* of the Mediterranean lands – always had its original basis in the rents which the landed princes and noble clans derived from their estates and from levies on their dependants. This was true to a degree unknown today except in the case of certain capitals centring on a royal court; a more appropriate comparison would be Moscow during the period of serfdom. The significance of this source of wealth, and with it the specific political conditions of the economic 'flowering' of the cities – and hence too their swift decline – remained very important throughout all Antiquity. The ancient cities were always much more centres of consumption than production, whereas the opposite is true of mediaeval cities.

Similarly the development of ancient cities, although producing numerous elements of 'an urban economy' (discussed below), never led to anything so closely resembling the 'ideal type' as appeared in a great many mediaeval cities. This was a consequence of the fact that ancient civilization was coastal in character. Hence these characteristics of the ancient economy: (1) cities exported certain articles of high labour input and quality; (2) cities were constantly dependent on grain imports from distant lands; (3) slaves were purchased; (4) city policies were shaped by specific commercial interests. In the light of these factors, one must then ask: although there were periods of Antiquity marked by a dramatic rise and fall in wealth, were these developments really part of an economic structure which we can call 'capitalist'?

Our answer will depend on our definition of 'capitalist' – and that of course can take many forms. However, one element must be emphasized: capital always means wealth used to gain profit in commerce. Otherwise the term loses any classificatory use. Therefore we should expect a capitalist economy to be based on commerce. This means that goods are produced (in part at least) to become objects of trade, and also that the means of production are themselves objects of exchange. This excludes all manorial charges levied in rural areas on subject groups, like the various tributes – rents, dues and services – extracted from peasants in the early Middle Ages, who had to pay dues in kind and money on their possessions, inheritances, trade, and persons. For neither the land owned nor the people subjected can be regarded as 'capital'; title to both depended (in principle) not on purchase in the open market but on traditional ties. This was a form of manorialism and was known also in Antiquity.

There also existed in Antiquity the commercial practice of dividing estates into parcels and leasing them out, in which case the land is used as a source of rent and capitalist enterprise is absent. One also finds in the Ancient world the exploitation of subjects as labourers in lords' workshops, as cultivators on the land (Pharaonic Egypt, Roman imperial domains), as purchased slaves in large enterprises and in combinations of the last two.

Analysis of domain agriculture (*Fronhofsbetrieb*) is difficult because one finds a great variety of gradations; they range from systems based on formally free transfer and lease of land to *coloni* on a market basis, to systems based on completely traditional social ties binding the lord and the cultivator owing him labour services to reciprocal obligations. Nevertheless the latter is by far the more common type wherever the land is worked by a colonate. In such cases the *coloni* are not themselves 'capital', for they are not part of an autonomous labour market, but their labour along with the land they work can become objects of trade, and in fact became such in the Near East and later Roman Empire. In these cases the system is intermediate in character: it is capitalist in so far as goods are produced for the market and the land is an object of trade; it is non-capitalist in so far as the labour force as a means of production cannot be bought or leased in the open market.

Generally the existence of domain agriculture is a transitional phenomenon, either from *oikos* to capitalism or from *oikos* to natural economy. It is always a symptom of relative lack of capital, especially risk capital. This shortage is reflected in the practice of forcing dependants to find their own working capital, and also in policies aimed at reducing capital expenditures on inventory and labour; thus instead of buying slaves or hiring labourers recourse is made to forced labour. Usually the reason for this lack of capital is a relatively low level of trading activity.

Slave agriculture, when the slaves are normal objects of exchange (it makes no difference whether particular labourers have been actually purchased or not), and the land worked is privately owned or leased, is of course capitalist in character from the economic point of view. That is because land and slaves are both acquired in the open market and are clearly 'capital'. The work force is bought, not hired as in enterprises conducted with free labour; or if labour is, exceptionally, hired, it is not from the slave but rather from his owner. Hence the capital needed for slave labour is significantly more than would be needed – other things being equal – for the same quantity of free labour. Similarly buying land demands commitment of more capital than would leasing it.

Finally there is the large-scale capitalist enterprise based on 'free' labour. It permits the maximum use of available capital at the same level of accumulation for the output of means of production. In general this form of enterprise was not a regular feature of private economic activity in Antiquity, either within agriculture or outside it. It is true that one finds 'country squires' in the Near East and in Greece, but precisely in those periods and areas governed by tradition – e.g. in inland regions in the Hellenic period, in references in the Talmud, and in certain zones in the Hellenistic period – not in areas marked by advanced economic development. Large enterprises which were on a regular basis and used only hired (i.e. free) labour existed in certain state undertakings, but private enterprises of this sort did not play a significant role in the social or economic systems of the centres of classical culture. This does not apply entirely, however, to the later period of the Near East.

Today the concept of 'capitalist enterprise' is generally based on this last form, the large firm run with free wage-labour, because it is this form which is responsible for the characteristic social problems of modern capitalism. From this point of view it has been argued that capitalist economy did not play a dominant role in Antiquity, and did not in fact exist. However, to accept this premise is to limit needlessly the concept of capitalist economy to a single form of valorization of capital – the exploitation of other people's labour on a contractual basis – and thus to introduce social factors. Instead we should take into account only economic factors. Where we find that property is an object of trade and is utilized by individuals for profit-making enterprise in a market economy, there we have capitalism. If this be accepted, then it becomes perfectly clear that capitalism shaped whole periods of Antiquity, and indeed precisely those periods we call 'golden ages'.

But we must avoid exaggeration. In particular, it is necessary to show the specific peculiarities of the various types of capital goods, and the manner of their valorization, which determined the course of ancient economic history. Among the types of capital goods we do not find, of course, all those tools of production which were devised during the last two centuries of technological advance, and which today constitute what we call fixed capital. On the other hand Antiquity had a form of capital goods now in disuse: debt or chattel slaves. Similarly among the forms of capitalist enterprise a very small role was played by the workshop in Antiquity, and an even smaller one by the factory. On the other hand a form of economic activity now of little significance was of absolutely dominant importance in Antiquity: government contract.

The most important forms of capital investment in Antiquity were as follows: (1) government contracts for partial or total collection of taxes and public works; (2) mines; (3) sea trade, with ownership of ships or part ownership, especially through bottomry loans; (4) plantations; (5) banking and related activities; (6) mortgages; (7) overland trade. The last only sporadically became a regular, large-scale enterprise – in the West only during the first two centuries of the Roman Empire and only with respect to trade with the North and North-east; most overland trade was in goods sent on consignment by caravan. Also important were: (8) leasing out slaves (sometimes educated slaves) or establishing slaves as independent artisans or merchants in return for a percentage of income (or *obrok*, as the Russians would say); (9) finally, capitalist exploitation of slaves skilled in a craft, either owned or leased, sometimes in a workshop and sometimes not.

That slaves were frequently used in private economic enterprises cannot be doubted. Artisans were to be seen working alongside a few slaves of their own. Capitalistic exploitation in the type of enterprise called *ergastērion* has been mentioned above and will be discussed further below. Although there is no proof of its existence in the classical period proper, we can certainly presume that there existed the 'domestic system', in which the master provides raw materials and tools, and the slave produces the finished product in his own family household and then delivers it to him. Certainly this existed in the Near East, and it was dominant in ancient Egypt. We may, therefore, presume such a system in the Athenian pottery industry, even though many exports bear the same name (so far the largest group numbers about 80). The name is of course that of an artist, not that of a 'manufacturer' or 'contractor'. The artist's name will have been that of a family of potters in which technical skill was passed on as an inheritance and as a secret, and the name would be kept as an eponym. In this connection we should note the existence of artisans' villages (*dēmoi*) in Attica, characteristic of the family-like organization of handicrafts.

The quantitative and also the qualitative importance of capitalist enterprise in Antiquity were determined by a number of independent variables which appeared in very different combinations at different times. These variables were as follows:

(1) It is clear that the supply of precious metals had great importance for the tempo of capitalist development. However, there is a mistaken tendency now current to overestimate the importance of this factor for the structure of the whole economy itself. Thus Babylonia had no mines and evidently very little precious metal supplies, as is indicated by the correspondence between Babylonia's kings and the Egyptian pharaohs, and also by the use of precious metals only as a measure of value; nevertheless from earliest times Babylonia's exchange system was as developed as that of any other Eastern land, and more developed than that of gold-rich Egypt. Similarly capitalism was not particularly important as a basic element of the economic structure of Ptolemaic Egypt, even though the Ptolemies had colossal hoards of precious metals (taking current estimates as at least approximately correct) and their economy was thoroughly monetarized. Indeed, capitalism developed to a greater extent in contemporary Rome.

There is also the strange theory that the rise of a natural economy in the later Roman Empire was the result of a fall in the productivity of the mines. This probably reverses the actual sequence of cause and effect; where a decline in mining productivity did occur, it was most likely caused by a shift from the classical period's mining system, based on a highly developed capitalist organization using slave labour, to a new system based on small contractors.

The foregoing, however, should not be taken as a denial of the significance of control over large supplies of precious metals and in particular the important effects for cultural history of the sudden appearance of such supplies. Some examples: (a) ancient customary kingship was supported by the 'royal treasure'; (b) without the mines of Laureion there would probably have been no Athenian fleet; (c) the transfer of many temple treasuries into the circulating money supply during the Hellenic period probably had much to do with price changes *c* 500 B.C.; (d) the release of the Achaemenids' hoard furthered Hellenistic city-foundations; (e) the well-known effects on Rome caused by the colossal influx of precious metals won as war booty in the second century B.C. However, the fact that this booty was used as it was and not otherwise – for example, it was not hoarded, as in the Near East – must have been due to prior existence of certain conditions. In other periods of Antiquity the presence of large stores of precious metals did in fact fail to have a 'creative' significance; that is, they did not lead to the development of qualitatively new forms of economic activity.

2. The economic specificity of the capitalist use of slave labour, as appears from comparison with free labour systems, is that a much greater amount of capital must be invested to assemble and maintain the work force. When low sales cause suspension of production not only does the capital invested in slaves bring no interest – as is true of capital invested in machines – but also the slaves literally 'eat up' additional amounts. The result is to slow down capital turnover and capital formation.

Furthermore there was a large risk in investing capital in slave labour. This was due first of all to the fact that slave mortality was very high and entirely unpredictable, causing capital loss to the owner. Then in addition any political upset could wipe out completely investments in slaves. This is particularly evident in the dramatic variations in slave prices; thus Lucullus sold prisoners into slavery at 4 drachmae apiece at a time when the regular market price, due to low supply, had risen to several hundred drachmae for an able-bodied labourer. The result of this was that capital invested in slaves could be drastically devalued at any time.

Moreover, there was no basis for reliable cost accounting, the necessary condition for large industrial enterprises based on division of labour. Along with this there was also the fact that patriarchal slavery, in the form prevalent in the Near East, either made the slave a member of the master's household or else conceded to him the right to have his own family household. In the latter case there could of course be no question of gaining maximum return on investments; the slave either paid dues, thus functioning as a source of rents rather than labour, or else performed work, possibly with his family, in which case he filled the role of labourer or unfree house worker with all the limitations on profit-making this implied.

Another limitation on the truly capitalist exploitation of slaves as a means of production was the fact that the slave market depended for supply on successful wars. For full capitalist exploitation of the work force was possible only if the slaves had no families, in fact as well as in law; in other words, if they were kept in barracks, which, however, made reproduction of slaves impossible. For the cost of maintaining women and rearing children would have been a dead ballast on working capital. Sometimes this could be recovered by putting women to work in textile production, but there were difficulties here due to the peculiarities of the consumption pattern and the importance of domestic spinning and weaving in Antiquity. As for the children there is evidence in a passage of Appian (*Civil Wars* I.1.7) that at least during certain periods of Roman history there was slave breeding on a mass scale for profit, as was done in the Southern states of the U.S., thus providing for use of part of slave capital for production and use of the other part for replenishment. However, this interpretation of the evidence remains open to question; the precipitous price fluctuations in the slave market must have made slave rearing very risky.

Furthermore, female labour was not suited for the major slave-labour industries – plantations, seafaring, mining, tax farming. Hence it was a general rule that profit-making enterprises depended mainly on male slaves when possible; indeed there is no evidence for females as farm labourers in the time of Cato or as workers in Athenian *ergastēria*. 'When possible' meant when warfare provided the market with a stable supply of slaves. In such periods female slaves were used for prostitution or house work. If, however, the market ceased to receive regular supplies over a period of any length, then the slave force had to be replenished through natural increase, leading to abandonment of slave barracks and establishment instead of slave family life. The slaves then became themselves responsible for replacement of slave capital, and this imposed limitations on exploitation of the work force. Slaves could then no longer be worked in chains and whipped in a plantation system; the result was inevitably to decrease profits, except where a way was found to use the economic self-interest of slaves for the benefit of their masters.

For not only was slave capital insecure and subject to unpredictable risks, there was also the fact that the slaves used in large enterprises naturally had no interest in any technical advance or in any increase in the quantity or quality of production. The moral qualities which render slaves amenable to exploitation are precisely those which make them most inefficient as workers in a large enterprise. Therefore besides attrition of slave capital there was also attrition of capital invested in draft cattle and work tools. There was also stagnation in technology: for example, there was no improvement in the plough.

Certain complaints are revealing. Thus we are told that it was impossible to use slaves for large-scale grain cultivation, because of its high labour intensity in Antiquity. Indeed, large-scale use of slave labour was in general really profitable only when the land was fertile and the market price of slaves was low. Hence slave labour was normally used for extensive agriculture. Further, a still more important consequence, this characteristic of slave labour hindered both technological advance and also that precise coordination of differentiated operations which constitutes – rather than simply the number of workers involved – the essential characteristic of modern industrial production.

Skilled slave labour, for the same reasons, was not regularly used in large-scale enterprises based on division of labour. Isolated cases are found, but always on a small scale; in general it was as infrequent in Antiquity as in other periods. Even the *ergastērion*, essentially an agglomeration of independent workers, developed mainly in thriving economic centres like Athens, Rhodes, and Alexandria, and then always as an annex to a trading firm or rentier establishment. Often princely and noble *oikoi* had more dependent labour or unfree house labour available than was needed, or an excess supply of products of their domestic production, and these surpluses then appeared on the market, but one must be careful not to confuse this phenomenon with the existence of 'factories' based on purchased slaves.

There were also half-capitalist formations, based on the use of forced labour to establish 'subsidiary enterprises' within the establishments of monarchs and great slave owners, and similar to many 'factories' in the Russia of 1700–1830. But these could exist only as monopolies, and only under certain conditions, among them being cheap food, monopoly prices for the products, and low slave prices. The rate of exploitation also had to be high enough (30–100 per cent in Demosthenes and Aeschines) to cover the risks of slave mortality, for it to be economically possible to use purchased slaves in the master's *ergastērion* on a regular basis. Even then however these enterprises had no more than a few dozen workers at most. Nor did they have the fixed capital which is characteristic of a factory. Loans were made on the slaves as collateral, but not on the workshop. The slaves in fact constituted the workshop or plant, and their maintenance by the master was the crucial factor, not their employment in a single production unit. The workshop, on the other hand, was a part of the *oikos*, and hence there is no trace in Antiquity of all those fundamental legal developments which resulted – many centuries before the appearance of modern factories – from the later separation of family household from workshop in mediaeval Europe, accompanied as early as the thirteenth and fourteenth centuries by separation of private from business property. Hence too there did not occur, with a few exceptions, any development of business organizations like our joint stock company which could ensure continuance of enterprises despite the uncertainties which accompany partnerships; the exceptions, as one might expect, occurred in tax farming.

Similarly the use of large numbers of slaves on an industrial scale in mines, quarries, and on public works was almost entirely a matter of exploiting unskilled labour. Unfree domestic labour was a type of corvée, and was subject to the usual economic disadvantages. It is therefore doubtful how much use it found in production for the market. Pharaohs and priests used house labour mainly to supply the needs of temple, court, and state, especially of course if the raw material was imported or mined by the temple (or pharaoh) itself. Some of the product may, however, have been marketed on the side. In any case unfree domestic labour, wherever it appeared, meant work within the slave's own small family household. Skilled slave labour was only used regularly in large industrial enterprises (save for the few large centres of commerce) in managerial positions. Thus slaves served as foremen and inspectors in mines and on plantations, and as cashiers and accountants (since they were subject to interrogation under torture) in offices, and the like. Men in these positions formed a kind of slave aristocracy, and they enjoyed the right to their own (quasi-) family (*contubernium*) and their own (quasi-) property (*peculium*); sometimes they were even allowed the right to dispose of their property by will (as with Pliny's slaves), and also – most important – were generally given the chance to purchase their freedom. All this was of course to the interest of their masters.

Such privileged slave labour formed a transition to exploitation of skilled slaves, both those trained before enslavement by war or bankruptcy, and also those trained at their masters' expense merely as a source of rents. They were then often leased out in large numbers as 'wage earners', with the lessee bearing the risks of slave mortality. Or else a skilled slave was set up in his own shop as an independent artisan or tradesman. This was yet more profitable, since it enlisted the slave's own self-interest. The master received a regular income (*apophora*) and could increase it up to the point where the slave's self-interest was discouraged. He could also allow the slave to amortize his own capital value, which was essentially what was involved in letting the slave use his earnings to buy his own freedom. In such cases, furthermore, the master reserved for himself certain levies and services still due after manumission, and also appropriated a portion of the freedman's estate at his death, sometimes all of it. The portion taken was fixed by law or contract or will; Roman law was especially rich in alternatives here.

The risk of capital loss caused by death was lessened once

the slave established his own business and family and trained his children. Slave law generally made the master liable for his slave's business debts only up to the amount of the slave's own property (*peculium*), which of course the master was legally entitled to appropriate. That this power was not unduly abused in Antiquity, at least by the *large* slaveowner, was probably due to the necessity of encouraging the slave's economic self-involvement, and also due to the skill with which slaves concealed their wealth; both were also significant factors in Russia before emancipation of the serfs.

Manumission was common in all periods of Antiquity, at times so common that legal regulation was necessary. Naturally it was never due primarily to vanity or to the desire to enlarge a political clientele; rather, its importance indicates how effective was the slave's economic self-interest. Manumission, in fact, provided a more secure way of realizing profit from slave ownership. Its economic effect, however, was to transform the capitalist exploitation of the slave as a means of production into the acquisition of profit from the slave as a source of rent and manumission money.

Hence 'the struggle between free and unfree labour' took place in the sphere of small business, both craft and trade. It was not a struggle between large-scale slave enterprise and small-scale free artisanal enterprise. When the above evolution occurred there was an end to the great economic and political risks which burdened slave capital used directly for production. This situation was very widespread in Antiquity.

The free but propertyless groups in Antiquity included peasants, tenants, shopkeepers, and wage earners. Alongside them there were two other groups: (1) a class of free, small property owners, engaged in trading and in small-scale production on order; often they were assisted in field or workshop by one or a few slaves ('fellow workers'), won as war booty or bought with savings; (2) a class of unfree skilled craftsmen, shopkeepers, serfs, and tenant farmers.

Members of the latter group functioned as unfree but economically autonomous agents. They stood to their masters in much the same relation as that between free peasants, shopkeepers, or artisans and their creditors, or that between free *coloni* and their landlords. In other words, the master was simply a recipient of tribute, and the slave was exploited as a source of rents. In order to realize profit for the masters this system obviously demanded an extensive division of labour within a local money economy. Once these conditions were satisfied this system was able to maintain itself in competition with the use of slaves as means of production, and even as a rule to expand. That was especially true when the masters were much involved in politics and could not direct their business affairs personally, for example full citizens of the *polis* as opposed to metics in Greece and members of the senatorial nobility as opposed to equestrians in Rome. Another condition propitious to this development was a continuously high price level in the slave market.

As for competition between free and unfree labour, tenant farming was in Antiquity as at present the most remunerative way to exploit landed property, where there was high population density and high land prices, and consequently an emphasis on intensive agriculture, with freedom of movement and absence of relationship of bondage. Small farming was certainly dominant in ancient agriculture, slave labour being used in general on plantations, including those devoted to oil and wine production. Grain cultivation, given the technology of Antiquity, demanded too much individual effort to allow the normal use of slave labour. Indeed the use of slave labour on a large scale was only profitable in agriculture at times when slaves were cheap and plantation products at the same time commanded high prices.

In trade and handicrafts, however, the opportunity for slaves to buy their freedom generally served as an effective spur, even more so when the privilege of keeping savings was also conceded. It was no accident that freedmen prospered, for they had acquired habits of industry and thrift while slaves. Their success was also due, of course, to their exclusion from politics.

Inscriptions of the Roman Empire indicate that slave labour was less important in the Near East than in the West, even in handicrafts; and that slaves were used in the main for heavy, unskilled work. The first phenomenon was partly the result of prior economic patterns inherited from the past (discussed below), but it was also a result of the fact that the Roman (i.e. Western) slave market had, for political reasons, a better supply. The second phenomenon was simply a consequence of the natural reluctance of masters to accept the risks and expense involved in putting slaves through a long apprenticeship.

Consequently one should not think of the effects of slave labour as simply – or even mainly – a matter of driving out free labour. Rather, its main effect was to discredit work because so much of it was done by foreign slaves bought in the market; there was, however, a general tendency to drive out free labour wherever armies were not recruited (as in the Hellenistic Near East) from professional soldiers, mercenaries, or alien ruling peoples. When wars were bitter and constant, when victory inclined now to one side and then to another, and when this kept the free population away on campaigns for years at a time, then the inevitable result – as Appian reports – was to favour slave labour as opposed to free labour, and indeed every form of slave exploitation.

On the other hand military expansion and great victories typically led to an increase in the slave supply, a reduction in slave prices, and hence furthered the capitalistic exploitation of slaves in private enterprises – plantations, navigation, mining, handicrafts, and so on. In agriculture capitalist exploitation of slave labour was profitable when another variable was present – cheap land. This occurred irregularly as the result of military expansion or revolutionary confiscation, regularly where a small population was settled on a large area of fruitful land alongside developing municipal centres of consumption. The latter situation obtained in Rome after the unification of Italy and Rome's first overseas conquests, to a degree indeed never matched either before or after. This, and similar considerations discussed above, bring us to a third problem, the influence of politics.

3. In each country political developments and conditions shaped the relative growth of free and unfree labour, and also the degree and manner in which unfree labour was subjected to capitalist exploitation. L. M. Hartmann has demonstrated the importance of military burdens imposed on free populations, and has shown that it furthered use of slave labour most of all where levies recruited from the farmers and small-owners had to equip themselves and fight a series of major wars. Well-known examples of this occurred during the flowering of Greek democracy and in the Roman Republic. Conditions were just the opposite when the army, or at least part of it, was a feudal levy,

or was an autocrat's professional or mercenary or serf army; these types existed in Egypt, many Hellenistic states, the late Greek *polis*, and the Later Roman Empire. From the variety of economic systems in the last group of states it is apparent that military organization by itself determined neither the degree to which slavery developed, nor consequently the degree or direction in which capitalism developed. On the other hand economic life was always much affected by the political systems of Antiquity, in particular by the type of administration which arose from the constitution in question. Most important of all in this respect was the financial administration.

For the organizations of public finance were the oldest large-scale enterprises of Antiquity, and they remained the largest. They developed gradually out of the *oikoi* of the city princes, and were at first hoards of precious metals. In part these enterprises functioned as substitutes for private capital accumulation, in part they were pace-makers for it and in part they throttled it. Let us examine each aspect.

1. Finance authorities were substitutes for private capital most clearly in the bureaucratically directed compulsory labour systems of pharaonic Egypt, which originally did not have private entrepreneurs. But even the financing of the large public projects of the Greek cities, which were let to private contractors (as the inscriptions show) was really made possible by advance of working capital from the state treasury, and this indicates that there were no private accumulations of capital sufficient to finance such large projects. In short, moneys raised as tribute by political or sacred authority had to fill the gap. In such cases the entrepreneur was essentially hired for a fee to organize the necessary clerical and labour force, as the cities – unlike the pharaonic administration – did not have the bureaucracy necessary to oversee building and had no pool of compulsory labour supply, since citizens had been freed from corvée and the city slaves were employed in government offices, registries, the treasury, the mint, and sometimes in building roads.

As for tax farming, it should be remembered that in many cases precisely that feature was absent which we are accustomed to think of as characteristic of the role of private capital: payment in advance. Often the tax farmers deposited their guaranteed payments only after they had collected all or – more often – an agreed part of the taxes. When the state possessed an executive officialdom, such as appears in the Revenue Laws of Ptolemaic Egypt, then tax farmers did not even collect taxes; the state did so, and the tax farmers either made up any deficit that appeared after converting taxes in kind into money, or else profited if there was a surplus. Here the purpose of farming the taxes was evidently no more than to obtain a secure cash basis for the state budget by insuring a minimum income in currency.

Now of course this was an aspect of the development of tax farming in Hellenistic times, and tax farmers did in fact often have the obligation of making at least partial advance payments. Nevertheless the sums paid, though often high, do not allow us to infer the existence of correspondingly large capital accumulations. On the other hand the system of state contracts, especially in the area of tax farming, was clearly an important factor in capital formation, and indeed in Greece one of the most important.

2. Public finance set the pace for private capital formation in city states which could do without a bureaucratic apparatus and, instead, used state contractors to administer domains as well as territories and tributes of enormous conquered areas. In Antiquity this was the case in Republican Rome, in which there developed a powerful class of private capitalists, undoubtedly based from the first on the state contract system. In the era of the Second Punic War – the time is significant – they supported the state with money in the manner of modern banks, and in return were able to determine the state's policies even during the war. Their thirst for profit was such that a reformer like Gracchus had to give them control of provinces and courts in order to win them over, and their struggle with the senatorial aristocracy (whom they economically controlled as money-lenders) dominated the last century of the Republic. Ancient capitalism reached its high point in this period, as a consequence of the constellation and of the unique political structure of the Roman state.

3. On the other hand the public finance of the ancient states could also retard private capitalism in various ways. Above all the general political basis of ancient states typically reinforced the great instability of capital structure and formation inherent in the ancient economies. There were many pressures working in the same direction. Among them were the liturgies imposed on propertied classes and the unrestrained and sovereign power of

the Greek city states – especially the democracies – over the private property of their citizens; in late Hellenistic times loans were still sometimes secured by mortgaging all private real estate in a city, a practice unknown in the Middle Ages. Furthermore there was the danger of confiscations, which occurred at every political upset and change of parties in ancient communities; and the not uncommon and wholly arbitrary expropriations of monarchies, such as the seizure of 'half Africa' by Nero.

However, much more important than these catastrophes which affected only particular interests or communities, was the general limitation imposed by public administrations on the profits of private capital, and thereby on capital formation. This limitation varied significantly. It was much more pronounced in the ancient monarchies than in the republics. The ancient monarch and members of his court were always great agrarian lords, whose position was secured partly in private law, partly in arbitrary domination exercised over conquered populations forced to pay tribute and denied any legal title to their land. The ancient *polis* could also control such possessions, and indeed the Roman Republic did so on a colossal scale.

Where a *polis* had such possessions they were primarily objects of purely economic exploitation by the changing cliques surrounding prominent political leaders, above all their financiers. Consequently city states, especially Rome, subjected their possessions to brutal exploitation by private capital through usurious tax farming, high mortgage rights, and slave trading. A monarch, however, had to act otherwise. In the first place he regarded the inhabitants of his domains essentially in more political terms – that is, as adherents of his dynasty. Furthermore a monarch naturally tended, in his own interests, to value security of revenues much more highly than would a republican government directed by officials elected for short terms; for the latter and their followers, immediate profit was much more important. Hence a monarch's financial policy would be oriented more towards political and state-economic objectives, and hence would aim at a prudent and durable rate of exploitation based on the actual resources and capacity of his subjects. City-states, on the contrary, looted subject populations for the benefit of capitalist interests. Thus royal domains were generally let to small tenants, whereas the use of large contractors and slave plantations was very much the exception. It is true that the Roman emperors preferred large tenants on their family estates for pecuniary reasons, but on state domains they followed the normal rule.

But the crux was tax farming, the most important form of capital investment in Antiquity. In republican communities it was so central that it always tended to make the state an enterprise based on tax loans and tax contracts, like mediaeval Genoa. In monarchical states, on the contrary, tax farming was always under control, often entirely or nearly entirely nationalized, and always restricted in its profits. This of course reduced its role in capital formation. In these states it was usually limited by a combination of bureaucratic regulation and (relatively) modestly financed monopoly administration. This process of control, monopoly, and bureaucratic regulation – often leading to the complete exclusion of private capital – developed inexorably in all the great monarchies of Antiquity. Gradually it transformed the administration of taxes and domains, and also the supervision of the mines and of politically important activities such as the grain supply and the delivery of provisions for the court, army and public works. Furthermore it led to the emergence of state and municipal banks enjoying monopoly status, for example governing all money-changing activities in the Hellenistic monarchies and municipalities.

Thus there was a sharp distinction between the city states and monarchies of Antiquity. In the city states there always remained the possibility of accumulating and investing capital. This was true even though the constitutional character of city states greatly heightened the unstable composition of capital, less because of repeated efforts to attain economic equality within the citizenry – efforts which were nearly always unsuccessful – than because ancient party conflict and ancient warfare constantly led to political and economic catastrophes of every sort.

In the monarchies, on the other hand, capitalism was gradually checked by bureaucratic regulation. Large private accumulation in particular fared badly, for its major sources of profit were blocked, and so it was slowly starved out. This eventually caused stagnation in closed monarchical areas; exploitation of rural areas by cities, as essential in Antiquity as in the Middle Ages, came to a halt, and expansion through conquest of new land and population stopped. This meant that there ceased to be a plentiful supply of cheap slaves and exploitable land, both essential for growth in a capitalist slave labour economy.

Stagnation and decline in capital formation were regularly accompanied by measures designed to ensure fulfilment of the needs of the state. This process, well described recently by Rostovtzeff, meant a steady increase and differentiation of the number of those made liable with their persons or property for the performance of tasks assigned by the authorities. Such persons were tied to their land and social function by administrative law, until eventually society was universally dominated by a system of obligatory services, which abolished all that men of the 'classical' periods called freedom, in a mutation typical of the so-called 'decline' of ancient states.

Thus monarchical regulation, though beneficial to the great mass of subjects, spelt in fact the end of capitalist development and everything dependent on it. Slavery as a basis of capitalist enterprise regressed and new capital formation expired, for the profit margin allowed had sunk below the indispensable minimum needed by ancient capital. Instead the economy became dominated by labour which was formally 'free', but was in fact subject to administrative law and direction. Wherever, in addition, the monarchy assumed a theocratic character, there we always find that religion and law sanction 'protection of the weak' as in the Near East, and this set rather precise limits to capitalist exploitation of men.

For agrarian history the results of this development were always the same. The relative importance of slave plantations declined while small tenant farming – especially share cropping – became the main form of land use. Estates exploited for rents by princes, and landowners holding their land from princes on a semi-private basis, became the predominant category of property in the countryside.

To sum up, the most important hindrance to the development of capitalism in Antiquity arose from the political and economic characteristics of ancient society. The latter, to recapitulate, included: (1) the limits on market production imposed by the narrow bounds within which land transport of goods was economically feasible; (2) the inherently unstable structure and formation of capital; (3) the technical limits to the exploitation of slave labour in large enterprises and (4) the limited degree to which cost accounting was possible, caused primarily by the impossibility of strict calculation in the use of slave labour.

It should be noted in passing that private accounting was by no means undeveloped in Antiquity. It was used in banking and also by country estates and extended households to keep inventory. Only the first kind was commercial in character. All other forms of private accounting were – as far as we know – still quite undifferentiated as compared with those of later mediaeval times, judging by the capitalist standard of how accurately profit margins were reckoned.

Large enterprises based on slave labour were not created in Antiquity for economic reasons – that is, in order to assure a form of production based on division and coordination of labour: rather, they arose from purely personal circumstances – the fortuitous accumulation of a large number of slaves in the possession of a single individual. This, then, is the correct interpretation of the *oikos*-theory. It explains why all large enterprises had a peculiarly unstable, evanescent character. Publicans, artisans, shop-keepers – these were the mainstay of the money economy in the Near East and in the Hellenistic States, and when political and economic stability arrived in the West, there too there was a decline in capital formation, and these groups became predominant.

Again and again we find that it is precisely in the periods of 'justice and order' – equivalent of course to periods of economic stability – that there occurred a swift decline of capitalism. Capitalist entrepreneurs, not to be confused with gentlemen rentiers, generally enjoyed only a rather precarious social position in Antiquity. Conditions differed somewhat at certain periods of Babylonian, Hellenistic, late republican and early imperial Roman history, but certainly in the classical periods proper most entrepreneurs were metics and freedmen. Another indication of low status is that men engaged in trade were often ineligible for office, even – or rather, especially – in democracies.

In fact, ancient political theory was based on the ideal of the 'independent citizen', which meant in practice a rentier able to live on his income and also – this was especially important in the 'free' communities – ready to serve in the army whenever needed. Ancient political theory was hostile to the profit motive, but not in the main for reasons similar to those of the mediaeval church, which condemned impersonal commercial relations because they could not be subjected to ethical norms. Political, rather than ethical, considerations determined ancient ideas on the subject. Reasons of state, equality of citizens and autarky of the *polis* were at the centre of these ideas, and there was also the contempt for trade and tradesmen cultivated by the leisured upper classes.

Businessmen, on the other hand, were not sustained by any positive justification of the profit motive. Only among followers of Cynicism and in the lower middle classes of the Hellenistic Near East do we find the beginnings of such an attitude. In early modern times the rationalization and economization of life were furthered by the essentially religious idea of 'vocation' and the ethic derived from it, but nothing similar arose in Antiquity. The ancient businessman remained no more than a 'common tradesman' in his own eyes and in the eyes of his contemporaries.

There were of course exceptions, most notably in the area of marine commerce. From the first the ownership of ships and their use to transport goods for sale by employees was 'respectable'; kings, temples, and aristocrats of coastal areas engaged in this in early Antiquity. Then there developed genuine mercantile operations (*Emporia*), involving the use of hired ships to transport purchased or consigned goods to centres of commerce, first as a joint venture and then for the profit of a single organizer. This too was considered respectable, although always with reserve, but only because it involved the irregular use of one's property and did not have the character of an 'established business', and so it does not really weaken our argument.

Another factor which checked the development of capitalism in Antiquity was the great variety of distinctions which divided the population into hereditary classes, especially in the 'free' ciy-states. Political considerations also caused differentiation in the law of property, especially as it concerned land and inheritance. All of these distinctions could and did become sources of income, equivalent to rents. Especially in the democracies the interest of the lower middle classes in safeguarding their incomes and food supply became the dominant factor in city politics; a good example is Athenian citizenship policy. Even in the monarchies this attitude was influential as long as it did not conflict with the state's omnipotent fiscal interests.

It should be noted here that the course of agrarian history in Antiquity was so closely connected with the fortunes of the cities that the two subjects cannot be treated separately. Although rural areas outside the municipal structure formed of course the greater part of the ancient world, little clear evidence about conditions there has come down to us. Even more scanty is our knowledge of conditions in the territorial possession of cities before they were conquered, and indeed virtually nothing of the sort has been preserved from the subjected peoples themselves. The most ancient tradition of the Hebrews must have its origins in a period before the municipal organization of the nation, but it arose in a milieu shaped by centuries of urbanism and alien domination of advanced nations, and it is also impossible to determine to what extent the oldest elements of the tradition were later revised.

As for the Occident, although we come upon peoples there living in stages of development much more primitive than those of Babylon or Egypt, nevertheless the problem is the same. For example, we cannot be sure what was the original character of the canton or village – that is, before military differentiation (to be discussed) affected them – because the little evidence we have about conditions and institutions in historical times may well be shaped by the influence of bordering urbanized areas. This applies even to areas without municipal institutions, such as Arcadia, Samnium, and Persis (modern Fars).

Nor can we arrive at conclusive answers to such questions as when did such institutions as the phratry, phyle, curia, tribe and clan appear. Before that is possible we must know whether the Greek phratry – generally regarded as especially ancient – is essentially similar in character to other such institutions known to us from ethnography, or is different. If different, then despite all contrary arguments it was probably the result of a secondary development conditioned by military factors.

Nevertheless one long-accepted theory about the early social history of Antiquity may now be regarded as disproven – the theory that the occidental peoples originally led a nomadic life, and that their economy was entirely pastoral. This theory was based on such facts as that cattle played an important role among all occidental peoples as the chief element of movable property, and was therefore the main type of wealth used for exchange and tribute; that cattle ownership was used as the basis for class distinctions and cattle formed a major part of royal wealth (along with metal jewellery and sumptuous weapons); and, finally, that cattle rearing was regarded as a specifically masculine occupation and was therefore not demeaning to a nobleman. Despite all this the theory is untenable, although perhaps exception should be made for some eastern groups living near deserts.

Another plausible theory which must be rejected is that noble clans arose out of the conquest of sedentary agricultural groups by pastoral tribes. Although individual examples may be proven, the general theory is nevertheless untenable, for it was on the coasts that the ancient aristocratic states especially arose and developed in very early times. Furthermore other sources of power supported the dominant position of kings and nobles.

However, we do not have any reliable evidence concerning the social organization of agricultural societies in their earliest period, although agriculture was practised by all the peoples with whom we are concerned from the earliest prehistoric times of which we have knowledge. But one thing is clear: there are certain *stages* of organization, and these were recapitulated by all the peoples in Antiquity from the Seine to the Euphrates among whom urban centres developed. These stages were:

(1) First walls existed to provide defence against attack, and it was within these walls that cities later arose, but at this stage household and village continued to be the centres of economic life. Clan, cult, and military associations still provided for security and shaped religious and political institutions. Little more than this can be said, for we have no reliable information concerning the structure and interaction of these associations in the period before Antiquity.

We do know that all free members of the community had a share in ownership of the land, and where slaves were not numerous they also did part of the field work. Chiefs were probably similar in (transient) function and status to those of the early Germans, for they were never present except where the threat of war existed, and as judges their decisions were backed – as among most primitive peoples – only by moral authority. Furthermore they always had to respect the tradition which entitled the elders of the tribe to give counsel. It was of course the particular political situation which determined whether general problems arose.

Originally the sense of community arose out of joint efforts to produce food. Later ties based upon blood developed, and they gained strength first among princely clans, since the memory of their military exploits or meritorious judgments conferred upon them an aura of divine legitimacy. Their economic position was enhanced by voluntary gifts, by preference in the division of spoil, and later by special allotments of land.

(2) Next there appeared a form of settlement with more urban characteristics – the fortress. At its head was a 'king', elevated above his subjects by possession of land, slaves, herds and treasure, and surrounded by a personal retinue, the members of which dined at the royal table, enjoyed the ownership or use of royal land, slaves, herds and treasure, and served under the king in wars or on plundering expeditions.

Relations between king and subject varied. If royal policy aimed at peace, then the monarch simply relied on occasional gifts; but if the monarch's wish was to conquer an 'empire', then the population was forced to pay tribute, perform labour services, and provide recruits for supply on infantry duty at command.

We have no evidence as to the status of the land (and inhabitants) outside the fortress at this stage. But we know that two factors were generally necessary for establishment of a fortress kingdom: (a) fruitful land, able to support rent payments; (b) profit from commerce. Furthermore we know that the members of a royal retinue always formed a new and foreign element in the primitive community of peasants; everywhere we find that royal law and feudal law were separate from tribal law.

Indeed, members of the royal retinue were often regarded as foreigners, even when in fact they were not. For example, the followers of David (*Krethi* and *Plethi*) and of Romulus were supposed to have been bandits; similar traditions are found among many primitive peoples. It is possible that traces of such an idea explain the position of royal vassals in Mesopotamia (see below).

Once a king emerged as a conqueror, however, the foreign status of his military followers often came, quite naturally, to correspond with the actual situation. Above all the royal bodyguard became, for various reasons, a mercenary body. Hence the formation of larger realms became possible, with the differentations in wealth of the fortress-kings; the king with the largest 'treasure' could make other kings his vassals. This was the original of nearly all ancient 'states'.

(3) The next stage, closer to the 'classical' traditions of the Mediterranean peoples in Antiquity, is represented by the aristocratic city-state. In this the dominant class possessed lands and serfs (or debt slaves) which enabled its members to train themselves for war, provide themselves with the costly weapons necessary, and live the life of knights. Aristocratic clans controlled a citadel and from there dominated the surrounding area. This stage too was reached only where two factors were present: (a) rich land, to sustain rental payments; (b) proximity to a coast, to allow profits from commerce.

It was at this time that the feudal nobility of the old fortress kingdom emancipated itself from royal authority and constituted itself as an autonomous, urban community, in which rank was determined by military criteria and rule was exercised either by a king who was no more than first among equals or else – and this usually developed with time – by elected magistrates. In any case, however, these cities were not administered by bureaucracies, a fact of decisive importance.

It should be noted in passing that the urban character of these communities distinguished the development of Antiquity from the analogous development of feudalism and manorialism on the European continent in the early Middle Ages; although in Italy early mediaeval institutions were somewhat similar.

The aristocratic city was in fact a league of great 'clans'. Only those men were admitted who could live the life of a knight and take part in the city's military institutions. It was at this time that great value came to be placed on 'blood' and high birth.

In this form of society the typical – though not the only – form of labour-power was the debt slave, for the aristocracy was at first a class of money-lenders and then became a class of landowners living on rents. Most peasants fell into debt, then slipped into a form of debt slavery. Thus the open land outside the city came to be divided, part of it being farmed by independent peasants outside the aristocratic families, the rest being worked by a large class of debt slaves. Sometimes the latter were legally distinguished from free men as a separate order, but generally the same effect was achieved by the debt and trial law of early times, combined with aristocratic domination of the courts and the associated institution of clientage.

4. Sometimes the fortress kingdom developed in a direction quite different from that just sketched. If the king gained sufficient economic resources to become master of his retinue and army to the extent that he could bind them to his own person, then he was able to take a step of fundamental importance: create a bureaucracy entirely subordinate to himself and organized on hierarchical principles. With the aid of such a bureaucracy the king could govern his subjects directly, and the city then became no more than the royal capital where he and his court resided.

Sometimes the capital had no autonomy whatever, as in Egypt, which supposedly 'had no cities'. Elsewhere, as in Assur, autonomy was conceded in religious affairs. In still other cases the capital enjoyed a degree of unpolitical local autonomy under royal control and had certain privileges; Babylon is an example for which we have documentary evidence.

What of the land outside the city gates? We have little evidence on conditions during the early stages of the authoritarian city kingdom. Sometimes heavy taxes and labour services were imposed on subjects to such a degree as to lead to a form of complete 'state socialism', as in Egypt. In other cases a rather large sector of private economy continued to exist. The decisive factor here was the manner in which the needs of the royal household were met – that is, whether through forced labour services or through 'taxes'. One can therefore say that the system would tend towards one or another of two types: a regime based on forced labour or one based on tribute. Generally the former developed out of the latter, and it in turn was transformed by a process of 'rationalization' into the tax-and-liturgy state.

Commerce played a crucial role in the development of types 2 and 3 (there were of course many variations of these 'pure' types). Always type 2 appeared only when the chief monopolized foreign trade or at least was able to tax it – more or less like the 'kings' in the Camerun before the German occupation and to some extent since. Such control was vital because it enabled rulers to accumulate a 'hoard', as essential to the primitive 'kings' of the Nibelungen as to those of Mycenae, Persia, and India.

Hence too the significance of the provisions in Deuteronomy by which the theocracy prevented the Hebrew kings from accumulating a hoard.

Accumulation of hoards went hand in hand with the economic subjection of the peasantry. A typical example is preserved in the legend of Joseph in Genesis 47. 15–26: first the peasants borrow grain in time of need to have food and seed; then in order to repay this they must hand over their cattle, land, and their own persons into debt slavery; finally, they receive them back and henceforth work their land as share croppers.

Whether further development tended towards types 3 (aristocratic *polis*) or 4 (bureaucratic city kingdom) evidently depended upon the interaction of a complex of factors, some of them geographic, others purely historical. In either case, however, the economic burdens laid upon the populace to satisfy the needs of the government were in inverse proportion to the development of private domestic trade. This was true whether these burdens were imposed in 'domanial' or 'public' form, and whether the proceeds went to a group of ruling families or to the royal *oikos*.

However, as soon as either regime (type 3 or 4) could depend mainly on taxes it then took a natural attitude towards transfers of land. There continued to be, however, laws protecting the rights of heirs, and there were also limitations connected with estate tenure (in the aristocratic *polis*) or military obligations (in the monarchical city). Then under bureaucratic monarchy (type 4) the matter came to be of little concern to the ruler once he could rely upon 'his own' army as well as a bureaucratic fiscal system, and so full freedom of trade in land was allowed. The aristocratic families desired this so far as peasant property was concerned, for their position depended in part on the practice of usury, but they did not wish this freedom to extend to their own lands. Hence the formation of extended aristocratic clans (*gentes*) led to entailment in law or in practice.

On the other hand despotic rulers had good reason to oppose the development of autonomous patrimonial lordships, except those they themselves sanctioned; Napoleon's attitude is a recent example. That is why 'tyrants' often checked the tendency to accumulation of land, where it threatened, as in Greece, or promoted division of lands, where it had occurred, as in the Near East.

To sum up: type 4 was the bureaucratic city kingdom or bureaucratic river kingdom; in it the army and bureaucracy 'belonged' to the ruler, while his 'subjects' owed him labour services and tribute. As the state's needs were met in increasingly rationalized manner a new form of state appeared, namely

5. The authoritarian liturgical state, in which the state's necessities were met by a carefully contrived system of duties imposed on the state's subjects, now treated as purely fiscal units. Using their form as a basis for analysis, we can divide these duties into the following three categories:

(a) labour services rendered directly to the court and state;
(b) monopolies based upon labour services and upon coercive laws of various types;
(c) taxes, often paid mainly in money or by delivery of goods of money value, but accompanied by a punitive system based on compulsory surety for punctual payment which betrays the functional tendency so often typical of oriental despots.

This type of state did not put limits on commerce, unless its fiscal interests were threatened. Quite the contrary; it fostered commerce by direct action whenever this meant increased revenue.

'Enlightened despotism' of this sort generally developed in the ancient Near East directly out of the more primitive forms of the bureaucratic city kingdom, and indeed differed from the latter type only in its more rationalized organization. On the other hand the third type (aristocratic *polis*) led to a great variety of transitional forms, among them

6. The hoplite *polis* of Mediterranean lands, in which the domination of the clans over the city and of the city over rural areas was legally abolished. Participation in the city's military institutions was relatively democratized by the predominance of a hoplite army, while military service – and with it full citizenship – now became entirely dependent on ownership of land. A self-equipped citizen army emerged. From this developed

7. The democratic citizen *polis*, in which army service and with it citizenship rights were no longer dependent on ownership of land. There also existed a tendency in the coastal cities to allow anyone able to serve in the fleet to hold office; since naval

service involved virtually no expense this meant in practice that all citizens could become eligible for office without regard to property qualification. But this tendency never wholly triumphed, not even in the most radical period of the Athenian democracy. In the hoplite *polis* (type 6) the core of the army was recruited from the free citizen yeomanry. Hence trade in this form of state was not unrestricted, especially trade in land. The legislative programmes by which, typically, hoplite *poleis* were founded had as their aim the establishment of a lasting, generally accessible system of law as well as the stabilization of the social order by the amelioration of class conflict between creditors (aristocrats) and debtors (peasants).

Hence land ownership was closely regulated, partly to sustain clan rights and partly to ensure that a maximum number of able bodied hoplites would be available. In short, the *polis* pursued policies designed to preserve its yeomanry. Expansion of estate holding was blocked by both direct and indirect means; e.g. limits were set on the quantity of land or number of slaves a citizen might possess, and old debt laws were repealed. Along with this went other efforts to reduce distinctions within the citizen body and to promote a 'civil economy'.

Nevertheless the interests of the wealthy and of the urban classes prevailed. By the time of the transition to type 7, if not sooner, all land had become entirely or almost entirely transferable and free from any entail. It is this basic development which shapes agrarian conditions in the periods for which we have written sources. What existed before is revealed to us by a great variety of survivals, ranging from extreme cases like Sparta to the limited areas in the late Roman Republic still subject to liturgies such as responsibility for road building.

To sum up: the 'classical' *polis* consciously did away with the institutions of earlier times. It cannot be a coincidence that neither in the Near East nor in the West did the private land law of historical times include any provision for entail or acknowledge any labour service or tribute obligations on the land to individuals. Indeed no obligations went with land ownership except those connected with (a) mortgages and (b) the absolutely necessary provisions for water and road maintenance. Furthermore the classical *polis* did away with all communal forms of ownership and with all forms of feudal tenure, and ceased to regulate the subdivision of land by testament or other means, while keeping the right to impose labour services or inheritance taxes itself. What remained in effect was the right to rent land for money or part of the crop, an arrangement made solely for profit and subject to cancellation by either owner or renter.

Once these conditions had been established the flowering of capitalism followed. Slaves ceased to be recruited from debtors, and were instead purchased. The subsequent development of land ownership and land use under the impact of the new slave system and of the city-state's political fortunes is the basic theme of the agrarian history of the 'classical' periods. That history is shaped by the decline of the free yeomanry which had prospered under the hoplite *polis*, and its replacement by slaves or sharecroppers. Parallel with this went the formation of mercenary armies or, as in Rome, armies of the proletariat.

Thus the free tenant and the slave mark the end of the 'classical' periods; the former was more common in the Near East, the latter in the West. Nevertheless neither group ever became exclusively dominant, for everywhere free yeomen remained present and often they were settled in compact groups and formed the majority.

Then came periods in which the city-state was completely displaced by universal military monarchy, and it was in such epochs that an entirely new institution appeared: the manor. Certain basic characteristics defined it: peasants were bound to the land to the profit of the lord (but also to his cost) with more or less traditional rights and obligations; judicial power was in the hands of the lord; public burdens, especially taxes and army recruitment, were met by the manors; and the manors enjoyed immunities of various kinds. These are phenomena which the citizen *polis* (types 6 and 7) naturally did not know, and indeed consciously excluded. The emergence of the manor therefore appears as an entirely new development.

In fact, however, the manor had never ceased to exist. Its sphere of influence and relative importance was much reduced after the time of the fortress kingdom, but in the large, unurbanized, inland areas there were certainly always present manors of more or less evident character. When the Near Eastern city kingdoms and liturgy monarchies developed into 'world empires', these manors maintained their character as domains or as fiefs.

Such empires were therefore really conglomerates of urban and manorial areas. This was true first of Assyria and later of Persia. Similarly in the Hellenistic monarchies the royal domains kept their manorial character, for there the monarch united in his person proprietary and public authority. Probably other areas also continued to retain manorial features, even though the Hellenistic monarchs – except in Egypt – strongly promoted and propagated cities as agents of control.

In the Roman Empire, the final phase of Antiquity, the centres of culture and population (the latter being of military significance) shifted inland in the West away from the coasts. This meant fundamental changes in the entire social basis and administrative problems of the state. These changes, their economic effects, and their influence on imperial policies, combined to foster new social institutions which mark the transition to mediaeval society. Therefore the major aspects of the agrarian history of this period and of manorialism in late Antiquity in general will be examined in a separate article under the heading 'colonate'.[2]

The analysis just presented depends upon the use of various 'types': peasant community, aristocratic *polis*, bureaucratic city kingdom, hoplite *polis*, citizen *polis*, liturgy monarchy. Needless to say, these types seldom existed in complete isolation. They are 'pure types', concepts to be used in classifying individual states. They simply allow us to ask whether a particular state at a particular time more or less approximated to one or another of these pure types. More than an 'approximation' cannot be expected, for actual state structures in the most important phases of history are too complex to be comprehended by so simple a classification as the one used here.

Indeed, one historically important type has not even been mentioned: the military peasant community constituted as a hoplite band. Examples of this in Antiquity are numerous, but

2. [An article on this subject by Michael Rostovtzeff appeared in vol. 5, pp. 913–21, of the *Handwörterbuch*. Its conclusions, in substantial agreement with Weber's argument, had already been sketched by Rostovtzeff in 'Der Ursprung des Kolonats', *Beiträge zur alten Geschichte* (= Klio), (1902), pp. 295–9, and were later discussed at greater length in 'The Problem of the Origin of Serfdom in the Roman Empire', *Journal of Land and Public Utilities Economics* II. 2 (1926), pp. 198–207.]

in my opinion are always secondary; that is, they appear in connection with the partial adoption of urban institutions, as among the ancient Hebrews, the Aetolians, and the Samnites.

Nevertheless, besides providing a useful terminology the classification presented here has the value of indicating how very different were the stages which each of the nations of Antiquity had reached when, as chance would have it, their history starts to be revealed to us by our sources. Mesopotamia had passed through several thousand years of urban development and Egypt had a similarly long history of semi-urban development when they first emerge in our sources; they are, in fact, already liturgy monarchies. When we first learn anything secure about the Romans they have already passed the stage of the citizen *polis*. For the Greeks, on the other hand, we have much fairly secure information going back to the aristocratic *polis* or even to the fortress kingdom stage. Our information concerning the Celts – which is unreliable; hence they have not been considered in our analysis – relates to all three earliest stages. Finally, our sources for the history of Sparta, of the Athenian democracy in its imperial period, and of Rome furnish in each case unique examples of development. Because of this basic aspect of our knowledge of Antiquity, we must be prepared to combine individual characteristics from various conceptual 'types' in order to describe the history of a single [nation] in concrete terms.

Finally there is one historical factor which raises particular obstacles to the application of our classification. That is the manifest or latent struggle between theocratic and secular-political forces, for often this conflict introduced military institutions from more than one of our 'types'.

Originally there must have been a union of political and religious authority everywhere, but with the development of theology and an educated priesthood functional specialization became inevitable. Great power remained in the hands of the priests, partly because of their wealth from temple lands and income, partly because the masses looked to them for salvation from punishment for sacrilege, and partly because they were originally the only men of learning.

From this followed two important results: (1) in general, since priests enjoyed a monopoly of legal knowledge, and since the priesthoods were held by members of the aristocratic families, these families enjoyed a position of unassailable dominance as long as the law remained uncodified; (2) all education, especially in the bureaucratic monarchies, where training was necessary for employment in the administration, was almost entirely in the hands of priests. Throughout the Near East the priesthood strove to gain control of education; we see this tendency clearly in the Egyptian New Empire, where the priests displaced secular officials and secular education.

Hence certain conflicts are characteristic of early Antiquity: temple priesthood versus military nobility and royal authority in bureaucratic monarchies, commoners versus the monopoly of legal knowledge enjoyed by noble priests in aristocratic states. All sorts of alliances occurred. These conflicts influenced social and economic developments, especially in periods of general secularization or restoration; the latter were usually due to usurpers striving for legitimacy. There were important differences in this respect between Near Eastern and Western societies, and these will be discussed below.

In the second part of this essay a sketch will be given of what is known about the agrarian history of those states which are historically most significant. Complete coverage of all known systems would be impossible, for the primary sources published during the last decade are so extensive and complex as to defy interpretation, by any other than specialized scholars trained in philology and archaeology.

II. The Agrarian History of the Major Centres of Ancient Civilization

Mesopotamia

Cuneiform scholars have astonishing achievements to their credit, but nevertheless the sources – including the Code of Hammurabi – have not yet been made available for interpretation by non-specialists. The scholar who has not mastered the field and must depend on translated texts cannot therefore reach definite conclusions regarding the Mesopotamian economy. Furthermore it is precisely the texts most important for legal and social history which often elude interpretation.

As for Old Testament texts, there is still the problem of distinguishing genuine evidence from the tendentious accounts of 'political fiction' written after the Exile. This difficulty remains despite the work of Wellhausen, Eduard Meyer, Guthe, Jeremias, and most recently, A. Merx. For these reasons what follows is no more than a brief and tentative outline.

Domestication of animals and intensive horticulture appeared very early in Babylonia, and then in the other societies of Mesopotamia. Large fortunes regularly included grain and date-palm gardens, and sesame became an important item of diet. In addition our sources mention a great variety of green vegetables and legumes: turnips, radishes, cucumbers, colocynths, and onions. Garlic was bought and sold in enormous quantities; our sources mention transactions involving several hundred thousand units. Dill, lettuce, beets, coriander, saffron, hyssop, thyme, and blackberries are also mentioned. All were raised in the royal gardens.

On the other hand there were no forests. The wood used for royal building projects in Assyria was won by conquest in Lebanon, and inscriptions report hunting expeditions of Assyrian kings in the northern forests in the same manner as military expeditions. Further, though cattle and sheep rearing have an important role in the Code of Hammurabi, it was the monarch who was evidently the largest owner of herds and flocks.

The basis of the economy was irrigation, for this was the crucial factor in all exploitation of land resources. Every new settlement demanded construction of a canal, so that the land was essentially a man-made product. Now canal construction is necessarily a large-scale operation, demanding some sort of collective social organization; it is very different from the relatively individualistic activity of clearing virgin forest. Here then is the fundamental economic cause for the overwhelmingly dominant position of the monarchy in Mesopotamia (and also in Egypt).

Canals and irrigation systems are already prominent in inscriptions from Sumer and Akkad, the oldest centres of civilization in Mesopotamia, and later inscriptions from Assyria in the north tell the same story. Labour services of various types were exacted from the population for building and maintaining canals and dikes, and work was done under the direction of royal overseers, so that very soon the ancient city kingdom began to develop into a bureaucracy.

Wars were fought by Babylon and Assur – especially the latter, an aggressive imperialist state – primarily with one objective: to conquer subjects who would dig a new canal for a new city. Then these new subjects were settled in the new city, granted temporary privileges with regard to taxes and labour services, and so contributed to the increase of the royal income and power.

Later, during Assyria's imperial period, its kings boasted that the peoples whom they had conquered 'pay the same tribute as the Assyrians', indicating that the latter themselves counted as royal possessions and no more. That however was not true in earlier times, nor was it maintained with all its implications in later times. The city of Babylon, for instance, addressed a memorial to the Assyrian king referring to immunities and privileges granted by his ancestors, among them a very generous grant of metic rights designed to encourage commerce. Other cities also had guaranteed privileges. On occasion the Council of Elders in Babylon and Sippar was summoned to advise the king on the construction of a temple, and similarly the Assyrian king consulted 'the nobles and commons' of the Assyrians when planning a new palace. But these exceptions could not alter the basic character of the political system.

The economic activities of the Mesopotamian monarchy constituted an *oikos* which far surpassed in size the private sector. The royal *oikos* drew its revenues from several sources: (1) the royal domains, including a large number of bondsmen and serfs (the king of Sumer, and evidently all later rulers, had his own shepherds); (2) the royal subjects, who (a) paid taxes in kind and (b) rendered labour services. We cannot be sure, however, as to how state burdens were divided between the two categories in specific periods. In earlier times flocks and herds seem to have supplied most revenue, later taxes in kind on crops.

Similarly we cannot be precise about the relative importance of the royal slave force and the labour services rendered by subjects, but the relationship clearly fluctuated, as one would expect from the character of the system. Like the pharaohs, the kings of Sumer and Akkad regulated the labour services of their subjects, provided them with food and drink, and then saw to it that they received payment in kind. There were all sorts of royal warehouses – for wagons, grain, spice, treasure – and all sorts of royal workshops. Thus the Sumerian kings imported gold and had it used to make ceremonial pots in their own workshops, and likewise stone was cut and made into statues by royal craftsmen. Above all, everything needed for official building projects was produced in the royal *oikos*. Wood, for example, was imported from distant lands.

Furthermore the royal citadel was surrounded with land holdings which were assigned to craftsmen bound to render labour services; they thus constituted a labour force always available. Later the Assyrian kings used war prisoners for their colossal building projects alongside the native craftsmen bound to labour service, the latter being given the tasks needing skilled labour. Sennacherib boasted that he had sponsored technical advance in bronzework, and he even sneered at his ancestors because 'their ignorance amazes all craftsmen'. From these inter-relations it is obvious that one cannot make a sharp distinction between royal slaves and subjects owing labour services.

(3) Another source of income was foreign commerce. A Sumerian king conscripted 'sailors and their captains' and then dedicated them to temple service, indicating a wish not to be directly involved in trade. His predecessors, however, had no such hesitation, and royal trading on the basis of exchange of 'gifts' with

foreign princes lasted 1000 years, as is well known. Indeed it was precisely the monopoly of foreign trade at the river mouths which constituted the foundation of the power of city kings in the southern lands. Hence it was there that royal *oikos* first appeared, as in the delta area of Egypt.

(4) In Assyria another source of revenue was booty. At the height of its power the Assyrian state sent out its armies on annual plundering forays.

One of the most important sources of state power was control of the temple treasuries, mainly because funds from these treasuries could be used for loans. This remained true throughout the ancient Near Eastern and Hellenistic periods. As early as the Sumerian-Akkadian monarchy, the state regulated these treasuries, fixing the temples' perquisites, and marriage fees (especially); rivals ('magicians') and heretics were persecuted in order to maintain the official cult's monopoly position.

As a result the temples gained great stores of precious metals and of supplies, and soon had large landed possessions as well. In fostering this development the monarchies gave the temple-priests a source of power which could be dangerous, and indeed there eventually occurred in nearly every state conflicts of priests versus secular lords and bureaucrats for control of the throne and the profits of power. Where the priestly clans gained power they behaved in a manner similar to that of the city aristocracies in archaic Greece.

Hence in the period before Hammurabi the old city kingdoms had to take steps to check excessive temple fees and to prevent the priests from seizing the lands of 'poor' peasants who owed them debts. At the same time the monarchies had to prevent abuses by officials such as: (1) exploiting labour services for their own advantage; (2) reducing payments due for fulfilment of labour services; (3) pressuring peasants to buy products from them at high prices and sell at low prices. The latter occurred often in sales of cattle to the rich, and was stopped by publication of an official price schedule.

When a Sumerian king claimed that he had 'done away with bondage' and established freedom, that meant in effect the following reforms: (1) labour services due the state were reduced or ended ('in area X there was henceforth no overseer'); (2) labour services due individuals were abolished; (3) finally, and most important, permanent courts were established to protect 'the poor' – that is, peasants, artisans, and tradesmen – against arbitrary appropriation of their property or profits.

Just what forms 'arbitrary appropriation' took is not entirely clear. But our sources mention one way the powerful oppressed the weak: officials, large landowners, and members of the great secular or priestly families demanded that small peasants pay their debts in cash. The economic situation was therefore somewhat similar to that of Greece before Solon's legislation and similar programmes. However, there was one difference: the dominant position of the priesthood and the state bureaucracy.

Consequently the kings sought, like the Hellenic 'tyrants' (at least in archaic Greece), to win the sympathies of peasants as well as artisans and tradesmen. Nevertheless, even though a king might have his differences with his officials he needed the support of the bureaucracy; despite his struggles with the priests, legitimacy remained indispensable, and such legitimacy could be gained only through apotheosis (in Egypt) or divine confirmation. Military monarchies founded on conquest were able to free themselves from priestly control, as in Assyria, but this was more difficult in the older 'civilized societies'. Thus in Babylonia, where theocracy was much more developed than in the Assyrian military state, the monarch was considered to hold his land as a fief from a god, and indeed he went through a ceremony of re-investiture each year.

Among the taxes exacted from subjects several were from the first paid in grain. To us the differences between them are unclear. Later they were adjusted according to the legal status and the fertility of the land. Other taxes in kind were also levied, and seem to have been rather onerous; mortgage contracts include mention of them, and fragments of cadasters have survived. A poll tax was also levied on free people, or at least on free women; perhaps originally it was levied on all not fit to fight. In addition there were various taxes levied on commercial transactions, such as sale of land and slaves. Where contracts specified that a penalty be paid the state for non-fulfilment, this penalty seems in earlier times to have been the performance of labour services for the king, a remnant of earlier systems.

One of the liturgies demanded of landowners was military service, which in the Persian period could be satisfied by providing a substitute. But we do not have a clear idea of how the army of militaristic Assyria was recruited and sustained, for this army was highly disciplined and not only displayed great fortitude in marching long distances but also did a great deal of construction work which was – even after allowing for the exaggerations of the inscriptions, and they are not obvious – of much economic importance. From Hammurabi's letters it is clear that military service was demanded of all subjects except temple personnel, members of the royal household, shepherds, and – it seems – royal *coloni*. But the conscript force so raised cannot have been used except as a home guard for defence in emergencies, for the military conquests of the Mesopotamian states were gained by chariot fighting, and only professional soldiers could have mastered the necessary skill. Furthermore the cavalry and infantry were very numerous – Shalmaneser II is supposed to have confronted an army in Syria of about 70,000 men, including 4,000 chariots – and one cannot imagine that in the wars fought every year over several generations armies of that size were recruited from yeomanry like the ancient Germanic *Heerbann* (which itself soon became fictive).

A national armed force which was thoroughly trained would have been a threat to the power of the monarchy, while the horticultural economy of the area must have made the creation of such a force impossible; thus a self-equipped hoplite force never existed in the Mesopotamian city-states which were from the first theocratic and bureaucratic in character.

Later, mercenary soldiers were used, but this surely was not characteristic of early times. Instead, we may assume that the king provided chariots, spears, and armour from his arsenals. Probably horses were similarly supplied from his herds or through requisition. As for the soldiers themselves, we find that in the time of Hammurabi the soldiers of the king held military fiefs, land to which professional military service was assigned as a liturgy.

But the men who held military fiefs did not constitute an order privileged above other groups of subjects. Daiches has even argued that they were branded for identification; this is just possible, for the same terms are used for them as for debt slaves, but in any case the terminological similarity is itself highly revealing. Daiches's argument depends upon a document which records that a soldier of the king was assigned to the service of a great personage, and indicates that a soldier sworn to the royal service lost his hereditary rights and had a status similar to that of an alien or slave. The proof of this is that when the individual concerned was discharged and returned home his family allowed him to settle on its land as a concession, not as his hereditary right. Low status is also indicated by the fact that one of Hammurabi's laws mentions military fiefs in the same connection as land granted to fishermen.

The reason for the plebeian character of fiefs in the Near East is that they were always small, just as were the lands granted cleruchs by the Ptolemies, since the equipment needed by a soldier was certainly very simple and in any case may have been provided entirely by the monarch.

Vassals holding military fiefs had to render service personally, under pain of death. Unauthorized requisitions or acts of violence were severely punished. Vassals served not only as soldiers but also as unskilled labourers; for example, they were used in building a new city. Some may have been settled in conquered territories to replace deported populations. They received from the monarch not only land but also livestock.

Vassals were, of course, forbidden to sell what the monarch granted. However, their holdings could be inherited by a son if he were fit for service, and provision was also made for the care of widows and orphans. If a vassal failed to fulfil his duties for three years then his fief passed to whoever assumed his obligations. Although the vassal served the king personally and received his reward from him, nevertheless he was also considered a servant of the community. Whoever gained the freedom of a captured soldier could claim repayment of the ransom from the temple treasury of his city if the soldier's own property was insufficient; in this matter the royal treasury had only secondary responsibility.

Besides these enfeoffed soldiers there were others who were not free in status – as is indicated by the fines levied for injury to them – but held property under special protection of the king, evidently to secure their availability. They lived at court and were always at the disposition of the monarch; hence Peiser has called them *ministeriales* after the analogous class in mediaeval Germany.

Still other armed groups deserve note. Assyrian kings garrisoned captured towns with 'cavalrymen and eunuchs', thus mixing retainers with bond servants. Prisoners were inducted by the thousand into the Assyrian army, and in resettled towns a certain number of soldiers were drafted, which must mean that either the settlers had to supply the recruits or else a corresponding number of military fiefs were distributed.

Soon the military system moved towards reliance on mercenaries, and the vassals were used as a reserve force. The reason for this was that as early as the reign of Sargon the regular soldier could marry, and this caused the extra expense in peace to the king, who had reinforced his army in time of war, since owing to their separation from their family relationships they had to be maintained by him.

Fiscal institutions show the course of development. As late as the reign of Artaxerxes distinctions in taxation were made between 'bowman land' and 'title land'. We can deduce from this that: first the possessors of certain lands had to serve personally, as a feudal obligation (see above); then the provision of recruits was attached to the ownership of these lands as a liturgy; finally, the liturgy was satisfied by the payment of a fee, with the proceeds of which the king hired mercenaries. How early and how completely this development occurred is not known to us. We do know, however, that the army of the last Assyrian kings was a completely heterogeneous force. Similarly the Babylonian corps of archers under the Persian Empire received its armour and food from the royal warehouses, and was therefore not a 'national' unit in the economic sense.

Private trading was at first hampered in Mesopotamia, as in Egypt, by the royal *oikos*, which was essentially an instrument of a barter economy. However this was only true for a period much before that from which we have cuneiform private documents. In the epoch immediately before and after Hammurabi there was a remarkable development of trade, and it became progressively more free. The theocratic monarchy did regulate the internal economy, especially wages, by official tariff-rates. such as we find in Hammurabi's Laws. But in principle, commerce in goods was virtually free.

Trade was, as one would expect, more developed in Babylon than in militaristic Assyria, for Babylon's rise was in large part due to international commerce. However, neither the exact sources nor the space available makes it possible here to distinguish between the economic development of the two states or to trace the successive periods which begin with the 'first dynasty' of Babylon and end with the Islamic conquest. In any case, however, the Mesopotamian economy remained much the same throughout its long history, the differences being due essentially to the degree to which a commercial economy (the term money economy is only conditionally applicable here) became dominant and then ebbed.

How the population was divided in earlier times is a difficult question which cannot be discussed here. Certain problems remain unsolved: to what extent was society based on the clan, as in Greece and Rome, or on occupation, as in Egypt? Both forms of organization are frequently found in the Occident in combination, and similarly both kinds of 'tribe' are found in Mesopotamia. Caste, however, is a term which applies even less to Mesopotamia than to Egypt.

Rather, it may be that here as in early Egypt the original liturgies imposed on trades gave rise to a form of social organization, since the members of each occupational group were probably jointly responsible for performance of liturgies and therefore – perhaps – gained certain rights to each other's property. It is at least probable that members of a weavers' association had legal rights of repurchase on (each other's) landed properties even after the land had been sold. Nevertheless all this remains hypothetical.

In the period of the fully developed labour service monarchy of early times the rule seems to have been that a parcel of land belonged to the man who fulfilled the obligations connected with it. Nor did this apply only to soldiers' land; it was a general rule, and indeed Old Babylonian law acknowledged performance of ploughing duty as proof of ownership. If the rule remained in force longer for land granted as a benefice to state servants, this was simply because the personal qualifications of these persons were especially important to the king. We do not have record of other lands being transferred into such ownership with royal or priestly permission, as occurred for a time in Egypt, but we do know that very often priests were in charge of dividing inheritances.

Whether residents of the same district had joint rights in land is not clear, but common responsibility for maintaining the peace did exist. Our sources do not, however, indicate definitely that there was joint responsibility for taxes and labour services, as there was in the Egyptian Old Empire. Inscriptions of several Sumerian kings mention changes in the legal status of subjects who owned fish ponds and cattle, but it is very doubtful whether this can be interpreted to mean that there was a sweeping abolition of services and restrictions connected with land ownership.

In general one can say that the legislation of the theocratic monarchies tended to promote private commerce. If there were restrictions on land ownership they were essentially liturgic in character, but in historical times the states's interests did not oppose the free transfer of lands other than those granted as benefices to office holders. Thus the Code of Hammurabi expressly assumes that purchased land can be freely sold. Inherited land, however, remained clan property for the benefit of all clan members. Documents indicate that originally such land could not be alienated; later it could be sold, but every member of the clan, including the seller himself, could reverse the transaction provided he paid the buyer the purchase price plus interest.

We know of the provisions for reversing a sale only because of formulas in the documents clearly devised to thwart the procedure; they call down curses upon whoever should initiate the procedure and promise special indemnities to the buyer. Thus in practice all private land eventually became subject to sale or division at the will of the owner. Records show that farm produce too was normally divided in inheritance proceedings, except when there was a temporary joint operation. Collective farming groups are, as one might expect, not mentioned in extant documents, except for common lands used for grazing and fallow lands; the latter are regulated in the Code of Hammurabi.

In general, then, land was divided into separate fields which were evidently fenced as a rule. Sale of land was accompanied by precise record of each field's boundaries according to paths, position, and neighbouring parcels. Generally the field's size was given in terms of area, sometimes too according to the amount of seed used. There are recorded cases where the terms of a sale stated that if the land was not as large as claimed the purchase price would be reduced.

Inscriptions from Assyria record expropriation of lands for building a temple. This may have been the legal process used by the king to make a gift; in any case he boasts that he has given compensation to the expropriated. But the fact that land put under cultivation by canal construction was distributed by the king indicates something akin to ultimate royal ownership of all land. In Assyria royal allotments were accompanied with instructions on how they were to be cultivated – e.g. used for garden vegetables; in Babylon royal ownership seems to have been expressed in terms of divine possession of the land.

Allotments given to resettled alien peoples were partly lands served by new canals, and partly service fiefs, whose former owners were moved abroad. There are also cases where land and bondsmen were granted as fiefs to reward officials, royal donations of land, and also cases of tax-free transmission to an official of his father's fief. These phenomena occurred over a long period in Babylon as well as Assyria. Normally however, a royal official as well as a temple official was supported by payment in kind from warehouses and by fees.

Although the beginnings of manorialism and feudalism were present in Mesopotamia, the political system did not develop in that direction. The state became essentially bureaucratic, with the trappings of a theocracy. Nevertheless the elements of manorial development were there. Serfs subject to private individuals are not, it is true, definitely attested, but in Hammurabi's letters there is mention of a class exempted from military service, and this has been rightly interpreted to refer to royal *coloni* bound to the land. Documents also mention gardeners and peasants on private lands, but it is unclear whether they were married slaves or semi-free persons legally bound to the land, even perhaps bound to the land against the will of its owner for the state's purposes.

When temple lands were mortgaged the peasants on these lands were included just as was the livestock. An inscription from the reign of Assarhaddon records royal confirmation of a private manor which the boundary descriptions show to have included entire villages. Similarly in imperialist states as early as the period of the city kingdom officials were rewarded with the grant of whole cities and their territories; later, as noted above, lands and peasants were granted, and there are documented examples of manorial 'immunities' granted by the kings as hereditary privileges subject to occasional renewal.

From all this it is clear that the state had strong feudal elements despite its basically bureaucratic and theocratic character. This is true without regard to the question of how far these feudal elements developed towards a colonate.

Family life was based on institutions originally found everywhere in Antiquity. The patriarchal family was the residential and economic unit, and was already nuclear in character (though there were of course many cases where heirs lived together). Women were given in marriage by the family head, and in early times were simply sold. Husbands originally had complete power to punish and repudiate their wives, but this came to be limited by contracts which prescribed forfeit money in case of divorce and the like.

Originally men had 'secondary wives', often sisters of the first wife. There were also 'serving maids', as mentioned in the Old Testament. Then the position of the dowried wife was protected by contract, as were the inheritance rights of her children, against the arbitrary power originally possessed by the husband. From this developed the institution of 'legitimate' marriage, as can be clearly seen in the Code of Hammurabi. Then this institution, originally developed among the wealthier classes, was gradually generalized by legislation as the only moral form of union.

Thus Sumerian kings (e.g. Gudea of Lagash) forbade the practice by which several men jointly purchased a wife, and they punished adultery cruelly (that is, adultery committed by women). By the time of Hammurabi's Code women had gained important rights: they could sue for divorce, and if repudiated were given compensation. Originally dowries consisted of household utensils, jewellery, clothes, and a few slaves; the slaves were used not only to serve the wife but also – as the Talmud indicates – to relieve her from waiting on the husband. In later times land too was included, military obligations having ceased to accompany land ownership. By the time of the Chaldaean Empire the legal form of marriage prescribed dowry, rather than purchase price, and provided for support in case of widowhood. On the husband's death the eldest son seems to have received the first and largest part of the inheritance, but this matter needs further study.

As in mediaeval Italy the development of commerce and expanded opportunities for private profit caused a change in the status of family property; from being entirely under patriarchal control it came to be regarded as the joint capital of all family members. The father's paternal authority remained in force, but his sons now counted as partners in a certain sense. Thus when a child was adopted, which involved buying the child from his parents, written stipulation was made guaranteeing the child a right to his adopted parent's property, especially in case the child was sent back.

Adoption itself meant simply that a purchased child assumed the status of a son rather than that of a slave. It was the primitive form by which a family operation expanded its work force. Adoption of slaves, marriage with slave women, and the like all contributed to diminish the distinction between free and unfree within the family group. One can compare this with the situation in mediaeval commercial family operations, in which sons of the family were treated in the same manner as agents and apprentices. Inheritance law allowed the transfer of property to children with retention of income by the parent, and from this there gradually developed division of property among children by will.

Slaves were not very numerous in the early periods of Babylonian history. Thus a dowry of one to three slaves was usual. Evidently however their number increased along with the growth of trade, and by the Persian period slaves were part of the money economy and were regularly used by their masters as a source of rent. Analogies can be seen in the use of *obrok* people in Russia and in the very different use of serfs in West and South Germany as late as the eighteenth century. Hence we find that slaves could themselves own property, could take part in all types of business, could buy their own freedom, and could even enter into contracts with slaves of the same master.

House slaves, however, continued to be few in number. This does not apply to royal and temple households, but otherwise four slaves seems to have constituted a respectable household staff. Furthermore even the class of slaves engaged in agriculture and business should not be regarded as very large.

Royal domains were originally worked by bondsmen, called

'peasants' and 'gardeners' in our texts, who were married and had to render labour services. It is still a problem whether there was a real legal difference between their status and that of slaves, as well as between that of coloni and slaves. These bondsmen also worked the fiefs granted to officials, and the great estates of Babylonian temples and of the leading commercial families in Babylonia and, to a much lesser extent, Assyria. Later all these lands, in so far as they had not been broken up into parcels for renting, were worked also by purchased slaves.

Hence slaves were an important item of commerce, in particular slave families. The reason for this was debt slavery, which was much developed in Babylonia. Since the law provided for swift collection – private arrest was allowed! – it became the basis for a great expansion of credit. The law also provided that when a man went into debt slavery his wife and children went with him, although according to a provision of Hammurabi's Code they became free after three years. If a propertied relative stood surety for him, a debt slave was set free, though his movement was limited, and he was given opportunity to earn money with which to pay his debt. Debt slaves formed part of the class bound to the land in the periods for which we have documents. But we do not know what proportion of that class they constituted.

The earliest way to expand the work force temporarily was to hire slaves or domestic youths in return for food, clothing, and rent – the latter paid originally in produce and later in money. Harvest workers in particular were procured in this manner.

Out of this developed the practice by which a free man could 'rent himself out', and this was the precursor of the free labour contract. But the original formula shows that the period of work was regarded as temporary slavery; cf. the Roman expression *in mancipio esse*. Furthermore the man who rented himself out needed a patron, who would if need be help him regain his liberty. Of course this temporary self-enslavement could also be enslavement for debt. It probably was this in historical times, for by the age of Hammurabi there were already many free men engaged in agriculture.

*

The impression that one gets from the Code of Hammurabi and from older documents is that there were two types of agricultural enterprise. There were small farms worked by their owners and producing fruit and vegetables, and there were also larger operations whose owners lived in towns and cultivated their land partly with unfree labour and partly with free labour hired by the year. Often supervisors of free status were used; their loyalty was secured by public criminal law.

Wages were regulated by law. This was evidently in the employers' interest, but it also benefited the workers and followed the theocratic principle of 'protection of the weak' – women, debtors, and slaves.

Livestock was private property and inheritable. Leasing livestock was governed by established rates and rules. There were also regulations governing the duties of shepherds to landowners, based no doubt on the theory that the shepherd served the whole community. The distraint of work animals was forbidden by the Code of Hammurabi.

To sum up, certain conclusions can be drawn regarding land use and distribution. If we compare the Roman agricultural economy of Cato the Censor's time, then we see that the Mesopotamian economy differed in the following respects: (1) agriculture was shaped by irrigation, as is still evident in Hammurabi's Code; (2) vegetable cultivation was much more extensive; (3) above all, the use of organized slave labour was much less developed.

The last aspect is undoubtedly due to the fact that in Rome as a result of her conquests an enormous number of slaves and a great quantity of land were thrown on the market and made available for private exploitation; nothing comparable occurred in the Ancient Near East. There slave prices were not high, but the number of slaves was clearly not great. Land and population won in war were royal property. The king did, it is true, like the pharaohs, distribute a part of captured livestock, prisoners, and land to his soldiers, but the land was regularly granted either in connection with garrison duty in conquered territories (the inhabitants being transported to Mesopotamia) or else with responsibility for canals and horticulture.

Thus conquered land was here exploited primarily as a source of royal revenue, and prisoners with their property were treated similarly. Matters differed greatly in the Roman Republic: conquered territories and populations were nearly always given over to exploitation by private capitalists, to whom taxes were farmed, domains leased, and slaves sold (especially for working plantations).

Furthermore the fertility of Mesopotamia's soil was limited and dependent on irrigation, and therefore did not provide the necessary basis for the peculiarities of large-scale slave farming. Hence the land possessed by the patrician rentiers of Babylon was mainly let to small tenant farmers who paid either a fixed rent (no claims for reduction allowed) or else a part of their crops. In either case the tenant was obliged by law to cultivate the soil with care.

Rental agreements, to judge from extant documents, were for rather short periods: one to three years. The tenant farmer, especially the share cropper, was necessarily interested mainly in the land's yield, and theoretically was able to move on; but generally he was in fact held fast by debts, and was really no more than a farm implement of the landowner, like the *coloni* of the later Roman Empire or the share-croppers of Mediterranean lands down to modern times.

How the tenant farmer fared over the centuries is a subject needing further study. One thing that emerges from our sources is the gradual increase in money rentals, but they never predominate. Similarly many contract provisions indicate that Mesopotamian rentiers were generally urban capitalists who either bought land and put it under cultivation or else used already cultivated land as a source of rent.

At harvest time silver was sometimes borrowed to pay hired labourers; there were also occasions when grain, dates, and the like were borrowed for use in sowing, to be repaid at harvest time. These are the earliest documented examples of production credits, and they were already known in Old Babylon along with the loan of grain for subsistence. Seed loans in particular were probably the oldest form of production credit, and were certainly older than the loan of cattle (contrary to Hainisch).

Commerce was much more developed in all the ancient Levant than in Egypt, the reason being the urban character of Babylonian culture and also its position as a centre of transit trade, always a spur to diversification of commercial organization. Indeed, Babylonia and its law set the pace for capitalist development throughout the Ancient Near East, and this too although the country had to import nearly all its precious metals. Once kings and priests realized that their tax revenues outweighed labour services they concluded that commercial expansion was beneficial and made no effort to curb it.

It has been argued that the Babylonian priesthood opposed special provisions for money transactions in commercial law, as in fact the Egyptian priesthood may (perhaps!) have done. But this is implausible; the argument is based merely on analogies with Occidental states. It is true, however, that as early as the Sumerian period measures were taken to soften the terms exacted of debtors; but a general cancellation of debts similar to Solon's is neither documented nor probable.

Debtors did indeed benefit from provisions of Hammurabi's Code which allowed postponement of payment in cases of necessity, but this corresponds entirely to similar clauses in private contracts and in general reflects the function which money had in the economy of the Ancient Near East.

For example, legal coinage in the modern sense of the term was not used by the Phoenicians during the entire period in which their commerce flourished, nor did coinage appear in Carthage until well into the fourth century. In Babylonia we find that in early times domestic trade was highly developed but nevertheless was based on the barter of crops; coinage was not used nor was any other money equivalent regularly employed.

Yet money existed in the Old Babylonian period. It circulated in the form of silver rings according to weight, and was used at times as a means of paying for goods, but primarily it functioned as a measure of value. That is, it measured the value of the goods which were actually exchanged in kind (as in Egypt), and generally only changed hands when it was necessary to make up for a difference in value between the goods bartered.

Only later did a form of coinage proper appear, at first evidently due to private initiative. Pieces are extant with legends such as the following: 'one-fifth shekel piece (weighed by) X'. Then money gradually began to monopolize the exchange function. In the Old Babylonian Empire dates were still often exchanged against grain, houses against fields, occasionally with some use of silver for price equalization. During the period of transition there continued to be complicated transactions, in which various goods were exchanged according to their respective values in silver. For example: land was exchanged for 816 silver shekels, of which 100 shekels was paid with a cart, 300 with six harnesses, 130 with a donkey, 50 with a donkey harness, 30 with an ox, and the rest with small amounts of olive oil, clothes and so forth.

For this kind of commerce, precisely because of its barter character, enterprises of a banking type were absolutely necessary to bring together buyers and sellers and also to evaluate exchanges. Consequently 'money man' is a term frequently found in the Code of Hammurabi. Produce was evaluated by brokers, who themselves handled grain, dates, and the like, besides dealing in silver as well. We also find a most unusual type of trade in produce, with warehouse warrants entitling the bearer to collect quantities of goods; this deserves further study. Perhaps the form of this trading was derived from the storehouses used for royal and temple tributes.

Babylonian temples loaned grain and money on a large scale and drew regular income from these transactions. Originally their only competitors were the royal storehouses, members of the royal family (identified as such in documents), and some important personages. But the temples had much greater resources than the private sector, for *coloni* had to send tribute in grain to warehouses and these were usually attached to a temple. Later, however, private banking firms arose and reached impressive size.

Nearly all the major business forms of a money economy were anticipated in Mesopotamia, albeit generally in archaic form. Thus along with the above-mentioned loans in kind (grain, dates, bricks) we also find loans of money at interest. Yet even here the number of shekels stated often indicate no more than the market value of the produce actually loaned. Interest charges varied, from 33⅓ per cent for a loan of grain to the distinctly low figure of 20 per cent for a cash loan, and the latter was not uncommon.

Borrowing on collateral was also known. Sometimes in connection with trade in slaves or real property, it took the form of reciprocal loans e.g. an interest-free loan of money in exchange for the rent-free use of a house. Mortgages were also written, though generally without a clear legal distinction between first and second mortgages. Later we find that a lender is sometimes expressly given first claim on the debtor's assets and that a mortgaged parcel of land is already encumbered; such phenomena indicate that at least by the Persian period Mesopotamian mortgage law was on the level reached in the Hellenistic states.

There are also examples of discontinuous capitalist enterprise, most commonly in the commenda, a primitive form characteristic also of Western Europe's mediaeval period. Its origins are varied, perhaps derived in part from agriculture. However, it is more likely that the joint ventures found in agriculture, for example in improvement leases, were themselves inspired by trading institutions.

As noted above some land was divided into small parcels and let to tenants who paid either a share of their crops (generally a third) or else a fixed rent in money or kind. In addition there also existed: (1) the lease of large manors by the temples; (2) the rent of land for a long period in return for an agreement to put the land under cultivation (a precursor of Hellenistic emphyteusis); (3) a variant of the above, in which uncultivated land was let, as it were, on consignment. In the latter the tenant appears to have built a cottage on the land and lived there on his crops. During the first years he made an 'advance payment' of whatever part of his crops exceeded his needs and later he shared profits with the owner. Such payments were made in kind, after five years according to the Code of Hammurabi.

Already in early Babylonian law there existed analogous provisions for commenda in goods and money as a form of capital investment in foreign trade. Many aspects are unclear but in principle these arrangements seem to have corresponded to similar institutions of mediaeval Islam and Genoa, except that the lender received one-half of the profit instead of the one-fourth typical in Genoa. Later we find examples of commenda retail stores as a form of capitalist internal trade.

To what extent tax farming developed in Mesopotamia before

the Hellenistic period is a subject which needs further study. So
far as I know its appearance has not yet been securely documented. As late as the reign of Artaxerxes, on the other hand, one
finds landowners advancing large tax payments in kind, collected
by a firm which was itself insured by the landowners through
mortgages.

This type of capitalist enterprise seems to have arisen mainly
where landowners owed the king grain or meal deliveries, but
had instead planted their land with another crop (e.g. dates). The
firm therefore bought grain or meal, delivered it to the king, and
then collected dates from the landowners and sold these on the
market.

We also find large-scale lending at usurious rates on rentals
(certainly in the Persian epoch), in which the lender was often
debtor in reciprocal loan operations as a kind of insurance against
non-payment.

Trade was divided between two groups which, following
Bücher's terminology, we can call hired workers and independent
workers. The former included weavers, tailors, smiths and gold-
smiths, whose pay was set by Hammurabi's Code. They received
raw materials from their customers. Independent workers on the
other hand purchased their raw materials and sold their goods
in the market for what they could get. Weavers of coloured goods
fell in this category, as did probably carpenters and other groups,
and later slaves were put to work on this basis. Normally slaves
did not work in large-scale enterprises, but instead were set up
in business by their masters who advanced them capital as an
investment. The one type of large-scale organized enterprise was
unfree domestic production, for which temple slaves in particular
were utilized. They were given raw materials and often the
necessary tools as well, then turned over their product in return.

It was mentioned above that in very early times some artisans
had to render the king labour services. Documents of later periods
(including the Persian period) also show kings and princes in
possession of skilled craftsmen, slaves in status, and along with
them were the slaves of private individuals who had been
entrusted to them for training. Our sources, do not, however,
indicate how the 'free' trades and work for private individuals

and the 'market' developed with respect to liturgies. The transitional stages naturally blended into each other, and the whole development depended upon the royal demands for liturgies, the number of artisans, and the presence of captured skilled craftsmen. But the documents do show that unfree craftsmen were used as the teachers of other owners' slaves apprenticed to them. The exploitation of slave artisans as sources of rent was in later times the rule, taking the Babylonian term *mandaku* as equivalent to Russian *obrok*. Prices for unskilled slaves continued to be moderate in later times; slaves trained in a craft, because of the length of apprenticeship (five years for weaving) were more expensive. Female slaves generally were higher in price.

Rent, profits and interest were therefore present in elementary form. Another economic institution also developed – the benefice. State and, in particular, temple benefices were already known to the law of the First Babylonian Empire as objects of exchange, mortgage, and dowry. An established trade in benefices developed, and investing capital in them was the ancient equivalent of buying interest-bearing public bonds. Benefice holders were in theory deputies entitled to payment in kind. This could take the form of the right to dine at the priests' table and receive free room and board from temple funds, or else the right to land allocated to officials; out of these rights then developed payments in kind which became inheritable and later transferable.

We find frequent mention in the documents of lands which had to pay the temples various dues in kind on certain days of the month (e.g. the 30th), either because of endowments made to the temple or because the land had originally belonged to the temple and had been granted on condition of paying the dues. From these and other revenues accruing to the temple were paid the meat, bread, beer, clothing, and other supplies due to benefice holders. These supplies were delivered on certain days, e.g. the 15th and 30th of each month, were then sold by their recipients, and so found their way into the general stream of trade.

What has been sketched above indicates that somewhat complex economic institutions existed, but it is not now possible for us to judge the relative importance of these phenomena for the economic structure of Mesopotamia. Although trade was technically highly developed, nevertheless prices were determined either by direct government regulation as in Babylonia in Hammurabi's time, or else by the overwhelming importance of the royal and temple storehouses. In Assyria under Assurbanipal cattle taken as booty were sold to Assyrians at fixed prices, and under Sargon grain and sesame from the royal storehouses were sold in times of scarcity in order to keep prices down. Sargon's rules setting limits on meals also seem to have been issued to reduce consumption when supplies were short, although they also reflected the policy of not allowing any class to play a prominent role which would compete with that of the king.

The temple storehouses must have played a role similar to that of the king. Undoubtedly, too, the lending activities of the temples must have effectively regulated the conditions and rates of private lending, though whether this was planned remains uncertain.

Therefore prices were not set by the market. When we find in old Babylonian law that caravans regularly had commissions to buy cattle and slaves, and that orders were given 'to buy at the going price', this hardly means a price set by competition in the open market; it is much more likely to mean the selling price set by the royal or temple storehouse.

About 200,000 cuneiform texts have been brought to light. Of these only a small part have been translated, and furthermore the translations themselves are widely scattered and those of important documents are still subject to conflicting interpretations. Because of these conditions the available material does not make it possible – at least for me – even to attempt to trace the actual history of the development of Mesopotamian society.

Egypt

(a) *The Old Empire*

Babylonian society was from the first shaped by economic institutions propitious to capitalism. Thousands of years before official money was issued, it had a strict debt law with harsh provisions for the servitude of defaulters, and later a developed money economy appeared. Egypt, on the contrary, was at least in early times completely dominated by natural economy.

It is not easy to describe how this affected Egyptian society. Foreign trade was entirely in the pharaoh's hands as far back as our sources reach, and indeed the pharaoh's position depended in part on this. As for domestic trade, money evidently did not exist in early times. Nevertheless as early as the fourth millennium there was trade, including trade in land, and it is fairly sure that property ownership was inheritable and, under certain conditions, transferable even before (or, rather, just before) the unification of Upper and Lower Egypt.

It is also probable that the *oikos* of the pharaoh and of the temples were not originally of dominant importance, but became so in the course of Egyptian history. The documents we have from the Early and Middle Kingdoms and – especially – from the New Empire are much concerned with the affairs of the royal and temple administrations because those are the sources of these documents, and so it is clear that the extent of temple properties has been much exaggerated.

Furthermore one must seriously question the view, once generally accepted, that under the earliest historical dynasties there were no private estates – that is, land which was neither enfeoffed nor worked by *coloni*. But unfortunately the interpretation of many sources is disputed, and also the readings of many documents, especially those in demotic, are still very uncertain In particular the standard reference works of E. Revillout, although useful, are nevertheless full of serious errors (e.g. he confuses marriage certificates with divorce documents) and are discursive rather than analytic.

The monuments do not allow us to reconstruct the early development of Egypt until the Thinite period, at which time (*c.* 4000 B.C.) the capital was moved to Memphis. The state was then in a transition from a fortress and labour service monarchy to a system centring on the great royal *oikos*, which at the beginning of the New Empire reached its height.

In the Old Kingdom social institutions were shaped by three factors: (1) the absence of any serious military threat and also the absence of possibilities for expansion; (2) the necessity, arising from geography and climate, to develop a somewhat sophisticated bureaucratic administration and to mobilize the population for large-scale work on the irrigation system; (3) the consequent dominance of society's economic interests and of court officialdom, and also, evidently connected with this, the absence of important families with their own names and internal ties, such as would have constituted a force for individualism. In fact the individual was above all a servant of the state. Thus when the pharaohs boast that they have established order and have visited every city of their realms it is clear from the context that they are thinking of the irrigation system and its demands.

There were of course rich families which possessed landed estates, but they owed their position to their role as part of a service nobility. This group was recruited more and more by promotion from lower classes as the position of the pharaohs grew stronger.

The administrative system of the Old Kingdom was relatively decentralized. This was due to the modest development of genuinely military institutions. Besides the pharaoh's guards and the police units of the temples there normally existed only district militias. The latter were used by local authorities against the desert tribes, which at that time did not constitute a serious threat.

Economic investment went mainly to construct systems for distributing, draining, channelling, and raising the waters of the Nile. The national economy was therefore completely directed

towards regulation of the great river, and so it was from the first
– that is, from the time the regulation began – necessarily shaped
by the economic needs of the society. The ancient division of the
land into 'nomes' was certainly connected with the organization
of irrigation and production, and the same is true of the public
granaries erected later in the nome capitals, just as the Assyrian
institutions of a similar character were instruments of fiscal and
price control policy.

Therefore the nomarch was responsible primarily for the irrigation system and for the assignment of labour services, and also
was charged with maintaining the incomes of the royal domains.
That these domains were from ancient times very extensive is
securely attested, and later a regalian right to all land may have
existed in theory, as will be explained below. But this is a long
way from the concept of a 'state socialist' direction of all production as the formative element in ancient Egypt's economy.

About economic conditions in the earliest period we know
virtually nothing, as one would expect. Barley, wheat, and millet
were cultivated with very primitive implements: hooked plough
drawn by oxen, hoe and hook instead of the harrow, sheep and
pigs used for sowing, the sickle for harvesting the crop, and
donkeys or cattle for threshing it. In addition wine, vegetables
and dates were raised; the olive was not raised until later and on
a small scale. In the marshlands of the Nile lotus seeds were
gathered for food, and papyrus was collected and used for a
variety of purposes, ranging from building ships to producing
sheets for writing. Diodorus noted that the pharaohs themselves
lived on a simple diet, mainly vegetables; the masses lived on
bread and sesame oil.

The horse is not mentioned in documents until the New
Empire, and evidently was imported from Syria. The camel is
securely attested only for Hellenistic times, although it appears
earlier on a cameo. Other domestic animals attested include the
donkey (used for transportation), cattle, sheep, goats, and various
breeds of antelope. The goose was widely raised, and was fed on
bread dough.

The delta marshes were thickly settled in later times, but originally they were used as seasonal pasture land for large herds of

cattle from the interior. Smaller marshes and swamps must from very early times have been divided among the nomes, since cattle raising was even then quite extensive. Later under the Ptolemies the royal authorities set aside lands in all parts of the realm which were reserved for grazing exclusively. The pig was evidently known from early times, but images do not show herds until the New Empire.

Timber was very scarce, but it was not needed for building since that was done with bricks made of mud from the Nile. Nor was timber critical in early times for building ships.

Cultivation of the land was always relatively simple. Manuring was not essential, nor did the land ever need to lie fallow. New crops could be planted at will. Hence the agriculture of pharaonic Egypt was of moderate labour intensity. A document from the eighteenth dynasty [c. 1580–1250 B.C.] seems to assume that a slave family could work 6 *arourai* of arable land, equivalent to 4.11 acres. However, a document from the reign of Shishak [c. 930 B.C.] reckons this at 0.7 *aroura*. As for garden land, Revillout estimates that five men rendering labour service were assigned 4 *arourai*; however, the Kahun papyri from the twelfth dynasty [c. 2212–2000 B.C.] reckons 10 *arourai* (2.15 hectares or 6.19 acres) per man.

Whatever the precise significance of these figures and also those of later periods (which differ, of course), it is clear nevertheless that Egyptian peasants had to spend only a relatively small part of their time working the land. It was because of this that the pharaohs could commandeer extensive labour services for their colossal buildings. Even so the peasants had considerable time free for secondary occupations, and produced goods partly for the market and partly as liturgy work for the royal storehouses.

It may be that this situation, which arose quite naturally from agricultural conditions, was responsible for the lack of a sharp division between agriculture and manufacture, and explains the fact that urban development occurred to a much smaller extent in Egypt than elsewhere. But of course another factor, then as now, was the geography of the country: the Nile, along with a thin strip of settled land on each bank, was the single great route of trade and traffic. Two other important factors were the social and military-political structure of the country: the unified system of labour services and liturgies, and the fact that the Old and Middle Kingdoms were peaceful states until the Hyksos invasion, while the New Empire relied on mercenaries and on the liturgies of a peasant warrior class.

When we say that the land had no cities, what is meant is that its fortresses and its larger settlements lacked certain attributes common to ancient cities, including those of Mesopotamia. Thus under both pharaohs and Ptolemies the land was administered on a unified basis, and was divided into regions. Furthermore, we find that privileges were not granted to the citizens of a city nor did urban institutions with administrative autonomy, however limited, exist – with the exception of the three Greek cities.

It is not certain whether or not the Egyptian language ever had a native word for slave. In inscriptions even the terms used for prisoners of war, escaped slaves, and purchased slaves (*boku, honu*) are also used for eminent officials and priests. As for the priests, this can be partly explained by the fact that by the Middle Kingdom there existed the institution of 'hourly priests', who were divided among the four priestly colleges and took charge of the cult in turn. This type of organization, incidentally, corresponds entirely to the 'shifts' of workers rendering labour service to the pharaoh.

In this connection it is noteworthy that often in the documents an extraordinary number of terms are used for what seems to be the same status, evidently unfree in character. So far no scholar, not even the meticulous B. J. Baillet for example, has succeeded in making distinctions on the basis of etymological origin or occupation or class of origin. There are a few exceptions, which will be discussed, but the distinctions made have always been imprecise. In fact this phenomenon reflects the essential characteristic of a liturgy-state: every individual is bound to the function assigned him within the social system, and therefore every individual is in principle unfree. Egypt emerged as a fully developed liturgy-state in the New Empire, but the beginnings of this development were already present in the Old Kingdom. Even in the oldest extant documents we can see that while there were privileged classes in Egypt there were no juridically free communities equivalent to the Greek *polis* or *kōmē*. In theory every slave 'carried a marshal's baton in his knapsack', and in fact those who succeeded as scribes could rise to the highest positions.

Purchased slaves were of course numerous, but slave prices, as compared to land prices, seem to have increased from the time of the New Empire. Thus a document from the Libyan period [Dynasty XXII, beginning with Shishak, *c.* 947–925] indicate that a slave cost nearly as much as the plot of land he cultivated. Under Darius a slave cost twelve times the price quoted in earlier documents whereas land was cheaper. It is true that for a time Egypt waged great wars for plunder and that slaves were sent as tribute to the conquering rulers of the eighteenth dynasty [*c.* 1580–1322 B.C.], but these slaves were destined for service in the royal household. The figures given for prisoners of war are – in so far as they are trustworthy – not high. In short: if we consider the scattered information available regarding the supply and price of slaves, and if we take this information to be representative, then it is clear that the conditions indicated militated against large-scale use of slave labour in private agriculture. Later the great rise in land values must have made it economically impossible. In this connection one should note that all unfree persons normally had their own families, the only exceptions being prisoners of war.

Our thesis, then, is that the functions of slavery were performed in Egypt by two other institutions: clientage and colonate.

Generally it is assumed that in both Upper and Lower Egypt the pharaonic monarchy was established by subjecting the individual local kings and transforming them into feudal nomarchs, similar to the *patesi* of Mesopotamia. 'Lord of the fortress' is found as an administrative title even in later times. The original independence of the local princes was reflected in the fact that many priesthoods continued to be monopolized by certain aristocratic families. Lords were surrounded by retainers, who were distinguished by the right to dine at the lord's table, and in Egypt as in early mediaeval Europe this was the beginning of a feudal aristocracy. These retainers were free born, like the mediaeval *ministeriales,* and were called *chamsa*; later the word was used regularly for slaves and services.

However, the institutions based on retainers and on relations of personal dependence in general eventually affected all spheres of society. This was due to the complete dependence of all upon the bureaucracy charged with regulating the Nile. Even the manner in which justice was administered made it inevitable that eventually the prevailing rule would be 'no man without a master', for the man without a protector was helpless. Hence the entire population of Egypt was organized in a hierarchy of clientages (*amach*).

From earliest times the pharaonic monarchy was based upon labour services. It seems, in line with our general theory, that in fact the conditions binding the peasants to labour services and therefore to the land were at first more oppressive in Lower Egypt, where the Nile has its mouth, than in Upper Egypt, where commerce originated and had its oldest centres.

Thus a royal *colonus* of the period before King Snefru – that is, before the age of the great pyramids – is supposed to have had his own seal. One must conclude from this that royal peasants were then less reduced in status, and that their degradation began with the period of monumental building. Nevertheless the situation is clouded by the loose use of terms, as noted above.

Originally labour services seem to have been exacted without much distinction between occupational groups. Rulers of the Old Kingdom used soldiers, sailors, and other subjects for transport duty, those of the twelfth dynasty used warriors and priests as well; Mentuhotep [eleventh dynasty, *c.* 2375–2212 (?) B.C.] used 3,000 warriors and priests to transport a sarcophagus lid. Later a levy limited to all construction workers of the land was made.

All the peasants of the Lower Nile seem to have had the status of royal labourers. They worked land assigned to them under the direction of royal officials, and their crops were then disposed of according to the pharaoh's instructions. As early as the fourth millennium there existed an administrative title for an overseer of peasants. When a royal estate was granted this included the estate's peasants – *retu* in Egyptian, equivalent to 'people', like the Ptolemaic *laoi*.

In Upper Egypt, however, feudal institutions seem to have continued, and most peasants were free – that is, they had mainly to pay taxes rather than to render labour services.

The same mixed situation existed with respect to artisans, some being free workers in the villages and towns while others owed labour services to the monarch and lived in settlements near the palace. However, it seems unlikely that this distinction was established in law. The fact that Egyptian wage-earners in practice enjoyed great freedom of movement cannot be used as an indication of their legal status; consider, for example, analogous phenomena in Russia when serfdom prevailed. The term 'worker' was used frequently in Egypt for all commoners – that is, all who were not part of the temple or bureaucratic aristocracies – and all commoners certainly had to render labour services.

In general, the individual in Egypt was from early times a tool of pharaonic power; he and his property were no more than entries in a cadaster. Members of a community were jointly responsible for meeting royal demands, and community leaders were liable to punishment for default. That this was the original order of things is proven by the fact that the law of the Old Kingdom already included the concept of *idia* [place of origin, in which a commoner was usually obliged to remain], as is indicated by a hieratic papyrus from the eleventh dynasty.

Idia, which later became of central importance, was based on the principle that every individual must have an official domicile; that is, he must be officially entered on the rolls of a community and hence be responsible for helping that community meet its assigned labour duties. He who did not have a domicile therefore had his property confiscated, and he and his family became directly subject to pharaonic authorities.

Later the labour services were generally equalized, according to Revillout, and so – for example – a worker would be made to cultivate 2,000–2,500 square ells of vegetable land. Such land was quite often part of a royal domain. On the other hand the taxes which subjects paid were in kind: grain, cattle, and cloth and other things produced in the household.

Land which was privately owned and inheritable seems to have been limited mainly to royal fiefs. 'Inheritable' here refers to land which was not only in effect inherited, as was the land of *coloni*, but was legally defined and protected as such. On the estates of royal feudatories inscriptions were set up to record the extent, origin and inheritable status of the properties. Documents tell us of royal grants, usually houses and gardens with slaves and perhaps *coloni* as well included; in one case the grant included

12 parcels of land totalling 200 *arourai*. Often the estates granted were really perquisites of the offices of priests and nomarchs, and they were always carefully inventoried and taxed.

However, from the Thinite period, the oldest in Egyptian history, we have tomb inscriptions which record the ownership of inheritable and divisible landed possessions; an example is the inscription of Mten, dated to *c*. 4000 B.C. Some properties were gained through royal concession, especially burial land, always very important in Egypt and indeed constituting an item of trade by itself. Other properties were held as fiefs (*ger* means beneficeholder) and could be transferred by private deed from father to son, still others were royal grants with peasants included. Finally, documents record conveyances of property; for example, 200 *arourai* with rights to a daily income of 100 loaves are given as recompense to an official for certain services rendered. Whether these properties could become objects of private trade is a question which extant documents do not answer, but it is more likely than not that they could. This is not, of course, to be taken as meaning 'sale', since that could not occur while there was still no money.

A deed for the conveyance of property included an inventory (*amit-per*, *ampa*), and this constituted a substitute for disposition by will. Later these terms for inventory were used as technical expressions for the transfer of property from father to son, husband to wife, and brother to brother.

Furthermore we can infer that the right to alienate land existed from the terms of certain bequests. Inscriptions show that as early as the fourth millennium land was left to religious foundations for the benefit of the deceased ('to have masses said for their souls', to make a bold analogy), and this with the express condition that the land should not be transferred. The priests are charged (as *honu-ka*) to leave the land only to their children, who will then inherit their function. Priests bound to a duty in this manner were called 'permanent children', – that is, they were free born but nevertheless not their own masters, like Romans still subject to their fathers' *patria potestas* and hence called *liberi*. Charters of religious foundations express this legally as a gift on condition of heredity, since the modern concept of a charitable institution did not of course then exist. This has been elegantly demonstrated by Moret and Boulard.

The inscriptions mentioned above tell us a good deal about the general character of ancient Egyptian society. They prove that not merely temple lands but official benefices, later so important, already existed, and that alongside them were also enfeoffed offices. We also find that the charters of religious foundations stipulate that their lands shall be exempt from the jurisdiction of notables – that is, the great feudatories. Only a member of a feudal class could have made such a bequest, and the stipulated autonomy is an indirect proof that a feudal class existed in the fourth millennium. It is also clear that the beginnings of the power of the priestly class also had their origins in this period.

Under the eleventh dynasty even peasants in flight from their lords appeal to the pharaoh. Later under the New Empire criminal jurisdiction over slaves fleeing from royal princes was again vested in judges appointed by the state.

In the Old Kingdom the monarchy had to share power to some extent with the nomarchs, who in Upper Egypt kept or even acquired a dynastic position within the districts which they administered. Already under the ninth dynasty these and other positions were usually hereditary, and many other offices had been still earlier made subject to the rules of *ampa*.

Because of the very wide usage accorded the concept 'office' this hereditary tendency must have strengthened the position in family law of the eldest son, who alone inherited office. In general Egyptian family law seems to be quite typical. *Mutterrecht* – that is, the absence of right to inheritance through the male line – is absolutely unattested in Egyptian society. Even the oldest epitaphs indicate inheritance on both sides.

Frequently only the mother is mentioned in inscriptions, but this was sometimes due to the fact that an office was inherited through her. Or it may have reflected a widespread reaction against polygamy, which caused marriage contracts to specify that a bride would be 'the principal wife' and that her children would inherit everything or else a specified portion. Another factor was connected with inherited rank. 'Son of X, made from [*sic!*] Y' is the correct patronymic.

In general then, one can say that the advantageous legal position of women in later times grew out of the development of these practices, and also resulted from the demilitarization of Egyptian society. Of course the actual position of women changed a great deal in history, and evidently also differed very much according to class. 'I am a woman' was a formula used to express political subjection. But in legal matters women were equal with men in everything pertaining to inheritance, and our sources indicate that women could conduct their own enterprises down to Ptolemaic times.

Thus as early as the fourth millennium we find in the inscription of Mten that a husband gave his wife property to divide among their children as she wished, and that a son received land from her (*amit-per*). Evidently the common practice of sibling marriage served to avoid divisions of a family's patrimony, in the upper classes as well as lower classes. In the royal family it served to maintain 'purity' of blood.

The names of landed estates in the epitaphs of Old Kingdom families of Lower Egypt, if traced through generations, indicate the degree to which possessions could be accumulated through judicious marriages and a dose of incest (cf. *Proc. Bibl. Arch.* 17, p. 244). One finds large and evidently scattered estates collected and transmitted by inheritance – through heiresses as well as heirs – and gift to a son. Some sources not entirely clear also indicate that fiefs or gifts from the king also contributed. These estates were worked by *coloni* from earliest times, and groups of them representing the individual manors are depicted in the graves of lords. The agricultural economy reflected in these monuments seems to be based on labour services of free peasants and the tenures of unfree *coloni*.

Most aspects of the economy are still very obscure. But it is clear that the economic framework of Egyptian society was constituted by the domains and *coloni* of the king, and by his hoards of treasure, his storehouses of grain, his barns for cattle, and his armouries dispersed throughout all the nomes. Along with this went a growing element of feudalism.

b.   *The Middle Kingdom*

Under the Old Kingdom the royal governors of the provinces – the nomarchs – were granted domains and also allowances in kind from the royal storehouses. These grants were kept legally separate from personal wealth in allodid dues and possessions. Then came a period of particularism and anarchy, after which Egypt was reunified under Thebes, the old centre of private manorialism. The Middle Kingdom was established under the twelfth and thirteenth dynasties (*c.* 2000 B.C.), and it was in this period that the nomarchs developed in familiar fashion into a hereditary aristocracy. At the same time the temples proceeded to appropriate lands and communities.

Under the new order villages were grouped together into large manors, and were organized on bureaucratic lines with their own scribes and so forth. The peasants had to pay taxes and were put under military discipline. Workers were unfree and tied to their profession; we find manorial carpenters, cabinet makers, potters, and smiths. There were great herds of cattle, several thousand in numbers, and there were also perquisites and allowances from the temple and royal domains. Together these elements were administered as possessions by the dominant nomarch aristocracy.

Peasants received seed from royal and manorial storehouses, and then delivered their harvests to them, or that part due. Already there existed the *uput* system, under which a census was taken of each household, in order to determine the number of people liable to labour services, the equivalent of what in the Later Roman Empire was called *capitatio plebeia*. It seems to have extended in principle over the whole land.

It is not clear whether there existed a unified, centralized administration of labour services. Tasks (*ahuit*) were assigned to the individual villages on instructions of royal officials, and all those liable were responsible. Scribes were not liable for labour services. At court and near the large storehouses there were walled workshops, and occasionally they functioned as labour camps. People liable to labour service were divided into groups of five and ten, and they seem to have worked in shifts; each shift normally lasted two months, holidays excluded. Public lands were classified as marshland or dry land, and were divided among workers, who received 10 *arourai*, 1½ of marshland 8½ of dryland. These allotments, we may assume, were essentially granted to those liable for labour services.

Owners of large manors must have managed their lands in essentially the same way as the pharaoh. They seem to have worked their best lands directly and assigned the rest to bondsmen in return for work or fixed rent; the two systems existed together and are not always easily distinguished. Peasants evidently transferred their labour services partly from the state to lords of the manors. It is not clear whether a distinction existed between peasants who were serfs and those who were personally free but bound to the soil, nor indeed do we know whether such a distinction had any real significance.

We do have a document in which at least 24 individuals, without specifying their occupations, declare themselves personally dependent on a lord. So far the only interpretation which seems tenable, though it is not precise, is one which assumes a distinction between those clients who were personally dependent on a lord and served in his household, whether actually or in theory (as *schemsu, boku, sodmu, keri-dot, amu, ketu*), and those who were bound to the soil, which is the interpretation Baillet gives to a number of terms (*honu, meratiu, nesitiu, satiu, sidiu, samdotu, uhuitiu*). In one extant document a peasant is warned that if he continues to disobey orders he will be reduced to the lowest class and become a simple agricultural worker subject to labour services (*awaitiu*).

So far as the state is concerned, the general rule was as follows: everyone who owned land or pursued a craft became thereby responsible for certain payments, the peasant for land taxes, the craftsman for licence fees and a part of his product. If a man could not fulfil his responsibilities, then he and his family became debt slaves of the pharaoh and henceforth worked under the direction of the authorities. Yet, despite this distinction between those who could and those who could not meet their responsibilities, all who owed payments to the state were just as dependent as simple workers, all were as controlled and subject to whippings as they were, and all were despised. Above them were the king's retainers, professional soldiers, who now become prominent; retainers of vassals probably had a similar position.

As for the temples, we have sure evidence that their lands and also – more important – their income from tributes and fees, were divided among the priests as hereditary benefices. Then the priests – willingly or unwillingly – transferred their lands to manor owners, who subsequently assumed lordship of the temple *coloni* as well.

c. *The New Empire*

After the expulsion of the Hyksos [*c.* 1580 B.C.] Egypt again moved into the foreground of history. This period is not marked by the introduction of essentially new institutions, but rather by the one-sided development of old institutions in a certain direction. Egypt was now subject to a unified system based on labour services (*Fronstaat*), in which only the pharaohs and temples had manors, with a few exceptions, and which eventually evolved into the bureaucratic liturgy state of the Ptolemies. The transition was probably quite gradual.

The New Empire emerged out of the struggles of the eighteenth dynasty (*c.* 1600) against the Hyksos. As long as it remained a national state – that is, down to the end of the Ramessids – the New Empire stood to the Middle Kingdom in much the same relation as that of the Princedom of Moscow after the expulsion of the Mongols to the pre-Mongol estate system centred at Kiev. Feudal institutions, aristocracy, and all or at least most of the manors disappeared in both cases. The major part of the land was in the king's hands, 'and another part – though much less – had come into the hands of the temple priesthoods through gifts.

At the same time a great number of war prisoners were brought in as result of great military expansion, so that 'the war storehouses were full'. The king continued to grant deserving officials fiefs – but of lesser extent than formerly – together with a few slaves. Part of the royal lands was viewed as fiscal domain and was worked for the royal household. The rest of the land – that which the temples did not hold – was formerly thought, on the basis of the account in *Genesis* and Greek tradition, to have been granted to peasants in return for a share of the crop. Today, however, we know that land taxes were not set on a quota system, but were levied in fixed amounts. Only *coloni* were sharecroppers.

Then, at the latest under the Ramessids, came the well-known division of the land among those who served in the army as a liturgy. Perhaps this may have been modelled on the Asiatic systems of royal service fiefs.

The lands of the temples and of the warriors were legally and permanently tied to the support of religious and military functions, and they were therefore freed from the general obligations to which the rest of the population was subject. The rulers of the Old Kingdom had bestowed temple lands as fiefs on trusted officials, but this must have become more and more impossible. (However I am not familiar enough with the relevant material to be more precise.) In any case, there were later attempts at secularization which led to sharp conflicts.

Members of the warrior class (equivalent to the Ptolemaic *machimoi*) received enfeoffed allotments, but these were of modest size, about 3½ hectares (8.64 acres) in Herodotus's time. Their equipment was light and cost little, and so they were able, like the cleruchs of the Hellenistic armies, to pursue gain in diverse civilian occupations and to lease their lands.

The army of the New Empire included a number of separate categories: (1) royal guards and recruited mercenaries; (2) members of the warrior class settled on the land (Egyptian *ma*, later Greek *machimoi*); (3) the conscripted and armed *coloni* of the pharaoh, settled on the land according to time of service and divided into seniors and juniors; (4) temple militias, formed from temple *coloni*; (5) the district militias, used as a general levy.

The army was, therefore, essentially an army of serfs. The royal sailors were foreigners, and were branded as the Assyrian peasant soldiers may have been.

The entire bureaucratic system, royal as well as temple, was run by scribes, most of them serfs. It was not, as before, in the hands of the old hereditary nomarch aristocracy. The priestly class increased in number, importance, and exclusiveness. In the Old Kingdom the priesthood had only begun to be a separate profession, and in the Middle Kingdom it had become mainly hereditary. In the New Empire the priests were divided into tribes, and membership in the priestly estate (rather than office) was inherited by sons if they were fit.

It is true, however, that the priestly tribes seem never to have been closed to recruits from outside. Marriage with members of other classes was also possible. Therefore one cannot speak of the priesthood as a caste. Nevertheless it developed into an estate with enormous influence, charged with educating the offspring of the administrative class, with which it was connected by many kin ties and by multiplication of offices.

Every attempt of the pharaohs to free themselves from the power of the priests was thwarted, because the counterweight of independent secular feudal families had now nearly entirely vanished. Under Rameses III we find that temple possessions included great masses of people, land, and cattle – the figures go into the hundred thousands. All these possessions paid tributes in kind, such as woven goods, which were collected and administered by the 'white house' of each temple. The latter was also charged with supervising the field work of the temple *coloni*. Thus the 'first prophet' of a large temple boasted of his measures to maintain the number of 'the offspring of the serfs'.

Thus the wealth of the Temple of Ammon in Thebes was already legendary in Antiquity, and no doubt with justification, even though Erman is right in his argument that the Greeks overestimated the extent of the temple's landed possessions. Often three-quarters to four-fifths of war booty was given to the gods. Temple land, no doubt like royal land and all other land, was divided into marsh land, dry land, plough land, garden land, and hoe land. The temples had many craftsmen bound to their soil, though less than the king, and engaged in foreign commerce with their own ships. Inscriptions also mention people who served the temples only for fixed periods; these were undoubtedly hired free men, not rented bondsmen. Indeed we find free workers also serving the pharaoh and paid in kind. (It should be noted here that the two Gurob papyri edited by Griffith are difficult to interpret, and his version of one must be mistaken; an ox and other items as pay for 24 days of housemaid service is simply impossible!)

Great synods of the higher ecclesiastical authorities were held annually in Ptolemaic times, but our documents do not attest their existence in earlier periods. Perhaps the synods, like the Jewish Sanhedrin, developed partly because the foreign rulers of Egypt sought support among the priests, partly because the synods on occasion served as an instrument of resistance to foreign domination.

In ancient Egypt the paraoh was the legal head of the priests. Even in such later times as the Ptolemaic period, the ruler had to approve appointments.

The royal *oikos* was administered by a large staff of officials, and it was supposed to meet the expenses of the court and state from its own income in kind. Each domain, temple, storehouse, and public works office had its own administration, and each administration had its own staff of workers bound to render labour service in return for rations from the royal hoards. Sometimes the rations were embezzled, leading to hunger and labour strikes. Spiegelberg has edited the accounts of the court storehouse in Memphis, which show that meal was delivered to bakers who were unfree, evidently, and engaged in domestic production. The bakers delivered over 100,000 loaves in three months, 480 a day of one type. Similar entries record deliveries of wood for shipbuilders, leather for commanders of mercenaries, clothes for black slaves, and black slaves for the service of important personages.

Grain due the pharaoh as a tithe or as the harvest from land worked on labour service was delivered to royal storehouses, threshed and stored in royal barns, made into bread, and issued to royal workers. In short the *oikos* was self-sufficient. In times of bad harvest the royal storehouses issued grain and seed to workers and peasants, as was done in Mesopotamia and is done today in Russia.

Whether the workers employed in the pharaoh's building projects were counted as slaves, or whether they were entirely or in part workers rendering general labour service, is impossible to determine with certainty. Those who were classed as workers, a rather large element of the population, had families like members of other groups, and often were literate. Probably they were distinguished from peasants only by having no permanent allotment of tribute-paying land – or, indeed, simply by having a smaller allotment.

In any case it is clear that the royal workshops were essentially labour camps, to which the peasants delivered raw materials produced at home. As noted above, agricultural conditions allowed the peasants much time for supplementary pursuits, and their production can be called either cottage industry or unfree domestic labour.

As to the legal aspect, however, the situation is unclear. What the status of artisans and peasants was under the national dynasties is, as can be imagined, difficult to determine. Nor can we draw any conclusions from conditions under the last dynasties before Persian rule, since the period of Assyrian domination intervened and before that the struggles between Ikhnaton, the religious revolutionary, and the priesthood of Ammon had caused profound breaches in tradition.

The royal household (in the wider sense of the word) met its needs through labour services and through the taxes paid by the entire population. References to various reforms of land ownership must be interpreted as referring to reforms of the system for apportioning state charges. Again and again the monarch orders that an administrator is to divide the necessary labour services among workers 'according to each worker's craft', or that he should assume the 'ordering' of the entire population of a district and divide this population into classes; this refers to making a census of the population to show each person's responsibility for public charges.

For large building projects and mining operations large numbers of people owing labour services were collected, as in early times. For example, under Rameses IV a force of 9,268 persons was collected; 5,000 of them were soldiers, 2,000 royal *coloni*. In such formations a distinction was made between seniors and juniors; the same distinction thus obtained in labour services as in military service. Just as the army was recruited in part from foreigners, so the ranks of the royal *coloni* were replenished with war prisoners. Examples of this policy, so reminiscent of Assyria, are attested as early as the reign of Amenhotep [I = 1557–1545]. As a punishment men could be conscripted for the gold prospecting expeditions to the Upper Nile, which were attended with immense loss of life.

Taking a census of the population made possible a change in fiscal administration. Whereas before village communities had been responsible for paying the taxes and fulfilling the liturgies connected with land tenure, now individual families were made directly responsible. This would help explain the important position of the *hir*, if Revillout is correct in regarding this as the title of the eldest man of a family rather than a land owner. In

any case the *hir* had important privileges in the inheritance law
of the period, and this with the contemporary effect of the inheritance of offices (see above) can be explained by similar fiscal
interests. However the subject needs further study.

Nor can we be certain about the transfer of land outside the
family in the New Empire, now that private manors had ceased
to exist. Nevertheless we do know that in a much-quoted peasant
story, written before the New Empire, there are peasants who
want to sell their houses. Nevertheless the ownership of arable
land and the exercise of a craft continued to be essentially connected with responsibility for liturgies or taxes. Hereditary ownership of land was therefore conditional on fulfilling one's duties
to the pharaoh. This sums up the position of that part of the
population which did not belong to the privileged classes (priests,
soldiers, vassals, officials, scribes) or did not serve the pharaoh and
privileged classes as landless serfs.

For a long time scholars were led by Herodotus to assume the
existence of castes in Egypt. However the hereditary character of
occupations was simply due to the fact that in the nature of things
the peasants inherited responsibility for liturgies and taxes in so
far as they were connected with their land or craft. This does not
mean that real castes were formed, for no occupation was regarded
as religiously 'impure', nor was marriage outside the group prohibited, nor was each occupational group closed to outsiders,
Even the military class was recruited simply from a group of
peasants charged with the liturgy of being ready for duty at any
time and, no doubt, like the Cossacks committed to regular
training. In principle free entry into any occupation continued to
exist. There did exist, it is true, certain hereditary income rights,
but these were not rights to a particular position in a particular
place, but rather special kinds of rent payments derived from
land, benefices, fees, and tolls.

Under the New Empire political offices ceased to be hereditary,
and were filled by men promoted according to bureaucratic
criteria. Similarly under the twentieth dynasty the rule of priests
was replaced by the administration of scribes. Nevertheless within
the bureaucracies each individual regarded his post as his station
for life, as indeed does every official today. An example would be
the supervisor of one of the labour groups mentioned above (the
post is the prototype of the Ptolemaic *hegemōn tou ergastēriou*).

We have documents in which governors boast, among other things, that they 'never dismissed a supervisor'. But of course in law and in theory these officials could be replaced.

On the other hand there continued to be other posts which remained as in ancient times hereditary and subject to division among heirs by will. Among these posts were many connected with religious burial, e.g. the 'body-washer', because this was a necessity for permission to use a burial place. Still, in these cases, the actual transfer of each office needed the consent of the authority concerned with the fulfilment of its duties, the state or, in most cases, a temple.

Under the New Empire the landed possession of the pharaoh and the temples continued to be immense. But now the documents regularly mention also the possessions of men who occupy royal or temple land (*nefer hotep*) as vassals or *coloni*. Hence these documents also mention transfer of lands to individuals, usually as inheritances but also as gifts, for example to priests. In each case consent of the landowner (state or temple) was needed. These documents are quite different in form from deeds of transfer dating from the earliest period (Thinite), but they are similar in form to the vassalage agreements concluded under the Old Kingdom by political officials, especially nomarchs.

Whether other types of deeds also demanded specific consent is not clearly indicated by the documents, but it is possible, especially for the period of theocratic rule at the end of the twentieth dynasty. Similarly it seems probable that consent of the landlord was needed for the sale of cattle and also slaves (if there were any) by *coloni*. The *coloni* themselves were of course bound to the soil, but seem to have been subject to the authority of state courts.

To sum up: ownership of land was inextricably bound up with duties, because each parcel of land had certain charges imposed upon it. This is illustrated most plainly for us by the traces of family law in our documents; they show that the eldest member (or members) of the family represented the family as a unit in dealing with the state or temple or landlord. Connected with this is the fact that property was regarded as belonging to the family rather than the individual; while occasionally we find extended families functioning as economic units (but census records indicate that this was not the norm). Also significant in this context are the rights to inheritance and prior purchase held by family members. The importance of this tradition is shown by measures taken later to circumvent it. Members of the privileged classes used formalized curses (only they could make divine images and therefore curse), others sought divine approval of untraditional inheritance arrangements, still others made deals with family members overlooked in wills.

It is within this context that one should place another phenomenon: the frequent appearance of partnerships in agreements for leasing land, even small parcels, in which one of the partners represents his group. Evidently this practice developed by analogy with family groupings.

Another aspect to be noted here, perhaps, is that even in very late times prices are not mentioned in documents recording land sales. Revillout may well be correct in arguing that this too sprang from the principle that ownership of land was sanctioned by fulfilment of duties, and therefore could not be considered an object of trade. Land, then, was supposed to change hands only through intra-familial transactions among those working it. But another factor was at work here: the special status of money as a medium of exchange in so far as religious institutions were concerned. The Old Kingdom had no money, and therefore the religiously sanctioned deed forms probably acknowledged the transfer of land only as an exchange for other land or as a bequest. We cannot be sure about these matters, however, until the time of Amasis [569–539 B.C.], and by then national character of the Middle Kingdom had been altered under foreign rule.

After the Ramessid period Egypt's development was marked by contradictions, due to successive waves of Asiatic and Ethiopian influence. This foreign influence resulted from the dissolution of the national army and its replacement with a standing army of mercenaries recruited from abroad. The national army had not been a sophisticated fighting force, but now the new warrior class, mostly foreign, was thoroughly professional and provided the main support for pharaonic power. During the Hyksos period Asiatic military tactics based on the horse and chariot had been adopted, and then wars of conquest were waged by the New Empire. These two factors led to the development of a professional military class.

Hence Egypt was subjected to foreign rule now by one group, now by another, for various periods of time. Foreign mercenaries joined with royal servants, often foreign themselves, in dividing up the priesthoods and dominating the country. After the Assyrian conquest Egypt was never again free for long. First the priests of Ammon usurped power, then Assyrian and Ethiopian dynasties ruled, with the intervening usurpation of Bocchoris, then Greek influence prevailed under Amasis, and thereafter came the Persian conquest followed by struggles between Ethiopian, Persian, and native (Greek-supported) dynasties. The result was that Upper and Lower Egypt were often divided for long periods and political stability did not return until the Ptolemaic period.

Under these successive regimes the degree of free movement of trade gradually increased. Greek tradition ascribes to Bocchoris a number of basic innovations, making him similar to the great Greek reformers. He is supposed to have allowed the purification oath, ended debt slavery, and – most important – allowed free transfer of land. Revillout has supported the validity of this account with arguments which are in part rather fanciful; yet it is nevertheless clear that the influences which profoundly changed Egypt's economy came from Asia first of all and were supported by the anticlerical forces of Lower Egypt. Opposed to the change was the priesthood of Ammon supported by the Ethiopians who had usurped the throne and the warrior class, part of which in fact migrated to Ethiopia.

Thus we see that about the time of Bocchoris there first appear demotic contracts, in particular those connected with transfers of land. Commercial law seems to have been changed, especially that relating to land, and a programme of secularization also was carried out. That is why when the allies of the priests of Ammon gained dominance, they burned Bocchoris for sacrilege, for they maintained divine lordship of the land.

In any case, whatever the precise circumstances, the evidence indicates that the private sector of the economy now increased steadily.

Down to the time of the Ramessides the royal *oikos* dominated Egypt's economy and naturally restricted the sphere in which commerce and division of labour might develop. Not that these phenomena were absent. Indeed in the Old Kingdom they may have contributed relatively more to meeting economic needs than they did in the periods of developed theocracy and bureaucracy. But foreign trade with Arabia, Somalia, and Syria was legally a monopoly of the royal *oikos*, and it actually had at least the major share. Later this role passed to the temples, which had their own fleets.

Hence for a long time foreign trade was conducted in the guise of an exchange of gifts between rulers. This is evident from the correspondence from Tell el-Amarna between the pharaoh and the king of Babylon. Egyptian sources from early times do not mention native merchants, and when they appear they are temple serfs. The name for them is derived from the word 'to empty' – that is, to empty a ship. Even under the New Empire most merchants were Semites from abroad.

Gold and copper were mined in Egypt itself, while silver was rare and had to be imported. Hence silver was valued more highly than gold until the New Empire was integrated into the international market. Tin and iron were also imported, the latter being used much less than bronze until the New Empire was established. Then, too, we find imports of ships, chariots, weapons, vessels, incense, cattle, and fish from Syria and Babylon. In return Egypt exported gold, later also linen. Under the Ramessides there seem to have been private shipping concerns.

A parallel phenomenon was the increased number of free workers. Originally the pharaoh's labourers had dominated the economy, and of course they did not disappear under the new order, nor were free workers a new phenomenon, for under the Old Kingdom there were craftsmen who worked to order, according to literary texts. This means that even then there existed, using Büchner's terminology, independent artisans as well as wage earners.

In ancient Egypt the crafts were highly developed. It is difficult to say to what extent this was due to the work of royal and temple bondsmen, or of *coloni* engaged in 'unfree' domestic industry, or of 'free' craftsmen responsible for liturgies. The craftsmen of a district had a chief master, evidently elected, and like the mayor of a village he was responsible to the treasury.

Originally, it seems, he was also charged with supplying men for labour service to the pharaoh or the nomarchs.

Later the status of craftsmen differed. There were some who worked for wages, yet had to do labour service when needed, and were given their raw materials. Others, however, were artisans who provided their own raw materials and paid for it with part of their products, a great variety of which are recorded. In so far as their raw materials were imported or their products were exported, we can presume that production was directed by a pharaoh or a temple or an aristocrat.

In any case the extant documents describe craftsmen as of inferior status. For example linen weaving, one of the major crafts, was evidently considered a typically unfree occupation, and in fact it was in the hands of slaves, first those belonging to households of pharaoh and the nomarch aristocracy, later of the temples. But of course linen was a luxury article for the court and the official class, since the mass of the population – originally even the pharaoh himself – wore only a leather kilt. It was also exported, and the export trade was a royal monopoly. The development and differentiation of products used, especially items of clothing, was clearly the result of the constantly closer ties between the New Empire and the Levant, especially Babylonia.

Private domestic trade was mainly in food and consumer goods such as fish, fruit, vegetables, sandals, and simple jewellery – all depicted in our documents as typical market wares. Barter was the basis of trade until, under the New Empire, round copper wires of definite weights (*uten, deben*) were introduced. They were generally used as measures of value for goods which were actually being bartered, but occasionally one of the parties in a deal would settle a balance in them. Workers were paid with what were essentially tokens, entitling the bearer to provisions from a royal or aristocratic storehouse. In foreign trade precious metal rings were used, as in Babylonia. Therefore the *deben* was mainly a measure of value, a theoretical – not actual – medium of exchange. In this it resembled the silver shekel of Babylonia. Furthermore we still do not have a clear idea of the relation between the *uten* as a unit of weight and as a unit of value (cf. *Bibl. Egypt.* X, p. 164).

Where barter prevails one usually also finds the payment of rent in kind. This is an ancient institution, and is indeed a precursor of the modern stock exchange. Lands were given to temples as endowments – for example, as payment for annual supply of consecrated candles for ceremonies honouring the dead and the like. From this period also come records of officials and others exchanging the pay they received in kind for other products; for example, a certain number of daily rations due from a storehouse, each 1/360th of the official's annual pay, would be exchanged for a delivery each year of so much bread and beer. Similar phenomena from Babylonia are known.

After the fall of the national dynasties the money economy expanded steadily, even though at the same time the intellectual and cultural life of the country continued to be dominated by theocratic and historical traditions and became stereotyped. The Hebrews of the post-exilic period still considered Egypt a great 'labour camp', and yet in reality the labour services exacted from the population were gradually being replaced with taxes, in fact if not in theory, and this may well have been the basic cause for the transition to money economy.

At this time, too, there seems to have been an increase in the number of slaves in the hands of temples and officials and in their use for field work. Estates now tended to depend more on *coloni*, who were given land and made to cultivate a definite part of the demesne land in return. Thus there appeared in Egypt the system based on two types of land tenure which became so important under the Roman Empire (for this system, see the article on the 'Colonate').

A document dating from the troubled reign of Bocchoris recounts a land transfer which seems entirely private in character, for it lacks any confirmation from an oracle or from the monarch. However, the transaction recorded involved members of the same family. Another document, dating from the reign of Psammetichus, records that some (former?) temple land was sold by priests in return for a permanent share of one tenth its product. The people who occupied the temple land seem, therefore, to have exchanged their position for that of hereditary tenants.

From time to time land sales are recorded in which divine confirmation is noted. However this disappears completely under Amasis, who was known as a legislator. This meant that a new hierarchy of ownership of temple land existed; instead of God, temple vassal or enfeoffed priest, and *colonus*, the hierarchy was now: God, hereditary tenant, *colonus*. From the reign of Amasis, too, we have the earliest written tenancy contract; it is a contract for sub-tenancy. Other documents, if our readings are correct, indicate private contracts, charging one-third of the product and also leases given to secure loans. The *colonus* appears to have had obligations but not rights; his tenancy was therefore similar to the later *precarium*. In this period we also find that property is frequently sold for money. However the deeds of transfer do not mention price, which was no doubt recorded separately. Generally payment was in cash.

As for leaseholds, one striking peculiarity is the number of leases assumed by groups of two to fifteen persons. Of course we are relying here on the accuracy of our translations (and the translator is Revillout!). But if they are correct, then it seems likely that the groups involved were generally not genuine collectives like the Russian *artel*, but rather came together for a speculative venture. The land would then be sub-let in small parcels. Most tenants continued to be smallholders.

Since rotation of crops was not necessary contracts were generally, though not always, for a year. The tenant paid all taxes and returned the seed he received for sowing. Temple tenants seem in many cases to have paid one-third their harvest as rent.

This sketch of economic conditions in Egypt is only provisional, since there are so few documents in reliable translation available for this period. In particular one cannot be sure about the importance and distribution of privately owned land, since many fiefs and grants had long been possessed extra-legally by influential persons. Greek writers report that the land was divided equally among king, priests, and warriors, but this is at best an exaggeration of actual conditions (although Eduard Meyer seems to accept it as trustworthy). That nearly half the land was possessed by the warrior class (*machimoi*), as Herodotus reports, is clearly inaccurate. Even under Rameses III the temples had only one-eighth of the land, or at most one-fifth, and they suffered the effects of political upheavals and secularization (as under Amasis) so that in later times they certainly had less land than under the Ramessides. That there was a noteworthy increase in the amount of land given as fiefs to important personages in the later period is a fact which cannot be doubted. The king however remained the largest landlord.

As for the peasants, the largest part of the population, except for those who were soldiers or otherwise entitled to privileges, their situation was hardly any better than that of the fellaheen in later times. Ancient writers all view the Egyptian peasant as a proletarian, for whom the bureaucratic state was as much a distant master as the Russian state was to its peasants. He is also depicted as paying little rent for his land, always ready to defraud the state of taxes, and proud of the beatings he received as punishment. Indeed the elaborate, omnipotent system based on forced labour and tax levies, which seemed so repressive to the Greeks, no doubt encouraged just this sort of attitude in every peasant, whether he was technically a tenant or owner. We know how an Egyptian tax levy was made: the officials arrived unexpectedly, the women began to cry, and soon a general flight and hunt began; those liable for taxes were hunted down, beaten, and tortured into paying what was demanded by the officials, who were themselves held responsible for quotas based on the official cadaster. This was the guise in which the state appeared to the peasants of the Near East, and as it appeared in modern times to Russian peasants. The profound feeling of alienation from politics found among Near Eastern peoples had its origin in this repressive relationship. Pauline Christianity responded to that feeling; that is its historical significance.

During the Ptolemaic period we find a linguistic distinction between land which is 'private' (*idiōtikē*) and land which is 'held as private' (*ideoktētos*). It is unclear whether or not this means that there was an end to the right to prior purchase, held by family members on family land down to the Ptolemaic period. But it is evident that from the first Ptolemies onwards official decrees presume the existence of private land available for purchase, and there is no reason to think that this was an innovation. Small-holdings probably arose in late pharaonic times, as is indicated by the fact that lists of properties inherited often mention gardens; one factor which may well have fostered this development was the long-standing divisibility of royal grants.

Because the land continued to be connected with families, and because polygamy continued to exist, it was very important to a married woman to have her position and that of her children acknowledged by contract, especially since the documents indicate that in this period full freedom of marriage and divorce existed. Hence binding contracts were written governing community of goods, dowry, income, and especially, as later under Islam, fixed household money for the wife. Especially effective were contracts by which the husband's entire estate was promised to the children, especially the eldest son, of the woman; this functioned more or less like the English entail.

That a 'trial year' of marriage existed in Egypt is pure fable. The 'unwritten marriage' of Ptolemaic times was evidently in origin a matter of man and woman living together without 'marriage contract', which means that the man had not paid for the woman and therefore did not have authority over her, although he did have – as in the Roman 'free marriage' – authority over their children.

In general, one can say that Egyptians used nearly all the important contractual forms found in Babylonian law, even, for example, sale of oneself for adoption. Slaves were included in inheritances along with cattle, houses, and gardens, but they were never plentiful, even in later periods, except in the households of the king, priests, and officials.

Nevertheless, despite all we know about particular aspects, it is still impossible to give a precise picture of agricultural conditions under the New Empire.

In conclusion, one can say that two institutional systems were basic to Egyptian society and reached a stage of full development never afterwards equalled: (1) the system of labour services (liturgies), under which each property was assigned a public charge and its owner was bound to his function in fulfilling this charge and to the property itself; (2) bureaucratic administration. Both systems spread out from Egypt and in Late Antiquity became dominant in the Mediterranean world, and with them spread that aversion to politics which was typical of subject peoples and which was certainly not due entirely to the suppression of their independence.

Furthermore it is possible that certain forms of technical labour organization important in Antiquity were developed in Egypt and spread from there, among them being: (1) production based on unfree workers under surveillance in labour barracks (*ergastērion* in Greek); (2) unfree domestic production; (3) manorial agriculture with the labour services of *coloni*. From Babylonia, on the other hand, derived forms of private enterprise and capital investment.

3
Israel

Reliable information on Hebrew society before the Exile is given only by certain legal codes in the Old Testament. They evidently date from earlier times, and their claim to divine origin made them unusually safe from changes in transmission. It is worth while briefly considering these codes, for they are the only documents extant from a people still at a stage of development before their political and religious leaders have settled in cities. Of course one can no longer maintain that even the oldest code (*Exodus* 19 ff.) is a product of a 'primitive' society of peasants still untouched by urban influences and money economy. This has been recently demonstrated by A. Merx, although he does stress the cultural differences between the period of the Exodus code and that of the Deuteronomy code.

One thing is sure: despite the great importance of cattle as the most important source of disparities in wealth, a widespread phenomenon, the Hebrews of history were never a genuinely nomadic people or Bedouin tribe, nor were their ruling classes. Nothing, so far as I know, exists in the sources which suggests a specifically nomadic law. The religious dedication of Sinai indicates only that the old cult of Jehovah had its centre on this highest mountain.

Not only the camel but the horse as well are not mentioned in our sources, and the ox is above all, as in primitive Rome, a work animal. Leather, as in Egypt, was the earliest clothing material. From the first the basis of diet was grain along with vegetables, wine, and olive oil. Only the king ate meat every day; his subjects slaughtered only on holy days, formally as a sacrifice. Cheese does not seem to have been especially important, as it was in ancient Greece.

Ownership of cattle was the sign of riches, a general phenomenon, and the royal herds were especially large. Sheep were important, because of the characteristics of the land and also the popularity of woollen clothing. Land was cultivated with the plough, little use was made of manure, and the production of bread was on a similarly primitive level, with the grain being milled by hand and then baked in a pot.

In any case we may say that, despite the greater attention to cattle ownership given by the old code than by the later one in Deuteronomy, the ancient Hebrews were at no time even primarily engaged in cattle breeding. *Genesis* 47.3 underlines the distinction here between them and the Egyptians. Before the monarchical period the Hebrews had come from East of the Jordan River, crossed the mountains, and descended to the coast, where they had a chequered history and felt themselves a mountain people. Thus they especially prized milk and honey, the characteristic products of the mountain slopes.

Only under Moses, a reformer in the Greek sense like Solon who gave them their law, did the Hebrews succeed in conquering some of the Canaanite cities of the river valleys. But the centre of their power was in the mountain valleys occupied by the tribe of Joseph, and from there they invaded the plains and conquered them gradually, in the same manner as the Aetolians and Samnites in Hellas. Sometimes they came under the sway of Philistine or other city kings, sometimes dominated them, and at the same time were attacked by desert tribes from the East and sometimes had to pay them tribute.

Did the ancient Hebrews actually live in Egypt and serve the pharaoh as peasants subject to forced labour in his work houses? *Exodus* 20.1 shows an excellent knowledge of Egyptian conditions, and even the title given Joseph is historically appropriate. But of course this proves nothing since Egypt was geographically so close, and therefore the facts remain uncertain. On the other hand, there can be no doubt of the great influence exerted on the Hebrews long before they entered history by the ancient urban culture of Syria. The Law presumes that the Hebrews are a sedentary, agricultural people, and it has no mention whatever of collective ownership. The land has been divided into private properties, but normally property is transferred only within a family.

Other provisions are more difficult to interpret. Vendetta is acknowledged, but this is no conclusive proof of an ancient stage of development, for it seems to have persisted in Athens until ended by Draco. Similarly the payment of fines in cattle is inconclusive, for this persisted in Greece and Rome until well into historical times, and in any case reflects a varying supply of precious metals rather than their scarcity.

Then there are the provisions of the Law regarding debt. The rule which was hated and feared by peasants in Sumer, Babylon, and Athens alike was that they must pay their debts in money when demanded. The Law shows a revealing effort to maintain the good old partriarchal ways in the interests of peasant debtors, an effort common to all the legislators of the Western Mediterranean lands, including Zalencos, Charondas, Pittacus, and Solon. The Ten Commandments enjoin – apart from purely religious duties – reverence for parents, respect for the marriage tie of others, punishment of murder and theft, strengthening of legal procedure, honesty in relations with others ('no conniving against others' property', as Merx puts it), and finally – the most original and significant of all – the keeping of sabbath rest and the extension of this to workers, slaves, and cattle. This last cannot of course be explained on purely 'socio-political' grounds, for it reflects most clearly the great power of religious motivations. Nevertheless this commandment clearly benefitted the debt slave as well as other classes. Furthermore the combined effect of the Commandments in their epigrammatic form indicates that at least one strong reason for the Law was protection of the mass of free men against the consequences of social differentiation in wealth and power.

In this connection one should note above all these aspects: (1) the time limitation on debt slavery of Hebrews; (2) the measures taken to avoid forcible enslavement; (3) a certain protection extended to marriages between free and slave (that is, essentially debt slaves, as the text indicates); (4) similarly, protection of the Hebrew woman bought as a wife from the treatment accorded purchased slaves in general; (5) protection of slaves (that is, debt slaves) against severe injury, especially fatal, from their masters; (6) protection against injury from cattle. The last provision is significant because cattle formed the major element of the aristocracy's wealth, and so this is an ancient analogy to our contemporary controversies over damage done by game. In many ancient legal systems punishment was meted out to animals as well as humans, as in the old Roman law prescribing punishment for an animal that caused damage 'while acting contrary to its nature'. A modern would find this very surprising, and indeed in this respect Hebrew law is more 'modern'.

Other important provisions aimed at protecting peasants, such as the rule (7) that the clothing of a debtor might not be seized for default; (8) likewise the later prohibition against taking interest, which grew out of the exhortation not to avail oneself of the punitory provisions of the debt laws against fellow-Hebrews; (9) provision for punishment of murder, acts of violence, and criminal conduct in general, which meant in essence regulating the right of retaliation. It seems, however, that no standing court was established. In general the criminal codes of Antiquity, the Hebrew among them, were aimed at protecting the mass of free-born persons from the consequences of the commercial economy which brought in its train social differentiation and made the aristocratic clans very rich and very powerful.

There are also provisions forbidding partiality towards rich or poor. These reflect a legislator's aim to end class conflict through impartial arbitration, which was indeed the aim of the great legislators of Antiquity. A significant feature is the exhortation not to oppress metics, reflecting the results of the commercial traffic which went by and in part through the homeland of the Hebrews.

Gold and silver money is clearly assumed by the Hebrew laws, but does not figure prominently. This is due primarily to the methods of commerce in the ancient Near East and the consequent legal regulation of money. Along with this, however, went the social aims of legislation which strove to maintain the natural economy of the peasants.

An important problem is raised by the commandment to let arable land lie fallow in the seventh year. Was this ever enforced in any way by a law to that effect? This naturally seems somewhat doubtful, and in fact the 'sabbath year' is first presented (*Exodus* 23.10–11) as a measure to benefit 'the poor' – i.e. the landless – since they would be allowed in that year to take the products of the land. Attempts have been made to deny the utopian character of this rule, even in the formulation extant, and to explain it on rational grounds as caused by agricultural technology. Others have seen social policy involved, viewing it as a measure to benefit the *colonus* working mortgaged land – as happened often in Babylonia and evidently in Athens as well – or as a general remission of debts on land. But these attempts are futile, for they can never explain the religiously motivated prohibition of sowing. Unless this is a later interpolation by theological authorities, it cannot be cited for the purpose of social history.

On the other hand the provisions for the so-called jubilee year came from a much later section of the Pentateuch and are primarily directed towards limiting the value of property mortgages, which have always been one of the ways land became in fact alienable. The jubilee year meant that a limit was set on the time within which a debt could be paid from the income produced by land. It could be explained by economic theory, but that would be neither interesting nor helpful here.

All the other provisions of Hebrew law share a basic principle which in fact characterizes many of the legal codes framed in the West to settle class conflicts. Looking at them one could believe that they were issued to counter the results of the debt slavery imposed on the peasantry by the powerful families of the cities, and with some imagination one could then interpret the urban Canaanite aristocracy (which existed for many years in Shechem, for example) as a patriciate, and the Hebrews as a plebs inspired to revolt by their priests. Then the Torah would be the Magna Carta of the Hebrews.

But such an analysis would be wrong. Rather one must conclude that the Torah was in part the result of purely religious forces, but mainly was meant to prevent the enslavement of the peasantry by the wealthy families, which had visibly occurred in the coastal towns, and to maintain the ancient freedom based on equality. This has more support from the evidence than many other theories now current, though one must admit that conclusive proof is lacking.

Certain aspects, however, deserve note. In the struggles of the pre-monarchical period the Hebrews fought on foot while their enemies were cavalrymen with chariots and were led by city kings, as is made clear by the oldest extant document, the Song of Deborah (*Judges* 5). It is also clear that the Hebrews regarded their victory as a triumph of poor free people over aristocrats, who would have used their victory to exact tributes of grain and 'multicoloured clothing'. Compare the Swiss view of their struggles with the Austrian feudal knights.

How long this free community remained peasant in character is difficult to say because the sources fail us here. The Song of Deborah mentions a Hebrew city which did not take arms in the struggle against Sisera, and it curses the city and its citizens. Now of course it is difficult to imagine just how a city emerged in the Hebrew society of the time. Our sources for the period of the judges mention great families which 'possessed' as many as thirty 'villages', and they also mention a Canaanite nobility centred in Shechem but allied by marriage with the Hebrews. Indeed the whole period of the judges is marked by a series of usurpations by aristocratic clans rendered powerful by their numbers, lands, and slaves. They armed their *coloni* and led them in repeated wars against the Philistine cities and the desert tribes. Analogies would suggest that this state of affairs was tending towards a unification (like the *synoikismos* of Attica), but there are also significant differences.

It was the war of independence against the Philistines which led to the monarchy. Saul's army was above all a national force, and a monarchy close to the masses was established. But this soon changed. The Philistines were led by men trained in war from their youth, as we are told of Goliath (1 *Samuel* 17.37). In the story of David's battle with him, emphasis is placed on the valour of untrained peasants guided by Jehovah, but the claim is suspect. Subsequent statements prove that the development of a permanent cadre of royal officers, along with a standing force of trained men paid by the monarch and owing him allegiance, was inevitable.

The division into twelve tribes was used to apportion tax payments (in kind) for army and court, each tribe being responsible for a month's expenses. The tribal system may have been inspired by ancient local bands, but it was itself established as an artificial division for the same purpose as that of similar systems in the Greek warrior states.

Already under David the Hebrew monarchy had begun to resemble a Near Eastern government based on labour services, and under Solomon the basic features of that system clearly emerged: a fortified capital, accumulation of a royal hoard, a foreign bodyguard in addition to the national levy, and public works for which the supervisors were imported and the material was collected from labour services.

At this point the Hebrews fell under the domination of cities and their armies were adapted to chariots, as is indicated by Biblical texts and also by Assyrian accounts of Ahab. Nevertheless the national army continued to be important, and our sources for the monarchical period indicate that it was recruited from men owning enough land to equip themselves. The account of the tribute collected by Menachem from 'the rich', equivalent to Roman *assidui*, indicates an impressive number – about 60,000 – of households able to contribute to defence. According to Assyrian sources Ahab put 2,000 chariots and 10,000 men in the field.

Samuel had warned that a king would take the Hebrews' land and give it as fiefs to his men, or at least to his chariot fighters (1 *Sam.* 8). Whether this actually happened is unknown to us; more probably his account was meant to frighten and was drawn from conditions prevailing in Egypt and [Mesopotamian] city-states. In any case subsequent developments indicated that here too the consequence of military organization was the domination of the great families rich enough to equip and train their men. One evidence of this is the new concern for purity of blood and ancestry, and the new interest in stories of heroes which we find reflected in the legends of the Patriarchs and – above all – in *Deuteronomy*.

Hence arose a distinction between those families which could not supply recruits and those which could, on the basis of property officially registered. The former class, which included at the least all families without land, was now classed legally as metic. The fact that again and again in the kingdom of Israel the monarch was selected by the army reflects this distinction. It was also the cause for the fall of the state, for the concentration of royal power and religious cult in the citadel of Jerusalem led to a phenomenon frequently found in Near Eastern political history: a conflict between the old military families and the priestly families of the new capital. The former naturally supported the claims of the local cults of their home districts and at the same time strove to keep the monarchy subordinate to the army. The priestly families, on the other hand, conferred upon the monarchy the mantle of legitimacy and with it a claim to dispose of the labour of its subjects; they strove to dominate the monarchy and to suppress the local cults.

These conflicts led to civil war upon the death of Solomon, who had been in effect a vassal of Egypt (as was his son too) and seems to have been the first to introduce an oppressive labour service on the Egyptian model. The old Israelite tribes refused to submit to the labour service state and seceded, and what was left, the kingdom of Judah, was now centred in Jerusalem and became essentially a city kingdom. At first it was dependent upon Egypt for varying periods, later it paid tribute to Assyria and this in turn caused a strengthening of its bureaucratic characteristics.

Then under King Josiah the city priesthood of Jerusalem gained control of the state. This was partly a result of the sinking international prestige of the monarchy, partly because of the fear caused by the barbaric wars of the Mesopotamian states; both factors contributed to an increase in religious sentiment and therefore strengthened the priesthood.

One result of this new order was the promulgation in 622 B.C. of the Law of Moses, that is *Deuteronomy*. Henceforth the monarch of Judah must be 'legitimate', of the line of David. At the same time he is forbidden to amass a hoard or surround himself with a mounted retinue, and his legitimacy is tied to the oracle controlled by the Jerusalem priesthood. The Temple in Jerusalem is designated as the only place where the cult may be celebrated, while the priests of rural areas are deprived of their function and reduced to the status of dependants of the priestly families of Jerusalem.

Along with this shift in power went a sweeping reorganization of political and social institutions. This reorganization indicates the great changes effected since the old law. Since tithes were now paid to the distant temple city they must have been collected in money, and this indicates an extensive money economy. The degradation of the local priests in favour of those in Jerusalem led to the establishment of secular courts in the rural areas. Thus the interests of the Temple priesthood conflicted with those of the peasantry and indeed also with those of the rural gentry; this was, indeed, a recurring phenomenon in the Near East.

Hence came, as perhaps was always the case in the Near East, an impulse to give judicial powers to the bureaucracy. In short: as theocracy increased, bureaucracy increased too. The administrative regulations of the Sumerian kings, which have been discussed above, were probably analogous in character. Similarly the establishment of local grain storehouses for the poor, in which were deposited every third instalment of the tithe, corresponds entirely to what one expects in a theocratic and bureaucratic city kingdom.

On the other hand there was a general revulsion at this time against an Egyptian-style monarchy, which, like that of Solomon, based its power in pharaonic manner on its business ventures, fortresses and storehouses (cf. I *Kings* 9.19: 'granaries, cities of chariots, and cities of horsemen'), through labour services and taxes levied on its subjects. (Anyone who doubts the historical character of the tradition of the Hebrews' sojourn in Egypt may assume that Egypt was simply used as a 'type' in popular protests against the oppressive nature of Near Eastern liturgy monarchy, as in 1 *Samuel* 8 and 12; an oppression from which the priests claimed to have rescued the people once through Moses the law-giver and again with *Deuteronomy*. I of course do not make that assumption.)

The essence of *Deuteronomy*, like that of the old law and of theocratic legislation in general, is that it seeks to increase the limitations on the misuse of power by the rich. Thus in the old law there were restrictions on distraint, while in *Deuteronomy* it is absolutely forbidden to distrain a debtor's home or private mill; the old liability of son for father and the reverse in criminal actions is abolished; kidnapping, now defined to include women and children, is punished with death; a day's wages must be paid on the day earned; collection of debts on the sabbath is forbidden (so Merx interprets, rightly, *Deut.* 15,3); and the rule is tightened that all who sold themselves into slavery must be freed in the seventh year. But the most far-reaching provision of all is that which forbids taking interest from fellow Hebrews. The

effect of this was probably to give a monopoly of the business of
lending on interest to metics and perhaps also, as in Babylon, to
the Temple. One can deduce this from *Deuteronomy* 15.3, which
stresses as a desirable result that Hebrews should lend to
foreigners but not borrow from them.

The sections of *Deuteronomy* relating to family law indicate a
change in the organization of the family and the assumptions
with which it was regarded. Respect for parents is strongly
emphasized, although the father can no longer execute a child,
but in fact the ancient patriarchal order has been much weakened.

For example, in the old law the woman who had been bought
at a price (*mohan*) became part of the husband's personal
property, and her daughters could be sold as an object of trade;
women not bought remained members of their own clans. Only
the wife was protected from being treated as a slave, and her
sons could not be sold into slavery. On the other hand bastards
and 'children of whores' could inherit from their fathers if
acknowledged by them, and indeed a father could divide his
property among his children just as he pleased. All this was in
many ways much changed by *Deuteronomy*.

But first, certain reservations: payment of a dowry did not
become the rule until the Exile, as the Babylonian word for
dowry shows, and the same is true for the rules making the
levirate an obligation (*ketubah*) incumbent on men. Furthermore
the exclusion of daughters from inheritance rights persisted long
after *Deuteronomy*, as did the limitation of their rights to a
claim to a dowry; this lasted, as with other peoples, as long as
the Hebrews remained independent.

Nevertheless, *Deuteronomy* marks the point at which patriarchal authority ceased to be unlimited. A father must now give
his first-born son the prescribed double share of his property, and
he cannot make a bastard or a son of a mixed marriage his heir.
The inheritance of the father's harem by the son, originally universal in the ancient Near East, is now forbidden. A form of
divorce is now prescribed, although it continues as before to
depend on the husband's will alone.

In these and other ways the position of women was improved,
and this was undoubtedly due to the power of the clans, which

ceased to regard their daughters as objects of trade and instead aimed to protect them when widowed, together with their children as heirs, against the arbitrary acts of husbands. This new attitude is connected with the views of the great families in the cities; notice, for example, that punishment for breach of promise is limited to urban territory (*Deuteronomy* 22.23). The great families were ever more insistent on purity of blood and the welfare of their children. Military concerns also played a role in the improvement of women's lot.

Naturally polygamy continued to exist, although the number of persons involved was limited. The children of female slaves given as part of a dowry continued to be reckoned as children of the mistress in the stories of the patriarchs. Nevertheless, as the legend of Ishmael shows, opinion among the upper classes tended to deny inheritance rights to 'the son of a servant'. Here as in other communities the desire to maintain the existence of the families which could provide equipped recruits for the army and were inscribed in military registers, served to strengthen the inheritance rights of daughters. It also justified the levirate, by which a childless dead man's widow passed by law to his closest male relative, in order that he might 'awaken' the dead man's seed in the widow.

Land ownership was naturally limited by the right of relatives to buy back land sold; later this becomes a right to pre-emptive purchase. Otherwise land was alienable in historical times and also could be used as collateral. As one would expect from the general pattern of development of the Hebrews and the military character of their society, it was considered disgraceful or even sinful to sell one's inherited land; hence the story of Ahab and Naboth (I *Kings* 21). The obligation to redeem family land even extended to agnates, but this provision undoubtedly dates from the post-exilic period.

Under the Hebrew monarchy the tempo of urban development increased, and this led to a greater demand for artisans. In *Exodus* 31.1 we hear of a family of artists charged with supplying the more highly-wrought decorations of the Temple, evidently on an hereditary basis, and when Solomon built his Temple he summoned Phoenician builders.

On the other hand, non-economic factors increased in importance; at the time of the destruction of Jerusalem smiths and carpenters, because of their importance for army supply, were counted as 'warriors'. This meant that they were subject to liturgies, like the *fabri* of Rome, and in fact they were deported as captives by the conquerors.

The other artisans – bakers, potters, fullers – were evidently quite few in number under the monarchy; only after the Exile did trade increase in importance. Apparently the development of large-scale landholding proceeded apace under the monarchy, and here as elsewhere it was caused by the inevitable indebtedness of the peasants to the great families resident in the cities. It was this feature of society under the monarchy which roused prophets to some of their sternest condemnations; See, for example, *Joshua* 5.8; *Micah* 2.1.

In the Talmud we find the principle that land and Canaanite slaves shall be the main collateral for business loans (whereas later Jewish business loans were taken out only on movables), and this reflects the conditions of a time when (as in archaic Greece) money was borrowed mainly in the guise of a pledge.

Since debt slavery was unprofitable for lenders due to the six-year limit set by Mosaic law, land was therefore the main object distrained, presumably according to contract. From this developed, we may assume, the legal mortgage described in the Talmud which is discussed later.

It is impossible to determine just how the large estates were managed. Perhaps the 'Canaanite slave' of the Talmud was bound to the soil like the Spartan helot or later client. But in addition to slaves there were also agricultural labourers paid wages; they are mentioned in both the ancient traditions and in the codes.

As for slaves, we find that as elsewhere unfree labour was drawn from various groups, reflecting the usual stages of historical development. These groups were: (1) children sold or hired out; (2) debt slaves; (3) prisoners of war and purchased slaves; (4) small tenants. But note that the stage in which small tenants were enslaved was not reached until Hellenistic times.

The fact remains, however, that among the Hebrews there was never much demand for slave labour and therefore the number of slaves was never very great. Thus we are told that Phoenicians accompanied the Hebrew armies in order to buy the prisoners, and this was of course for export. Furthermore slavery among the Hebrews always remained in fact as well as in law hereditary slavery, the milder form prevalent in the Near East. Experience showed, it was argued, that slaves reared in the household were far more faithful than purchased slaves. Slaves often had families, and indeed may well have been expected to do so. The codes take into account the possibility that slaves offered their freedom in the seventh year might decline the gift; this, it should be added, indicates that probably there was little demand for free wage labourers and also that they did not enjoy a very advantageous position.

To sum up: we cannot write an agrarian history of the Hebrews before the Exile because we have no evidence regarding ownership and production in that period. The prophets were only occasionally concerned with social questions, for they were religious leaders and were mainly interested in what they considered the theatre of action of their universal god, foreign affairs. Nevertheless we find in their writings the picture of a typical development of ancient urbanism under the influence of a money economy, a development bringing social differentiations which the codes, despite provisions to the contrary (six-year limit on slavery, prohibition of interest, and so on), could not check. So much is clear.

The 'reform programme' of Hezekiel was nothing but a vision in the Exile. The deportation of the military class, that is, the great families of the cities, meant that there remained only the peasants engaged in agriculture and viticulture. The so-called 'restoration' under Ezra and Nehemiah was really the foundation of a theocratic city-state on the basis of a *synoikismos*. For further on this see the section below on the Hellenistic age.

(a) *Pre-classical Period*

The Greeks raised spelt, barley, and wheat, alternating this in each field with grass (hence leases were for an even number of years). This system continued to be followed except in those areas specializing in a particular crop. Occasionally, it seems, the three-field system was used, but there was no change of crops, except that legumes were grown on fallow land. The use of manure is mentioned in Homer (but green manure was not used until later times); in general, however, agricultural techniques were stabilized at a rather primitive level and thereafter did not develop.

Thus the main features of Greek agriculture continued to be ploughing with a hooked plough (for long entirely of wood) drawn by oxen, sowing seed in furrows, hacking and weeding the grain fields, and harvesting with sickle and threshing board. Hence labour intensity was considerable, and since virgin land was no longer available, it was difficult to shift from subsistence agriculture to market production, even though grain prices were high in later times.

Cattle raising does not seem to have been much reduced in extent by farming until the age of the tyrants, who favoured the peasantry. The Homeric epics indicate a diet based mainly on cheese, milk, and – among aristocrats – meat. Clothing was made of wool and skins. Noble and royal wealth was measured partly in herds (partly also, of course, in precious metals and objects made from precious metals and bronze), and the herds included goats, sheep, pigs, and cattle. The latter were used mainly as work animals, since milk and cheese were supplied by the sheep and goats. Horses, on the other hand, were mainly used for military purposes. On the large plains of Euboea and Thessaly horses were raised in great number and were also used for travel and for sport. Shepherds were considered the highest class of royal servants.

Here too, moreover, irrigation was important from early times, but with this difference: no centralized, bureaucratic control of it was needed. Thus even the continued struggles over water rights, such as that between Tegea and Mantinea, although they led to stoppages, never led to the catastrophes which similar disturbances produced in Egypt and Mesopotamia.

In historical times the prevalent form of living unit was the patriarchal nuclear family. Women and children were in much the same position as among Semitic peoples: women could be bought or else married with dowry; husbands had the right to send away their wives, and could sell, rent, expel, or kill their children. Later the laws governing legitimacy, and the feeling for kin ties cultivated among the great families, combined to reduce these powers of the father over his children; by the time when the Gortyn Code was first framed these changes had all taken place.

But whereas the masses lived in nuclear families, nobles and kings – at first the same (see below) – lived as elsewhere in large households including agnates of a clan (*genos*). The purpose of this was to preserve the unity of inheritable landed estates. Thus both separate and group inheritance are mentioned in the Homeric epics; see the *homosipuoi* of Charondas, equivalent to the *homogalaktes* of Attic law. The description of the house of Priam is well known. It was only later in the course of history that the legal structure of the large patrician household was developed in the cities, very much as a similar structure of large households appeared in Italian cities during the Middle Ages. At first complete family communism existed, but as the money economy gained ground this gave way to a new concept; the household came to be regarded as an association for making profit. Gradually separate account was kept of dowries, of children's earnings at their fathers' disposal, and of women's personal property. This development, already present in the Gortyn Code, had its counterpart in the Near East but not in Rome. As in mediaeval Italo-Sicilian law there is some indication that a son could demand his share even while his father was alive; the Gortyn Code implies this in forbidding the use of force in such cases. In short: more and more wealth came to be regarded as the product of family members' work, and thus the basis of the ancient patriarchal household diminished.

An individual's personal safety was the responsibility of his *agchisteis*, a group defined more narrowly than the clan (usually extending to the children of one's brothers and sisters) and mentioned as early as the Homeric epics. Its members were bound to revenge each other's injury or death, and in later law they came to be secondary heirs when the nuclear family died out. Probably this group arose out of ancient conditions, and it is certain that close analogies are to be found in the laws actually governing kin relationships among other peoples ('actually' because in these matters theory and practice are often not the same).

Those people who did not belong to a numerous and economically established clan, who were in short without land, found themselves forced to enter the clientele of one or another aristocrat. This was a later development, as the supply of new land declined and differences in wealth developed; originally membership of the community and ownership of land each presupposed the other.

In historical times the Greek tribes (*phylai*) were divided into 'brotherhoods' (*phratriai*), territorial units with administrative and religious functions. Originally, however, they like the *agchisteis* were united by kin ties and the obligation to defend and avenge each other; this is clear from survivals in historical times. However, it is uncertain whether the phratry was the 'oldest' social unit, that is, the dominant primary group in the purely peasant stage of the Hellenic peoples. Although there is some evidence to support this hypothesis, analogies from non-urban areas in historical times must be treated with caution. It should be remembered that radical contrasts already existed among what for us are the 'most ancient' Germans, for example between fighting peoples such as Ariovistus' Suevi and others.

Of course it is perfectly clear that the phratry was very ancient. One cannot, however, assume that the communal features mentioned in historical times are 'survivals' from a primitive stage shaped by the collective economy of a nomadic society. The opposite is probably true: like the Germanic 'protection guilds' they indicate rather the artificial formation of the association, for common ownership of food sources ('household' in the economic sense) was the original basis for mutual obligations, not kinship, and this is evident also among the Arabs. Therefore the stress on kin ties, at least in the symbolic sense, must in fact have been characteristic of later organizations formed by choice. Such associations belong to a stage of development in which landowners organized themselves as a community of warriors and regarded their land as 'won by the spear'. This explains why later the phratry had the function of training its children for war and determining their eligibility to inherit.

However, we know very little about the relation between phratries and aristocratic clans and also, much more important, between phratries and the ancient village (*kōmē*). We know that Athenian law imposed the acceptance of both aristocratic and non-aristocratic groups, and we also have the fourth-century documents relating to Demotion and the lists of phratries from the fourth century published by Kastriotis and explained by Körte. But all of this is inadequate, for by the time of these documents the phratries had long been merely artificial groupings shaped from above by state policies. Above all we need to know what were the ancient relations between the two local units, *kōmē* and *dēmos*.

Indeed, it is possible that the phratries too may have been no more than the creation of a period of differentiation, a phase marked by basic political changes in which available land needed constant military protection, and hence the disposition of men and money for defence became of decisive importance. Perhaps phratries arose out of the institutions created by free peasants settled on conquered or threatened land in the period of the Dorian invasion.

In all *poleis* we find that the population was divided into tribes or *phylai*. Later they were used by the state as administrative and military units, and were defined as federations of phratries. Originally, however, the tribe was connected with an earlier stage of the polis, and in fact was normally a feature accompanying the union of villages to form a *polis* (*synoikismos*), related to military organization. Therefore the use of tribes to blur class divisions or to shift burdens from the warrior class (now organized as a 'state') was entirely secondary.

Szanto has argued that the three Doric tribes were connected with territorial divisions, but this implies a purposeful agrarian policy for which there is no evidence whatever. Of course there were cases where an area was conquered by an army already divided into tribes and was then apportioned among the tribes, which in turn assumed the task of subdividing the land among its members. An example of this was Rhodes. There were also cases where several rural districts of similar size formed a *polis*, and then constituted tribes corresponding to the old districts. But neither development was predetermined.

The Dorian cities were fundamentally military states, and so everywhere they maintained the same three tribes. Elsewhere there was great variety, but everywhere and always the formal division of a community into tribes signified one thing: that a people had constituted itself as a *polis* ready for war at any time. It should be noted here that the proper word for a tribe in a non-urbanized community was *ethnos*, as is shown by the documents of the Delphic Amphictyone. This is true even though the word *phylē* is itself older than *ethnos*.

More precise information is not available for the political and social structures of autonomous communities in early times. If, however, we rely on analogies with other peoples, then we can assume that in each community the position of ruler (*anax*) came to be hereditary in a family made prominent by wealth in cattle and marked out as favoured by the gods by success in war and equity in judgment. An *anax* received a larger share of booty, gifts on special occasions, and presents from parties involved in disputes brought before his court. Since tradition was the only source of legal knowledge, an *anax* had to rely upon the aid of a council of elders, and this was recruited – as one would expect – from great families ennobled by wealth and military prowess. The authority of the *anax* varied according to circumstances, depending above all on how great was the threat of military attack from abroad.

These local families who provided the rulers and elders were regarded as favoured by the gods, and were entrusted with the communal cults. Here too they formed the kernel of the aristocracy, and among them arose – as elsewhere – the ideal of the kin tie as the source of legitimate authority.

Every aristocrat belonged to a large lineage group – the *genos* – held together by the kin tie; this was an extended clan, and its economic aspect was the *oikos*, property held in common. Indeed *oikos* is often used as a synonym for *genos*, and the two institutions characterized the life of an aristocrat as opposed to that of a commoner.

It was once argued that from the first all members of a community were also members of the clans, though with varying rights. But now this is generally regarded as mistaken. In later times, it is true, such was the situation, but this was an artificial arrangement instituted from above for administrative purposes.

There remain several knotty problems: whether the clans originally stood in a definite relation with the phratries, and – if so – whether within a phratry members of a clan had certain privileges, and whether these privileges were gained with or without a struggle with the commoners in their phratry. General agreement on these problems has not been reached, and perhaps never will be. In any case only the specialist trained in archaeology is entitled to an opinion on these matters.

Originally the Greeks settled in villages, which were unfortified. Walled citadels were also built, to offer refuge for men and cattle in time of need. Ownership of land was regarded as an aspect of membership in the community of warriors. We see this in the law of associations, under which the phratry was involved in the designation of heirs (see above), and also in the form prescribed by classical law for complaints regarding property ownership. Like early Roman property law, classical Greek law made no provision for a simple petition regarding ownership of a property or inheritance. Instead a challenge was entered against another person, and the decision went to the party with the relatively better case (the *diadikasia* procedure). Similar methods were used in disputes involving an individual's social rights and duties, such as liturgies, right to a name, and membership in a phratry. All these phenomena sprang from the same cause.

There was an accepted procedure allowing a complainant to

have someone deprived of the use of a property. This procedure, *dikē exoulēs*, was quite similar to the Roman *interdictum* in function (although unlike it in form). However, only a few were entitled to use this procedure, that is those who had manifest rights based on judicial or state action, or who enjoyed special status, or were mortgage holders (cf. the Roman *precarium*). But even here the procedure did not involve appeal to fixed rules, but rather a claim to have the relatively better title.

In passing it is worth noting that G. Leist is, in my opinion, quite correct in his contention that the reason why there was no procedure for claiming absolute property in Greek law was that there was no equivalent in Greek law to the Roman *usucapio*.

As to land use, there is no reason to assume that the Greeks originally possessed a system similar to the primitive German division based on hides (*Hufen*), and indeed the same is true of the old Roman system. Nor have we any evidence on which to judge whether or not cultivation of the land was ever the work of joint labour groups. What is clear is that originally there cannot have been any sort of unconditional appropriation of land, for there is much evidence that in Homeric times the political community had rather autocratic control over the division of land. One clear indication of this is the frequent mention of a family's property being removed from the common lands as royal land (*temenos*) when that family was raised to monarchical dignity. Even in the fourth century, Attic village communities (*dēmoi*) still owned considerable lands, and clearly they must have been commons for a very long time. These lands had originally been used for grazing, but in the fourth century they were rented out and used for agriculture and horticulture.

It has been argued by Ridgeway that there were communities holding collective land with power to assign work at will, similar to the German villages. However, the evidence cited is not convincing. In fact the opposite is probably true, if one can judge from Near Eastern analogies, from the method of ploughing used by South Europeans, and from the fact that slavery is hardly ever mentioned in extant sources.

There is of course the term *klēros*, which does seem to refer back to a distribution of land by lot when a settlement was founded, but it certainly does not indicate that there were periodic redistributions. In Homer the term has two meanings: (1) land which a prince assigned to one of his household, as in the case of Eumaeus; (2) the land to which a warrior was entitled.

Pasture lands were very important in the society of the Homeric poems. Nor is this surprising, since sheep were absolutely necessary for clothing supplies (flax was not raised until the time of Thucydides, and hemp is first attested in the time of Pliny, in Asia Minor). Hence the rules prohibiting the slaughter of sheep before the first shearing and the first litters. Hence too the fact that large areas probably continued to be reserved for grazing in historical times; where inscriptions exist for common grazing lands, the latter are of considerable extent. Likewise the forest areas continued to be quite extensive even in the time of Theophrastus (end of the fourth century), despite the development of mining and shipbuilding.

The first great change in social relationships in Greece was due to the establishment of city-states (*poleis*). This seems to have been due to the arrival of Near Eastern cultural elements by way of the sea, and to the participation of coastal areas in overseas commerce.

At the same time military technology shaped developments. In the Greek states, as everywhere else, the legal position of an individual depended upon his role in the army. Hence a sharp differentiation developed within the population because of two factors: (1) the spread of chariot-fighting tactics, with heavy or light armour, over all the ancient world accessible to commerce, from India to Gaul, which tended to enhance the position of wealthy and athletically trained warriors; (2) the monopolization of barter trade by the fortress kings on the coast, just now rising to a dominant position.

Fortresses like Mycenae and Tiryns were the capitals of kings who fought in chariots at the head of their companions, often quite numerous but sometimes – because of local resources – numbering only a few dozen. These companions dined at the royal table and were recompensed with land, slaves, and cattle. They were similar to the military court aristocracy of the Assyrians and Persians, the *hetairoi* of the Macedonian kings, the *soldurii* of the Gauls, and the *degen* and *antrustiones* of the early Germanic kings.

The fortress was surrounded by settlements of artisans and shopkeepers. Although the Homeric poems depict the rural population as simply a mass of serfs (*thētes*) and slaves (*oikēes*), this does not mean that we should assume that in fact the peasants were all in servitude. What actually happened was that the masters of the city fortresses and their retainers used their military superiority to subject the peasants, exclude them from aristocratic society, and levy assessments at will; see the description of Phaeacia in the *Odyssey*. Although the common people kept the formal right to approve declarations of war and other decisions of their masters by acclamation, any individual who dared to express his own opinions was liable to be treated with the contempt and violence visited on Thersites.

Because the peasants had no military role except that of camp followers they were powerless, and so they were often unable in practice – sometimes even in theory – to defend their legal rights. As a result they were compelled to seek the protection of powerful men. Clientship was legally expected of men without property and hence without means of self-defence, and often it was advisable for a commoner of reduced means to accept it too.

But the extent of oppression often must have been greater. The astonishing fortifications of the dominant cities indicate clearly that a great deal of forced labour must have been exacted from the subjected peasantry. Military domination was the key to this.

Economically this domination was sustained here too by the participation of the rulers – in their public capacities – in overseas trade. Hence the creation of dominant fortress states started on the coasts and then moved inland. At first this trade was with Near Easterners visiting the coasts; it was monopolistic and deficitary. Gradually, however, rulers began to develop their own commercial organizations. When these proved successful, the next step was to send out overseas raiding expeditions, then to occupy distant lands in the manner of the Normans, and finally to pursue colonial expansion. For example, the Mycenaean export trade in metal work and pottery was undoubtedly a royal enterprise, as it was originally in the Near East. About the Mycenaean king's fortress lived subjects bound to labour service who supplied finished goods for sale. A later example is provided by a well-known vase from Cyrene which shows a king carefully measuring out silphium; it is clear that he is acting as not as a controller of trade, but as a commercial proprietor, and indeed silphium production continued to be a state monopoly at Cyrene in late Antiquity.

Such enterprises enriched the treasuries and graves of members of the small ruling class, enabled them to dress in linen imported from the Near East, and in general allowed them to maintain a way of life quite different from that of the unarmed masses living outside the fortresses. Political institutions reflected this. There were rather large states in the Mycenaean world, but each was essentially no more than an agglomeration of fortress fiefs under a high king. Thus Agamemnon offered to invest Achilles with lordship over a number of so-called cities whose population he comments have large herds of cattle (the main source of tribute from them).

Various groups were dependent upon the aristocracy of the fortresses. There were the men without land and those from abroad; they formed what might be called a 'feudal' element. Then there were free-born men held in debt slavery and they formed a 'capitalist' element; their ranks were augmented by prisoners captured in war and slaves purchased in the market. Clients, the feudal element, predominated in earlier times and continued to do so in the establishments of the inland rural aristocracy, whereas in later times and especially on the coasts the capitalist element of debt and purchased slaves prevailed. It should be noted, however, that in ancient Greece there was no clear distinction between purchased slave and client. Thus Eumaeus was purchased by Odysseus, hopes to receive from him a piece of land (*klēros*, equivalent to Latin *precarium*), and has his own servant.

Colonization in the Mycenaean Age was also shaped by this combination of feudalism and commerce. It was undertaken for agrarian expansion only in so far as a controlled peasantry was needed for establishing a *polis*, but the great families in charge of colonies aimed like the aristocrats of the motherland at profits from commerce. On the other hand it is not very likely that the Asia Minor coast was gradually colonized by the Greeks for the purpose of setting up trading posts, in the Phoenician manner. Eduard Meyer argued for this, but there is no evidence that payments were ever paid to the natives for use of their land, as was done by Carthage, and an argument against the theory is that a dominant position was held by the conquering aristocracy, in some parts centred in separate fortresses as in Greece. It is true however, that many of the later Corinthian colonies were established as trading posts; an example is Epidamnus founded in 627 B.C., where the oligarchy traded with the hinterland through an agent (*polētēs*) and did this on a joint partnership basis. But this cannot be taken as typical.

On the other hand it is clear that colonization was connected with a transition from a negative to a positive balance of trade, with the development of Greek-owned shipping, and with the search for foreign markets by Greek sailors. In other words, it was part of the great transformation from which emerged the characteristic features of Greek civilization.

The decisive turning point in Greek social history is the development of a military urban particularism which led to the *polis*, in contrast to developments in the Near East where city monarchy existed at first but then developed into bureaucratic territorial monarchy and finally 'world monarchy'. The crucial factor which made Near Eastern development so different was the need for irrigation systems, as a result of which the cities were closely connected with building canals and constant regulation of waters and rivers, all of which demanded the existence of a unified bureaucracy.

There was an irreversible character to this development, and with it went subjection of the individual to the community. Hence the dominance of religious tradition in Near Eastern society and the political power of the priesthood. Then, too, the peoples of the riverine cultures were repeatedly conquered by foreign invaders from Arabia and Iran, and as a result were held in permanent subjection and powerlessness.

Hence in the Near East the city king's companions, the men who fought at his side and dined at his table, developed into a royal army which was equipped, fed, and led by a bureaucracy. At the same a royal bureaucracy developed out of the growing body of the king's clients. Then there was a struggle between these bureaucratic formations in the Near East, and out of that struggle came the first 'world power', the Assyrian Empire.

On the other hand in Greece the retinues of the fortress kings diminished in size. It was only with the table companions of the conquering Macedonian monarchs that they again became an important political element. As the retinues dwindled the position of the monarchs declined too, and so began a development which ended – at the start of the Classical period – with an army recruited from yeoman farmers who provided their own arms. Political power necessarily passed to this class, and therewith started to emerge that purely secular civilization which characterized Greek society and caused capitalist development in Greece to differ from that in the Near East.

The process by which Greek society was transformed is not known to us, and in any case it differed greatly from state to state. Consider, for example, the Homeric account of the kings of Lacedaemonia with their horses and with their treasure hoards (as enticing to adventurers as their women); then compare with it the Spartan hoplite state, which lacked cavalry entirely, strictly forbade possession of precious metals, was without a citadel, and obliged the ephors elected by the army to swear each year that they would not attack the monarchy provided that the kings would swear that they would not interfere with the traditional institutions of the army.

From this comparison one can conclude the following: (1) that Spartan institutions were consciously reformed as part of a compromise between kings and army; (2) that this was in some way connected with the rise of disciplined armies using iron weapons for close combat, replacing warriors using bronze throwing spears and arrows in single combat; (3) that this was also connected with the decline in importance of the royal treasure hoard. In the Near East under all regimes, including the Persian, the royal hoard continued to be as important as it was for the Nibelungs. An accumulation of precious metals allowed monarchs to reward members of their retinues and to hire mercenaries when needed, and so it was always an important factor in the power of Near Eastern rulers.

In Greece the kings of fortress states had hoards, one of the results of their close relations with the great states of the Near East. Then towards the end of the second millennium these great states declined, and it has been rightly assumed that the eclipse of Mycenaean civilization was connected with this. It is of course perhaps also true that Greece's geographical characteristics would have ultimately sufficed to ensure the triumph of particularism.

In any case the economic decline of Greek monarchy was made manifest by the disappearance of Near Eastern magnificence. This meant that kings' retinues could not develop into royal bureaucracies, and so the first steps towards formation of large states were never taken. Furthermore the relative decline of the royal clans must have been even more striking, for at the same new social classes were coming into being and these enjoyed an economic position which rivalled that of the monarchy. For example, the practice of recruiting mercenary soldiers, which filled the Egyptian armies with men from all parts of the Mediterranean as far as Sardinia, seems to have led to the development of a new class in Greece, a stratum of trained and propertied soldiers socially independent of the monarchy, which played no small part in plundering expeditions and colonial occupations.

But even the kings' fighting companions must have essentially freed themselves from dependence as the importance of the royal hoards diminished. They gained possession of lands and became a self-equipped warrior class, following a pattern similar to that under the Merovingians. Then when the Greek fortress kings turned to overseas adventures in search of booty, their companions became even more independent. Thus the wrath of Achilles alone brought defeat close. The fortress king who led an expedition overseas was no more than commander in chief, for the weapons and provisions of the army did not come from him alone – as it did in the Near East – and therefore authority was divided.

Hence a constantly shifting relation between king and army. Agamemnon acts sometimes with authority, sometimes arbitrarily, sometimes he depends on others, sometimes he strives for compromise. The same was true of Alexander, the first Hellenistic rulers, Chlodwig, and the early Merovingians. The result of these shifts was to the disadvantage of the Greek kings once the royal hoard and table ceased to play a central role; that is, once a negative balance of trade with the Near East was replaced by a positive balance and military expeditions overseas. The personal retinues of the kings must have been present in the Mycenaean states, but even in Homer, they are much reduced in importance and seem to be recruited entirely from members of the community. Indeed the Homeric retinue seems to have been formed on a temporay basis as need arose, much like expeditionary forces of German princes described by Tacitus.

Henceforth the Greek king shared power not only with his lieges but also with members of great clans, like himself owning castles and lands, living in the same city, and serving in war at their own cost. These clans therefore had the right to advise the king in council, share in the booty, and participate in the exercise of political authority over the masses. Hence the ancient aristocracy of the royal council became more important in Greece, whereas in the Near East it disappeared and was replaced by bureaucrats and priests.

In the Homeric poems the term 'city' varies in meaning, as one would expect from the different times in which the poems were composed, but in general it stands for something between the ancient fortress state and the later *polis* formed by the union of several urban centres. Eduard Meyer has argued that in Homer the aristocrats are generally settled in the country and are quite distinct from city dwellers. I am not convinced, however, and in fact many of the passages Meyer cites use 'country' in the sense of native land rather than rural area. Rather the situation was this: many of the local chiefs of the peasant period and others who gained riches became aristocrats with landed possessions and clients. The king now counted as simply first among equals, a measure of how far Mycenaean kingship had been reduced, and the aristocrats were organized and urbanized. The city was now the sole centre of political power. Aristocrats visited their rural properties only to supervise their shepherds, slaves, and clients. He who, like King Laertes, lived permanently on the landed estates reserved for his old age thereby gave up any claim to political authority.

All the aristocratic clans had accumulated treasure hoards from their share of booty and from trading profits, and with this treasure they accumulated land and were able to use their clients as attendants or infantrymen in war. The king, therefore, was now no more than an equal.

Thus royal power first declined in areas engaged primarily in sea commerce, and then declined even further in inland areas where the development of royal hoards and retinues had always been slower. This process was substantially hastened by the Doric invasions, for whatever else these caused they certainly led to the establishment of political communities such as Sparta in which the warrior order allowed the royal clans only one privilege: leadership in war. Nor did this apply only to their own *polis*, for each ruling class used its strength to intervene in neighbouring states to defend warrior rule, prevent the establishment of monarchy of the Near Eastern type, and so maintain its own position.

Thus there arose 'the states of the Greek Middle Ages', as Eduard Meyer called them. Even putting aside Sparta as *sui generis*, it is clear that they had a very distinct social structure. A common Hellenic feature is the appearance of a knightly society which organizes military sports and national contests, thus providing the material for poetry about heroes and lovers, which as in the European Middle Ages aimed to define the style proper to knightly contests. For example, there was an attempt to prohibit the use of long-distance weapons (a sufficient indication of the military technology of this knightly society!). Certain forms of courtesy were observed in battle, much like the mediaeval '*Messieurs les Anglais, tirez les premiers*'.

Also as in our Middle Ages the warrior class divided into rival camps cutting across national lines, like the Guelfs and Ghibellines, as in the Lelantine War, and there were also unending feuds between the clans within each *polis*. Then again as in mediaeval times, a number of clans chose to make an alliance with the people and so establish a leader as *aisymnētēs* or tyrant – the distinction was not a sharp one.

But the possibility of such an alliance exists only when there is a 'people' able to make one, as in mediaeval Italy. In Hellas this arose out of a development in which three factors were crucial: (1) the use of iron weapons for close combat in place of the Mycenaean bronze throwing spear and the arrow; (2) the resultant increased importance of discipline, already apparent in Homer, and of battle in closed formation – especially infantry fighting in the hoplite phalanx (Brasidas ascribed the discipline of the Greeks to this, as opposed to the battle tactics of the barbarians); (3) hence in those states which were intent on expansion, such as Sparta at the time of the conquest of Messenia or Athens of Salamis, political power passed to the class which manned the hoplite army; (4) finally, paralleling the last, there

developed what one could call 'bourgeois business', which provided the economic basis for a class able to outfit itself with
hoplite armour.

In early times the *polis* citadel was surrounded by the dwellings
of merchants and artisans. In the Homeric poems we find mention of masons, carpenters, cabinet-makers, wheelwrights, gold-
smiths, potters, and workers in bronze, horn and leather. It is
true, however, that these references all occur in the later sections.
Still, the idea that in Homeric times Greek craftsmen were all
unfree workers for the citadel aristocracy is as untrue for Greece
as the similar view once held for the early Middle Ages, but now
rejected. It also is unlikely that Greek craftsmen were in still
earlier times employed by the villages, as were East Asian
village artisans, or that after the development of the *polis* they
became slaves of the *polis*. In Epidamnos commerce was organized by the oligarchy on a cooperative basis, and the system may
have been expanded, while similar developments may have
occurred elsewhere. But that this was a general tendency is a
hypothesis for which there is no evidence whatever.

Artisans were, however, certainly made to render labour
services to the Mycenaean state, just as in its Near Eastern
models. Like the pharaoh and the Mesopotamian city king, the
Mycenaean city prince with sufficient resources will also have
had artisans settled about his citadel in return for labour services.
We can even posit the existence of a royal *oikos* in Mycenaean
times with its own artisans, but with the disappearance of the
foundations of Mycenaean civilization this disappeared too, as
changes in workmanship indicate.

Later, cities without industries may have imported skilled
slaves and used them as state workers to pursue a form of
'mercantilism'. But it is far more probable that all the phenomena
which are taken to indicate state employment or the state slavery
of all artisans (*dēmiourgoi*) were in fact aspects of the military
organization of the *polis*. We can assume that the craftsmen who
produced articles needed by the state were organized and burdened with public liturgies, just as were *fabri* in Rome. The
Greek term *dēmiourgos* is much broader than our term artisan;
it includes all whose occupations served indeterminate large
groups, including doctors, singers, seers, and so on.

These plebeian settlements of craftsmen round the citadel

were unfortified, as was Ecbatana in the Near East and as Athens remained down to historical times. In Sparta the royal citadel was entirely destroyed, and the whole city became an open camp. The only valid generalization here is that the *polis*, like Near Eastern cities, retained a fortress or became a fortress; but that this fortress, contrary to the situation in the Near East, was controlled by the community of warriors and not by the king. The process of synoecism signified, therefore, the consolidation of the warrior class as the rulers of the *polis*. It is also quite probable that in most cases union meant an actual consolidation of settlement, and we have explicit instances from later times to confirm this supposition. Local fortresses were destroyed, or at least ceased to be centres of political power, and the great clans were joined together in a single community, very much as were rural aristocracies in many mediaeval Italian cities.

However, the main significance of synoecism in Antiquity was that it created an army organized into tribes and subdivisions, an army suited for the chronic warfare which henceforth was deemed normal by Greek international law (which did not include the idea of permanent peace between non-allied states, and indeed rejected it because it demanded oaths sworn for eternity, hence full of religious dangers). Synoecism did not necessarily mean that everyone had to move away from outlying areas, but rather that people had to reside *also* and primarily in the city, the centre of political life.

Very early, too, the city was also given staple privileges and other laws regulating commerce were enacted, for the *polis* was not only a political but also an economic centre – a market. From the times of the pharaohs to the Roman Empire the establishment of a market was a prerogative of sovereignty. As in the Middle Ages, so in Antiquity every city was a market, though there were also markets outside the cities.

We noted above that trade developed in the Near East even without the use of coinage. Much more evidence exists to show that the Greeks had commercial life as active as that of the Phoenicians hundreds of years before the first state coinage. The more significant, then, is the fact that the Greeks were the very first to exploit fully the invention of coinage. For there can be no doubt that the Greeks owed much of their superiority to the Phoenicians in commerce to the fact that they had used coinage several centuries earlier. (Carthage started to issue coins in connection with a military reorganization involving the use of hired mercenaries, which initiated its period of great expansion. Before then Carthage, like other Phoenician colonies, had been essentially a trading depot and had an economy based on the barter techniques similar to those of the Ancient Near East.)

But the introduction of coinage into Greece in the seventh century occurred when a money economy already existed there, and only served to accelerate its development. For a long time there had existed an intensive local market alongside an extensive international trade. There existed the 'public artisan' (*dēmiourgos*), that is the person engaged in organized production for anyone who chose to be his customer rather than simply for his own needs (as *autourgos*) or for a master who commanded his labour service, and this type, a 'wage worker' in Bücher's terminology, multiplied in number and became more specialized. There was also a class actively engaged in overseas trade, which adopted and spread capitalist forms of trade developed in the Near East. More and more domestic trade in necessities was conducted on a money basis.

These developments made possible an increasing production of cash crops. Thus the individual elements of the 'city economy' were present in Greece [by the seventh century B.C.], though of course only in an early stage and mingled with feudal features. Because it was the basic military unit, a dominant position was held by the *polis*, which meant the military aristocracy assembled in it.

At first the *polis* ruled the countryside very much as had the castle lords before. Then, however, the development of outlets for cash crops along with changes in military technology caused an expansion in the class of landowners with economic resources sufficient for them to purchase hoplite armour and weapons. Because of constant danger from abroad the state was forced to call upon this class for military service.

As a result of these developments the *poleis* assumed different characteristics, each according to the degree to which its military system had been democratized. Where the armed forces were still mainly cavalry, there as one might expect a relatively small class of large landowners remained dominant, and continued to hold the inland population in strict serfdom, as in Thessaly; even in Attica this class dominated the city as long as it was of military importance. But when the development of military technology shifted the leading role to disciplined hoplites, equipped with heavy armour and trained to fight in formation – and that is what happened in Greece (the cavalry disappeared in the time of the Persian Wars) – the number of full citizens nevertheless very often remained small, a few hundreds or 'the thousand' wealthiest. The number of positions in the council was often fixed in proportion to defined groups and the councillors were often chosen in co-option (in which case sons were chosen, like masters' sons in a guild, the older before the younger).

Since military service fell upon those economically able to equip themselves, it was natural that possession of land should become the economic qualification for admittance to the community, especially when it expanded. For example: Hesiod's father came from Cyme to Boeotia, accumulated a modest sum of money in sea-trade, and then moved to Helicon as a yeoman farmer. Here we see an example of freedom of movement, especially with respect to land law, which should be compared with the later guild-like citizenship and land policies of the democracies in order to see the greatly strengthened tie between property and person in the later period. At the same time there disappeared the ancient class of wandering knights – akin to the mediaeval *ministeriales* – of Homeric times, and their place was taken by the closed and local aristocracies of the *poleis*.

In this period, then, restrictions were placed upon those lands possession of which had allowed a warrior class to usurp power. Such lands are mentioned by Aristotle as 'the first allotments' or 'the old allotments' or 'the ancient portions' and there were many survivals in the historical period. Most important: sons had prior right to ownership of the family lands and sometimes even the herds as well, the only condition being that they had to dower their sisters. According to the Gortyn Code sons inherited land in the city because it was they who exercised political rights. If there were no sons then the daughter inherited, and for a daughter in that position (*epiklēros*) the law prescribed, in the manner of inheritance rights, the order in which agnates might ask for her hand. In these cases an agnate might even break an existing marriage, and originally (as with the Jewish levirate marriage) this was a duty, later in some cities (e.g. Athens) replaced by the duty to provide a dowry. All this indicates that the marriage of an heiress, because it involved disposition of an allotment (*klēros*), was of military significance and therefore of public concern. If no relatives had any claim to her hand then the matter was referred to the magistrates, in Sparta to the king.

In order to ensure that warriors retained property appropriate to their station, the *klēros* could not be divided or sold in many states. This was certainly true in the military states of the Dorians, and in many others as well. It was so, for example, in Leucas, which was founded as a colony in the seventh century B.C., and this continued in force until late times. This militarist land regulation is entirely opposed to the land law common to the Greeks, for in the age of Homer and Hesiod the rule was that inherited goods were equally divided. No trace of primogeniture is to be found. (However, there may be a reminiscence of very ancient conditions, in which the eldest son was house priest in the legend of Iris and Poseidon. When he cited general Hellenic practice against primogeniture to Zeus, Iris replied that the Furies favoured the older brother.)

In any case the legal prohibition on division of the *klēros* must have had the practical effect of forcing the choice of a principal heir, and it must also have encouraged the maintenance of extended facilities. It led, at least in Sparta, to limitation on the number of children reared and even gave rise to polyandry – that is, shared possession of a woman, hardly 'a survival of very ancient conditions', as Eduard Meyer thinks.

Wills could be made in Athens only from the time of Solon, in Sparta not until the Peloponnesian War. In Sparta wills originally served mainly to solemnize adoptions and ensure maintenance of the warrior family and the family cult.

We cannot be sure whether the limitations on military allotments were everywhere written into the laws. It is enough to note that these limitations shaped the ethos of the military class, and we see its effect in the general condemnation of the sale of inherited lands. It should be noted, however, that there is mention of limited rights to sell allotments, for example in Elis and in Thebes under Philolaus (*c*. 728 B.C.). We also are told that Pheidon of Argos made the allotments equal.

The economic basis of the warrior class differed greatly in particulars from place to place. The most extensive provisions in the interests of military power were made where the warrior class was supported by a natural economy, for example, on the Lipari islands, in Crete, and, above all in Sparta. There the conquered population was held in state slavery or serfdom, and their tributes in kind were used to support the warriors. These tributes were distributed partly in a communal manner, partly in such a way that an individual warrior was assigned the produce of a particular piece of land and its slaves. Such lands were in varying degrees appropriated by the warriors and tended to become hereditary.

New distributions and redistributions of allotments were not regarded as impracticable in historical times, and instances seem to have occurred. These were of course not allotments of land to be cultivated, but rather assignments of income properties from which rent was collected. Military considerations, especially military population policy, decided specific arrangements. If there was no heir then the law sometimes required adoption, sometimes marriage, or else imposed the duty of finding a third party 'to provide offspring', as in Israel.

The organization of the citizen army found its fullest expression in the common meals of the warriors, meals eaten by groups (*syssitia, hetairiai*) similar to modern men's clubs. Another typical institution was the common training given by the state to children to make them into warriors. Under this sort of regime the role of army units (phratries) was enhanced so that they became true brotherhoods, to the detriment of family life.

It is to this context that we must refer the power of phratries to decide on the destiny of the new-born and also those sons just coming of age for military service. There is nothing 'primitive' about this; the primitive rule was that the father's will decided.

Sparta developed most the natural economy basis of its city militarism and also the *esprit de corps* of its warriors based on the comradely equality of privileged members of the Spartan community. From youth on Spartans had to devote themselves exclusively to training for hoplite service. Hence the spirit of solidarity among its warriors.

This solidarity, however, also set limits to the Spartan state's development. Again and again down to late Antiquity Spartan kings tried to expand the number of those eligible for military service and so increase the state's power, but this was blocked by the institution of the ephorate. Since a money economy tended to destroy social unity it was arrested by artificially maintaining the natural economy and restricting the consumption of the warrior class. Hence the use of money in trade was discouraged, hence the prohibition on the sale of military allotments, hence the maintenance of the club community. This did prevent the number of warrior lots from increasing, but not from diminishing through inheritance by women, and impoverishment. Other Spartans secretly engaged in foreign commerce. At the same time these artificial policies had the effect of limiting the political options of the state, due to the well-known anxiety to avoid the loss of Spartan lives.

Finally the conservative military policies of Spartan tradition could no longer be maintained after the Peloponnesian War, for the dominant position Sparta had won meant that the state had to meet its increased obligations with the use of money. Then the money economy affected the structure of the military state, for it created private fortunes, revolutionized the consumption of the ruling caste, and so in a very brief time destroyed the economic basis of the entire Spartan system. The democratic restoration established by Cleomenes, on the basis of a redistribution of property, collapsed at the battle of Sellasia (222 B.C.).

However, Sparta's militarism was not typical of Greek tradition. It was based on a barter economy, and the form known to contemporaries was the result of a unique legislative programme. For us, however, the truth lies deeper. Sparta was in reality only an extreme example of the ancient city-state's drive to rule. What was actually unique in the situation was that the feudal substructure of the state did not serve a ruling class set apart by membership in aristocratic clans, but rather one chosen and shaped by an educational system. This system trained men to be experts in hoplite fighting, and because of the particular demands of such training it instilled a life style which was the very opposite of aristocratic.

Whoever belonged to the caste of Spartiates was obliged to keep up his professional military training, just as were mediaeval knights, and the state made adequate provisions to render this possible. To keep in training was a condition for living in the city, at least for those warriors who formed the core of the army. Daily training was what made Sparta's army 'invincible', and later the Holy Battalion of Thebes. Any men in these strictly militaristic communities who left the city thereby gave up the practice of arms; he became a 'rustic' (*agroikos, perioikos*), and his political status was reduced. Participation in the training of the gymnasium and political citizen rights were inextricably connected.

However, it is very likely that the system of Sparta and Crete in historical times was by no means a general stage in the development of Greek society. This system was a barter economy militarism, and it involved a democratization of Greek city-state feudalism so extensive that members of the ruling warrior class were obliged to exist entirely on the produce of allotments of some 8–12 hectares worked by helots. Now we do not find such equality elsewhere, and in fact the record shows that the characteristic militaristic institutions of Sparta were maintained with more rather than less rigour as time went by, the reason being that as Sparta's subjected territory expanded and the number of Spartiates declined its military position became ever more perilous.

Institutions such as the public meals in the Prytaneum at Athens (which was a substitute for the ancient royal table) certainly do not prove that anything like the Spartan messes (*syssitia*) with their specifically military character were once found everywhere in Greece. In Hesiod, for example, there is no trace of feudal restrictions on the free peasants, who are pictured there as working the land themselves with the help of a few bondsmen and day labourers. His complaints mention only the misuse of judicial power and the fact that it was necessary to become the client of a rich man either temporarily or permanently in order to defend one's rights in court. Debt law is also mentioned by Hesiod, and that is the decisive point. Whereas in Sparta, Crete, and other feudal states based upon conquest the population was enslaved, this change was achieved in other states by debt bondage; men were of course usually forced into clientage everywhere (e.g. the *pelatai* at Athens), but this declined as debt slavery took root.

The fact that an urban military class possessed political power did not necessarily lead to the formation of a large rural class of helots, just as the domination of military monarchies in the Near East did not necessarily lead to the establishment of labour service regimes such as we find in Egypt. Similarly one finds whole rural populations reduced to serfdom in areas other than the Dorian states of the Peloponnesus (Sparta, Argos, Sicyon) and Crete – for example, in Thessaly, Locris, Byzantium, and the two Heracleias. But these are only the places for which there is extant evidence from historical periods; serf populations seem to have existed also in many other places, but we cannot say anything definite about their legal systems.

In Sicyon and Argos the origin of serfdom seems to have been conquest, as at Sparta, or else a transformation of clientage owing to the monopoly of armed force in the hands of the city's citizens (the serfs went into battle as light armed infantry). Here and in the colonies based on conquest (such as Crete, Byzantium and the two Heracleias) the serfs were evidently considered as tribute-paying dependants of the state, holding a position guaranteed them by state treaty at the time of the conquest, as in Pontic Heracleia. Their status was midway between that of helots and of perioeci; like the latter, they paid tribute and owed military service but were personally free. In Thessaly a mild form of personal serfdom seems to have existed. Thessalian and Cretan serfs clearly had well-defined rights in family and property law.

Therefore it is virtually certain that this reduction of politically subject rural populations to a state of serfdom was not a stage of development found generally in Greek societies. City feudalism led to such institutions only in particular cases, and they were mainly if not entirely in states based on conquest. On the other hand it is also quite probable that the reduction of elements of the population to a dependent status was much more common than our scanty sources indicate. Certainly it is clear that clientage existed everywhere, and was used by the aristocracy as a source of tribute. On the other hand we can be sure that during the Greek Middle Ages the city aristocracy procured the manpower it needed for economic purposes in much the same manner as was used in the Ancient Near East, in archaic Rome, and in the older city-states before the advent of great numbers of purchased slaves.

Men were hired to reap at harvest time, and this type continued to exist in later as in earlier times. But most work was done by permanently employed labourers, part of them paid by the year, part of them working as debt slaves; the latter group was increasingly more numerous on the estates of those aristocrats who farmed the land directly rather than renting it. Debt slaves were free men who had lost status, and as such were distinguished from personal clients and political subjects – what we would call serfs. This distinction is quite clear in Cretan law. (As to the controversy among legal historians about such persons, see below under Athens.) Serfs generally appeared in Greece, as elsewhere, as soon as the great clans of the cities established their rule and before purchased slaves were an important factor.

Purchased slaves seem to have been rarely used for field labour in Greek lands, and their use on larger estates was evidently not common. Of course, it is unlikely that there were many large estates at this time. Ancient representations of the harvest show a landowner standing by, staff in hand, but this merely indicates that country squires existed in Greece as elsewhere and that they did not join in the actual field labour. On one occasion the Delphic oracle characterized the Corinthians as 'slaveholders' (*choinikometrai*) because of their many slaves, but it is doubtful whether the existence of large enterprises is implied (see further discussion below regarding Athens).

In any case it is clear that during the Greek Middle Ages the land was worked mainly not by slaves but by tenants, some unfree and some half-free, by debt bondsmen, and by holders of mort-gaged land. There were two classes of landowners, the peasants on the one hand, on the other those who had large holdings in land, cattle, and money. The indebtedness of the first to the second group is the characteristic feature of all of early Antiquity, and distinguishes the social conflicts of that age from those of our own. To describe the situation in modern terms, one must imagine the Prussian landowners as urbanized moneylenders and the peasantry as their debtors.

Hence the mortgage stones placed on peasant properties and the debt bondsmen on large estates were parallel phenomena. Similarly we find that later in Babylonia individual capitalists disposed of an astonishing number of city lots; it is probable that they did not actually own them but instead held them from debtors in lieu of interest, and rented them back to the debtors. The sharecroppers (*hektemorioi*) of ancient Athens were probably in a similar situation. They paid one-sixth of their crop to the landowner, not much less, in fact, than the one-third paid by Egyptian *coloni*, considering how extraordinarily fruitful Egypt's land was. (For further discussion see the section on Athens.)

The aristocratic clans of the Greek cities, especially coastal cities, were always involved in shipping. Some aristocrats, such as Solon, engaged directly in maritime trade. They also owned large grain-producing estates, and as such were the ones who advanced loans to peasants in lean years. This situation was further affected by the effects of money, after coinage had been invented.

Trade was a somewhat minor factor in the society of early Antiquity, looking at it in terms of its absolute extent. However, we should not under-estimate the relative importance of commercial profits in a society still dominated by a barter economy. Furthermore the fact that the aristocracy lived in the cities – the Attic Eupatrids were in fact called 'the city dwellers' (*astoi*) – was a source of economic as well as political power.

Two developments in the cities involved in sea trade led to a crisis of the clan state: (1) the increase of wealth in money and land; (2) the growing indebtedness of the peasantry. The commoners of Homeric times, in so far as they served in the infantry, were led by the aristocratic clansmen, who fought from chariots and dominated them much as Segestes said the aristocrats of the Cherusci dominated their own people (Tacitus, *Annals* 1.55). However, this situation became untenable as hoplite troops became more and more important.

The most important factor was that the debt bondage of the peasantry now posed a threat to the military force and political power of the state. At the same time the money economy led to a differentiation in income and the creation of new classes: rich parvenus, poor free men without property, and impoverished aristocrats. From this sprang bitter class conflicts within the *polis*.

Everywhere in Greece the most fertile land, especially valley land as opposed to mountain land, came into possession of the aristocracy by purchase and foreclosure. This of course followed the laws of rent, for only the fertile valley land could support both the men who cultivated it and the rentiers who owned it, and so the aristocrats bought valley land with their surplus cash, just as in Germany aristocrats prefer to entail only the best land. This explains why the aristocratic *polis* was rarely found in mountainous areas, whereas the characteristic centres of aristocratic society were the plains: 'hollow Lacedaemonia', and the Messenian, Elean, Thessalian, Boeotian, and Attic plains. The mountain slopes, on the other hand, were left to the peasants (*agroikoi*). So there was even a territorial distinction between peasant democracy and aristocratic oligarchy; we see this especially clearly in Attica.

There was another factor, the development of a new class in the port cities of the coast where there were export industries (e.g. pottery production in Athens) and shipping business. This new class stood outside the traditional circles of those who lived on the land and whose interests were bound up with agriculture, and they were ready to give political support to anyone who promised to further their economic interests. There was also the class of free-born men who had lost their land and been reduced to debt slavery. These two groups, sometimes in alliance and sometimes acting alone, formed the basis for movements aiming to overthrow the aristocratic regimes.

On the other hand there also emerged a new group which took its place beside the ancient landowning clans, commoners who rose out of the lower middle classes and gained wealth. It was possible even in the days before capitalism developed for an artisan (*dēmiourgos*) to become rich. So we must at least assume, since the well-known Solonian compromise of 581 B.C. provided that two artisans should be archons, and these two would necessarily have been possessors of an income of at least 500 drachmae, a high income in those days (although at the poverty line in Demosthenes' time). One must remember that among the artisans of early times were those from families with inherited secret skills, skills which (as in myth) were highly prized for their rarity. These artisans undoubtedly lived in large extended families like the aristocracy and so could accumulate wealth. It was capitalism and slave labour, along with the decline of the ancient family communities, which destroyed this basis of their position. Furthermore one should also remember that about 581 B.C. the artisans' party also included the merchants, who stood outside the aristocracy and all those who owned rural property. For example the father of Demosthenes was all his life called 'the cutler', although he probably knew no more about cutlery than the average stockholder in a Bochum firm knows about mining. In fact, the family of Demosthenes senior had been a wealthy merchant family for generations, and he himself owned, among other things, a workshop with slave cutlery workers.

The city's domination of the countryside could not be maintained when the propertied class itself was divided by bitter conflicts. Naturally the manner in which the change occurred, and the degree to which it occurred, varied from place to place. In general, however, the first great reforms in ancient Greece were shaped by the desire to reach a compromise with the indebted peasants, primarily in order to preserve the military power of the state and so serve its political interests. We see the same tendency in Near Eastern codes.

The most serious threat to the aristocracy was the radicalism of the peasantry, caused by the loss of political rights, social degradation, and economic insecurity suffered by the hoplite yeomanry. The Draconian and similar codes as well as the establishment of tyrannies were the results of this radicalism, for they meant that the city ceased to be a semi-feudal fortress dominating the countryside and that the aristocracy lost its political privileges. All landowners, to the degree that they could afford to arm themselves for military service (*hopla parechomenoi*, says the Code of Draco) became citizens, and the civic burdens of citizens were distributed according to the income derived from property (as in Athens).

Thus the city-state in its original form disappeared, ownership of land alone determined a man's political status, and the city became officially subject to the countryside. Very much like the later Twelve Tables of Rome, the various Greek codes bear an agrarian stamp and testify to the emancipation of non-noble landowners.

The causes and indeed even the means of these changes were analogous to those which had earlier manifested themselves in the inscriptions of Sumerian kings and in the oldest code of the Hebrews. The peasants and petty bourgeois who could afford to arm themselves now fulfilled a militarily indispensable function, and they demanded (like the peasants and petty bourgeois of the Near East) that there be an end to the vestiges of legal vendetta (the 'right to feud', one might call it), as well as jurisprudence based entirely on custom and privilege, and the institution of patronage in court procedures. Furthermore they demanded that these institutions be replaced with legal codes and an administration of justice equally available to all citizens. They also pressed for the elimination of personal liability for debts, and in particular for measures to end the burden of money debts and the danger that small propertyholders would lose their lands, demanding that debt bondage be abolished, interest rates limited, and foreclosure checked.

The radical leaders of the dispossessed demanded redistribution of the land and remission of debts. Since most of the land had been mortgaged and so fell into the hands of the aristocracy, the first demand was essentially a sharper version of the second. (In this connection it should be noted that in Athens only land free of debt [*ousia eleutheria*] entitled a citizen to membership in one of the property classes.)

The great reformers sought compromises. On the one hand they instituted fixed legal fines and either removed or lightened the burden of debt, but at the same time they strove to check attacks on existing property relationships and to arrest the processes leading to social differentiation. The most ambitious programme was that of Solon, who took the revolutionary step of cancelling all debts for which land or persons had been offered as collateral (the famous *seisachtheia*), a great boon to the peasants. Along with this went liberation of Attic debt bondsmen who had been sold abroad. Both measures reflected the political motivation of Solon's programme: the maintenance of the hoplite army's strength, for this was henceforth the foundation of the state's military power.

Naturally this political tendency did not have equal and similar effects throughout Greece. Tyranny was, of course, above all a form of unconstitutional government, though it originally enjoyed the support of the oppressed classes, and as such it used a variety of novel methods.

One unmistakeable feature of tyranny in Greece was a

tendency towards theocratic authority. Just as later the oracles favoured Persian rule, so in the earlier period a great many prophets, though not the ancient aristocratic priestly clans, favoured the tyrants, just as in the Near East. Tyranny came later to Sicily, and was different in character, being closely allied with the aristocracy of money which had emigrated there. Also the political methods used by the first generations of tyrants in Sicily differed from those used in Greece; the incorporation of entire city communities and even of foreign mercenaries in the tyrants' cities were measures of a Near Eastern character which were possible in Greek colonies but not in Greece itself.

Nevertheless it is clear that the important innovations of the tyrants share certain characteristics with those of the great law-givers. Both represented the city economy and its interests as against the monopoly of political power by the ancient aristocratic clans, and also as against the monopoly of economic power by the old and new classes which controlled men and money. Both were allied with the peasants. One expression of this alliance was the principle that 'All Attica is one city'. Both aimed to secure guaranteed legal rights and the independence of the law from the traditions and class interest of the patrimonial-sacral courts of the aristocracy, and legal codification was carried out to that end. A related aim was to make sure that justice in the villages remained in official hands; thus Peisistratus personally visited the villages of Attica to hold court, and later minor matters at least were handled in the Attic countryside by travelling courts (*dikastai kata dēmous*). This, incidentally, has a close parallel in provisions of the code in *Deuteronomy*.

The same tendency is manifest in many of the measures of the tyrants (Periander, Theogenes, Cleisthenes, Peisistratus) and the lawgivers (Zaleucus, Solon) on matters where economics and politics intersect. For example the strict limitations on luxury, often extended to include sweeping prohibitions, sprang partly from class feelings and partly from petty bourgeois values, and was directed against differentiation in life styles because it represented a threat to the equality of citizens. Attempts were made to arrest concentration of wealth by measures such as Periander's law prohibiting the purchase of slaves (similar laws in Phocis and Locris lasted into classical times) and Solon's law limiting the accumulation of land.

One particular aspect, however, was this: the abolition of imprisonment for debt and the removal of legal distinctions between all landowning citizens (equivalent to a liberation of the peasants) were correlative with laws aimed at preventing peasants from emigrating to the cities. Often attempts were made to maintain the peasantry by using state authority to limit transfers of land. Thus laws were passed prohibiting the sale of land 'to the city' (*pros to asty*), which meant in effect 'to aristocrats'. The many laws to prevent the purchase of land for speculation or for resale (e.g. Zaleucus), or to prevent the export of grain, all belong in the same category. Analogous measures were taken by mediaeval cities, among them laws to fine people for being idle or for begging. All these efforts have in common the aim of preserving the typical bourgeois forms of earning a livelihood.

In the final analysis the measures of both lawgivers and tyrants in at least the major coastal cities had the effect of bringing together the ancient clans with the new classes which had gained wealth from commerce and money operations, wealth of a distinctly urban character. Thus Solon's legislation seems to have based property class divisions on income as expressed in terms of money, as Bruno Keil argues (but this is not certain), and if so he had already moved away from the basic principles of the peasant hoplite *polis*. Similarly the privileges extended for mercantilist reasons to metics in industry in Attica, making it easier for them to become citizens or to buy land – just the opposite of the policies of the democratic regime later – testify to the alliance between the classes which controlled money and therefore men. Another instance was the permission given to export olive oil from Attica, while the export of other products of the land was prohibited; this too was a product of ancient agrarian mercantilism, which was essentially plantation in character.

Therefore one can say that the laws passed to favour the peasants were merely means to secure political aims. The same basic motivation was present in the law enacted by Periander which prohibited peasants from wearing city dress – namely, the desire to keep them from settling in the city. It was also evident in the prohibitions on peasant emigration mentioned above.

At the same time efforts were made – similar to those later at Rome – to send abroad the rural masses driven into the city by debts and dispossession. Thus the Athenian colonists settled on Salamis were assigned lands which could not be mortgaged. Such regulations were later made also for some – not all – of the colonies sent out for political purposes, and they served both immediate military needs as well as the desire to alleviate the social problem at home. Similarly the colonies sent out by the tyrants were aimed at putting the unemployed to work just as much as were their domestic public works programmes. Another feature of the age belongs in this context: the constant efforts to stabilize the food supply and so avoid the creation of depressed classes among the citizenry; hence policies aimed at regulating commerce without unduly reducing opportunities for profit.

Because of these factors the conflict between classes did not everywhere result in the creation of states with relatively clear characteristics such as Thessaly, Sparta, and Athens. Instead, as one would expect, a great variety of compromises and alliances took place. Unfortunately, there is little evidence for these developments.

Democratic movements aimed above all at destroying the close association of great clans (founded on ownership of land by extended households) and so ending their preponderance in the local and tribal associations, namely the village and the phratry. The village (kōmē, later dēmos) had of course always existed as an economic community, but the clan state ignored it in politics, and the clans undoubtedly stood outside the village communities with their landed possessions, very much as did the Junkers in Prussia. They formed their own kōmai out of their clients, debt bondsmen, or tenants. Their lands, however, were largely acquired through mortgages, and were therefore in great part scattered. Hence the aim of peasant movements was to incorporate clan estates into the villages and to put obstacles in the way of owning lands in many villages.

The phratry was the smallest unit of the military community and as such controlled bestowal of citizenship and the right to own land in military states. Phratries were entirely controlled by the great clans, although they included all able-bodied men, not just clan members (Wilbrandt is certainly correct on this point). This explains why peasant movements aimed at democratizing the phratries or else abolishing their functions.

Concessions of various extent were made to the hoplite classes. For example in Elis there was no *polis* until the *synoikismos* of 471. The upper class of fertile 'hollow Elis' was an exclusive, horse-breeding council aristocracy; its members lived scattered in their castles as in ancient times and acted together only for the purpose of administering the Olympic sanctuary and Games, the latter being (incidentally) a source of profit. At no time was there any significant degree of commercial activity. As a result relations between the social orders (*Stände*) were quite amiable.

Thus the aristocracy of Elis joined with their hoplite army to conquer the Pisans in the Peloponnese, and just as the Roman patricians made concessions to the plebs, so the Elean aristocracy granted each village (*dēmos*) a share of the subjugated territory. The Pisans remained tributaries of the Elean state. Aristotle mentions a prohibition against debt, designed to protect the peasants from loss of their land, and it belonged undoubtedly to this period of compromise.

The villages (*dēmoi, kōmai*) of Elis remained the constituent elements of the community. They, not the state or the phratries, were the agencies which controlled the right to own land. On the other hand the hoplites allowed themselves, evidently without protest, to be led as in ancient times by the aristocrats until 471.

In short: no *synoikismos* had taken place at Elis, as a result of the low level of commercial activity, and this meant that for a long time there did not appear the phenomena typical of the aristocratic *polis*, namely: (1) indebtedness of the peasants; (2) concentration of land ownership; (3) disappearance of the *dēmoi* in administrative law; (4) rise of a new aristocracy. What happened after the *synoikismos* of 471 is discussed below.

Things were very different in two neighbouring commercial cities, Megara and Athens. In both, as in other harbour cities, the peasants fell into debt and at the same time an important political problem appeared: the role of the new clans which gained wealth through the development of commerce. In Megara these new families became rich from the export of woollen goods made from wool supplied by the herds of the aristocracy and worked in their workshops (*ergastēria*). Their pretensions aroused the scorn of Theognis, although in fact the old aristocracy had made its money in much the same way.

In Athens a new class arose out of the export trade in olive oil and pottery. There, as in Megara, this new class for a time joined with the rural masses against the aristocracy in order to gain equal status. In Megara warnings against this were issued by Theognis, and he seems to have supported oligarchy because of such an alliance.

However the real revolutionaries everywhere were the debt-ridden peasants. In Megara (as in Athens) a political revolution enabled the peasants to gain a typical and limited reduction of debts (*seisachtheia*); that is, the interest paid to lenders was returned. Whether at the same time the Megarian aristocrats were 'degraded' and forcibly incorporated into the demes as in Athens we do not know. In any case Athens destroyed Megarian commerce and this prevented further development towards full democracy.

In Athens too democracy was achieved only by fundamental changes. The basis of the development was provided by the creation of new clans by Cleisthenes. We still do not know whether members of the new groups could participate in the ancient clan cult of Zeus Herkaios and Apollo Patroos, which was demanded of archons on taking office (they also had to declare their local community as in the *Hantgemal* of mediaeval Germany). However, this may be of no more significance than the rule that only a native American can be president, for the hereditary incorporation of all aristocrats and all new citizens into particular demes by Cleisthenes must have ended the importance of this matter. Cleisthenes 'made all Athenians noble'; that is, everyone henceforth had his 'home community'.

The necessity of stating one's community indicates, however, that before Cleisthenes the great clans admitted to the royal council selected the archons from their own ranks. Once the clans were drawn from their fortresses – Deceleia, for example, was one of these clan centres – by a synoecism, they functioned within the framework of the clan state until it was reformed by Cleisthenes.

The so-called Solonian classes undoubtedly existed before Solon. They served to rank citizens according to their fiscal, military, and labour service obligations, just as in the early period of Rome. Draco admitted to active citizenship all men able to arm themselves. Solon then admitted those below the yeoman census, and at the same time extended eligibility for office to all yeomen (*zeugitai*). But nevertheless it must have been necessary for citizens belonging to the commons (*astoi*), not of the old city aristocracy (*Eupatridai*), to be formed into new artificial clans (like the Roman *gentes minores*) in order to become archons. That is the deduction to which one is led by the semi-revolutionary compromise made after Solon, by which the archontate was exercised by two *dēmiurgoi*, a compromise reached with regard to participation in the cult of Zeus Herkaios.

It is clear that before Cleisthenes clan membership presupposed landownership as a qualification for office, for one cannot imagine a clan without landed possessions. But, unlike the situation in Elis, the *dēmoi* were not yet the lowest political unit. The phratry, dominated by the aristocracy, continued in Athens to have the important function of preparing the citizen list, rather than the *dēmos* as in Elis.

Furthermore the village was still absent. The naucraries were not real communities, but rather geographical units for apportioning state burdens. Solon's policies for furthering the export of olive oil and pottery, as well as his monetary reform to promote commerce and his prohibition of the export of grain, all show clearly that his programme was not primarily designed to benefit the peasantry.

Therefore it is not surprising that the ancient aristocracy continued to dominate the phratries even after Solon's reforms. Again the peasants fell into debt, and again there developed what one might call a struggle between the lands which paid rent and those which did not – that is, between the Pedia (aristocracy and new tenants) and the peasants, between the coastal population and the yeomen of the hinterland.

Peisistratus followed policies hostile to the ancient clans and based his power on the support of the peasants. We do not, however, know what measures he took against the aristocracy (besides his confiscations); Cauer's account is not supported by firm evidence. Then Cleisthenes sought to incorporate into the community of citizens the wealthy aliens living in the city, freedmen as well as metics, in order to enhance his own political position, and at the same time he aimed to destroy the framework of the clan state. His method was to incorporate the aristocracy into the village communities [*dēmoi*] and at the same time build up the influence of non-aristocrats in the phratries.

For this purpose he sponsored an entirely new, territorial division of the state, which cut across the old tribal units. Henceforth everyone, even the city-dweller, had his own local village community (*dēmos*), to which he belonged by birth according to public law. The foundation of the state on these *dēmoi*, the extension of the popular courts' jurisdiction, and the institution of ostracism – these were the three elements of what men then called 'democracy', which at that time was in no way equivalent to 'sovereignty of the people'.

The Areopagus was originally a council drawn from the clans and, according to Aristotle, appointed the magistrates; later the situation was reversed and it was recruited from the magistrates. Even before Cleisthenes it had lost some of its ancient powers over the magistrates, especially those connected with finance; the establishment of an elected council of the Prytane (*boulē*) took place during the period of aristocratic rule. Hence the Areopagus did not gain powers similar to those of the Roman Senate, to which it corresponded, but it did continue to be a court of appeal against unconstitutional acts of the popular assembly (*ekklēsia*), especially acts infringing on sacral law. It was the legislation of Ephialtes and Pericles which did away with this prerogative, and the resulting situation corresponded to the radical concept of democracy.

Athenian 'democracy' did not resemble English democracy, based as it is on the sovereignty of Parliament, so much as American democracy; in both, a change in constitutional law must follow prescribed rules. In Athens every citizen had the right of appeal against an unconstitutional action of the people's assembly; it was heard by the people's court! Even so the sovereignty of the Athenian *ekklēsia* was significantly more complete than that of the Roman assemblies (*comitia*), for according to Roman constitutional law an assembly's act might be voided not only if it violated sacral law but also if it was directed against an individual and did not establish a general norm. This characteristic of Roman law is seen in the Twelve Tables, which clearly exclude adoption of the Greek institution of ostracism.

The 'sovereignty' of the Greek *polis* was also expressed in its power over the property of its citizens. This was taken by Von Wilamowitz as an indication that private property was a recent institution in Greece. It should be emphasized, therefore, that the *polis* had control of its citizens' landed property in Homeric times, that in historical times this power did not diminish but in fact increased, and that this tendency continued into Hellenistic times (as is shown by the debtors' document from Arcesine, discussed below). The ultimate origin of this power over citizens' property must be sought in the military character of the *polis*, for the *polis* was essentially a camp and the *ekklēsia* was essentially an assembled army. This is the explanation of the phenomena just discussed; they have as little to do with survivals of primitive communism as does the Prussian bill for the acquisition of Polish-owned farmlands.

Democracy in the form of the Attic deme-organization spread to other cities under Athenian influence and came to dominate most of the maritime cities of Ionian speech as well as some – such as Rhodes – of Dorian character. However a further analysis of the Athenian constitution would be out of place here. The sharp divergences between distinguished scholars such as Von Wilamowitz and Eduard Meyer, the frequent changes of opinion by the same scholars, and the studies of Bruno Keil, Friedrich Cauer, and Martin Wilbrandt, all indicate that much is still unclear to philologists and, of course, still more so to us outsiders. Even the recent discovery of Aristotle's *Constitution of the Athenians* has left many problems still unsolved.

All classical Greek history was characterized by the social contrasts between aristocracy and commons, and this itself was inextricably connected with the economic opposition which separated oligarchs from democrats. Changes in domestic policies meant changes in foreign policy, and the reverse was also true. Naturally there was no question of a conflict between an industrial proletariat and industrial employers such as exists today. It was, rather, an opposition based upon differences in wealth – whatever the economic structure of this wealth – and upon conflicts between debtors and creditors; another factor was the contrast in life style between those groups which were shaped by ancient chivalry and those which were not.

Here it should be noted that the property of the ancient clans was mainly in lands bringing in rents, and that these lands (as has been emphasized) were accumulated partly with profits from commerce. The latter is a general conclusion, and of course not all clans engaged in commerce. Originally, indeed, the aristocracy was recruited from descendants of local chiefs, but those who subsequently gained riches generally did so through owning ships in whole or in part and through investing in joint ventures. We can see this economic process in action in the so-called Lelantine War, which was conducted at sea by merchant patriciates of the large commercial cities, but was in fact fought for possession of the fruitful, rent-paying, Lelantine Plain.

As one would expect, the ancient clans tried to prevent incorporation of the new clans into their midst, and so they tried to discredit the accumulation of money. In later Antiquity, even in the ports, only the emporia and firms doing an overseas wholesale trade were considered respectable. The landed aristocracy in theory condemned any sort of profit, and of course it also reproved any personal participation in buying or selling for profit and indeed personal labour in general.

Thus in Sparta, as a consequence of its military organization, artisans and merchants (both retail and wholesale) were ineligible for office, and indeed did not have the status of full citizens, for these groups were perioeci. Furthermore the Spartiates themselves were explicitly forbidden to use their labour for profits, which would conflict with their social rank; this is comparable to the rules which govern the conduct of officers in the army of the German Empire.

At the same time Spartan law – in complete opposition to the law of democratic Athens – allowed the admission of illegitimate children and even helot children into the community of full citizens; for military training, not blood, was the basic characteristic which distinguished the order of Spartiates. In Thebes, where chariot fighting was long maintained, debtors as such were regarded as *déclassés* – as in ancient times – because they had either pledged their persons or had alienated their property to redeem a mortgage. To be eligible for office in Thebes a man had to have been absent from the market (*agora*) for ten years.

In Athens, on the other hand, all offices were filled by lot (with the exception, perhaps, of the commanding general), and the *dēmos* was freed of burdens by liturgies levied on the rich. Nevertheless, there remained a clear distinction between the gentleman living off his rents and the man who earned his income. This was not abolished by Athenian democracy; indeed, it is evident, for example, in Demosthenes' *On the Crown* even though this speech was delivered as a plea before representatives of the *dēmos*.

The upper class of the hoplite *polis* was a community of warriors supported by rents from their lands. It was of decisive importance for the development of the characteristic features of Hellenic civilization, including its art, that members of this order did not lead the life of grand seigneurs. Rather, they were compelled to live in a simple, unpretentious manner, and this precisely in the period when they were developing self-consciousness as a class. Thus there arose the national games, and the gymnasia under Spartan influence gained acceptance of nudity, with its significant implications. Such phenomena would have been unthinkable at the courts of Etruscan or Roman or Near Eastern grandees, for they would have found such things repugnant to their 'dignity'. For example, experts agree that Etruscan athletes, as evidenced by their physiognomy, were professionals who performed before Etruscan aristocrats for pay. The same was true in the later Roman Empire.

Political development followed a certain typical course: first the particularism of the aristocratic *polis*, then the hoplite *polis*, and finally (in the richest cities) radical democracy. This evolution determined the characteristically secular character of Greek civilization (and of Roman too) in contrast to the theocratic civilizations of the Near East. This difference was certainly not due primarily to variations in the economic resources of temples in the two areas, for Greek temples too had large landed possessions for a time. The outstanding example of this was Delphi after the Sacred War of 590 B.C., as a result of which the lands of

Cirrha and Crisa were ceded to the temple and later divided among tenant farmers. Greek temples also had treasure hoards which fulfilled the same functions as those of the Near East, and they (like Egyptian temples) owned workshops and made loans. At other times they served as deposit banks. Incidentally, it is probable that the procedure by which slaves bought their freedom through the temple god is to be explained by the fact that the temples held the slaves' savings deposits, since the slave's personal property (*peculium*) was safe there (provided his master took no legal action to confiscate it). Another factor, of course, was that under this procedure the god guaranteed the slave's liberty.

Furthermore, in classical times (though not in Hellenistic) the only important sources of state loans in Greece were the temples, and they also served as depositories for war booty. Such were the functions performed by the Parthenon and by the temples at Delphi and Olympia. In Thucydides we find a discussion by Pericles of how important the temple treasuries were for the Peloponnesians.

Nor were ethnic differences in susceptibility to superstition the factor which made Hellenic civilization more secular than Near Eastern. The Greeks, and even more so the Romans, were just as superstitious as Near Easterners – or, at least, the Near Easterners of earlier times, before general political levelling and theocratization. Political leaders in Greece and Rome always had to take this tendency to superstition into account.

The real reason why religion was so much less dominant in the Occident was that the priestly order there was not organized, ranked, and unified. Hence many consequences: there was no special training for the priesthood, nor was there religious instruction for laymen, nor were priests bound by a special code of ascetic and ritual rules (though there were steps – relatively minor ones – in that direction). Above all, laymen were not summoned to a sectarian ideal of ascetic purity as in Judaism.

Priesthoods in Greece were often hereditary in certain aristocratic clans even in historical times, an example being the priesthood of Dionysus in Delphi (but not that of Apollo). Undoubtedly this was the rule in early times, but it ceased to be so later, especially after the triumph of the hoplite *polis*. Then, in a few cases, priesthoods were filled by election or else – more commonly

– lot was used to choose from a field of qualified candidates. But the most frequently used method of filling priesthoods was to sell them.

Generally tenure of a priesthood could be combined with other occupations. Originally a priesthood was held for life, but in later times often only for a year. Serving as priest was in fact often a kind of business transaction, so that we know of a case where it was difficult to fill a priesthood because the temple's olive groves had been burned down.

To sum up: in the Occident there was absolutely no tie binding priests together as an order, nor was there any tendency to build a church or to develop a sense of priestly unity and self-consciousness. This cannot be explained simply by the strong competition between local divinities; consider mediaeval parallels. The explanation is that these phenomena were the results of the political subjection of the priesthood by the military power of the aristocratic clans and then of the citizens of the *polis*, with their entirely secular orientations. Thus Delphi was not controlled by a Delphic priestly clan but rather by a *polis*, and indeed the cause of the Sacred War was an attempt by this *polis* to exploit its control of the temple by levying tolls on pilgrims. After the war the Delphic temple passed under the control of a league of originally rural communities (*ethnē*), but gradually the *polis* asserted more and more influence.

Even after the subjugation of the priesthood there continued to be tendencies in the Greek world towards theocracy, mysticism, and ecstasy. Indeed, even the Persian Wars can be regarded – as Eduard Meyer has brilliantly argued – as a decisive struggle between these trends, supported by the Persians in Greece as elsewhere, and the secularism of Hellenic civilization. All the tyrants and the aspirants to tyranny had ties with temples or prophets; an especially well-known example is the alliance of the Alcmaeonidae with Delphi.

Nevertheless, the power of the priesthood was insufficient to legitimize the position of usurpers, whereas it was sufficient in the Near East, and this is why tyranny in Greece failed to establish itself. The weakness of the priesthood was an inheritance from the Homeric age; we can see in the Homeric poems the lack of respect felt for both gods and priests. Whereas in the Near East the martial clans of the army monarchy were subjected by the allied forces of royal bureaucracy and theocracy, in Greece the clans remained in control over kings and priests. Then the victory of citizen-peasant hoplite forces meant the definitive defeat of all theocratic tendencies in Greece, for the priesthood had been enlisted in the service of the aristocracy and hence the victors were hostile to any sort of religious or traditionalist jurisdiction. In the Near East, on the other hand, the masses regarded the priests as a protection against the despotic power of kings and men of great wealth, and they therefore supported theocracy.

With respect to the history of Greek law, it is probable that temple properties were so important that they gave rise to the institution of the hereditary lease, the later emphyteusis. It is most unlikely that in early times there was any need to lease urban or village properties on a hereditary basis, for these properties were either divided among the young or else held in common. The temples, however, would not have followed either course. Only in Elis do we find hereditary leases, these being assumed by a part of the conquered Pisans. Therefore we may conclude that as in pharaonic Egypt some of the temple peasants may (we cannot, of course, be sure of this) have assumed hereditary leases. Certainly it is not a coincidence that in Greece, where a hereditary lease is first documented by an inscription from Olympia of the fifth century, the temples were to such an extent the landlords of hereditary tenants. Common lands were also let on a hereditary basis in the classical epoch. But private owners did not engage in the practice (the only alleged instance is not clearly documented and is unlikely).

As Mitteis first saw clearly, hereditary leases were used for two economic reasons. The first was to rent wasteland on the specific condition that it be developed by planting either olive trees or grape vines, at the cost of the tenant. Here a hereditary lease was simply an extension of a form of agreement found often in Greece and in the Near East, under which a tenant was given a long or even permanent lease on condition that the land must be cultivated and that otherwise the lease could be revoked. Under this agreement a lease would not lapse unless the leasee died without heir. Incidentally, it was shown above how the ancient Babylonian law handled values added by such improvements in a much more primitive fashion.

A second reason operated where hereditary leasing was used as a way of 'buying revenue', as Mitteis calls it on the basis of a justified analogy with Germanic institutions. This refers to the type of transaction in which developed land was bought by (or for) a temple and then leased back to the seller for rent. This was advantageous to the temple, for it was a secure investment, while for the former owner it meant that he had increased his investment capital and also had the legal security conferred by the temple's ownership of his land. Whether or not the lease could be sold was determined by the contract, and at times it was forbidden. In a very late contract from Thisbe sale was permitted, but only to citizens of the local community; this corresponds to ancient Hellenic principles.

b. *Classical Epoch (especially Athens)*

Thus land was let on hereditary lease only by juristic, public entities, not by private landowners. Indeed Greek law, like Roman, denied this power to private persons. In Athens during the classical period hereditary lease was the only form of limited land ownership, and the same is true in other communities of similarly radical democratic structure. For as a rule the development of the citizen *polis* meant the development of full freedom of trade in land. This was true in Athens and in the cities of the Athenian Alliance. Indeed, one of the chief advantages which the Alliance brought Athenian citizens was that it gave them the right to buy and let land in the allied cities. Elsewhere too, outside Sparta and seigneurial states like Thessaly, the laws giving clan members a pre-emptive claim were repealed in the classical period.

Furthermore, the limitations on land transfer imposed by hoplite states at the time of their establishment were abolished. These limitations included an absolute prohibition on the sale of an allotment, prohibition on accumulating properties, limitation on dividing and mortgaging property, and so on. They had been instituted in order to maintain the economic basis of a citizen army, and of course they disappeared entirely when defence was later entrusted to mercenaries.

Thus in Elis, which had been constituted in 471 B.C. by a

synoecism, a political compromise made in 350 B.C. provided that exiled aristocrats might return and that sale of their properties was forbidden. The latter provision indicates that in fact such sales had undoubtedly been hitherto permitted and, indeed, for a long time.

Free trade in land necessarily meant that once again there existed in the free *polis* a tendency to differentiation in agrarian wealth, something which not even Sparta avoided. This tendency was made stronger by the fact that the prohibitions and limitations on slaveownership made by the old hoplite *polis* were not maintained anywhere. As a result commercial slavery penetrated steadily into an ever larger area down to the Hellenistic period and became a normal feature of the age. We find this, for example, in Phocis after the Peloponnesian War; indeed, a single shipment received of 1,000 slaves is recorded, since the number aroused surprise at the time. We also find slavery among the Aetolians in the Hellenistic period, after they had organized themselves as a military, hegemonial state and in consequence found themselves compelled to pursue 'flexible' economic policies.

Now the questions we must consider are these: what effect on ancient Greece did this free trade have; and, in particular, did it promote the Roman type of development towards the concentration of land ownership and the formation of large slave-labour enterprises?

From the sources available we can only reach indirect conclusions. This applies even to such a well-documented area as Attica. First of all one must remember that there were no large buildings in rural areas besides the ancient castles of the aristocrats and the local chapels. When enemy troops appeared, the wooden houses of the countryside were taken down and carried into the cities for safety along with slaves, flocks, and implements. Furthermore participation in politics made it necessary to leave the countryside and live in the city, so that bailiffs were used not only by landowners with more than a certain number of field slaves but also by men who were simply full-time politicians. The same sort of consideration applied to hoplites: to keep in training they either had to live in the city or else visit the city frequently, and this became necessary as soon as a city started to pursue an ambitious foreign policy. For example, Argos took this course and the first measure adopted was to recruit 1,000 hoplites for an elite force destined to challenge the Spartiates. For similar reasons Thebes established the famous Holy Company.

We do, however, have evidence from the speeches of the Athenian orators that the 'capitalists' of coastal cities had landed properties, but that these properties were regarded as investments and very often were in separate parcels, not manors. Capitalists of the classical period, for example Timarchus, bought and sold properties readily, whereas aristocrats held onto their land. Hence the development of free trade in land was precisely what capitalists wanted.

During the fifth century and after, land in Attica could be sold and mortgaged at will. Free disposition by testament existed if there were no legitimate sons; otherwise property could be left to anyone under guise of a legacy, and in such cases Athenian law (unlike the Code of Gortyn) did not prescribe that a fixed part of the estate had to be left to heirs. A passage in Lysias has been taken to indicate that there survived a distinction between inherited and acquired property, but this is unjustified. In the Athens of Lysias' day it was a matter of good form – no more – not to sell inherited property. Elsewhere, however, such a legal distinction may have persisted even in the fourth century, for example in Thera.

It is, however, true that when an Athenian divided his property personally he normally gave his sons the land he had inherited (in contrast to the land acquired). This is analogous to the institution of *Inkyo* in Japan and the inheritance customs of the primitive Germans known to us from Tacitus. All may have had a similiar origin in the conditions of a community of warriors. In the hoplite *polis* the citizen too old to fight had to turn his allotment (*klēros*) over to his son and retire to that part of his property reserved for his old age; at this point, in early times, the old warrior lost his vote in the army assembly and henceforth participated in the council of elders.

It was because of the military character of the *polis* that sons retained a privileged position in Greek inheritance law, which favoured relatives and in particular those in the male line. No secondary rights were accorded other members of the clan or phratry so that the laws governing inheritance and vendetta were at variance.

Furthermore, all non-citizens were denied the right to own land. In Athens from the time of Pericles this applied to anyone whose two parents were not full citizens – that is, neither could be a metic or a freed slave. An important economic consequence of this was that all aliens and metics were thereby excluded from dealing in mortgages, since this business sometimes involved purchase of mortgaged land until the mortgage was retired and of course it was also necessary at times to take possession of a lender's property. As a result this basic form of capital investment was reserved for wealthy full citizens.

In Athens foreigners were not granted the privilege of lending on mortgages until the time of the Decelean War; this concession was then granted from necessity. Indeed, we can judge the significance of the exclusion or admission of foreign creditors from the fact that when the Second Athenian League was formed Athens had to assure her allies specifically that no Athenian would be allowed to own land or write mortgages in their territories. Mortgages and state loans were in fact the two major forms of capitalist investment, and it is fair to say that the Confederacy of Delos had in effect given wealthy Athenians a kind of financial hegemony over the allied cities.

To understand this fully one must remember the terms under which loans on land were made. The most common type of mortgage was the *prāsis epi lusei*, 'sale upon repayment'; this provided for sale of the land offered as collateral to the creditor, who then sold it back upon repayment of the loan. (This was in fact closer to the corresponding German legal form than to the Roman *fiducia*.) There also existed a simple mortgage loan similar to our own, and the two forms continued to coexist in the classical period. A third type of mortgage also existed, the *apotimēmata*, applied to loans on dowry property and property held by a ward; this differed from the second type merely in the terms used.

It was only in later times that the simple mortgage loan became the more common. It is possible that at first only public or semi-public obligations could be secured by collateral without actual transfer of ownership, and so the origin of the simple mortgage loan may be connected with the liturgy system.

Inscriptions on the Attic boundary stones [*horoi*] indicate that even in the fourth century, the *prāsis epi lusei* was the normal type of loan, not the simple mortgage.

Szanto has argued that the simple mortgage developed out of the institution of debt bondage, after the laws against it excluded the person of the debtor from liability, basing his analysis on a well-known inscription from Halicarnassus (published by B. Haussoullier, *Bulletin de correspondance hellénique* 4 (1880), pp. 295–320). He also believes that the *prāsis epi lusei*, like the Roman *fiducia*, arose out of the actual sale of land for a price held on credit. However, I do not find this theory convincing, despite Szanto's clever arguments. Short-term debt bondage, with limitations and transfers for cause and with other forms of agreements in return for money, have played an important role in many legal systems, indeed in legal systems which are quite different otherwise and include the most ancient known to us. Furthermore the use of lands as collateral for loans is important even in rather primitive societies. Finally, personal debt bondage continued to exist alongside the simple mortgage in several Greek states. These facts thus disprove Szanto's theory and also the variation of it developed by Swoboda in his otherwise valuable studies.

Instead, I would argue, it seems more likely that the *prāsis epi lusei* is a very ancient legal form, as ancient as the pledging of wives and children as collateral. Indeed, it is probably the oldest form of mortgage, as it was in mediaeval times; the debtor usually (as so often in other connections) held his land as a *precarium* or on lease (especially as a sharecropper: *hektēmorios*) from his creditor, and his right to redeem his property was recorded by a mortgage inscription (*horos*).

Extant mortgage inscriptions, it is true, are no older than the fourth century, but Solon mentions them by name. Solon prohibited the enslavement of debtors, even those found in default, and in general ended the practice of borrowing on one's own person (elsewhere, however, these practices continued in use).

Therefore, the development of the simple mortgage was merely the natural result of this softening of debt law in Athens and elsewhere. This explains two features of Athenian debt law: a creditor could on his own authority take possession of a defaulting debtor's property, and there was a legal procedure (*dikē exoulēs*) providing for ejection of a debtor who had not vacated land adjudged to a creditor. These can be regarded as survivals connected with the old precarial tenure of debtors. The theory that the simple mortgage developed out of the *prāsis epi lusei* also explains why originally a mortgaged property could not be alienated without the creditor's consent. Later it gradually became possible to use that part of one's property not mortgaged as collateral for another loans, and here too consent of the first creditor was initially needed, as it was for a second mortgage.

Buying and selling land and mortgages was very simple. There were very few land registries, despite the statements of Aristotle and Theophrastus; there was one in Tenos and also, as in Chios, a register of mortgages. Elsewhere, as in Athens, a simple contract sufficed for the conveyance of property. In Athens (contrary to Egypt and the later Roman Empire) there were no legal mortgages, but the tax lists and land cadasters of the demarchs (after the reform of Nausinicus in 377) gave information on the proceeds of each property, and public announcements had to be posted before a sale with a declaration that anyone with a prior claim to the property should state this publicly. This was a common provision in ancient Greece, and outside Athens we often find the provision that a public announcement or a public sacrifice be made. From this it is clear that real estate transactions were sufficiently regulated and publicized, considering the limited territory of a *polis*. There remains, however, this question: granted that there existed great freedom and security in the sale of land, what influence did this, along with the deme organization, have on the social structure of the countryside? Let us examine this problem with special reference to Attica.

Free trade in land was by no means first established by Solon; the novelty of his legislation consisted in allowing a testator to dispose of his property freely. Indeed Solon may have instituted as many limitations (e.g. prohibition of conveying property in trust) as he removed. Recently a number of scholars, including Fustel de Coulanges and Martin Wilbrandt, have maintained that Solon did away with clan land, until then the general form of land ownership in Attica and as such a definitive obstacle to trade in land and private property in land. However, the sources do not support this theory, and it is contradicted by the traditional account of Draco's hoplite census and the Solonian classes. Indeed, the Solonian classes unquestionably existed before Solon and were used for apportioning tax and military burdens. They presuppose existence of individual economic differentiation.

Analogies also disprove the Fustel-Wilbrandt theory. In Antiquity the clans were everywhere of much later origin than private property in land, as indicated by the fact that private ownership of land was limited usually by the pre-emptive rights of family rather than clan members. Private property in land was the result of economic differentiation due to the influence of commercial profits and booty.

Furthermore, the Fustel-Wilbrandt theory presumes a set of conditions for which there is no secure evidence. Wilbrandt's discussion of the limitations placed on trade in land dates these to early Antiquity, when in fact they were imposed later by legislation in order to maintain a large yeomanry for military service. His ideas on the *prāsis epi lusei* overlook the fact that under this form of loan the creditor did not acquire property but only a title which could be redeemed, and furthermore this title was to the land, never to the income from it.

I must also disagree with the theory of Swoboda that the *hektēmorioi* formed a class of serfs similar to the helots of the Spartans. That they were not simply hired labourers has already been noted here, but what Swoboda adds concerning their status in inheritance law, their being bound to the land, their rights to legal representation, their labour services and so on, is all a series of hypotheses and no more.

Furthermore, Swoboda's related statements about the rise of large-scale enterprises seems to me not only a hypothesis but a most unlikely one at that. I think he was led to this, as was K. J. Neumann in his similar work on Roman society, by the fascinating studies of our common teacher G. F. Knapp, and read back into ancient times a process which Knapp described brilliantly for modern conditions.

In any case, it is clear that there is no evidence whatever that Solon 'ended' any institution of serfdom in Attica, and our sources would certainly mention this if he had. The evidence indicates, rather, that Solon ended the necessity of having a patron in legal proceedings, but this of course indicates that the commoners were already free. Solon gave full parity in court to the landless workers (*pelatai*) who were previously in clientage to patrons. This does not, however, mean that the *pelatài* are to be equated with the *hektēmorioi*, even though this assumption appears already in the ancient lexicographers.

That part of Swoboda's work which, in my opinion, is valid can be harmonized with the hypothesis suggested: that the *hektēmorioi* were debtors, that their lands were transferred to their creditors, and that they were allowed by them to work the land as share-croppers. The fact that a sixth part [*hektos, moros*] was the rule indicates that the matter was already governed by legislation, a limitation on the powers of creditors.

It was, then, this institution which Solon ended, for when he reformed the debt laws he cancelled all outstanding mortgages at the same time, and so wiped out the *hektēmoroi* relationship. This at least is clear: after Solon the institution does not exist. It should be noted here that the only passage connecting Solon with sharecropping (Pollux 7.151) says that he removed mort-gages on the land being sharecropped (*gē epimortos*); thus the land is mentioned, not a class of *hektēmorioi*.

As mentioned above, Solon also put restrictions on the accumu-lation of land, but what these were our sources do not reveal. From Aristotle, *Politics* 2.4.4, it seems likely that there was no direct prohibition. Aristotle mentions a general ban on the sale of land far away from the city to city-dwellers (that is, to aristo-crats), but while such legislation seems quite appropriate for the time of party struggles between *pedianoi* and *diakrioi*, one would expect it to be connected with Peisistratus rather than Solon.

On the other hand it seems quite probable that limitations were placed on the purchase of land outside one's own deme at the time when the administrative reorganization of Attica was carried out by Cleisthenes; it may even go back to Peisistratus, under whose regime there must have been a division of the great estates still existing in Solon's time. At any rate we know that as late as the fourth century those Attic demes which maintained a cadaster collected a tax on the land of every individual who did not belong to its people (*dēmos*). This tax (*egktērikon*) meant, of course, a significant restriction on the investment of capital in land and in mortgages as well.

Furthermore, this tax is an indication that local government remained vigorous in the countryside of Attica. Throughout the fifth century and also the fourth, despite great devastation during the Peloponnesian War, the Attic demes remained a real force, as is shown by the inscriptions. It is true that the source of their finances is not clear, since the 22,000 drachmae mentioned by the Plotheia inscription may represent capital or an annual expense.

Nevertheless we know that the deme owned, administered, and rented land. We have a contract showing the deme Aixone concluding a rental agreement for 40 years, and other contracts mention fields, vineyards, theatres, and shops of all sorts. The deme was the unit of conscription; thus a sick man could choose a substitute for the army from his fellow demesmen. The deme was also the lowest unit of tax collection, and therefore drew up the list of those subject to the *proeisphora* [money levied as a loan, to be repaid from proceeds of the property tax]. Finally, the deme was involved in the election by lot of members of the Council (*boulē*). The prytany documents indicate the participation of all the demes of each tribe, and indeed it seems that the principle of proportional representation was followed.

Incidentally, in the procedure for choosing members of the Council the hereditary character of deme citizenship worked against the purpose of Peisistratus' and also Cleisthenes' policies. The latter aimed at giving political domination to the class of yeomen, the men of moderate property able to arm themselves as hoplites, and at the same time they sought to destroy the power of the great clan groupings. For this purpose every aristocrat was enrolled in a deme, just as in the democratic communes of mediaeval Italy every nobleman was assigned to a guild; properties lying outside the deme were subjected to a special tax.

Furthermore the phratries, which had once been the preserve of the old stock (*homogalaktes*), were now made to accept the 'new Athenians' (*orgeones*) from the new, artificial tribes. We do not know when this took place, nor when – except that it was later – the phratries were also made to accept *thiasoi*, members of voluntary associations made up of immigrant citizens, associations without any clan organization whatever.

It should be noted that nearly every particular here is subject to controversy. Thus the phratry list mentioned above from the early fourth century with 20 (!) names probably did not include all members of the phratry. One must also keep in mind, however, that while every new citizen was allowed to choose his deme, phratry (later the choice was subjected to limitations), and tribe, it was also true that only membership in the deme, which kept the citizen register, and therefore the tribe was automatic. Formal admission to a phratry was important only to those who intended to leave property, especially landed property, by will, and it was evidently not affected by admission to a deme, as the *dēmotioi* documents show. From all this it seems very probable that many citizens, indeed the great majority, did not belong to a phratry in later times.

In the earliest group of *dēmotioi* documents (beginning of fourth century) the old Eupatrid clan of the Dekeleiai had a legal function in connection with drawing up the citizen register; thus an aristocratic clan preserved a remnant of its privileges in the performance of the phratry's most important function. However, in the second group (mid-fourth century), the decision on citizenship has been put entirely in the hands of the *thiasos*, without any role being assigned to the aristocracy. In short: phratry and deme have been democratized.

It was the demes, in fact, which manned the strong hoplite army of Athens in its period of greatest power (480–460 B.C.), and here 'demes' meant above all the yeomanry. Eduard Meyer has reckoned that in 431 the Athenian citizen population was divided into census classes as follows *c.* 2,000–2,400 were in the upper two classes (*pentekosiomedimnoi* and knights), 30,000–33,000 were yeomen (*zeugitai*), and *c.* 20,000 were proletarians (*thētes*); most of the yeomen lived in the countryside.

However the countryside was no longer dominant in 431. Citizenship in a deme had become permanent and was not connected with actual residence or occupation, very much as in Czarist Russia the peasant remained a member of his mir. There was this difference, however; citizenship in a deme did not involve limitations on one's freedom of movement. Still, it was in his deme that an Athenian paid his taxes, irrespective of his actual place of residence.

But most important of all was the fact that it was only those members of the demes living in the city who could regularly attend meetings of the assembly. As a result the propertyless masses who supplied the sailors (hence called *nautikos ochlos*) could exert decisive influence in the assembly on the policies of the democracy. Nor is this contradicted by the fact that most of those who held office in the council or served as general or ran the financial administration were men of property, and that even the men recorded in the inscriptions as moving bills in the assembly were to a large extent wealthy. The professional politician in Antiquity generally had to be a man of means (indeed, even in modern times the first leaders of the socialist movement were wealthy men, even though paid positions as editor and party secretary are today available).

On the other hand it is significant and indicative that the propertied classes played an increasingly important role in the local administration of many demes, and naturally even more significant is the question of how the land was divided within the demes. Despite the strong influence of the propertied, the government of the demes does not seem to have become pluto-cratic even in the fourth century. In the fifth century, we are told, about one-fourth of Athenian citizens did not have any landed property, and this included a majority of all those living in the countryside. However we do not have firm evidence to support this. The figures which have been transmitted to us regarding land ownership indicate that properties such as a peasant might own today were then considered substantial, while properties more than 50 hectares in extent – large, it is true, for olive raising – were very few.

Fifty hectares may well have been more or less the figure set as the minimum for membership in the highest census class, the *pentekosiomedimnoi*. (Today, using average figures for Prussia, about 22 hectares are needed to raise the equivalent of 500 *medimnoi* of barley; in ancient Attica at least double that area was needed. However, extraordinary as well as ordinary yields were reckoned together in Attica, and when conversion to money was made the census based on the equation 1 *medimnos* = 1 *drachma*.)

Using these figures, it is noteworthy that an aristocrat such as Alcibiades inherited only about 30 hectares. As early as the time of Cimon we find that when he had to pay the fine of 50 talents levied on his father Miltiades he did this, as one might expect, not from his rents but from the proceeds of his investments in international trade. Leading figures in the Peloponnesian War, both conservatives like Nicias and radicals like Cleon, were not landowners but slaveowners, and later the same was true of Demosthenes. (But this does not mean that they owned 'factories', as explained below.) The properties let on hereditary lease were generally only medium-sized farms; larger properties are found only in areas where new lands were divided and in such cases are really examples of leases conceded in return for undertaking development (*emphyteusis*).

To sum up: one should remember that in Greece – as opposed to the Near East and Rome – the prevailing life-style was marked by great simplicity, and this was true of the creative figures of Hellenic culture in the period of its greatest achievements. Greek art in particular was not stimulated in any way by a demand for material luxuries.

There is the problem of explaining why the hoplite forces of Athens declined – that is, why the great losses of men during the war could not be replaced. These factors were essentially responsible: (1) decline in the number of those economically able to purchase hoplite armour because of division or concentration of landed properties; (2) decline in time spent in training by those able to buy the armour because of their growing economic connection with business. These two factors seem to have worked together, though one cannot tell which had more effect on developments in Athens. Sundwall has demonstrated that there was a movement of population within the demes; the distribution of prytanies among the trittyes indicates that during the fourth century the inland demes remained stable in population while the coastal demes increased and the urban demes declined. This is interesting, though it can lead to different conclusions regarding residence, occupation, and – most important – the question of the density of population in the countryside. It does indicate that families from the cities and suburbs died out more quickly. The increased population of the coastal demes, where radicalism was strongest, was perhaps the result of a higher rate of marriage due to the employment opportunities offered by maritime commerce.

One thing, however, is clear; there was no increase in the number of peasants. The stability of the inland demes' population does not mean that their citizens remained peasants or even that they continued to live in the country. The decline of the urban demes' population, moreover, was probably not caused by any emigration of particularly large numbers of their citizens to the colonies. What was involved here was, rather, the narrowing of occupational opportunities for free labour by slavery. But of this we can be sure: that during this period many country demes were in fact dominated by hereditary groups of landed clans, and also that after the end of the fourth century the political life of the demes began to lose importance. Thus we find that deme offices were sold, and that monopoly of these offices by the landed classes went hand in hand with this phenomenon. The most convincing evidence of the decline in political and social importance of the rural middle classes is the disappearance of deme inscriptions in the third century. This must have been the result of a shift in the distribution of property during the Hellenistic period (see below).

On the other hand we cannot say to what extent slave labour in the countryside increased during the classical period, nor do we know how much importance to ascribe to tenant farming. As to the latter, the extant sources indicate a great contrast with the Near East. We have only a single private lease (in mutilated condition) from Athens; otherwise we have only lease contracts with public corporations. It is quite clear that throughout all of ancient Greece there was a strong preference for leases at fixed rent as opposed to share-cropping agreements, which seem to have been a minor factor for a long time; also that money leases (especially, of course, in Attica) were quite common as compared to rentals paid entirely or partly in kind. Furthermore, the relation between the capital value of land and its rental was rather low by our standards, due no doubt to the high interest rates paid in Antiquity. Thus the rental of a farm property in Thria amounted to 8 per cent of its estimated value; in other cases the relation between rental and value cannot be determined because non-agricultural objects were involved. In hereditary leases the relation between rental and value was always much lower – 4 per cent or somewhat more – but these are naturally not comparable.

Compared with Near Eastern and Roman conditions the situation of the Greek tenant seems to have been relatively favourable. This however may be because the extant leases mainly concern public lands. When rental periods are stated they are longer than those known to us from the Near East: five years, often ten years. But many agreements do not state a period, in which case they are either for life or else terminable at will. Public land leases undoubtedly obliged the tenant to put the land under cultivation and his use of the land was not only supervised but also sometimes regularly inspected. How much of this also applied to private leases cannot be determined.

Finally we must, for better or for worse, take up the question of the character and significance of slave labour in the classical period (that is, in the fifth and fourth centuries B.C.). Earlier scholars overestimated its importance greatly; now, under the influence of Eduard Meyer, a strong reaction has set in which is essentially correct so far as the quantitative aspect is concerned. As for slavery's qualitative importance, however, Meyer's followers have not gone far enough, for they retain the concept of 'slave-labour factory', although at the same time they have been led by Francotte's book to underestimate seriously the effect of slavery upon the condition of free labourers. Something has been said above on these subjects, and now some further aspects must be examined.

Slavery, it is clear, increased greatly in ancient Greece. This did not lead to autarky of the *oikos* and weakening of consumer demand to the degree which I once assumed, but that effect was certainly present and was of great importance. For example: (1) We are told of Pericles that for political reasons he satisfied his needs as far as possible 'outside'; in other words, he purchased goods from free artisans. This is a clear indication of the reduced opportunities for employment caused by seigneurial slave-households, for the larger they were the more specialized workers they had to produce the goods and services which would otherwise have been purchased from free wage-earners.

(2) Clothing and, in the cities, food for the slaves were to a large extent purchased in the market (as they were in the slave states of the US). It was the competition of slaves which had an

effect upon the living standard and buying power of landless
free workers and thereby limited the development of the market
for consumer goods, for slaves could be kept to a living standard
reduced to the essential minimum for subsistence. The demand
for industrial products was necessarily very precarious in Antiquity because of the poverty of the masses. We can see this from
the fact that Athens had to allow its allies to postpone payment
of tribute because of a bad harvest in the Pontus area; everything,
we can see, depended upon the current price of bread.

The great building inscription of the Erechtheion indicates that
the hired free workers were paid the same wage as the slaves:
1 drachma a day. In the fourth century we hear of wage rates up
to 2 drachmae a day (but this was for skilled workers), whereas
in Eleusis during the fourth century the temple paid its own
slaves a food allowance of only 3 *oboloi* a day, which was the
same sum allowed a contractor in Delphi in 338 as a food
allowance for each worker. Later in the century it was reckoned
at Delos that a worker could feed himself for 2 *oboloi* a day. At
this point it should be noted that it was the democratic regime
of Athens which paid such high wages for its public works,
though of course these wages meant substantial profits for the
owners of slaves hired, whether the slaveowner received a sum
of money from his slave (*apophora*) or rented him directly to the
state. In any case the wages which Athens paid may well have
just barely sufficed for the needs of free labourers with families.

Furthermore, the figures cited above – further analysis is
impossible here – fail to support Francotte's conclusion that the
competition of slave labour did not depress the wages paid free
labour. There are even examples of free labourers being paid in
kind or in food – and this was not in the country – just sufficient
for bare subsistence; this was familiar in Egypt and the Near
East, and occurred in Greece too – for example in 282 B.C. in
Delos, at a time of fully developed money economy. Such cases
indicate a tendency to reduce wages to the subsistence level,
though this did not operate where skilled labour was concerned,
or where there was an acute labour shortage or political factors
intervened. In particular there was a need for quality work; thus
skilled workers were receiving 2 drachmae at virtually the same
time when unskilled workers were receiving only food for subsistence.

In fact, the social degradation of free workers was inevitable when slaves worked side by side with free men, as was the case with the Erechtheion, where citizens, metics, and slaves worked together, just as even contractors worked along with their employees. These facts indidate the full significance of a passage in Xenophon's *Memorabilia*. Socrates having remarked on the prosperity of Athens' citizens, Aristarchus comments that they use their wealth to buy barbarian slaves to do their work.

It is clear, therefore, that domestic slaves as well as working slaves reduced the opportunities for employment available to free workers. If we remember the restrictive citizenship policies and also the recurring attempts in all parts of the ancient world to give citizens a monopoly of opportunities to profit from contracts, then we see the significance of this: although limitations were placed on the use of slaves in the period of the tyrants and law-givers, throughout the whole of the classical period no attempt was made to limit employment on public works to native craftsmen. This alone shows that by the classical period free labourers were already powerless, a situation undoubtedly caused by the expansion of slavery.

It is of course also true that it would have been impossible to maintain such a limitation, since a sufficient free work force in the modern sense simply did not then exist. The great state projects could not be implemented with workers drawn from the free craftsmen and workers, and most certainly could not rely on only the citizenry (partly because of the restrictive citizenship policies followed). Consequently the idea of limiting employment on public works to citizens would have been very popular, since the Attic masses still thought of themselves as above all craftsmen, but it was too impractical ever to be seriously considered.

Slaveowners were naturally unwilling to shoulder the costs of long training, and so slaves tended to do mainly unskilled labour. There were certain tasks, such as milling, which were never performed by free men in Antiquity except in times of dire need. On the other hand the free crafts retained the organization of family work until late, and indeed never emancipated themselves entirely; a structure akin to mediaeval models never developed.

Still it is evident that the word *synergos* and others as well could on occasion indicate something similar to our term 'journeyman'. But we cannot be sure, for example, whether or not the apostle Paul was in the pay of his fellow craftsman Aquila, in whose house he worked (*Acts* 18.2). When we read that the goldsmith Demetrius roused craftsmen other than those with whom he worked in his own shop, against the Christians who threatened the cult of Diana (*Acts* 19.25), it is more probable that we are to understand independent artisans in other crafts connected with the cult.

In Hellenistic times, then, it is quite possible that there were skilled artisans without capital who worked for others and received from them tools and raw materials, but the same is not true for the classical period. When we find an individual of the classical period called *hegemōn* or find artisans working as a group, we are usually dealing with temporary associations, and certainly this is true in all cases (the great majority) where the tools used were not of significant value – that is, did not constitute a form of capital. Doubtful cases, of course, are numerous. An example is the men who worked in groups under foremen on fluting columns for the Erechtheion and were paid in groups; they were partly slaves of the foremen, partly other slaves either hired from foremen or working on their own account, and partly free metics and citizens. Now since one of the foremen was a slave and one of his men was free, one can hardly speak of a master–journeyman relationship here. Evidently the groups of workers were simply crews organized by the construction supervisor for purposes of efficiency, as the differing performances of the groups seem to indicate (as argued by Francotte). Probably each foreman received extra pay.

Most frequently we find the foreman–worker relationship within slave workshops (*ergastēria*), therefore in a form of unfree production community. An example is the *ergastērion* of Timarchos; the *hegemōn* paid the master a higher *apophora* than the others, therefore evidently was an especially skilled craftsman. He was either slave or freedman, ran the workshop, and dealt with others as a manager and as such made extra profits.

These phenomena represent the beginnings of an internal structuration of craft industries, and deserve further study. This, however, can be said with confidence: whereas mediaeval crafts were articulated, the free crafts of Antiquity were amorphous. *Ergastēria* were briefly discussed above in the Introduction; here let it be added that there were of course permanent *ergastēria*, buildings made of stone; one is mentioned, for example, in a contract as a property held on hereditary lease. Such properties were 'work areas' like the 'selling areas' in our market halls, but the former was no more a factory than the latter is a retail firm.

Finally, let us summarize the types of slave labour. An owner could exploit his slaves in these ways: (a) by renting them out; (b) by employing them himself, at the same time feeding them and providing them with raw materials, tools, and work area (in so far as they were used to produce articles for sale); (c) by employing them, but giving them a lump sum for sustenance; (d) by letting them find employment on their own, receiving in return a fixed payment (*apophora*) from their earnings; (e) by putting them to work producing goods for sale but letting them find their own work area, raw materials, and tools, and receiving from them a payment from their earnings; (f) finally, by a mixture of (a) and (e), under which the owner received an *apophora* but also provided work area, raw material, and tools. Timarchus used the last arrangement, but Demosthenes (*contra* Francotte) did not.

Obviously every form of exploitation which enlisted the slave's self-interest tended to increase slave labour's productivity, and indeed on large building projects slaves seem to have been no less productive than free workers. More productivity meant more profits for the owner. Although the problem of estimating slave-owners' profits is much more complicated than Francotte would have one believe, still it is clear from the innumerable temple inscriptions recording emancipations that owners counted on rather quick amortization of their investments in slaves.

The industrial use of slave labour to produce goods for the market, and in particular the establishment of workshops owned and managed by slaveowners, were both evidently pioneered by merchant importers of raw materials. One of them was Demosthenes, who imported ivory to be inlaid into knife handles and wood carvings. One can compare this with the manner in which exporters of finished products called into being domestic industries in the Middle Ages. The import of ivory helps explain why Demosthenes' workshop did both goldsmith and carpentry work. Probably Demosthenes senior did not originally work raw materials, and later used only part of them; at all times the greater part he sold on consignment (*tō boulomenō*). Still, at his death his stock was estimated by his son to be worth 11,250 marks out of a total estate of about 62,000 marks. Of the rest, about 13,200 marks was in loans (mostly to banks and on sea ventures), about 17,550 marks was in working slaves, 2,250 marks in a house, and 18,000 marks in treasure.[1] Note that there was no landed property, and that the treasure, which amounted to more than the two 'factories' together, was simply a quantity of precious metals and other valuables which were hoarded and not used as capital. The specifically mercantile origin of the fortune is obvious. Thus, one of the workshops had been acquired by chance in the course of business, when the slaves employed in it came into Demosthenes' hands as security for a *prāsis epi lusei* loan and then the debtor (perhaps a dealer in ivory) defaulted. Both workshops were clearly set up mainly to capitalize on a merchant's stock. Sometimes even a combination of professions occurred entirely by chance. Timarchus, for example, owned tanners, embroiderers, and other craftsmen – all purchased simply because they were good investments. In general it is quite clear that in historical times the number of purchased slaves in Athens was greater than the number of those born into a household (*oikogeneis*), for the reasons explained above in the Introduction.

All these conditions were not analyzed by Francotte, and in fact what he says about the economic structure of Antiquity only develops the ideas of Bücher and others. His book is, of course, very valuable, for it is evidently the first on the subject to attract the attention of historians. Still, the matters just discussed have as yet been examined only in a few good monographs and should now be given systematic analysis, for it was as a result of the individual character of its development that the industrial capitalism of Antiquity led to virtually no improvement, as compared to craft work, in the technology and organization of production.

Naturally there existed from earliest times division of labour

---

1. These are Schäfer's estimates: the absolute sums are disputable, but here we are concerned with the approximate relationships.

and coordination of production, as noted above. Should anyone doubt this let him look at the numerous Egyptian and Pompeiian frescoes which show groups of workers cooperating in organized production within workshops. The number of distinct functions coordinated in a single workshop was not large, and – what is much more important – this number did not tend to increase in the period when capitalism took over industries.

Industrial 'progress' takes place when large production units are developed in which technological innovations can be introduced to differentiate production tasks and so rationalize the use of labour. Such innovations were few in Antiquity, and were connected with agriculture and the secondary enterprises of the countryside in the West, where first in Carthage and then elsewhere capital created the plantation. Nothing similar is known for private industries – that is, for those not connected with military and building technologies (building was partly connected with military and political interests, partly state directed).

Slaveowners were affected by the extraordinary variations in the market situation and in the cost of maintaining slaves, and also by the insecure position of property. Because of these factors a slaveowner always wanted to have the option of dividing his slave property or converting it into money in other ways. In short: the slaveowner of Antiquity was interested in rents from his property, not profits from business; he was a rentier, not an entrepreneur.

Another factor, even more important, was the low level of consumer demand in Antiquity. This was caused by the manner in which wealth was distributed, political in origin and conditioned by slavery, which was an obstacle to the organization even of domestic industries, let alone 'factories'.

Today capital has enlisted science in its service and uses it to develop large units of production with internal division of labour and concomitant technology. One cannot, however, assume that this relationship existed in the past or that it will continue to exist in the future; it is entirely the result of historical development and is certainly not to be ascribed to the essential character of capital. For the essence of capital is that it seeks profits in the place and manner in which they can be obtained most easily, and the easiest way to achieve profits in Antiquity was *not* the creation of new methods to divide the production process in order to have larger, more disciplined, and better organized units of production. Slave labour was not suited for such a development either technically or 'ethically'. Nor did there exist a growing market for industrially produced consumption goods, because of the manner in which wealth was divided in Antiquity and the low level of consumer demand.

During the course of capitalist development in Antiquity there was, it is clear, an increase in the exchange of agricultural, horticultural (in private, non-state controlled trade), and mining products. It is, however, extremely doubtful whether trade in industrial products kept pace with this, and it is certain that the development of capitalism did not raise the economic and social position of industry as a whole, but instead destroyed its ancient foundations. The commoner of the archaic *polis* may have been considered the social inferior of an aristocrat, but nevertheless he was militarily indispensable in so far as he provided his own weapons or served in a ship, and as a craftsman he was highly valued by the community. For example, the smith is assigned a role in the village by Hesiod, and Solon mentions this craft as one of the ways to gain wealth. For a time craftsmen, benefiting by membership in extended families and from the mastery of a secret art, could become rich enough to strive for the offices reserved for the wealthiest; but this ended when a money economy was established, followed by the development of the nuclear family. Capital's search for profit led to the formation of a class of unfree skilled craftsmen as well as landless *coloni*. The capitalist, not the craftsman, became the model of respectability.

In the capitalist period the skilled industrial slave was simply a form of capital investment, and was in every respect except legal status very much equivalent to the free craftsman. Industrial slaves passed from master to master through purchase, mortgage, and rent; when convenient they were grouped together in large units of production. Free craftsmen and shopkeepers (*banausoi*) inevitably tended to be assimilated towards the level of slaves; the formal private and public law of the democracies did not succeed in protecting them from this tendency. The only escape for a *banausos* was to become a capitalist himself, but because of the competition of slave labour this was rarely possible.

The propertied drew their income from land rents, slave rents, and interest. Foreigners, metics, and freedmen were prohibited by law from owning land, unless a personal exception was granted, and so the ownership of both rural and urban property was a monopoly of full citizens. The development of land rents, so far as this was shaped by economics, was primarily dependent on commerce (and the same was true of slave rents and interest). Manors and lords never appeared simply because the land was fertile. Political coercion transformed many tribal chiefs into lords (or made the citizens as a whole a master class, as in Sparta); otherwise manors always appeared in Antiquity because of the need to profit from trade, in Greece especially sea trade. Foreign trade led to the development of slave property in the classical epoch just as earlier it had led to the formation of royal households based on labour services.

Exporters and importers assumed a dominant position [in commercial centres]. Evidence of this is the legal privileges accorded them, especially the provision that debts due them remained binding until paid; only debts due the state were similarly treated. They also enjoyed speedy judicial action in special courts for commercial matters.

Sea trade, then, was the most important source of new private wealth. It must be again emphasized that this statement is not contradicted by the fact that maritime commerce was quite limited in volume. One must remember that the zones of civilization in Antiquity were small, that ancient civilization as a whole was centred on the coasts, and that monetary wealth and capitalist exchange in the classical period were islands in a sea of traditionalism. Capitalism and the exchange mechanisms dependent upon capitalism were surrounded by the residues of a distant past, not just in neighbouring communities but coexisting in the same *polis*.

For example, there were groups (*eranoi*) which collected money by subscription to be loaned to fellow citizens in need. These groups played a very important role throughout the entire Hellenistic age and down to the end of Antiquity; compare the Roman *mutuum*. They may have shaped Christian ideas, and in any case were a real link with the primitive times when all peasants regularly helped their neighbours. It is clear that the *eranoi* were not originally associations for mutual aid. The mutuality (clearly expressed in *mutuum*) did not spring from the legal norms of a particular type of association, but rather from the primeval ethic of the peasantry and the citizen workers and small craftsmen of the cities, which justified loans 'among brothers' without recompense on condition that help received should be repaid in kind. In Attica this ethic was so expressed in the ancient 'curses of Buzyges' (*bouzugeioi arai*). Throughout Antiquity this very old economic morality was never forgotten by the lower classes of citizens, for whom interest was always part of foreign and aristocratic law. Similarly in the Near East the lower classes always so regarded the bureaucracy, 'the servants of the Pharaoh'. Today the Russian peasant is closest to these ancient attitudes.

We now come to the problem of whether there was in the classical period a 'capitalist invasion' of the countryside in Attica and in other Greek states outside of Sparta (though even there concentration of wealth occurred), and whether this took place in the fifth century or – as is most often argued – in the fourth. No sure answer can be given, but most students agree for good reason that in fact this did occur. Conditions were not the same in the Hellenistic age, when great private fortunes arose so that at times rich men made loans to cities on harsh terms and then held them in a form of debt bondage; this may be contrasted with the classical period, when the temples were the normal source of state loans.

Furthermore, the cities of Greece, especially Athens, more and more came to be dominated [in post-classical times] by rentiers; they had the amenities of Weimar and Heidelberg, and also that civic freedom which set Greece apart from the Near East and later Rome. Along with this went a tendency for wealthy and successful men 'to return' to Greece, acquire citizenship, and then invest their capital in land. This was a safe investment, safer certainly than in the past, as we can see from the fact that in the late classical period interest rates fell to about 8 per cent. For long Athens' port, the Piraeus, was a sort of staple and monopolized re-shipment trade, first because of political privilege and then because of superior facilities. However, when this leading role passed to Rhodes the result was that at Athens there was a great decrease of opportunities to invest in overseas trade, banks, and other forms of capitalist enterprise. After Athens finally lost its domination of the seas in the League Wars, there was a rapid decline in the number of metics, to whose financial resources Athens had owed so much of its prosperity. Since commerce now ceased to be profitable, investments tended to be made in land, and this tendency was strengthened by the great numbers who emigrated to the colonial areas of the Hellenistic world.

It is therefore not surprising that the Attic demes, so important in the fourth century, began to fall into obscurity from the third century on. The immediate causes of this were a decline in local demand for Attic agricultural products and the replacement of yeomen by tenants.

During the fifth and fourth centuries, however, there was no tendency towards concentration of land ownership. There is nothing whatever in the sources to indicate that there were private *coloni*. Furthermore, the returns from slave labour in industry were rather favourable then: slave prices were not particularly low, though there were frequent fluctuations. Yet in the time of Demosthenes a horse sometimes sold for twice the price of a slave; if this is compared to conditions in the slave states of the US, it seems a very low price for slaves, but for Antiquity it was in fact only moderate, since the slaveowner had to assume costs arising from training and from risks. Furthermore, it is always a bad mistake to draw firm conclusions from the mere facts of slave prices at any particular moment; for example, low prices may indicate low demand for slaves, but they may just as well indicate large supply.

Colossal influxes of slaves were the sequel to the wars of the Sicilians, Carthaginians, and Romans, but such a phenomenon was exceptional in ancient Greece. Therefore it is unlikely that a dramatic rise in the number of field slaves ever occurred there. We hear of 20,000 slaves running away from Attica during the Decelean War, but of these a large part is explicitly said to have been craftsmen and of course another group would have been domestic slaves. Then once the Peloponnesian War was over there were no more large influxes of slaves at least into Athens. Another indication that the slaves lost during the Decelean War were not primarily occupied in agriculture comes from statements made by Xenophon in his well-known financial proposals.

Xenophon has also left us his *Oeconomicus*, a work not concerned with specifically Attic conditions but rather describing an ideal type of estate management anywhere in Greece (his own property was in the Peloponnese). In this Xenophon takes it for granted that work on the land was usually done by slaves. He speaks of no other labourers, and there can be no doubt that slaves were also hired and leased. We also learn something from him about estate management, though his knowledge of the subject was about what one would expect nowadays from a Prussian officer who has retired to an estate in the country. Anyway, according to Xenophon the overseer (*epitropos*), who would be unfree or perhaps a freedman, should be encouraged by the hope of profit, a hope evidently to be fostered by his master. To give slaves incentive good food, drink, and clothing should be promised to the most productive; from this, and from the fact that they are called 'members of the household' (*oiketai*), it is apparent that they had no families of their own and formed part of the master's own establishment.

It is most important, says Xenophon, that the master should personally supervise management of the estate. From other statements by him, it becomes clear that this was done much as in Cato's epoch – that is, by checking the accounts from time to time. In general the conditions reflected in Xenophon's work seem very similar to those found in Cato's, the only difference being that in Greece things were much smaller and simpler than on Roman estates even in Cato's time.

The Romans, indeed, borrowed from the Greeks many terms used in connection with managing large slave enterprises; for example, the term used for slave, *instrumentum vocale*, was simply a translation of the Greek *organon empsychon*. However, this does not prove close contact between Greece and Rome in the classical period; the source of Greek terms may have been Hellenistic Sicily. In classical times the only Greek land with a slave economy like Rome's was Chios, where there existed wholesale enterprises, the largest private fortunes in the Greek world, olive oil and wine were produced, and purchased slaves were used on a large scale. Note too that Chios also had slave uprisings, as early as the seventh century!

For these reasons, then, it is unlikely that there was a sizeable expansion of large-scale slave enterprise in Attic agriculture. Slaves worked in the fields in Attica under the direction of farmers and alongside them, in the old patriarchal fashion. So much we know from the comedies, and in any case it is clear that military conditions made this unavoidable, for the farmer had to serve far away in long campaigns. (The armies of the Peloponnesians, on the contrary, returned home for the harvests.) However, we can be sure that the field slaves so employed were not numerous, for agriculture in this period was not an object of capital investment. Indeed, the statement was often made that it was ruinously unprofitable, as Xenophon comments in the introduction to his *Oeconomicus*.

Still: although the speculative purchase of land for improvement and then resale actually occurred rarely, it is indicative of the mercantile mentality dominant at the time that even a reactionary like Xenophon recommended this form of speculation. In his day the profitability of Attic agriculture must have been greatly limited by the prohibition on the export of all agricultural products other than olive oil. Perhaps the struggle between interest groups in the sixth century was partly connected with this special favour accorded the plain (*pedia*).

Furthermore, grain imported from abroad, drawn to the Piraeus in the fifth century by the staple privilege accorded that port and the pre-emptive purchase right of Athenian citizens, must have tended to some extent to depress domestic production. Thus, during the years from Solon to the Persian Wars the price of cattle increased by a factor of ten to twenty, whereas grain rose only to three times its original price, the reason for this discrepancy being that cattle could not be imported from overseas but grain could.

Then during the fifth century grain prices rose to four times their level in the sixth century, at first due to population increases and then because of wartime insecurity. However, Attic cereal producers were able to profit from this only in the years between Sphacteria and the beginning of the Decelean War [425–413 B.C.]. Furthermore, stock-breeding was always limited mainly to small animals, though the aristocracy raised horses. After the Decelean War the ruin of the hoplite class was so complete that no real recovery ever took place. One sign of the social and political decline of the yeomanry is the fact that the judges assigned to demes were again drawn from residents of Athens. At the same time the mercenary army grew in importance.

As for the extent of cultivation we can only make estimates. Demosthenes tells us that Attica imported in 355 from the kingdom of Leucon in the Pontus area about 400,000 *medimnoi*, whereas according to the calculations of tribute at Eleusis in 315–318 Attica produced about 400,000 *medimnoi*, of which about one-tenth was wheat and the rest barley. Eduard Meyer has calculated that this indicates a cultivated area of about 14,250 hectares, and that if allowance is made for fallow about 12 per cent of Attica's land was used each year to grow grain. These are estimates, but no serious objections have ever been raised against Meyer's line of argument and so we accept it.

Now the figure of 12 per cent for grain land is a very low one, and probably it cannot be explained simply by the geography of Attica. But if we look at the list of prices paid in the market at Delos we see that for a time grain prices were stagnant in the fourth century, then declined steadily until *c.* 290. Therefore it seems that during the classical period the only branch of the Attic rural economy which could attract capital investment was olive cultivation.

Just how olive raising was organized we do not know, for the necessary documents do not exist. Possibly a slave system similar to the Roman was used, but a tenant system like that of modern Italy is also possible and perhaps more likely. Yet Xenophon in his *Oeconomicus* gives a good deal of attention to planting trees, and since he always presumes the use of slave labour this indicates that a slave system was more probably used at least in his time.

To sum up: we must think of Greece in the classical period as a country near the great trade centres, its land divided into rather small parcels, with significant areas in the plains used for horticulture and intensive agriculture on the hillsides. In the river valleys of the Peloponnesus the scene was dominated by masters of small manors; Elis was a 'squirearchy'; Thessaly was a land of large estates, serfs, and horse-breeding; in Boeotia a yeomanry with large farms dominated; and in the North-West the country-side was still in the stage of a natural economy.

One must also remember that the years *c.* 425–350 B.C. were marked by bitter political struggles. Sparta's armed hegemony checked this only briefly, then the struggles started again and with them came revolutions, restorations, and hence repeated confiscations. Property became insecure as never before. Other phenomena of the period included the establishment of purely urban cleruchies with the rural population reduced to the status of *coloni* (as in Mytilene), massacres of entire aristocracies and then redistribution of the land, then brutal restorations. The old party names, 'oligarchs' and 'democrats', did not always keep the meaning which they had once had in the fifth century before the Peloponnesian War. For example, Theban 'democracy' was based on the hoplite yeomanry which achieved the political unification of Boeotia and then sought peace, just as did the farmers of Attica under their 'oligarchic' leaders, whereas on the contrary the radical democrats of Athens were centred in the urban classes which lived on the proceeds of war, since war meant high pay for the sailors recruited from the proletariat, and victory meant new tributes from which to finance public works. Victory also meant that house-owners received higher rents and capitalists had new opportunities for investment in the conquered areas. In Sparta there was a short-lived 'democracy' (until the battle of Sellasia) dominated by a militarist class of landed rentiers. The feudal oligarchy of Thessaly and the mercantile oligarchy of Chios could not have been more unlike in their economic structures; the same is true of the mercantile oligarchies of Corinth and Corcyra as compared to the feudal oligarchy of Sparta, and yet the three joined forces against democracy.

The class character of the debtor–creditor relationship, always so crucial to party formations in Antiquity, also changed. As always the debtors were agrarians (just as today), but whereas in early times creditors had been drawn from the landowning and military aristocracy, in later times they were merchants and rentiers, while among the debtors a great number were now estate owners. The degree of tension between debtors and creditors varied but was always significant. Cancellation of debts and attempts to bring this about became the ideal of the old landed aristocracy, and was no longer a political and economic demand of an armed yeomanry.

During the classical and Hellenistic periods *polis* organization continued to spread throughout Greece, and with this went union of local authorities, inclusion of wealthy landowners, division into tribes, and popular representation in council and assembly. The *polis* became dominant in all of central Greece except Aetolia and in many areas displaced the ancient ethnic names. Once the full schema of *polis* organization was established it could never be destroyed; thus exiled groups which lived abroad for centuries would, on return, go right back into their old divisions of tribe and phratry.

Most of the newly formed *poleis* were states similar to the Athens of Cleisthenes, sometimes simply unions of landowners. Thus in 408 Rhodes was united for military reasons, due to fear of Athens; this meant that three Doric tribes were united and in part settled together. When these three tribes had initially settled Rhodes they took separate areas and each had established its own *polis*; now they joined to form one single Doric state with tribal units. Small towns were formed in the mountain valleys of central Greece, and again this was done by bringing the citizen farmers together to live within a fortified area. The effects of this development can still be seen today in the social geography of Sicily, where the population of the inland areas is entirely settled in 'cities'.

Wherever this process of organizing larger areas into a *polis* by concentrating settlement took place, the inevitable long-term result was an agricultural system marked by absentee ownership and production by *coloni*. Furthermore, it was only by concentration of settlement, at least in classical times, that an army trained in hoplite tactics could be formed. Military and economic motives therefore often came into conflict and compromises were sometimes necessary, for example in the mountainous areas of the Peloponnese where the same difficulties arose as had led earlier to formation of the Mountaineers Party (*diakrioi*) in Athens. Nevertheless, in general military motives were decisive. The *poleis* formed by uniting tribes were generally 'democratic' hoplite states; examples include Mantineia and Megalopolis in Arcadia, Elis (founded in 471), and Cos. Only in Elis did the squires remain largely in the country, which was rich and developed. In Arcadia, because of the danger from Sparta, compulsion was used to settle people in the cities.

In Cos and in Elis the demes controlled eligibility to serve in the army and to own land, just as the gradually democratized phratries had this function in Athens. In all cases the purpose of settling peoples together in a city was to establish a new military organization. In Elis this had the result of reviving a policy of conquest. Nevertheless, the military reputation of the Eleans seems to have been always rather low, despite the successes they gained at times; no doubt this was due to the absence of a fully developed *polis* organization, for Elis always remained primarily an agricultural area, while its commerce was insignificant. The Arcadians provide an instructive contrast: they were the chief commercial travellers of Greece, and they were a formidable military power from early times.

In Elis and in Arcadia hoplite military organization was based – partly in theory, partly in reality – on the union of tribal groups in *poleis*. This basis was entirely lacking among the Aetolians, the last major Greek people to depend on an army recruited from all the people. The Aetolians lived in villages, and they never changed. Thermon was a fortress, a place where great masses of booty were stored, where annual fairs were held and where the federal authorities and the assembly of the federal forces met, but it was not a *polis*. In the classical period the Aetolian army was simply a group of light-armed peasants; hoplite organization and tactics were adopted later, but the *polis* remained lacking. Nor did the Aetolians have an aristocracy, because the differentiation caused by commerce was absent.

In the Macedonian period the Aetolians pursued a policy of conquest. Because of the character of their military organization they handled their conquered neighbours in this way: some they made subject to conscription into the Aetolian army; others they forced to pay tribute and controlled by means of garrisons stationed in the cities, just as the Eleans dealt with their conquests and the Swiss with the Thurgau. But the latter method seems to have been a transitory phenomenon, for admittance to the Aetolian League was readily granted, even when it was at its strongest; this was just the opposite of the policy pursued by the democratic citizen groups, especially those of Athens.

Here then we have an instructive contrast. Generally the introduction of hoplite tactics and the hoplite state implied destruction of the old clan state, and meant that the city dominated the countryside. In Aetolia, however, hoplite tactics were introduced but the populations of the villages were not brought together into a *polis*; this was because the clan aristocracy and therefore the clan state did not exist. The Aetolians consciously sought to avoid creating a *polis* with its differentiating effects, and instead created a non-urban but powerful state.

However, the conquests of the Aetolians led to the development of a money economy, and this in turn led to social differentiation. As early as the time of King Perseus [179–168 B.C.] there were sharp contrasts between the propertied and the debt-ridden classes (Livy 32.38), similar to those which had existed 500 years before in Athens.

Thessaly was the second largest area which remained largely untouched by *polis* organization. There the aristocrats, strong in their castles, retained unchecked dominance until late times.

Finally, the most powerful of the Greek states, Macedonia, remained until the reign of Philip II a fortress kingdom with conditions very similar to those described by Homer. For example, the Royal Companions had much the same role in Macedonia as in Homer. The so-called cities of Macedonia, even the royal residences such as Pella, were probably very much like Persepolis. Later hoplite tactics were introduced, as may be seen from the speech which Alexander is supposed to have delivered at Opis to his veterans; also a permanent military organization of the hoplite army was established on the basis of landed property, and *poleis* were founded in great numbers by uprooting people ruthlessly and settling them as colonists. These reforms prepared the way for the great conquests of Macedonia, which in turn revived the old tie between king and army. The army, as under Chlodwig, was sovereign alongside the king; this was the first step towards creation of an aristocratic clan state in place of the monarchy. Thus members of the royal family appealed to the army for justice, as did Queen Olympias; the king himself, when he charged a general with treason, put the matter before the army.

Of course the size of the Macedonian state was greater than any other in Greek history, and indeed the extent of Alexander's conquests made him and his successors more like Oriental monarchs than anything else. Nevertheless, the victorious Macedonians held fast to the principle that even in the Near East the Hellenic *polis* must and could be the only basis of political organization, and so they presided over the last great expansion of the basic institution of Greek civilization.

5

Hellenistic Age

In the Near East Persian rule did not bring any significant changes in social and economic structure. The fact that the tribute levied by Darius on the individual satrapies remained unaltered throughout the remaining years of the empire is no less characteristic than the fact that in the ancient home of the ruling people there continued to exist rural military associations similar to the Swiss. Similarly the old agricultural economy was maintained: debtors were reduced in social status, being regarded as owing tribute and no longer free; army service included even peasants working their own land; a feudal class did not exist, it seems, only a group of aristocratic clans whose members were distinguished by possessions and knightly education, and as such were qualified to hold royal office and, through their clan chiefs, to participate in the royal council. Judges were appointed by the king, succeeding the tribal chiefs who administered justice earlier (as in *Deuteronomy*), but no steps were taken towards codification of the law and in general the masses were subject to despotic-theocratic authority.

Tribute was paid partly in money, partly in kind. The largest monetary tribute, 1,000 silver talents, was paid by Babylonia, and the total was 7,600 silver talents, equivalent to 53½ million marks; but this included services rendered in the provinces. These sums are not an index of the development of the money economy, for the fourteenth satrapy on the Iranian plateau, although half wasteland, paid nearly as much tribute as Egypt (Eduard Meyer assumes, no doubt rightly, that mines must account for this).

Tribute in kind was paid partly by giving quarters and rendering other services to garrisoned troops, partly by entertaining the ruler or his representatives on their travels (a duty which fell on the cities, as in mediaeval Europe), partly in fixed tributes. These fixed tributes were generally assigned according to the needs of a gigantic *oikos*; they were divided and assigned by locality. Thus certain cities or towns had to deliver wine or wheat for the king's table or provide for specified needs of the queen's household or toilette. Similar provision was made for the most important item, payment of the support due to members of the royal staff ('those who dined at the king's table'), the officials, and the king's permanent army.

In addition to these payments in kind the monarch also rewarded his servants with enfeoffed land, a practice especially common in Mesopotamia, where it corresponded to ancient traditions, but used elsewhere as well. Fiefs were granted to men in the military reserve, and those of higher rank received fiefs with feudal rights and various immunities, including private courts, seigneurial conscription, and the duty to provide recruits.

These fiefs differed greatly in extent and in legal character. Some were simply private estates enjoying immunities, others were large patrimonial manors exempt from local authority, and some were vassal principalities which paid tribute but were otherwise autonomous. These varied institutions had origins going back to the Babylonian Empire, and they were the forerunners of later private authorities which probably existed in Hellenistic and certainly in Roman times. There was this difference, however: later the bestowal of political and governmental powers (exceeding simple patrimonial immunities) was much more unusual than it had been in Persian times.

Naturally political as well as patrimonial aristocratic rule extended mainly over the inland areas lacking all urban institutions, but not exclusively: there are examples of political and feudal powers over cities being conferred. Private manors worked by *coloni* were regularly found in areas with an urban culture. Little is known of the legal position of hereditary serfs.

First let us consider agrarian conditions under Persian rule in the lands of the earliest civilizations: Mesopotamia, Egypt, and Syria. Only now are we beginning to get some primary evidence on these lands from excavations and demotic papyri. Babylonian documents mention large shipments of dates from private landowners, indicating that extensive plantations had developed and that they had been formed from land recently tilled, since they paid tribute in grain.

The evidence also shows that Persian magnates rented out estates for long periods, in one case for sixty years. These estates were evidently held on feudal tenure or were grants from the royal domains, and the leases indicate that the Persian laws strictly demanding attendance at court had the effect of making the magnates absentee landlords.

We distinguish between private manors and royal domains, but in fact the former were all granted from the latter. The domains included forests, orchards, pastures, and arable land; they had been acquired by confiscation and by succession to the possessions of pre-Persian rulers. Besides royal herds there were also numbers of slaves in royal and princely possession, among them skilled craftsmen who undoubtedly worked on occasion for private individuals and also trained slaves for private owners.

The domains were run by professional administrators, much as in Carolingian times. Large areas do not seem to have been let out for sub-leasing, just as the taxes were not farmed. But we can see the presence of capital in certain arrangements for tax payments in Babylonian documents; for example an investor assumed a landowner's tax liability and bought on the market the grain owed the royal treasury as taxes on his land, then took in return the dates actually produced by the land and sold them for a profit, thus circumventing the limitations on productivity imposed by taxation in kind.

From the evidence available it seems that the Persian period was a time of pronounced economic stagnation in the areas we are discussing. In fact the Babylonian canal system was in noticeable decline by the end of the period, and we do not hear that either the Greek or the Phoenician cities flourished under Persian rule, even though this meant peace and unity throughout a vast area.

The reason for this stagnation was that the particular stimuli needed by ancient 'capitalism' were lacking, stimuli always connected with political expansion. Further the payment of taxes in kind was an important limiting factor, as was the requisition system used by local officials (described by Nehemiah) and the arbitrary command in this matter to which even the cities were subjected. At the same time there were not the opportunities for profit regularly available in Greece.

Little of specific character can be said of individual areas. At present the documentary material regarding Egypt in the Persian period is still too little understood and translated to allow any conclusions about its economic history. Revillout has argued that the revolutions of the 'national' dynasties led to new legal codes and such phenomena as the revival of family pre-emptive rights; but the laws regarding those rights may never have been repealed, and in any case Revillout's statements can only be considered hypotheses without evidence, since the source on which he relies (the *Demotic Chronicle*) has not yet been carefully interpreted and evaluated as evidence.

Although the Persian monarchs evidently secularized temple property at various times, they did nothing to change the basic position of the priesthood, and they certainly made no changes in the national laws. Neither in Egypt nor in Babylonia do there seem to have been important modification in the social structure and legal system.

The state sector of the Persian Empire's economy was not dynamic, and this must have had an effect on foreign trade. In fact economic development evidently came to a stop throughout the vast area which was unified for 150 years. There was no commerce on the Persian Gulf, and very little growth was registered by the Phoenician coastal cities in the Empire, or by the Greek coastal cities annexed after the Peloponnesian War.

As in many other areas, so in Jerusalem the Persian government sought to base its rule on the support of the priesthood. Jewish favourites of the Persian monarch succeeded in gaining permission for their people to return to Jerusalem, to rebuild the Temple and the walls of the city, and to centre the cult in the Temple. Furthermore, and this was historically the most significant aspect, they were allowed to make generally binding the rules for ritual purity and the so-called Priestly Code, which had become of central importance in Jewish life during the Exile, when the old form of the cult of Jehovah could not be maintained and which now justified the dominant position of the Jerusalem priesthood.

Before the Exile the Hebrew priesthood had been a profession outside the clan groupings; it soon became hereditary and was supported by certain defined taxes. Now under Persian rule the priesthood was enriched with authority to collect tithes. At the same time it was also organized as a distinct tribe, the tribe of Levi; this explains why Hebrew tradition traces two tribes to Joseph [whereas only one tribe each is traced to the other sons of Jacob].

Furthermore, the entire Jewish people, once repatriated to Jerusalem, was newly divided on a clan basis such as existed in Athens during the period from Draco to Solon and also in early Rome. The Jewish 'clans' were named after localities or persons, and often included several thousand people. They had been created artificially for political purposes, and they were in fact groupings of the landowners prosperous enough to arm themselves. Alongside the clans there existed (as usual) 'guilds' – that is, groupings of craftsmen which fulfilled functions similar to those of the clans.

The country to which the Jews returned was largely unpopulated. It was surveyed and divided among the clans. Then Nehemiah implemented the equivalent of a synoecism, settling groups from the clans (supposedly one tenth of each) in Jerusalem as their representatives, with compulsory residence.

The principle remained that whoever lost his land lost his membership in the community. However, the metics, among whom the landless were counted, were given careful attention in Jewish law and literature, if they accepted the Jewish faith.

The new state was clearly a theocracy. Alongside the lay clans there were the clans of the city priesthood, with temple servants (Levites) subject to priestly authority. As a group the priests amounted to one-seventh of the population, an unusually high proportion. Membership in the Jewish national community now depended upon adherence to the ritual laws regarding circumcision, Sabbath, purity, and so forth; hence the priestly clans were leaders of the community, even before the High Priest formally became the chief of state. But it should be noted that the community's economic centre clearly remained in Babylonia, as is indicated by many documents.

The political institutions of the Jewish state were designed to serve a single purpose: preservation of the sacred centre [the

Temple]. As in Hellenistic states the symbol of political unity was the ruler's table, at which clan chiefs dined together. Marriage with 'country-people', once allowed, was prohibited; that is, all those who had not accepted the law and so integrated themselves into the sacred *polis*, even if of Israelite descent, were now excluded. At the same time Judaism began to proselytize among gentiles in Palestine and abroad.

As to the agrarian development of the Jewish community, we know that at first it was rudimentary and rather laborious. Otherwise our information is indirect and late, coming from Talmudic law and the Gospels, and it is both sparse and unexceptional. Some further comments will be made later.

The 'national war' of the Macedonian military monarchy made Hellenic civilization dominant in the ancient world. In the economic sphere it caused sweeping changes in the Near East. Above all there was the extraordinary expansion of the Greek *polis*, with autonomy in internal affairs, as a form of political organization even in inland areas up to the Turkestan border. Until then very few Greek cities had been more than a day's journey from the sea. Along with this went the introduction of money economy into new regions. This was especially apparent in public finance. Thus whereas the visit of a Persian king to a city had been an economic burden because of the requisitions made for the court, now a monarch's visit brought profit; this is noted in our sources as a striking characteristic of the new order.

It was at this time that state farming of taxes began to spread to the East. We noted above that as late as the reign of Artaxerxes private capital was used by debtors, and Beloch is certainly right when he interprets Aristotle, *Oeconomica* II. 33, to mean that in Egypt the nomarchs themselves had to convert into money the taxes paid in grain; it was in order that they might be able to remit the taxes that they urged that the export of grain be allowed, for otherwise they could not collect sufficient money.

Hence the Hellenistic states, Egypt above all, began to farm out the collection of taxes in kind. Tax farmers guaranteed to pay a fixed sum of money, and so the state was able to balance its budget in money. The great hoards of the Persian kings were distributed as donatives to the sovereign army, its leaders, and members of the staffs of the Macedonian princes, and so vast sums of money were poured into the economy. The Seleucid Empire, essentially the heir to the Persian Empire, evidently never had a royal hoard of any significance, but it seems to have received a greater revenue from money tributes than had the Persian Empire from all its lands outside India. Egypt had a large state treasure, but certainly not as huge as the absolutely unreliable figures recorded would indicate (many modern historians accept an estimate that is impossible). In addition there was the royal bank which, as in most Hellenistic cities, controlled money exchange and, with its branches, collected all sorts of payments.

Another feature of the Hellenistic age was that everywhere cities began to issue their own coinage. Under Persian rule even a city such as Babylon did not coin, and in fact Persia's imperial coinage, the gold daric, had been issued primarily to be hoarded or to be used for bribes. Only a few coastal cities had issued coins in the Greek manner, and in general the money system had remained more or less similar to that of China: token money of small value was used along with precious metals which fluctuated in value and were weighed out at each transaction.

We can see the development and influence of money economy best in the case of Egypt, for its conditions are especially well known to us thanks to the work of Ulrich Wilcken. Consider first the differences in tribute. Darius received 700 talents and 120,000 artabae of grain (these figures supposedly remained stable), while Ptolemy II Philadelphus received 14,800 talents and 1.2 million artabae. In the first century, after a notable decline, 6,000 talents were collected, a figure quite credible. Of course these figures cannot be used to indicate a proportional increase in total state receipts. First of all there was a decrease in the value of precious metals, and then too all our sources agree that under the Persian Empire the heaviest burdens fell on the satraps and local military units, so that only a part of all taxes paid went to the Persian court and naturally an especially small part of the taxes paid in kind. Nevertheless it is also true that the value of taxes paid in kind to the Ptolemies was only one-fortieth of their total tax revenue; this is a measure of the extent to which the money economy had grown.

Furthermore – as Wilcken first pointed out – whereas the expenditures for army supplies in the third century B.C. were divided between money and products in the ratio of 1 to 2, this relationship changed in the second century to 3½ to 1 and for naval expenditures at the end of the second century it stood at 20 to 1.

As to the categories of natural economy, distinguished by the Chaldaeans more on the basis of form than function, there still continued to exist throughout the entire Ptolemaic period the loan in kind, wages in kind, and so forth. They are mentioned mainly in demotic documents, but not exclusively. Leases for rents in kind were an important factor in private trade down into Roman imperial times. Yet during the period 300 B.C.–A.D. 150 the money economy continued its irresistible advance. Extant fragments of account books indicate that households were conducted entirely on a monetary basis in the third century B.C. and then in the time of Vespasian. People bought goods in the market for money, sold their products for money, received wages in money, and paid interest in money; this was the dominant pattern.

Above all, taxes were assessed and paid mainly in money. This was true of most land taxes, with the exception of those on crops subject to state monopoly (sesame croton), and on cereal cultivation. Similarly money was used to pay the taxes on trades; these had been instituted in place of the old pharaonic labour services and taxes in kind on products. Everywhere one finds a tendency to commute payments in kind into money payments – *adaeratio*, as it was called in the later Roman Empire.

Indeed, this is the key to the extraordinary development and complexity of the Ptolemaic finance system, under which virtually everyone from prostitutes to canal superintendents paid specific taxes on their occupations and transactions. The only exceptions were the Greeks, priests (up to a maximum per temple), and military settlers (*katoikoi*: see below). This system took form as the planned continuation of the Ramessid labour service system, based on the use of cadasters recording labour services owed, land owned, and classification of soil. The only difference between the two systems was that the Ramessids levied labour services while the Ptolemies in theory (the actual practice is discussed below) levied money taxes.

From these facts we conclude: state demands in Hellenistic times were met increasingly in terms of money, and this indicates that the economic structure which made this possible was or was becoming a monetary economy.

Then, however, a reverse tendency set in. The administrations of the Hellenistic monarchies were bureaucratic, and they became more so with time. Soon they instituted an ever expanding system of liturgies with which to ensure the receipt of state revenues, and this precisely because of the money economy. More and more wealthy individuals were made personally liable for the full payment of sums due the state, and these individuals were tied to their functions. This system was most fully developed in Egypt, but all the other Hellenistic states made some use of it.

Even in the autonomous *poleis* such as Athens the state slaves increased in importance. The Attic administrative system had certain procedures worthy of note, such as having an individual advance money (*proeisphora*) to the treasury to pay the taxes of another, forming a group of taxpayers (*symmoria*) subject to joint assessments, and handling the demes as discussed above. Here were the origins of the system which five hundred years, later in the age of Constantine, governed the levying of taxes and the handling of the urban masses (*populus plebeius*) in the munici-palities.

Another feature of the Hellenistic states was their adoption of feudal institutions from the preceding Near Eastern states. These institutions existed alongside the *poleis*. This adoption was due to Hellenism's conquests and, in particular, its expansion into inland areas, and it took place in practice even when not admitted in theory. For example we have a contract from Ptolemaic Egypt for the hereditary lease (99 years) of private land, very similar to those in Mesopotamia under Persian rule. Not a single instance of such a contract has so far been documented for Ancient Greece or Rome, and this indicates the stronger feudal element in Hellenistic Egypt's social structure. Despite various policies designed to bring the nationalities together, the mass of the natives were in fact the conquered subjects of the Greek army, and that reality was reflected in society's institutions.

It is true that outside Egypt the Hellenistic states energetically promoted urbanization, but it is also true that the cities were agents of Hellenization. People in the countryside remained 'natives' (*ethnē*), and so the desired Hellenization regularly occurred only in the cities. This was achieved partly by settling

Greek emigrants and veterans in them, partly by uniting these colonists in a *polis* with Hellenized native clans (old temple families and military aristocracy).

Inscriptions seem to indicate that everyone had to place his land under *polis* authority if that land fulfilled or under law could fulfil any sort of state charge. This meant in practice all private persons, even those who had received their lands from the royal domain (which was not subject to *polis* jurisdiction). This indicates that the Hellenistic rulers consciously used their colonists to undermine feudal and also, especially, priestly privileges. This was very different from the pro-theocratic policies of the Persian Empire. Thus in Egypt the Ptolemies, officially so solicitous of religion, used the apotheosis of Arsinoe in 265 B.C. as a pretext to deprive the priesthood of its traditional share (*apomoira*) of horticultural products (one-sixth), evidently as compensation for a large grant, and transfer it to the new goddess – that is, the state. Later, of course, came the great national rebellion centred in the Thebaid [under Ptolemy IV Philopator, 216 B.C.] which led to more conciliatory policies.

We can also see evidence of Hellenistic policies in the foundation by synoecism of new cities such as Pisidian Antioch and Stratonice in Caria. The latter was founded on land belonging to an old sacred league centring round a temple, and in fact the league's territory was effectively splintered by the foundation of Stratonice and other cities. Thereafter each new city had representation in the league's council in proportion to the number of old villages it had absorbed. Similarly, the Herods in later times founded cities to counterbalance the power of Jerusalem, a *polis* which was unique in its clan and theocratic character. One of these Herodian foundations was Tiberias, and Josephus informs us that those who settled there received arable land, houses, and privileges: in return, however, they had to remain there. Another Herodian foundation was Sebaste, which sent a contingent of 3,000 men to fight in one of the Herods' wars. This points to another aspect: the new Hellenistic cities were the strongest military supports of the Diadochi rulers; they were, after all, Greek islands surrounded by natives of other races, and as such they were completely dependent upon the Hellenistic states.

Furthermore, the Hellenistic *polis* played an important role in increasing taxable resources. Hellenistic monarchs were mercantilists, pursuing policies similar to those of German territorial princes in the seventeenth and eighteenth centuries.

Generally the foundation of a city by synoecism meant that the classes concerned with business (including, let it be noted, municipal administration, a source of business profit) were in effect forced to concentrate in the city. An example of this is supplied by Cassandreia; one of the villages included in it was Mende, and Kuhn has pointed out that whereas before the synoecism Mende had exported wine, this ceased after the synoecism and henceforth the wine was exported from Cassandreia. In short: the Hellenistic *polis* enjoyed staple privileges.

Here it must be stressed that the enormous areas under urban jurisdiction in this period indicate that the Hellenistic cities must have been very different in their social structure from the classical *polis*, and indeed that they were often really only complexes of large manorial estates brought together artificially by a legal synoecism. Furthermore, the vast domains of the monarchs remained outside urban jurisdiction, and alongside these there existed many estates held by private individuals through royal favour. The latter were not incorporated into cities, especially in those areas in which *polis* organization had not been generally established.

So much is securely attested. No sure evidence exists, however, to document the existence of a class of *coloni* legally bound to the soil and attached to private manorial properties. This is not only undocumented but also unlikely to have existed in the Seleucid Empire or in the early Hellenistic period in general, and that applies both to Greek tenants (rare outside *polis* territories) and to natives.

But the situation is very different if we turn to matters involving administrative law and the duties owed by subjects to the state (that is, to the monarch). In so far as his relations with the state were concerned, the Hellenistic subject was bound to his home community; in Ptolemaic Egypt this was formulated in the laws regarding *idia*, undoubtedly a continuation of pharaonic practices discussed above. It was also similar to the ties binding the Athenian to his deme. The Athenian, however, retained freedom of movement, but in Ptolemaic Egypt a man's *idia* was the

community where he had to pay his taxes to live for the performance of personal liturgies. If he moved to another community
he lived there as a 'stranger' (*epixenos*) and could be sent back to
his *idia* at any time.

In general, of course, freedom of movement existed in Antiquity
only in so far as it was guaranteed by specific treaties or privileges. Otherwise, so far as the state and law were concerned, the
individual was tied to his community very much the way the
Russian peasant is today. Hence we find that subjects were sent
back to their home communities to fulfil public charges. There is
the well-known example later mentioned in the Gospel of St
Luke, and in fact it took place throughout this period in all the
Hellenistic states. In particular the Hellenistic state depended
upon labour services – though not as much as had the ancient
Near Eastern states – and whenever emigration seemed to en-
danger their fulfilment it acted without hesitation to force the
emigrants back.

Now on the extra-urban domains of the kings and similarly on
the extra-urban private manorial estates held by favour there
was a strong tendency for the duties of the *coloni* towards the
state to be confused with those due the owner, due partly to
tradition and partly to the way in which leased domains were
run. This was especially the case in Egypt, where the tradition of
labour services went back to pharaonic times. For example, the
old rule of five days' work on the canals continued in Ptolemaic
times. It is true, however, that, as the money economy grew in
importance, there was a trend to commute labour services into
payments in kind or money. But where this conflicted with the
state's interests, it reversed the trend; thus Ptolemy II did not
hesitate to limit the freedom of movement of workers in the state
olive oil presses, although legally they were autonomous labourers
hired by contract.

Such measures were not justified by general legal principles
but rather by the king's administrative powers, and the same
applied in time of need to the order issued to *coloni* on royal
estates. Thus a document recording the sale of a village on a
domain in Asia Minor by Antiochus II to his wife Laodice in
256 B.C., the importance of which was first noted by Rostovtzeff,
assumes that the village inhabitants actually enjoy freedom of
movement but also indicates clearly that they are legally bound

to their village (contrary to P. M. Meyer) and of course in case of need could be brought back. Very much the same powers were held by private estate owners when they were conceded any local jurisdictions.

In fact, the private law of the Near East from Snefru and Hammurabi down to the Talmud always regarded tenants from the owner's point of view; the tenant held his land at the owner's grace, he did not even have a prior claim to profit from the land (this applied mainly but not exclusively, to share-croppers). It can easily be imagined that nobody was much concerned to separate the powers such principles conferred from those connected with labour services owed the state, especially when kings or patrimonial lords were concerned. Even in pharaonic times it had been difficult to distinguish between the labour services owed by *coloni* on the domains and those owed by his peasant subject to the pharaoh for public purposes, as discussed above.

Some effort, however, was made to clarify this distinction in Hellenistic times, at least in so far as the natives (*ethnē*) were concerned. In the Ptolemaic *Revenue Laws* and other sources the official terminology distinguishes between the *laoi* on the domains and the *geōrgoi* on private land. (*Laoi*, incidentally, was the word used for *coloni* in the Near East, and it undoubtedly corresponds to the pharaonic *retu* and *miritiu*.) Under this distinction *geōrgoi* were legally free farmers, owners or tenants, including royal tenants (*basilikoi geōrgoi*), whereas *laoi* in the *Revenue Laws* and elsewhere was used for the native Egyptian *coloni* of the king. However, this distinction was probably not substantive nor is it likely that it persisted, for as in pharaonic times the royal *coloni* seem to have been treated in administrative law in just the same way as the great mass of landless natives were, being legally defined as landless or else assimilated to them in status. This is what one would expect.

Laoi paid poll taxes, and were liable for such labour services in their home community (*idia*) as the community or the state might demand. In Hellenistic times, however, these labour services were generally commuted into money payments, and as a result *laoi* enjoyed actual freedom of movement, though of course this was legally quite insecure. But if *laoi* were needed actually to render labour services – as in crises when the state was hard pressed or money was lacking (as happened in the second century B.C., first noted by P. M. Meyer) – then they were excused from other liturgies, such as cultivation of land assigned by the state, in order not to impede work on arable land already.

One aspect of the agricultural economy about which we know little is this: whether *laoi* settled on royal domains simply fulfilled traditional obligations or else had written leases. Peasants on private estates holding written leases were termed in later legislation *homologi coloni* (though some deny this). Wilcken found a group holding leases (*geōrgountes homologoi andres*) in the second century, and thought they were settled on state properties; but unfortunately no more precise information is available. In general it is probable that originally *coloni* of Greek origin held their lands on lease while natives paid rents determined by custom.

These phenomena clearly were connected with the type of state apparatus which the most rationally organized Hellenistic state, Egypt, had erected on the basis of pharaonic social structure. As shown above, alongside the Hellenistic money economy there existed feudal institutions as well as the bases of the ancient Ramessid labour service state. Furthermore, the money economy was also heavily burdened by the manner in which the state financial system functioned. The state maintained a great army of salaried bureaucrats and also a rather large standing army, paid more and more in money exclusively. There were also large expenditures for the court and also (especially in Egypt) for the state religion; finally there were the sums demanded by an active foreign policy. All these things needed money.

Now just as today in contemporary Europe, so in the Hellenistic period it was precisely the need to find money for state expenses which tended to lever the entire economy back towards social controls which limited the role of the market. In Antiquity this tendency found its fullest realization in the liturgy state. This subject cannot be examined fully here; certain aspects important for agricultural history are discussed in this *Handwörterbuch* in the article on the colonate by Michael Rostovtzeff.

Let it suffice here to note that Ptolemaic Egypt was the model Hellenistic state – the Seleucid Empire was much more loosely organized and therefore declined relatively quickly – and that in Egypt many important industries were state monopolies. Among them were the production of oil (from sesame, croton, and pumpkins; the olive spread to Egypt later, in the Roman period), salt (with appropriation of a small quota, like the French gabelle), natron, and also, it seems, fine linen (connected with institutions in pharaonic Egypt, discussed above). This meant that the cultivation of oil-producing fruits and (probably) flax was strictly controlled, the state purchased the entire product, and therefore all the harvest was stored in royal warehouses. Oil was sold at prices fixed by government fiat on the basis of various considerations and after the prefects (*kapeloi*) of the towns and districts had indicated their areas' needs and the court had deducted enough for its own consumption.

Oil and wheat were the most important foodstuffs, and both were regulated by the state administration. Banking, especially currency exchange, was likewise monopolized and farmed out. State monopolies increased constantly and included more and more products, in particular: (1) 'heavy products', that is, those closely connected with raw materials, (2) items of mass consumption. Thus in Roman times we find that the brick industry was a state monopoly, as were also most basic consumption articles: bread, oil, building materials, and in part clothing.

In addition there was the system of liturgies, in a form which shows a combination of pharaonic and specifically Hellenistic institutions. The state aimed to make someone financially responsible for the performance of each public service. In order to make this possible all private fortunes of any size and permanence were so registered that their owners were assigned a certain number of tax units (*poroi*, equivalent to the *capita* of Diocletian's time), and on the basis of this local authorities determined each individual's qualification and liability for office. This system reached down to include village night watchmen (assigned a *poros* of 300 drachmae).

This liturgy system affected the most important source of capital formation, state leases and in particular state tax farming (as has been demonstrated by Rostovtzeff). In Athens and in Rome the tax farmer had a free hand, because there was no bureaucracy; in Egypt, on the contrary, the state was in charge. In the last instance the state needed tax farmers only to guarantee the collection of a minimum sum, thus enabling a budget to be drawn up. Guarantors took a risk, for which they were compensated with a 5–10 per cent share (*opsonion*) of any surplus over the minimum (but many aspects of this are still unsettled). Nor did the tax farmer pay the state a lump sum and then collect the taxes; rather, the state itself did the collecting. On the other hand the tax farmer did not have to make any advance payments (or only partial ones), and therefore he needed very little capital; he and his associates needed, rather, property in order to be useful to the state as guarantors.

Therefore this sort of tax farming was qualitatively different from that practised by Roman *publicani*, and this is indicated too by the fact that more and more it was regarded as a liturgy and in bad times as a particularly onerous one. By the end of the Ptolemaic period compulsion was regularly used to force individuals to assume tax farming agreements, and the edict of Tiberius Alexander shows that it was an intolerable burden. Eventually compulsion was also used to impose the lease of state domains, and this is shown to have become a normal phenomenon by agreements among leaseholders explicitly made to protect themselves against the consequences of such forced contracts.

Royal domains, in fact, provided a very important part of the state's revenues. In the beginning, when the dynasties were not yet firmly established, the old domains must have been used to a large extent partly to raise money; for example, we know that Antiochus I sold land for 300 talents to the city of Pitane; or they were used to gain and endow allies. Cassander mentions in inscriptions large gifts of land from Philip and Alexander, and sizeable gifts were also made by the Diadochi, especially the first. One general received from Antiochus I about 600 hectares of land, and this was certainly not an unusually large gift.

Later, however, the royal domains were used for other purposes, especially in Egypt, and these – apart from temple gifts, discussed later – were as follows: (1) permanent allotments were granted to soldiers, partly to add to the royal guards a reserve always ready for duty, partly to have a recruitment cadre available (but some scholars argue against this) and so save money; (2) lands were leased in order to secure an income from rents.

The military aspect, especially with respect to Egypt, has been greatly illuminated by the work of P. M. Meyer; nevertheless much remains insecure, and therefore it cannot be discussed further here. A few remarks must suffice to indicate those features important for agrarian history.

In a broad sense all the agricultural regulations issued to settlers in the new cities of the Diadochi can be regarded as having a military character, for the new *poleis* were fortresses. Formally, however, the *polis* had a military duty towards its sovereign and the citizen had a military duty to his *polis*, which remained autonomous in internal matters. The situation differed, however, with respect to the lands allotted soldiers. Thus in Pergamon soldiers received allotments of 12½ or 6½ hectares (of which 1½ or 1¼ hectares were vineyard land), and military obligations were attached directly to the lands. The same is true of veteran settlements; these appear from the time of Alexander on and were revivals of an Ancient Near Eastern institution (discussed above). In fact these settlements provided for an hereditary warrior order, as a substitute for the Macedonian national army.

Especially in Egypt there was a tendency to build on old institutions. Side by side there existed, as in the later Roman Empire and in the Dark Ages, these two forms: (1) quartering of troops (*stathmoi*), and (2) settlement on allotments (*klēroi*). Only the latter is of interest here. Allotment land, in turn, was given to two groups: (1) native soldiers (*machimoi*), only called up in crisis, settled on small plots such as prevailed in pharaonic times (the *heptarourai machimoi* of Cerceosiris had 1.8 hectares, but native cavalrymen had larger allotments); (2) Macedonian and Greek soldier peasants (*klēruchoi*).

Other aspects must be neglected here, in particular the allotment of Greek military land to police and, later, civilian functionaries, as indicated by the Tebtunis papyri. Another is the relation between the various groups of military that were given allotments – regular troops (*syntagma*), reserve (*epitagma*), privileged descendants of Alexander's conquering army (*epigonoi*, as recently established by P. M. Meyer and Reinach), and military peasants (*kondrouchoi, katoikoi*). These matters are still debated by scholars, as in fact the following is too.

Those Greek soldier peasants, especially the *katoikoi* (the usual term for the largest group), who were settled on the land seem to have received allotments, when possible, from royal possessions in the uplands (*chersos*), not from the old flooded delta lands (*sporimos*), and consequently they received rather large areas. In Cerceosiris the allotments ranged from 20 to 100 *arourai* (5.6–28 hectares), but some as large as 320 and even 500 *arourai* are known. On the other hand men settled on suburban delta lands received plots as small as .83 hectares. When delta land subject to lease was allotted to soldier peasants, and therefore drew no rent, this was entered in the cadasters as an irregularity and figured as a deduction on the rent rolls.

Generally three types of land were distinguished: royal domains (*basilikē gē*), subject to lease; private land (*idioktētos*); 'granted land' (*gē en aphesei*), consisting of two sub-categories – temple land (*hiera gē*, discussed below), and military peasant land. Lands of the last type were tied to certain state functions, but were nevertheless no more exempt from taxation than was private land.

Indeed the taxes imposed on military peasants of all groups were sometimes so heavy, the land itself often being merely reclaimed wasteland, that they could be forced to give up their allotments. This was so even though the taxes were originally, as indicated by form and name, no more than registration fees and occasional contributions to the king for his army. When taxes were not paid the land was distrained, as the sources show, and then if possible assigned to someone else ready to assume its fiscal obligations. In particular the land was unquestionably confiscated when a military peasant failed to report for military service, just as with military fiefs in the time of Hammurabi.

The cleruch did not have to work the land himself; he could rent it out. Alienating it was probably illegal at first, but it could be arranged, the peasant resigning ownership in favour of someone else with consent of the authorities. Land was inherited by the sons, and wills were not yet used, it seems, in the third century B.C. We know of instances in which the land was divided between father and son, evidently simply to assign work and profits. Parcellization of land was very unusual, but occurred in connection with inheritance and no doubt needed official consent. We do not know whether the military peasant was from the first legally free to raise what he chose, but in practice, judging from extant documents (especially leases), there was no official interference. The cleruch paid money taxes and served in the army when needed. Only when he failed to cultivate his land or allowed its productivity to decline below the minimum necessary to pay the state its taxes (as indicated in the Tebtunis papyri) was the land taken back by the state, and indeed such was the practice with all hereditary leases in Antiquity.

Among the military peasants the most privileged group were the Greek *katoikoi*. They were no more pure ethnically than were the Egyptians and with time these groups became more mixed in accord with Ptolemaic policy. Indeed there seems to have been a policy of advancement by merit, allowing an individual to rise from the lowest to the highest class within the cleruchy. Allotments would then be successively enlarged and new grants made; at the same time an individual would be promoted to the class of *katoikoi*, but to gain such promotion one had to be Hellenized.

Probably the *katoikoi* were not very numerous, judging from the many mercenary soldiers employed by the Ptolemies and also from the large size of their military allotments. Cleruchies were, naturally, distributed quite unevenly over the land, being concentrated where the royal administration had reclaimed it through irrigation and drainage works. This was exactly in the tradition of the Ancient Near East, especially Mesopotamia, just as mass transfers of conquered populations reminiscent of the past were also carried out by the Ptolemies. Thus in Cerceosiris, an entirely reclaimed area, there were absolutely no private properties outside the sites of houses in the village and a mere 5 per cent was temple land; military land, on the other hand, amounted to 1,564 *arourai* out of a total of c. 4,700 *arourai* (1,300 hectares), or a third, while the rest was royal land.

The *katoikoi*, from the time of their first appearance in the second century B.C., counted as a privileged class. This privileged position was with time extended to include their allotments, which were in practice private property, indeed property exempt from taxes and also, as is documented, labour services. In the third century A.D. *katoikoi* seem to have paid the very low tax of 1 *artaba* per *aroura*. On the other hand they were subject to *epikrisis*, which with P. M. Meyer I take to mean registration for conscription; Wessely, however, interprets *epikrisis* as referring to registration of the ethnic groups subject to taxes. In any case the *katoikoi* class was ethnically mixed in Roman times, and as mentioned above it was probably so long before.

Only a few remarks can be made here regarding the royal domains (*basilikē gē*) in Egypt. As early as the New Empire royal lands had been cadastered, surveyed, and divided into square parcels. The manner in which the land was to be cultivated was defined and controlled precisely for each village, as the documents indicate.

Domains were scattered over the entire land, and had been since pharaonic times, although the distribution was uneven. So far we have no primary evidence to explain how this occurred. Domain land was leased, and as in pharaonic times the great majority of tenants were small farmers; under the Roman Empire this changed to some extent. Leases were not on a share-cropping basis, but rather called for fixed rents paid in kind and graduated according to the land's fertility. Wheat was the main medium of payment; other crops were accepted only up to a certain state maximum, the rest being reckoned as the equivalent of wheat according to a fixed formula – e.g. barley/wheat $= 3/5$. Thus in practice a certain freedom in choosing crops was allowed, while at the same time the treasury's aim of securing as much wheat as possible was sustained.

As a result the royal domains were mainly planted to wheat, and in this differed from the lands farmed by other groups, the cleruchs for example. For while the latter raised crops partly to meet their own needs and therefore cultivated legumes and the like, the domains were meant to raise crops for export. Thus Egypt became the great granary of the Mediterranean. Often more than half of domain lands was planted with wheat, and cereals accounted regularly for two-thirds; the remaining third was left fallow (*anapauma*) and was sown with grass, lentils, and the like.

For sowing it was reckoned that 1 *artaba* was needed per *aroura* [about 48 litres per ¾ acre]. The yield rose in one case to twentyfold; today the average is twelvefold (in this connection compare rents, discussed below). In order to ensure grain production, so important for both political and economic reasons, royal warehouses were used as in pharaonic times, and from these (as today in Russia) seed was given to the peasants who leased domain land and also to those who paid taxes in kind. The whole system rested upon the royal grain inspectors (*sitologoi*) who were quartered in the villages, supervised the cultivation and harvesting of crops, and distributed seed. The grain was threshed on the threshing floors outside the village and then delivered to the royal warehouse. If transport to Alexandria was needed, it was undoubtedly entrusted to a monopoly run by a state-disciplined corporation.

Domain rents seem to have been moderate compared to private rents, so far as we can judge. On the other hand remission of domain rents was very rare, and was conceded only in times of great disasters such as failure of the Nile to flood.

A cadaster of domains for each locality was maintained, and it indicated those domains which drew rent and those which temporarily or permanently did not. The latter category included land not cultivated (*hypologon*) due to natural causes or to chance, land 'under judgment' (*en sygkrisei*) because its tenants had asked for remission of rent, and land granted with privilege. Such privileged grants of domain land were made (contrary to rules) to cleruchs, as noted above; they were also made for specific purposes such as support of temples or priests (*en syntaksei* seems the term for this), and they were made as fiefs bestowed on courtiers (termed, evidently, *en dōrea*). Such fiefs often included several villages. These practices were certainly derived directly from pharaonic administration.

In general there are still controversies about many aspects of domain land. For example: was 'waterless land' (*gē abrochos*) irrigated upland? Was 'seed land' (*gē sporimē*) flooded delta land? Or, less likely, was the latter marshland and the former drained land?

Then there was the *gē prosodou*, which Mitteis interprets as land leased to hereditary tenants, while he takes the group called 'village farmers' (*geōrgoi dēmosioi*) to be tenants holding leases with time limits; some scholars think the 'village farmers' were tenants on village land, but that is certainly a mistake. In any case Mitteis has shown (*Zeitschrift für Rechtsgeschichte*, vol. 22, pp. 151 ff.) that a document mentions hereditary lease with hereditary rent, which indicates corresponding conclusions for Roman institutions, as discussed below. Hereditary lease is found where uplands have been forcibly occupied and the occupants have been allowed by the government to keep possession of these lands, with the obligation to improve and cultivate them.

The Ptolemies were very lavish in assigning revenues and in bestowing lands on temples, native Egyptian temples just as much as Greek ones. The great wealth of the Temple of Edfu was increased 150 per cent by a single grant! Accordingly the extent of temple lands (*hiera gē*) was very considerable, especially in Upper Egypt where from ancient times the national priesthood had always had its centres. Yet it was not as great as in pharaonic times. Even in the four southernmost nomes of Upper Egypt only one-twenty-fifth of the cultivated land can be reckoned as temple property, and Otto estimates the figure for the second century B.C. as one-tenth. Nevertheless the Temple of Edfu alone owned over 18,300 *arourai* there, and along with a few other temples owned 21,400 *arourai* (6,000 hectares) altogether, mostly the best land.

Sometimes demotic contracts mention the private sale of land formerly owned by a temple (*nefer hotep*), but this does not indicate secularizations by the Ptolemies; rather, some lands had been sold voluntarily by the temples, other lands had been confiscated under earlier dynasties. Nevertheless there were exceptions: temple revenues (*apomoira*) were confiscated to benefit the cult of the apotheosized Arsinoe (but compensation was paid; see above). In general the apotheosis of a sovereign was used in the Near East as a pretext to justify expropriation of temple property without incurring the danger of being judged guilty of sacrilege, for ostensibly the expropriated property was only transferred to 'colleagues'.

Furthermore, it should be noted that the state did no more than assume the administration of temple incomes. The national synod of the Egyptian priesthood continued to meet, and indeed the synod does not seem to have consistently supported anti-Greek nationalism, although of course it is no accident that the last nationalist revolution again centred in the Thebaid, the ancient capital of theocracy and the area in which the temples had their most extensive properties.

The ancient traditions of the Egyptian temples were stereotyped but not aggressive. Entry into the priesthood was controlled by the state. The priests were not well-educated, and therefore were at a disadvantage in Hellenistic society. They were distinguished from Greek priests partly by their organization in a unified church, partly by their greater 'asceticism' and partly – as a result of the latter – by the fact that they less frequently engaged in secular occupations.

The Egyptian Church of Hellenistic Egypt, along with the Jewish synagogue, influenced the Christian Church not only in many aspects of ecclesiastical organization and life but also in its economic activities. There are striking similarities between monastic and temple enterprises. Certainly not all of these similarities need be taken as borrowings, but rather proceeded from comparable situations. Nevertheless, the economic activities of early Christian monasteries in Egypt is so identical to those of the pagan temples that there can be no doubt of continuity here.

The temples' economic activities in Ptolemaic times clearly grew out of the *oikos* of a natural economy, in which income was used mainly or entirely for domestic consumption and cult purposes. From this a complex of money-economy enterprises developed, elements of which undoubtedly go back to pharaonic times (see above). It is certain that from early times Egyptian temples possessed mills which were used to convert the grain they collected into foodstuffs, and they may also have had bakeries. Sometimes temples purchased grain to be milled (as in Heliopolis) in order to make use of their mills, and sometimes the reverse occurred: having no need for its mill, a temple would lease it. We have an example of this from Soknopaiu Nesos, in which a mill was leased for an annual rent of 120 drachmae.

We do not know for certain whether the temples did milling with paid labour, nor whether they did baking for third parties, but there is no doubt whatever that often the many temple breweries produced for sale in the market. Linen was different, however: although in pharaonic times the temple and pharaonic *oikoi* had produced it for the market, in Hellenistic times the temples were allowed to produce it only for internal use. This was probably because it was a state monopoly, for we know that a similar limitation was enacted in the Revenue Laws when oil became a state monopoly. When olive cultivation spread in late pharaonic and Roman times, the processing of olives from temple lands, outside the monopoly, probably became of major importance.

Furthermore, the temples from earliest times had need of a great variety of skilled masons and painters. Documents indicate that craftsmen paid their permit fees to the state through temples, but it is not clear whether this meant that Ptolemaic temples used these craftsmen for profit-making enterprises, as Otto argues. If these craftsmen were free, then it is difficult to understand why they did not produce for the market on their own account. If, however, they were temple *coloni*, this would explain why they worked for the temples and why the temples collected their permit fees; but we have no evidence that the temple workers were serfs. Another possibility, and this is the most likely, is that these masons and craftsmen were free men, hired by the temples to produce goods exclusively for temple needs, and were bound by contract. This would explain why the temples collected the permit fees and paid them to the state, the temples in this as in other cases (as Otto rightly notes) being treated by the revenue authorities as business owners. To what extent these temple workers in fact produced for the market is a very obscure matter, but in any case the principle remains that production for the market is generally incidental to the size of an *oikos*, and always incidental to its foundation.

We can, however, be sure that the temples used permanent production equipment, such as the fulling mills sometimes found, not only for their own consumption needs but also for sales for profit; this applies in particular and above all to oil presses. No evidence indicates whether temples engaged in wholesale trade, but we do know that they made loans as Near Eastern temples had done from earliest times. Interest of 6 per cent was charged, probably a purposely low rate as in fact all state rents were kept low; collateral in kind was accepted.

The extent of all these temple enterprises was so great that Otto is justified in saying, from a purely technical point of view, that the temples constituted an 'industry' in Egypt second only in size to the royal monopolies. A small temple paid business taxes to the state of 1,295 drachmae, an eighth of its monetary income. Nevertheless, it must be added that the extent to which temple production was destined for the market is completely unknown, and therefore Otto's use of the term 'factory' is questionable, especially since the contractual status of the employed craftsmen (Otto calls them 'workers') is as unknown to us as is the manner in which production was organized.

Furthermore, it is clear that there were no large-scale agricultural enterprises run by temples. All temple land was leased.

Rents were paid in kind, and whatever was not needed for internal use was sold.

These aspects – the great royal and temple *oikoi* existing side by side, the liturgy system, the treatment of native peasants (*laoi*) – all combine to indicate quite clearly that here too one must be sparing in the use of modern concepts. For example: it is probable that in Hellenistic times there existed the letter of credit (essential for travellers of high status), and state bonds were issued which could be cashed by a designated representative (though probably not the bearer); nevertheless, it is most unlikely that in Hellenistic times there were bills of exchange (as Caillemer believed), even though there were undoubtedly initiatives in that direction which were later perfected in the Byzantine and Arab periods.

It is true that banking was highly developed in Hellenistic times, as Gradenwitz has shown, and that there was short-term speculation, especially in grain. Also we find in this period the sharpest imaginable contrasts in wealth, with some individuals possessing fortunes equivalent to several hundred thousand marks, sometimes even millions, such as were surpassed only in the Later Roman Empire.

Yet one need only glance at Genoese documents of the eleventh and twelfth centuries or at the account books of Florentine merchants of the thirteenth or fourteenth centuries to see that in those periods the techniques of finance were far superior and also that the economy then was far more shaped by capital than was that of the ancient world. For example, in mediaeval times there was a significant progression of public finance: first the propertied classes were forced to buy interest-free bonds to help a city in deficit; then the propertied classes exploited civic deficits by having the cities issue interest or dividend-paying shares in the state debt; finally, the cities raised loans by selling annuities. Now if we turn to Hellenistic times we find that besides the property tax the only device available to cities in need of cash was the loan from an individual, and such loans were secured by collateral ranging from the castle (Lampsacus), the commons (Orchomenus), occasionally the customs (Cnidus), to (on one occasion) the entire public and private property of the city plus the personal fortune of the treasurer (Arcesine).

Furthermore it is only in Rome that we find the first steps

towards development of something really resembling a true joint-stock company. Elsewhere in Antiquity we find superficial similarities, but in fact there were only merchant partnerships with shares which were only partially negotiable.

Capital not invested in rent-earning land or slaves was generally invested in trade, and the transit trade of Egypt was quite large. We have already mentioned in the introduction the extent of transit trade from the Indian Ocean in Roman times, and the 25 per cent *ad valorem* customs tax imposed at Leuce Come was meant to deflect transit trade from Arabia. We have record of a single shipment of goods paying a customs tax of nearly four talents, and according to Wilcken's calculations the Alexandrians paid half the taxes raised in Egypt. Yet even the large industries of Hellenistic Egypt were fundamentally the same as those of classical Greece (although of course there were certainly significant quantitative differences). For example: we are told that in Alexandria there were individuals who could field whole regiments with their own resources. Modern historians call them 'manufacturers', but in fact this story is clear proof that their wealth consisted of accumulations of slaves, similar to those that had existed *c.* 425 B.C., when Nicias the son of Niceratus possessed 1,000. These Alexandrian nabobs may also have possessed land, as an investment outlet for their capital earned in commerce, and recruited soldiers there too. They were certainly not 'manufacturers' in the modern sense.

As to the papyrus industry, it seems to have been dominated by Alexandrian papyrus merchants. How the workshops were organized and what was their economic function we do not know, for the subject has not yet been investigated. Workshops in general are known to have been rented out with necessary equipment. For example a document records that in Soknopaiu Nesos an oil press (*elaiourgiou*) was leased for 100 drachmae for seven months, the working season, and in fact we have many such transactions recorded with provision for compensation to cover the wear and tear of equipment. Let the student ask himself whether the lease of a modern factory would have provisions regarding term and limitations similar to those presented by the ancient documents; he will then see clearly the difference between ancient and modern conditions.

Another factor was that in Ptolemaic times most of this type of fixed capital was held by the monarchy or the temples. Private oil-presses are only found later, although other types of private workshops did exist. Only in the large cities (in Egypt limited to Alexandria) did businessmen have significant numbers of skilled work slaves. Indeed, evidence for many country towns and villages of Egypt indicates conclusively that slaves were relatively few – in 192 B.C., in one village slaves constituted only 7 per cent of those liable for labour services – and were mainly domestic slaves. This was primarily a consequence of the historical legacy of Egypt's social structure, as it took shape after the Middle Kingdom and the end of the wars of conquest of the eighteenth dynasty – in other words, after the supply of prisoners of war was cut off. The slave owners mentioned in the documents are mainly, though not entirely Greek (later Romans), and this is connected with the fact that evidently all economically rising bourgeois elements, in response to the social milieu, became Hellenized in names and speech, whereas conversely the declining elements tended to blend with the Egyptians in names and customs – a tendency which explains the obvious decline of the Hellenic element in Egypt during the time of economic regression under Roman and Byzantine rule.

But the most important factor in the situation was slave prices, which reflected the lack of supply. In the peace treaties signed in Greece in 304 and 194 B.C. the ransom for captured slaves was set at 500 *drachmai*, and in Roman times a female slave cost 2,500 *drachmai* (and prices were generally higher). The rearing and training of slaves for hire must have been a profitable business (see the passage from Appian quoted in the Introduction) and was found in Egypt as in Greece. One can see the high risk involved from the documents; for example, a contract with a woman for the rearing of a slave child specifies that if the child dies his place must be taken by the woman's own child. Relatively few slave women had children, and of those that did some had been made prostitutes and the others knew that their children could be taken away at any time, so that they often had as little personal interest in rearing their children as the woman mentioned in this contract. Throughout Antiquity, it should be noted, children remained to a large extent simply items of trade except where they were a valued possession for religious, military, or economic reasons, or where the law intervened for similar motives. This is true even though there undoubtedly exists evidence indicating instances of close family life among the petty bourgeoisie.

To sum up: production based upon slavery, especially large-scale production, played no role whatever in Hellenistic Egypt. Except perhaps in agriculture (see below) even debt bondage was not exploited, even though Hellenistic law continued to acknowledge seizure of a defaulting debtor's person (as Mitteis has demonstrated) with all its consequences, and in fact the evidence shows that this continued, especially in Egypt. Craft work was carried on by free men in small shops. Now and then a craftsmen hired one or more slaves from a slaveowner or else took on a slave as an apprentice for a fee, just as in ancient times.

It is true that there were large enterprises based on free labour – namely, those temple workshops which were discussed above. It is also certainly possible that occasionally others appeared. For example, we hear of a wool workshop in Upper Egypt in the Byzantine period which employed several hundred free workers paid entirely in kind. We must first ask, however, whether these 'workers' were not in fact small peasants engaged in cottage industry or even simply rendering labour service; such is often the true explanation in such cases.

Furthermore, we do not know to what extent unskilled workers really were free in the use of their labour-power, and in view of the decree of Ptolemy Philadelphus mentioned above it is doubtful whether they had much autonomy. Grenfell, commenting on a wage contract, takes it to indicate that the Ptolemaic administration had advanced social policies because the lessee of the oil press received one drachma and each worker two; but Grenfell is mistaken, for one-third of each worker's pay gives the entrepreneur quite a respectable return on his investment. The government did, it is true, seek to guarantee workers a traditional level of compensation, but this was in its own interest, for the aim was to prevent worker's strikes which were already frequent in Egypt and always had one single demand: 'Give us our bread' – and that meant, 'the daily bread' to which they were accustomed by long tradition.

In general, we need further studies to throw light on the technological and economic conditions which governed the use of free labour in Egypt. For the present we can say this: if, as noted in the Introduction, the capitalist concept of the employer seems to have developed in Egypt, we must understand this with emphasis on 'seems'. For example: the term 'work-giver' (*ergodotēs*) in the sources does not refer to what we call an employer, but rather to a customer who puts in an order; exceptionally the term refers to a building contractor who in fact often had a role – as today – resembling that of an employer. But in fact those who actually were employers and ran the largest enterprises – the public works – appear in the documents not as 'work-givers' (*ergodotoi*) but as 'work-takers (*ergolabontes*).

Further study of the papyrus sources should also indicate to what extent agriculture in the Ptolemaic period was characterized by large private concerns and whether such concerns mainly or entirely employed free labour under contract. (For the Roman period see the article 'Colonate'.) Hellenistic law had brought into Egypt the procedure allowing a mortgage-holder to distrain a debtor's goods personally, and had in particular introduced a legal warrant authorizing this, something which was as alien to the ancient Egyptian *sanch* documents as to the other theocratic legal systems. We do not, however, know how to interpret in quantitative terms the statement by Varro that debt bondsmen (*obaerati*) were used in Illyria, Asia (this was due to Rome's tax-farming system; see below), and Egypt. Incidentally, *obaerati* are not to be identified with the *coloni* of later times, as does P. M. Meyer. They are legally quite distinct.

Extant documents show harvest work being done by free workers on contract. One contract gives us an idea of the extent of a farm; it had 54 *arourai* in grain and an unstated area lying fallow. The workers were paid ⅚ *artaba* of threshed grain for each *aroura* harvested (including, evidently, threshing), and they were also given water and, on the last day, beer (for the harvest festival, so to speak). The owner himself had to collect the sheaves (using his own team and cart, of course). From the figures given we can estimate that the farm was probably about 25 hectares. Generally the extent of the larger farms (that is, individual units of production) was much smaller than that of larger estates, and in fact extant private leases are very often for sections of an estate. Really large plantations in private hands are found in some number, but this belongs to the Roman period when great accumulations were formed from imperial gifts and private purchases, and provincial officials regularly acquired vast properties (one case, and this in an imperial province, amounted to 7,000 *arourai*).

In general, however, the typical Egyptian working on the land continued to be the small peasant, especially the farmer leasing his land. Often the land was divided into very small plots; for example, a document (*Pap. Rainer* 1428) records the sale of four plots between ½ and 3½ *arourai* in area, lying in two village districts (neither the birthplace of the seller), and separated from other plots the owner had there. This division of property into small plots, and the even more frequent subdivision of farms, are phenomena – as Wessely's researches show – which are connected with the cultivation of a great variety of crops, and this too despite the pressure exerted by the state taxation system to grow wheat.

As to changes of crops or, rather, the use of the two- or three-field system along with horticulture, something was said above. Cattle holdings in this period seem to have been fairly large. The camel was now common, and because of its importance for public labour services and military transport (the camel and the donkey were the only animals suited for transport work) all owners of camels were registered. We find record of up to five camels in the possession of small and middle landowners, all carefully cadastered. Cattle, on the other hand, was generally not owned by small farmers.

As to social conditions in rural areas, we have at present no clear evidence regarding the distribution of land in the village districts (*kōmai*), nor do we know whether villages really held arable lands in common, as has been argued on the basis of a papyrus published by Barry. Documents do show that villages owned beasts of burden – perhaps because this was demanded of villages near the grain transport routes – and rented them out. In general here too memories of the ancient communal economy played a role among the lower classes of the rural population. Indeed not only among them; the propertied petty bourgeois classes were economically active mainly in groups: several would jointly give or take out a mortgage, and would often own houses in groups, each individual having one-tenth, one-thirtieth, and so forth of several houses. As a result we find that property was owned not only for use but also for rent. Groups were also involved in leasing (an old practice; see above), and this applies from tax farming to tenant farming. For example, an extant contract shows a state domain rented to a partnership; cf. *P. Amh.* II. 94, on which see U. Wilcken, *Archiv für Papyrusforschung* II (1902), pp. 131–2.

Partnerships were numerous because they served two economic functions: they collected capital, and they also provided security (in this resembling many institutions of the early Middle Ages), since they shared risks among several debtors or tenants, and also shared property ownerships among several creditors, lessors, or owners. For example, divided ownership of a house meant less damage for each owner if the house burned down.

Family groupings had tended to be mainly of the nuclear family type since pharaonic times, although often this was larger than the parent-and-children unit found today. Greek rule brought a change in this area, for the Hellenic institution of the family guardian was imposed on Egypt; this institution was derived from the militaristic *polis* and was foreign to the Near East. Otherwise both kinds of marriage continued to exist side by side: 'recorded', legitimate marriage (*eggraphos gamos*) and 'non-recorded', common-law marriage (*agraphos gamos*), discussed above. In legitimate marriage the partners were expected to live together and remain faithful to each other, their children had full inheritance rights (common-law children inherited after legitimate children), and the wife had (in fact or at least in theory) both dowry and jointure.

In general there were no laws against sexual relations by mutual consent. If a man slept with a girl, her family tried to get hold of him and beat him into promising to support her; that was what happened once to a saint! This changed in Christian times, however, for marriage contracts increasingly stipulated fidelity on the part of the husband as well as the wife.

Illegitimate children (*apatōres*) were in no way discriminated against socially or legally, as was the case in the Greek citizen *polis*, because of its 'guild' character (discussed above). Through Wessely's laborious researches we now have available directories for entire sections of Egyptian cities, and from these we see that in fact people of illegitimate birth were often quite prosperous. This was in the nature of things, since it was generally the woman of means who could indulge in free love, just as today it is only such who can take advantage of this freedom. Sibling marriage continued to be common, and served to prevent division of inheritances. A Berlin papyrus records one such marriage between siblings of 15 and 13. The Greek will was imported, but alongside this there continued to exist the native Egyptian marriage and inheritance contract, a legacy of polygamy.

From ancient times private land ownership had been entered on cadasters. Starting with the Roman period (not, it seems, the Ptolemaic), a record was also kept of all mortgages and it was revised every five years. It is indicative of conditions in both pharaonic and Ptolemaic Egypt that time and again scholars have argued (Maspero most recently, for the Ptolemaic period) that private property did not really exist in either. In fact this is wrong, as is sufficiently shown by the many extant documents recording the purchase or mortgaging of land.

Nevertheless, the great severity of Hellenistic mortgage law made the lot of the small property owner extremely difficult, for it allowed a creditor to distrain a defaulting debtor's goods personally; this was not softened until Roman times. Furthermore, in many districts most of the land – sometimes nearly all of it – was taken up by cleruch allotments, temple lands, and royal domains. In such districts the village (*kōmē*), which remained the basic local unit, was reduced to nothing except the old village common.

But the factor most responsible for Maspero reaching his mistaken conclusion was undoubtedly the type and high level of taxes levied. From ancient times private property in Egypt carried with it responsibility for the fulfilment of duties owed the state, and it was therefore different from domain land and cleruch land only in that its inheritance and sale was not subject to state control. Apart from these two matters, the economic situation of the small property owner was not much different from that of tenants on state land, for both had the same type of financial burdens and these burdens depended upon the improvements on the land and at times amounted to about two-thirds of what rent would have been. In general only privileged land, especially that held by Hellenized *katoikoi*, could be leased profitably.

On the other hand heavier burdens were imposed on those

who leased private land than on those who leased state land. Documents from the Ptolemaic and early Roman periods show that share-croppers paid between one-half and two-thirds of their harvests, while those paying fixed rent in kind gave 3 to 7½ *artabae* per *aroura*, which was three to seven and a half times the seed needed. Later documents show rents somewhat exceeding 1–9 *artabae*. State taxes amounted to as much as 6½ *artabae* per *aroura*. The properties involved in these leases ranged from 2 to 36½ *arourae* (0.56–10 hectares). Leases were for terms of one to four years, once for five; in this respect the tenant's position had improved since pharaonic times.

Besides share-cropping there were also leases calling for rents paid partly in money, partly in kind. During the Roman period money rents became more common, until the great economic retrogression of the third century A.D. Along with these changes went modifications in the general position of tenants, and these can be deduced to some extent from the type of lease used, as has been demonstrated by the valuable work of Waszynski. The pharaonic tradition was for one-year leases with obligations resting on the tenant alone, but in the Ptolemaic and early Roman periods the leases became longer; with this went the right of the tenant to make offers which then became binding without formal action if the owner accepted. Leases were concluded by the exchange of personally written statements that indicated the equal status of the two parties, as did the use of notarized contracts and mutual agreements (*homologiae*). But there also existed the 'unilateral agreement', issued by the lessor, and eventually, from the fourth century on, this form reflected the supremacy of the landowner; henceforth the tenant was again essentially subject to the latter.

This is most clearly seen in the form used in the Byzantine period for share-cropping; in effect it amounted to a contract for labour paid in kind, a contract which the landowner fixed at will. This reflects the fact that the lower classes lost the rather advantageous position which they had enjoyed in early Ptolemaic and again in early Roman times, a change which occurred, it should be noted, before the collapse of the third century A.D. From documents such as the Greek papyri in Berlin which Schubart has edited, the change can be dated roughly to the time of Marcus Aurelius.

Here it should be stressed that it is this change, rather than the physiological theories so popular today, that explains the decline of population in Egypt under the later Roman Empire. The millennial vitality of the fellahin hardly supports those physiological theories, to put it charitably, and in addition there is the fact that rents rose even as population declined. It is clear, therefore, that the decline of population was a process which is not to be explained by supply and demand nor by temporary economic depressions, but rather by the effects of the social structure of the Roman Empire.

Even though it is necessarily imprecise, this brief sketch of the administration and economy of the most 'rationalized' Hellenistic state indicates clearly that 'capitalism' in the modern sense existed there only to a very limited extent. Indeed, the state's fiscal system (especially its revenue policies) so restricted the profit-making opportunities of capital that one is entitled to speak of capitalism being stifled. The temples were no more centres of capitalism than were the monasteries of the Middle Ages; rather, they further reduced its opportunities for expansion. There existed a money economy, but its basis was petty bourgeois, small peasant, and small artisan. There was a wholesale trade in transit goods, although it was limited by substantial internal customs duties. But the most important factors were the state system of liturgies, the state monopolies, and state regulations. All in all, then, the economy was anything but modern, unless one wants to call the contemporary Constantinople of Abdul-Hamid modern.

In short, Hellenistic society is a perfect example of how mistaken it is to identify 'money economy' and 'capitalist economy'. Carthage in the days before any coinage existed, even the Rome which depended on crude pieces of copper (*aes rude*), were far more capitalist in structure than the national economy of the Ptolemies.

When we turn to the large Hellenistic areas in Asia we find that it is impossible to give as clear a picture as for Egypt. Even the sources for civil law are nearly all lost. It is true that Mitteis has conclusively demonstrated that the so-called Syro-Roman Law Code is not based on Near Eastern but rather on Hellenistic and Roman law, but the little information it gives for agrarian history and for understanding manorial conditions in Asia Minor will be discussed elsewhere with more advantage. In general, however, it can be said that the continuity of traditional Babylonian economic institutions was not broken either by the Seleucid or by the Sassanid Persian regimes. Some limitations were imposed by Parthian rule, for despite Hellenistic influences the Parthians were essentially barbarian, but in general the fundamental break only came with the advent of Islam.

The Seleucid Empire lacked the territorial unity and the disciplined administration which Ptolemaic Egypt possessed. It included areas of very contrasted economic character, and this was the cause of its decline. The fact that the attempt to impose Hellenism on Jerusalem failed is not in itself conclusive; even the Ptolemies never made a similar attack on the Egyptian priesthood. However, the fact that the priestly clan of Maccabees was able to wrest autonomy even in secular matters indicates that the disintegration of the Seleucid Empire was inevitable.

Then, the rule of the later Maccabees having become a purely secular tyranny, struggles arose between the Maccabees and the Sanhedrin, the council of elders controlled by the aristocratic priestly clans, the Sadducees. This in turn became a conflict between the rule of an aristocratic theocracy and the rule of a theology that regulated all life's activities and was taught by professionals, 'the separated ones' (*Pharisaioi*), and which gained the support of the petty bourgeoisie. The rural population was considered immoral by the Pharisees, and in fact country folk have at no time and in no place (with a single exception: the Donatists) supported Puritan doctrines.

But we cannot pursue these matters further.

Talmudic law, at least as it appears in the Mishna, is the code of a people which is in the process of becoming a commercial nation. Already it contains certain very characteristic statements directed against those defenders of ancient tradition who had effectively praised the security and dignity of agriculture. The constituent elements of Talmudic law need to be analysed, so that we could tell which really stem from ancient rabbinical tradition going back to the time of the theocracy or to the provincial conditions of Hellenistic and Roman times, and also which reflect influences from Mesopotamia. Furthermore Talmudic law needs to be studied to indicate which parts of it represent real practice and which simply reflect theological scholastics.

It is in fact clear that rabbinical scholastics could have a remarkably conservative influence on certain institutions, as in family law. For example, the form for refusing levirate marriage, the *chalitsa*, must date from the ancient clan state, and it has remained part of Jewish law until the present day. Also, the custom of giving a dowry, which arose in ancient Near Eastern law because daughters had no claim to inheritance, still exercises an influence on Jews making their way today as employees of commercial firms, for dowries give those who marry an early independence; this explains why Jewish clerks lack class feeling and solidarity, and also (in part) why their Christian fellow-workers are anti-Semitic.

But agrarian law is less likely to be shaped by purely theological considerations. Rabbinical speculations on the sabbath year, the 'poor man's corner', and the like were exercises in logic without practical effect. Other sections of the Talmud, however, undoubtedly grew out of the law actually prevalent in theocratic times and give us valuable information. For example: from the Mishna we can see that there were field slaves as well as house slaves, but the Mishna assumes that hired workers rather than slaves would be used on most small and medium-sized properties. These workers were protected in a manner typical of theocracies: after the code of laws there is an appendix giving principles which specify that they are not to work overtime, that they are to be paid promptly and fed properly, and that they should maintain their rights to a share in harvests. It is also stated that while no sacred law guarantees the right to strike nevertheless they should have the right 'to protest' – that is, to strike in the Egyptian manner. These provisions indicate the complete dependence of free workers, and also show, by their constant reference to the ancient traditions of the localities concerned, that social peace prevailed in the period in which these rules were formulated.

Leases are also discussed in the Talmud, to be more exact 'leases among neighbours', meaning among fellow-countrymen, men with whom one may not deal according to the law of foreigners or rulers. The tenant (*mekhabbel*) is either a share-cropper (*aris*) paying a half, a third, or a quarter of his crop, or else a contract tenant (*choker*) paying a fixed rent in kind or, evidently less often, in money. The tenant had by contract to weed and cultivate the land, and he could sow wheat instead of legumes but not the reverse. The latter provision recalls Egyptian conditions, and in fact grain was the principal crop in Palestine as well and its cultivation was encouraged because government policy aimed to keep the cost of food low.

In connection with share-cropping the Talmud also treats of the status of piece-workers hired to plant a field with trees. There is no mention of payment with land in return for its cultivation (*emphyteusis*); here again we see that the latter is distinctively Greek. In ancient Babylonian law, too, planting was handled in another manner, that of the joint partnership, evidently because there the most common task was to plant palm trees on land already under cultivation, whereas *emphyteusis* was used mainly for planting olive trees on new or waste land. Later Islam developed a casuist defence of the business practices allowed in planting the date palm; in Antiquity the plantation was a major centre of 'capitalist injustice'.

No limitations on the sale of land appear in the Talmud, nor is any distinction made in inheritance law between real estate and movables. The ancient limitations of the Law on the period for which land might be sold, and Jehovah's reminder that the land is His and should not be traded, are treated as no longer binding on the basis of a passage in *Jeremiah*. It is stated that a man should not sell his inherited land if he is not yet twenty, on the grounds that this would be displeasing to God and would rarely be propitious for the seller, a clear echo of the ideas of the clan state.

No legal form of trust for land similar to the Prussian *Fideikommiss* existed in Talmudic times. Land was conveyed either on payment in cash of the full price or by written contract or by official transfer of ownership, but the usual method was cash payment. If only part of the price was paid then only a corresponding part of the property was conveyed and the transaction was regarded as incomplete (*negotium claudicans*), thus avoiding money debts; this procedure reflected theocratic influences, as in Egypt. Otherwise the buyer was expressly allowed to pay the purchase price later as a credited purchase; this was done by arranging a fictitious exchange involving loan documents (like the German '*Mantelgriff*'). Land and slaves had no market value (a characteristic indication of the low importance of purchased slaves as a factor in the economy), so consequently the buyer could not make use of his right of liquidation (*ona'ah*), which the law guaranteed if an object bought on the market was found to have been overvalued by a sixth and so caused the buyer great loss (*laesis enormis*).

Land could be alienated for a specified period, and this seems to have been done as a way of giving usufruct instead of paying interest (*antichresis*). The Talmud mentions mortgages only in passing, and the term used – *iphothike* – shows its Hellenistic origin; it was in any case superfluous, since land and Canaanite slaves were legal collateral for all written, sealed, and witnessed contracts (*schetar chob*). As to the origin of this legal liability, compare Genoan documents from the early Middle Ages. Only land and slaves were legally liable as collateral; the rabbis explain this on the grounds that with other objects the fact of liability was not obvious to third parties, but the slave would say that he was mortgaged. There were, incidentally, no registers of land and mortgages.

Rabbinical law regarded the legal liability of land and slaves as applying from the moment a debt went into force; this must have been a serious limitation on dealing in land. One result of the fact that only land and field slaves were regarded as collateral was that an heir was not responsible for debts left unpaid so far as the inherited movables were concerned.

Debt law was unusually mild. For example, a debtor's food for a month was excluded from his liability, and also excluded were the clothes, bed, and bedding which he needed for a year, and all his tools. However, if debts were assumed on oath then all the debtor's goods were regarded as collateral. This innovation was presumably due to the onset of a commercial economy.

These regulations show the great influence of the old theocratic restrictions on trade, especially in debt law; so do the arguments against profit and interest (*ribbith*). Moreover the whole tenor of the Talmud shows more clearly than could the analysis of Hellenistic social structure one thing above all: that throughout the Hellenistic world of the Near East there did not exist a 'social problem' or a 'social movement' in any sense in which those words are used today, and that in fact nothing of the sort could have existed.

There were 'social problems' in Antiquity, which were subjectively felt as such, among them being: the political problems of the free citizens of the *polis*; any threat to the equality of *polis* citizens; and degradation in class status because of debts and loss of property. When the bureaucratic state and then the Empire invaded the sphere of civic freedoms and the *polis* citizen was transformed into a subject, then the worker demanded his accustomed 'daily bread' when he found it reduced and the tenant complained of his landlord's exactions, and all joined in complaining against the burdens imposed by taxes and publicans. But these were perceived as injustices directed against individuals, not as 'social problems' which could be solved only by restructuring society. That is why the injustices of the age did not call forth visions of a utopia in the future (like Plato's) or in the past (like Lycurgus'), as in the Greek *polis*, but instead reinforced the general political apathy which ever since has been a characteristic of subjects in the Near East.

In particular this applies to periods like the later Hellenistic Age, in the first period of the Roman Empire, when the economic situation of small farmers and petty bourgeois was in general more advantageous and more secure than ever before. There is less cause to speak of 'social problems' in that period than in any other time in world history. It is not only mistaken, it is absolute nonsense to maintain theories such as that Christianity was the result of 'social' conditions or was a product of ancient 'socialist' movements. It is enough to point out that, like every redemptive religion, Christianity held that worldly aims were dangerous and so was the wealth which made these aims attainable. It is also the height of folly to interpret the injunction 'Give unto Caesar what is Caesar's' as a commandment calling for a positive attitude towards the state; on the contrary, it is an expression of the most complete indifference to all politics, as has been rightly argued by Troeltsch (*Archiv für Sozialwissenschaft*, vol. 26).

These, then, were the two basic factors which made Christianity possible: the abandonment of the idea of a national and theocratic Jewish state, and the absence of any 'social problem' in the consciousness of its supporters (and in the consciousness of Antiquity). Indeed it was just because of the belief in the permanence of Roman rule until the end of time that men felt it was hopeless to strive for social reform and therefore rejected all class struggles; and this was the source from which flowed Christian love – purely ethical, charitable, and transcendental.

6

Roman Republic

(a) *The City-State*

It would be pointless here to examine Italic and, in particular, Etruscan prehistory, and it would also be beyond my competence. In Etruscan studies all Helbig's conclusions have been challenged by archaeologists, but no resolution of these differences is possible as long as the *c.* 8,000 extant Etruscan inscriptions remain undeciphered. Furthermore, it has been argued convincingly by Furtwangler, Modestoff, Skutsch, and others that the Etruscans came by sea from the eastern Mediterranean; but to an outsider this seems like saying that the Normans came from Sicily because documents show that they lived there, as documents show that the 'Turscha' known to the Egyptians lived in the eastern Mediterranean and fought sea battles there. The Greeks too were active as far as Corsica and even beyond.

Etruscan culture centred on the *polis*, and expanded swiftly inland from Tarquinia and Caere. This fits the general pattern we have met elsewhere, and was probably the result of commerce and Greek influence (the latter is not doubted by any scholar). However, other aspects of the problem touch on topics accessible only to specialists. The close similarity between Etruscan haruspices and their Babylonian counterparts, along with an old tradition among the Etruscans themselves, are the two strongest arguments for an East Mediterranean origin, while the two strongest arguments against it are the lack of any trace in the East of a related people or culture and also the fact that although the Etruscans from the first assumed the role of cultural intermediaries in Italy, they borrowed their script from the Greeks rather than from an Eastern people.

The Etruscan state was strictly aristocratic and theocratic, and the people were divided according to clan and descent. Certainly the Romans were much influenced by this, and they themselves believed that they had learned surveying from them. Etruscan influence may also lie behind the development of clientage, the authoritative position of Roman magistrates, perhaps also that of the family head (Etruscan society was metronymic). These influences would have been felt when Rome was a city ruled by Etruscan kings; note, too, that the name of Rome is now considered of Etruscan origin, as are the names of its old tribes: Tities, Ramnes, Luceres. But the extent of Etruscan influence is still as sharply disputed as ever. In any case the Etruscans did not keep pace with the Romans in developing into a hoplite *polis*, just as the Sabelli did not develop from a peasant state into a city-state, and as a result both peoples were subjected by Rome's disciplined hoplites.

I shall not attempt here to advance hypotheses about the regal period and the nature of the monarchy. Nor can I solve such problems as: whether the *celeres* (from Greek *kelēs*; horse) were the old royal bodyguard (the legend about the robbers who joined Romulus suggests other analogies); whether the position of the artisans (*fabri*) in the centuriate army (in which they voted with the first or – as others argue – the second property class) arose out of military liturgies owed by artisan clans who had been settled by the king, or was rather a result of the reorganization of the states on the basis of a hoplite army.

Little is known, too, about the early period of agricultural development in the free Roman *polis*. We can, however, see that the patrician clans were the only ones to have full political rights in the feudal city-state of early times, and that their position rested on the same economic basis as did that of the dominant clans in Greek cities: cattle and slave ownership, and a monopoly of non-local trade. Thus the pre-Servian and even more the Servian Wall (fourth century B.C.) included an area which bore no relation to the actual territory of Rome, and the disproportion is even more striking if one regards as Roman only the actual *ager Romanus*.

But Rome in its early period did not advance beyond the stage characterized by a deficitary balance of trade, at least not to any significant extent. Foreign merchants controlled the import of Greek, Phoenician, and Carthaginian goods, as well as the export of slaves and raw materials sent in exchange. Even when Rome was involved in an extensive Mediterranean trade it lacked for a long time a navy and also a gold and silver coinage. The feudal city-state dominated the open country, and in general it resembled similar Greek cities in its basic military and political institutions, the main difference being that at Rome hoplite discipline and − consequently − magistrates' powers were maintained with extraordinary rigour. But, as with most Greek communities, we know very little about the agrarian foundations of Roman society.

K. J. Neumann has advanced clever arguments to show that the entire Roman commons (*plebs*) up to the time of the Twelve Tables (457 B.C.) was composed of serfs similar to the hereditary serfs of modern times. This is in my opinion historically unlikely. In order to support his theory Neumann is forced to change the traditional chronology rather frequently, a practice which should be avoided by any scholar who wishes to publish an interpretation of archaic Roman history. Of course anyone who cares to follow the ingenious, destructive critical methods of Ettore Pais will find no problems too difficult to solve in Rome's early history, for he can date the beginning of the Roman people as an historical formation at *c.* 450–400 B.C., he can label the Twelve Tables as a forgery of the second century B.C., and he can situate the upper limit of the historical tradition at 300 B.C.

In what follows, however, an attempt will at least be made to reconstruct some of the major features of Roman society's development, while at the same time keeping as much as possible of the ancient tradtion. Furthermore this reconstruction is advanced as merely tentative, and the reader is urged to preserve a healthy scepticism.

(As to Pais, I do not consider myself entitled to pass judgment on his methods. It should be pointed out, however, that while there may be clan legends in the tradition as well as tendentious retrojections of agrarian struggles and class conflicts into early times, the instances in which similar conflicts recur, the *duplicazioni* which Pais often uses to question the authenticity of a passage, do not in themselves prove anything. Such recurrences actually happened; for example, the agrarian struggles of later

Greek history recapitulate those of earlier times though under somewhat different conditions. These recurrences arise from the essential character of Antiquity.)

If one accepts Pais' methods, then of course criticism of Neumann's theory would be pointless, but if one uses the opposite method and tries to keep as much of the tradition as possible – as Neumann ought to have done – then his theory cannot be accepted, because it cannot be reconciled with the position of the Roman commons (*plebs*) as one can reconstruct it by studying properly the Roman historical tradition.

(This does not, of course, mean that everything in Neumann's work is mistaken. For example: I cannot judge whether or not important changes in the political position of the hoplite army actually took place in 457 B.C. But I cannot accept his theory about 'the end of manorialism'. Nor is it demonstrable that the rural tribes kept the legal status acquired at their foundation; see below on Dionysius 4.14)

The Roman plebeians do not appear in the tradition as helots, but rather, I think, as simple peasants similar to the Greek *agroikoi*. Of course the dependent peasants (*clientes*) are to be distinguished from the *plebs*, and I do not dispute that they may have been a source of tribute paid to the ancient patrician clans, on which more later. As for the Roman aristocrat, it has long been known that he was lord of manors, as was every city aristocrat in Antiquity, but Neumann has added that he was also lord of the plebeians, and that he was not.

(Here it should be noted that even the concept of manorial lord – *Grundherr* – has been too widely used for Antiquity. It is more than doubtful that the Roman client was tied to the land in the sense that even the owner could not take it from him. If we take the Spartan helots (and similar cases of genuine serfs) we see that the owner could not sell them abroad, whereas in the period after the Twelve Tables a Roman owner who enslaved a defaulting debtor had to sell him abroad. Furthermore a Roman owner had to let an indentured debtor (*nexus*) work off his debt. Similarly children sold or rented by fathers (*personae in mancipio*) were in a position in Rome quite different from that which they held in very early times when (as in Babylon) they were an important source of workers for large landowners. This demonstrates sufficiently that one must be very cautious in using the concept

Grundherr for the Roman patricians, in particular the legal aspects of the concept.)

We must, therefore, hesitate to think of the Roman aristocrat as a lord, and we must certainly refuse to picture the Roman plebeian (i.e. commoner) as a peasant owing labour services and cultivating his master's land like a Prussian serf. Neumann of course does not suggest that, but if we accept his argument that the plebeians were clients, and if we remember that the Twelve Tables confirmed clientage (rather than ending it, as Neumann assumes), then we must think of the plebeians along with their equivalents the clients (for example, those of Atta Clausus, discussed below) as helots or serfs. But serfs do not train and equip themselves as hoplites, and it was as members of the hoplite army that the plebeians became more and more indispensable to the state's military system and gained corresponding privileges. Nor do serfs become indentured debtors [*Schuldknechte*]; it is, rather, the opposite transition which is normal. Yet the imposition of indentured servitude for debt was the typical lot of the poor plebeian. The hoplite army system must have been based on free commoners owning land and on moneyed plebeians, as Eduard Meyer pointed out. This system was older than the Republic according to tradition, and it was certainly older than the consulate.

Furthermore, the dominant position in rural areas enjoyed by a number of partrician clans was evidently due to political factors, these clans being in part former tribal royalty and castle owners. Note, too, that not all patrician clans had such positions in the countryside (as in Athens), but only a minority of sixteen. Nor was the Roman countryside, any more than in most Greek cities, taken up entirely by manors or large estates. Besides much other evidence to the contrary, there were in later times many remnants of the autonomy once enjoyed by rural communities, sufficient indication that an original and general serfdom of the plebs is most unlikely.

Some may feel that this argument is contradicted by the sharp quarrels over the right of intermarriage (*connubium*) between plebeians and patricians, but it should be remembered that Theognis too felt that it was disgraceful for a nobleman to marry a girl from the commons. Later, after the development of the clan (*gens*), it was in the interest of clan members – in order to keep their properties intact – to marry their daughters with rights of inheritance to men of their own order. Indeed, according to one line of tradition, intermarriage between plebeians and patricians was not illegal until the Decemvirs so decreed. It is in fact probable that limitations on marriage developed late in Rome as in Athens during the democratic period, in both cases the economic reasons just mentioned being the cause. This seems the more probable if one remembers that everywhere the most ancient laws gave the father absolute discretion in determining the legitimacy of his children, whether born of wife, concubine, or slave. One finds this in ancient Greek law. The principle of equality of status among a man's children undoubtedly developed in the course of time at Rome, as the documents prove it did in Greece. It was the corporate cohesiveness of the urban citizenries of Greece and Italy, something which did not exist in the Near East, which led the *polis* to promote monogamy.

Above all, however, I must insist that the problem of serfdom at Rome ought to be studied without dragging in the circumstances and conditions connected with the nineteenth-century emancipation of serfs in Prussia. We are all familiar with this procedure from from the justly famous book by G. F. Knapp, a work which has had an unfortunate influence on Neumann and on Friedrich Cauer and Swoboda as well (just as Meitzen's categories were mistakenly used by me as general truths). The Roman Campagna is an area with irrigation works dating back to prehistoric times (the modern meaning of *rivalis* arose from the frequent quarrels involving water rights), with numerous cities from early Antiquity. Consequently there can be no question of making analogies between the Campagna and East Germany, an area shaped by manorial grain production for export, and in fact the way in which manor lands were divided among the peasants is unlikely to have parallels in Antiquity for historical as well as technological reasons.

It is of course probable that in primitive Rome, as in Greece and the Near East, the community held land in common and the peasants acted together to exercise sovereign authority over members' lands (as in Greek *poleis* in historical times). This was certainly the case, reasoning from analogy, where the group saw itself as a military community. In such a polity it was necessary to reach communal decisions regarding members' sons, either to assign land or else make some other provision. If a son did not emigrate to conquer land for himself, then his father asked the clan council of the city-state to assign him land; otherwise he joined the landless masses (*proletarii*; from *proles*, 'offspring').

We cannot know how these matters were first handled in the rural districts (*pagi*), but certainly new divisions of the land could and did occur. It is also probable that the ancient princely houses of the tribes, later transformed into aristocratic clans, used their power to intervene in the disposition of land among the peasants while at the same time withdrawing their own lands from community control, as occurred in the Greek phratries. This would explain the passage in Pliny the Elder (*Natural History* 19.19.50 Loeb) in which he says that in the Twelve Tables the term *villa* – traditionally used for an aristocrat's estate – was replaced by *hortus* (fenced garden) and *heredium* (hereditable land), indicating that all *villa* land became fenced and inheritable. The removal of land from control of agricultural communities and the transformation of all allotments into *hortus* land subject to private ownership (*dominium*) – that may well have been the historical significance of the reform of Rome's legal system by the Twelve Tables so far as agricultural conditions are concerned. Yet all these matters are entirely different in character from those connected with the manors worked by serfs in mediaeval and modern times.

Furthermore, we must distinguish carefully between clientage and serfdom – the bondage, that is, which appears in Rome as the result of indebtedness secured by personal liability (*nexum*). Clientage arose in Rome, as in Israel and elsewhere, when a person without property put himself under the protection of a prince or a landed fellow-citizen, as will be explained later. It is quite true that any citizen of low status not acquainted with the law – in other words, any peasant – might find himself obliged to seek the help of 'gift consuming' dignitaries in a legal matter; see Hesiod's remarks on this. But such recourse did not make a man a serf; on the contrary, the free clientage of the later Roman

Empire probably developed out of this, and in fact the voluntary patron–client relationship existed at all times.

Thus we see that in all our sources there is a sharp contrast between clients and plebeians, so much so that, for example, Oberziner regards the *plebs* as a conquered, non-Italic people and the clients as an Italic people that had immigrated with the aristocracy. Oberziner's theory is attractive, and apparent support for it is afforded by certain phenomena such as the absence of legal marriage (*connubium*) between clients and plebeians, the two methods of burial attested by the Twelve Tables, and so on. Other sources, however, seem to indicate the equivalence of clients and commoners, namely those passages in a few late texts which appear to assert that in early times all commoners were divided among the clan chiefs (*patres*) as clients – that is, much like the helots in Sparta or the serfs (*oikees*) in Crete.

But in fact it is exactly these passages which prove that the texts are obviously projections into the past of later theories. Certainly it is clear that if the peasants were treated as clients of the state (like Sparta's helots), then they could never be used for private farming operations; the Spartans were rent-receivers [*Rentner*], not landlords [*Gutsherren*]. Even in these tendentious texts, patronage is presented as an institution designed to protect citizens of lower rank who were at a disadvantage, it is implied in legal proceedings. In one of these sources it is even stated explicitly that the choice of a patron was free; cf. Th. Mommsen, *Römisches Staatsrecht*, vol. 3, 1 (Leipzig, 1887), p. 63, n. 4.

To sum up, then: from the evidence of the sources and also on the basis of what the facts indicate as probable, one can say that while the Twelve Tables and the legislation which followed reflected a victory of the peasants over the aristocratic clans, it did not mark in agrarian life the dissolution of a 'lord–peasant' [i.e. patron–client] relationship, but rather the elimination of the ancient local communal groupings for individual settlements in *villae* which later became dominant. The significance of this change is discussed below.

The village, which later became completely foreign to the Roman administrative system, had from earliest times been the unit of human settlement. Some have maintained that village settlement was not everywhere the original form, and that in contrast to Germans and Greeks, the Italic peoples originally settled in separate farm units. There is also an old formula still used by many archaeologists, that the Germanic peoples settled on farms while the Mediterranean peoples settled in villages; but this comes from complete ignorance of German settlement and from a misunderstanding of a rhetorical expression in Tacitus.

The idea that the individual farm (*villa*) stood at the beginning of Italic and, especially, Roman development, a thesis which even Schulten supports, is not sustained by any text or probability, and it is contradicted by Greek analogies, by the conditions of the other Italic peoples, and by the patterns of prehistoric settlement. The division of the land into separate units (*fundi*) comes late in Rome, and the fact that the Roman surveyors term these units 'contiguous occupied properties' (*continuae possessiones*) indicates clearly that they were formed when the old system of land use gave way to individual settlements. The *villa* derives from the feudal castle lord, not the peasant.

Schulten's valuable monograph has demonstrated how the power to make allotments (*assignatio*) was used to abolish the old rural communities and villages root and branch. Greek city-states such as Athens were able to use the rural districts (*dēmoi*) as units of local administration, but Roman practice avoided this completely. When allotments were made the ancient rural units (*pagi*) were ignored and sometimes even cut across; we see this in the field systems of Piacenza and Velia as described on the alimentary registers.

Confusion has arisen from the fact that for administrative purposes *vicus* was used for a city ward while *pagus* was used for a unit of a city's rural area to which specific burdens (*munera*) were assigned. The sources also indicate that in later Roman law both *vicus* and *pagus* counted as legal bodies, and had the right to own property, reach autonomous decisions regarding their own affairs, and institute legal proceedings; the *pagus* was also a territorial corporation. The *vicus* was always a compact settlement, and as such in the pre-urban period it was either the centre of a *pagus* or one of several villages in a *pagus*, as occurs in all ancient settlements. Festus calls the *vicus* the place where the community's market was held.

Originally, however, the *pagus* had a role similar to that of the

Greek *kōmē*; such, at least, seems to me the most probable view. All our difficulties in interpreting the sources spring from the fundamental contrast between 'city' in the Roman sense and village. Schulten's monograph reveals this contrast. It was the later field system which caused this contrast, for it was the very opposite of a village system.

From this it follows that the *pagus* had no function in historical times in registering the ownership of private property, as Schulten justly maintains against Mommsen. In particular its main function, the purification of the district (*lustratio pagi*), was a purely religious ceremony designed to ward off evil and had nothing to do with ownership. Similarly the power to issue ordinances possessed by the *pagus* in later times was, so far as is known, concerned entirely with religious matters. For example, the ordinance on women's hair style issued by a *pagus*, as Pliny records, is expressly motivated by religious considerations.

Of course it is also true that the limitation of the *pagus* to matters of this sort not only sprang from Roman reluctance to erase ancient cults but also preserved rudiments of an older social system in which the *pagus* counted for more. One also sees this in the fact that sources show *pagi* owning public carts, and it is quite probable that they originally had the market monopoly within their districts.

The pasture land of the ancient village survived to some slight extent in the later common land (*ager compascuus*). The right to graze cattle on it was an ancient law (*ius*) says Cicero, an individual right of each member of the community. Alongside this there was the public land (*ager publicus*); later this was land that had been conquered, but in early times it was evidently the undistributed wasteland (this has been doubted, but for no good reason). As in the primitive period of the Germanic peoples, every member of the tribe had the right to clear a share of this common land and he kept possession of this 'occupied land' (*ager occupatorius*) as long as he kept it cultivated. This ancient right of occupation was later extended by the hoplite state to cover conquered land, even though it might already be cultivated and fruitful, in so far as this conquered land was not set aside for private allotments or financial exploitation through leasing. The fact that a regulated form of land development was established, similar to that used in the United States when the Indian lands were made available to settlement, and also the fact that a certain tax on crops was levied as compensation for the state, does not alter the reality that this represented an extension of 'squatter's rights' over an enormous area which had been conquered. The crucial element in the matter was the 'occupation' of the land, as the terminology used reveals; the legal regulation of the process was secondary.

We know very little about the particulars of life in those settlements of long ago, when the peasants lived entirely from the fruits of their labours. Very likely there was no land entirely inheritable and entirely alienable as in later times, but there were probably some lands tied to families here as elsewhere; we can be sure that some patrician families had these rights, and they probably were also held, in weaker form, by peasants too. There is, however, no secure evidence on these matters.

In the legal procedure which was used to declare a person unfit to manage his affairs there is a reference to dissipating one's ancestral estate (*bona paterna avitaque*). This reflects the disapproval felt towards selling one's inherited land, a trait found in all legal systems shaped by militaristic considerations; it is, however, not a sure proof that originally there was a legal distinction between inherited and purchased land with respect to alienability. Probably developments at Rome were not fundamentally different from those in Greece, and in any case it is certain that in Rome as in Greece there existed landed property both hereditable and transferable at the dawn of recorded history. The legend that Romulus gave each citizen a *heredium* of 2 *iugera* as their only hereditable (note: not alienable) property is no proof against this, for it is clear that this was not the only land in peasant ownership.

On the other hand one cannot accept the idea that this land was cultivated by labourers for daily wages, as Eduard Meyer argued. The *heredium* was, rather, a garden plot (*hortus*), hereditable land set aside for the cultivation of a single small family, the sale of which outside the family was restricted for political reasons. As to its origin, there are three possibilities. The first is that when a city was founded by union of villages (*synoikismos*) or by executive action of a city government, the plebeian living in the city and not part of a clan (*gens*), but nevertheless valued as an artisan or merchant, was granted a garden and rights to the city commons but not a farm. Such grants were made in many new German towns of the Middle Ages. We can also imagine that grants of this kind were made by the Romans when citizen colonies were founded in early times. These colonies (*coloniae maritimae*) were not established to relieve agrarian unrest, but rather to settle and garrison the coast so as to maintain Rome's monopoly of trade, and their settlers had to remain there very much as did the Athenian settlers sent out to Salamis by Solon.

Now it is precisely in a colony of this sort, Anxur, that we find a securely attested example of 2 *iugera* per colonist (*bina iugera*) allotments, along with which each colonist naturally was entitled to use the common pasture. That the colonist received additional grants, as I once assumed, now seems to me unlikely in view of conditions in the Hellenistic Near East. Furthermore, any conception of the settler having a share in some sort of land community (*Flurgemeinschaft*) of the Germanic type must, in my opinion, be rejected entirely in so far as Rome and the whole of Antiquity are concerned. The *bina iugera* would then be the allotment of all those free plebeians accepted into the newly created city community.

There is a second possible explanation of the *heredium*, which can be combined with the first: that it was the allotment given to an infantryman, or, more precisely, the accounting unit used in making such allotments. At the end of the Second Punic War, the veterans of the Spanish and African campaigns were promised as many times 2 *iugera* as the number of years of service to their credit. (Uneven numbers occur in accounts of land allotments reported by the annalistic tradition, but the name alone of *centuria* for 100 × 2 *iugera* indicates clearly that the normal unit was 2 *iugera*.)

There is still a third possibility: that full citizens sent out in early times to occupy a subjected area were given allotments quite different from 2 *iugera* units. This is supported by the facts concerning Antium: after its conquest the hostile inhabitants were reduced to helot status, subordinate to the Roman colonists. In this case, then, 2 *iugera* was merely the urban plot assigned to each of the Roman colonists, who (like the Athenians on Mytilene) were concentrated in the city. These Roman colonists were, of course, not artisans or merchants (as in our first hypothesis) but rather warriors, and their role was to be city-dwelling landlords, not peasants.

Furthermore, what of the land rights of the peasant families living in the country, as opposed to the city-dwellers, whether patrician or plebeian? We know nothing about them, nor do we know to what feudal privileges they were subjected. The same is true for Rome itself.

In historical times the citizenry of Rome was divided into tribes (*tribus*) and federations of clans (*curiae*), just as in Greece there were tribes (*phylai*) and brotherhoods (*phratriai*). The clan (*gens*) here too was found only among the aristocracy (a long-debated point), and here too there was nothing 'primitive' about it. Rather it arose out of social differentiation, the process in which aristocrats came to possess cattle, precious metals, land, and slaves, and on the basis of this wealth developed a life-style characterized by knightly manners and military training. There can be no doubt that here too clans were formed by accumulating property, stressing kinship, and the associated phenomena, and here too they developed first among the families of the ancient tribal chiefs, which had become castle lords as in Greece.

Indeed, it was the unification in a single urban community of these castle lords which constituted the political achievement of archaic Rome. Some families entered the community voluntarily; the most famous example was the clan of Atta Clausus, which was incorporated into the clan federation as the *gens Claudia* and received a stretch of territory as a land allotment for Atta and his clients. Other groups entered under compulsion after their castles had been levelled.

This development explains why the 16 ancient rural tribes each had the name of a clan. But of course that cannot be taken to prove that all or most of the land involved was held by the 16 clans, for then the great majority of patrician clans would have been landless; nor does it mean that originally all free men belonged to a clan. In fact Roman tradition itself indicates that land outside the city gates remained for a long time divided into *pagi*, the ancient unit, until is was assigned later to rural tribal districts (*tribus rusticae*).

We can assume that the rural peasantry was just as powerless politically under clan domination as was the peasantry in Greece when the aristocratic *poleis* flourished. In Rome too – indeed, more strictly than in many Greek states – the aristocratic clan possessed lands in the country but lived in the city. The soldiers of Rome's large armies in the period of conquests were peasants, but always the officers were of urban origin.

As in Greece, too, the aristocratic clans nearly always had cults that were different from those of the commoners; this was first emphasized by Eduard Meyer. Hence it follows that the clan cults were private, and indeed the clan was essentially an institution which functioned parallel to the state rather than as part of it. On the other hand the cults of the clan federations (*curiae*) were public cults (*sacra publica*), and in fact the *curia* was an officially acknowledged part of the citizenry.

Even in Antiquity the *curia* was generally considered equivalent to the phratry, but modern scholars are as perplexed about the origins of the one as the other. However it is attested for historical times that the *curiae* supervised the execution of wills and the adoption of sons, which means that they controlled entry into the community of warriors and – consequently – also the right to own landed property. The only other thing we know about the *curiae* is that their ratification was essential for the transfer of military power when supreme magistrates were elected. This makes it probable that in the Roman military system the *curiae* were the local recruitment authorities. In this respect, then, they resemble the phratries, but in others the Greek tribes (*phylai*).

For example, unlike the Greek phratries the *curiae* had no corporative status and therefore no validity in the courts; they were purely sacred and administrative entities. But even apart from that, those who consider the Greek phratries to be of primitive origin would never compare the ancient, original phratries with the Roman *curiae*, but would instead compare the later artificial phratries which arose out of ulterior amalgamations. For the *curiae* were essentially institutions connected with the city-state; for example, they convened in the *comitium* of the forum, whereas the tribes did not. *Curiae* are found in all the Latin cities, but it is doubtful whether they existed in the citizen colonies (*coloniae civium Romanorum*).

The three ancient tribes with 10 *curiae* each and the clans (*gentes*) attached as subdivisions were, of course. institutions established to facilitate the allocation of state functions. Perhaps they assumed this schematic form in the period of patrician–plebeian rule, when the entire citizen body was organized in *curiae* and artificial clans. If we accept the argument that the *curiae* were each assigned separate and defined common lands in historical times, it remains true that we do not know to what degree this localization was the result of an original tribal division or – more probably – of a later reallocation of land among the *curiae*; or this localization may have taken place only in the newly founded Latin colonies, just as similar changes occurred in tribes of the Greek colonies.

Roman political practice always differed from the Greek in the status accorded the state's constituent elements, and this is particularly apparent in family law. In Athens and other Greek *poleis* a legitimate son's military status and his legal standing were inextricably connected; at Rome they were completely separate. The Roman citizen as soldier was subject to the magistrate's authority, as son he was subject to his father's authority so long as the father was alive. The state's authority ceased at the house's threshold, and the head of the house's absolute authority (*dominium*) over his women, children, slaves, and cattle (*familia pecuniaque*: the relation between *familia* and *pecunia* cannot be considered here; cf. L. Mitteis, *Römisches Privatrecht* [Leipzig, 1908], pp. 81–4) was the origin of the abstract concept of ownership. There can be no reasonable doubt that the extreme patriarchal authority of Roman family law developed out of the organization of the *gens*. Similarly the position of the *pater* ('father'), the clan head in the ancient political structure as preserved by tradition, is paralleled by the position of the *pater familias* ('father of the family'). Nor can we doubt that this patriarchal authority originally served to maintain single ownership of family property. In other words the extended family, organized on a strictly authoritarian basis, was in Roman law assumed to be the normal form.

There remains the problem of how the position of clan chief was transmitted according to public law and with respect to the clients. Was it governed by inheritance or by vote? Lack of evidence precludes any answer, but it is relevant to point out

that the division of an extended family, which in the law of historical times followed the death of a *pater familias*, most assur-
edly would not have been ordained by original clan law; instead
it would have provided for the choice of a new clan chief in place
of the old. The discrepancies exhibited by the law governing inheritance of patronage as opposed to regular inheritance law
seem unreliable as evidence, although in fact they do go back to
the ancient regime of the autarchic clan.

This strictly authoritarian organization of the family is a factor
from which arose certain feudal elements in the Roman political
system, and as long as the Roman state existed these elements
shaped its character to a great extent.

Rome's social structure was distinguished in particular by one
element: fedual clientage. In the earliest stages of Roman history
known to us, as well as in the latest, clientage appears in unusually developed form. It was by no means absent in the Greek
city-states, but it began to decline markedly there even in early
times and lost all importance in the democracies. The influence
of clientage on Roman family law can be seen from the fact that
an allotment of land to a client is in ancient law equated with
one to a legitimate son (*filius familias*). The patriarchal authority
of the clan chief was the source of the Roman laws governing
clientage, and it is essential to discuss this institution further here
since it has led to so many misconceptions about ancient society.

Everywhere in Antiquity, and of course not only in Antiquity,
the original state of affairs was that those who had no property
had no rights. Property here means a share in a community's
common lands.

Thus in Egypt the pharaoh complains about the 'man without
a residence', who put his belongings on a mule and went from
landowner to landowner in order to get the most for his labour.
In ancient Israel the landless man was the archetype of the metic,
in Greece he belonged to the class of bondsmen (*thētes*) and
dependants (*pelatai*), and in the Rome of the clan state he put
himself by appeal (*applicatio*) under the protection of a wealthy
clan chief (*pater*) ready to accept him or else appealed to the
king for protection (as is reported for the regal period). When the
process was completed by the formal acceptance (*susceptio*) of

the patron, a relationship was established which, like the *amnach* of ancient Egypt, differed from slavery on the one hand and vassalage on the other in this: the reciprocal duties of patron and client were regulated by a traditional, rather rigid code of rules, but this code had a religious sanction and was therefore not included in the civic and secular law of the city-state. Nevertheless, because it was of such great importance this code could not be simply ignored.

Thus the Twelve Tables curse the patron who is not true to his obligations to his client (*si clienti fraudem fecerit*), just as the son who strikes his father is cursed. In both instances the case was not within the competence of a state court. As late as the laws against extortion, enacted in the period of democracy and world empire, attention was paid to the question of whether there existed between two persons the patron–client relationship (*in fide esse*), and even in the *Digest* the slave laws use the expression 'to be under the protection of his master' (*in fide domini esse*) – though of course by then slavery was crumbling and the expression was used wrongly, without any direct bearing on ancient clientage. The concept of 'honour' (*fides*) governed the relationship between patron and client, just as in mediaeval times, but in mediaeval Europe (and Japan) it is the *fides* of vassals which is mainly praised, ethically valued, and clearly defined by feudal law, for the vassal was a self-reliant knight or even prince who equipped himself and was in fact not dependent on his lord, and so he was always subject to the temptation to break away from his obligations. In ancient Rome, on the contrary, stress was laid mainly on the *fides* of the lord, for in historical times the Roman client was like the holder of a bureaucratic or service benefice under the Mesopotamian kings, or like the warrior (*machimos*) of the pharaohs and Ptolemies, or even the *colonus* of the Later Empire – in short, a man of low status, a vassal subject to plebeian law so to speak, who was nothing without his lord and certainly could do nothing against him.

There is extant a law from the regal period (*lex regia*) which stresses mutual *fides*. This may indicate that in early times there existed a more elevated form of vassalage, similar to that of mediaeval Europe, and that the position of the client was depressed later in the hoplite state; but that problem cannot be discussed here. In historical times the client owed his patron respect (originally it was 'obedience'), attendance in war, and economic aid for special expenses; the latter included dowries for daughters, public liturgies (*munera*), and ransoms from imprisonment. The need to raise a ransom was an important matter in Antiquity; it figures in Hammurabi's Code as it concerned vassals, and at Athens a special procedure for collecting ransoms through subscriptions (*eranoi*) remained in use. The client for his part had a claim on his patron for (1) aid in economic emergencies and (2) protection, in particular protection against court proceedings, for as long as the law classified him as a metic (in other words, a foreigner), he was legally unable to defend himself in court, and indeed in later times he was in actual fact powerless to do this anyway.

This explains why even in the law of historical times every sort of legal proceeding between patron and client is excluded, because of the feudal and honour-bound relationship existing between them, and this extended even to matters involving penal action. Originally, of course, any sort of complaint was excluded. Similarly neither patron nor client could appear as a witness for the other in court. The feudal tie between patron and client is particularly evident in the fact that a client's estate was inherited originally, it seems, by the patron or his *gens*, and also in a connected phenomenon, the prohibition against a client's female dependent marrying outside the circle of clients of the patron's *gens*.

Clients could be of advantage to the patron in various ways: (1) The client might be a source of income, for he paid contributions, escheat fines, and marriage consent fees. In later times it was considered improper to exploit a client as a source of income, but of course we cannot be sure that was always so, and considering the fact that clientage changed its nature completely in the course of time the reverse is probably true. (2) The client could be a source of labour services on his patron's manor, but here again and for the same reasons one cannot be sure whether this was originally so. Nor can one make use of analogies here with the freedmen clients of later times, for this institution – so fruitful for later developments – did not make the duty of protection incumbent on the patron, and that was the crucial element in ancient clientage. This question is connected with another – the significance of clientage for agrarian developments.

It has been argued, and it is very likely correct, that the institution of *precarium* arose out of the law of clientage; or, to put it more precisely, *precarium* was the concept in civil law which covered leasing according to the laws of clientage. 'Property held by grace' was involved, that is, property held on lease but without any contract which a civil court would acknowledge; the tenant was protected by the law against any third party, but his landlord could turn him out at any time. That is a characteristic way of solving the problem of the relation between feudal law and civil law, even to the provision which protects the *precarium*-holder against third parties, something the *colonus* of later times did not have in civil law (see below). So characteristic is it, in fact, that we can be sure, though no source attests it, that the *patres* (the chiefs of the clans of the city aristocracy) were so called because they were accustomed to assign (*attribuere* is the technical term of feudal law) land to men without property (*tenuiores*). We see this in the legend of the Claudii, the historical core of which need not concern us here; Atta Clausus is presented either as a tribal chief or – what is more likely – as lord of a castle in the Sabine country who voluntarily came to Rome with his people 'in the sixth year after the kings were expelled' and joined the community. (It should be noted, incidentally, that his Sabine home, Regillum, has never been identified, indicating no doubt that it was a lord's castle, not a *polis*.) When he came to Rome with his clients – the legend exaggerates their number to a ridiculous degree; one need only see the country round the Tiber to realize this – he received a burial place on the Capitoline and a large expanse of land; of this he kept, we are told, 25 *iugera* for himself and gave each client 2 *iugera*.

Now 2 *iugera* never and nowhere sufficed to support a family, especially in a natural economy. This land would have been enough only for the nourishment of one man. In order to make sense out of the account, therefore, one must assume that the land was given for use as house gardens, and that in addition the client families rendered labour service, cultivating the 25 *iugera* of the Claudian clan's estate (*fundus*) in return for food. Who can maintain that an arrangement of this sort was impossible? If one turns to the origin of Germanic labour services – voluntary assistance given for ethical reasons to neighbours in times of serious need such as harvests – then it will seem very likely indeed that clients were expected to give help in emergencies.

Nothing of course can be deduced from the Claudian legend, in particular from later versions, about the size and use of this earliest estate of the Claudians. Furthermore any idea of an estate run for profit on the regular work of clients is to be rejected, for it is unlikely that the patron's relation to his client was shaped mainly by such economic exploitation. Rather, landowners used purchased children and slaves (*mancipia*) and indentured debtors (*nexi*) as labourers; these groups were, of course, quite separate from the clients. It is somewhat more likely that if indeed clients had some form of permanent economic duty towards the patron it took the form of tribute payments. From a remark in Plutarch we can deduce that a Lycurgan law established reciprocal obligations between Spartan and helot, and comparisons can also be made with the 'serfs' in other Greek states; the *oikees* of Crete seem, as one might expect, to have resembled Roman clients in their position. The Spartan as well as the Cretan serf paid traditional and fixed tributes (the helot paid one-half his harvest) and along with this also rendered purely personal services, and yet they were not an economically exploited labour force on land worked for profit. Yet one must not forget that Rome's social structure was from the first entirely different from Sparta's. Thus the aristocratic *gens* at Rome did not have any institutions similar to the Spartanism which rested entirely on education.

In ancient times the Roman client was equated with the Athenian dependent (*pelatēs*), and rightly so (though the present tendency to equate the Athenian dependent with the Athenian share-cropper – *hektēmorios* – must be rejected). The dependent was a man without land, therefore a metic in need of protection such as could be afforded by a landowner. But, despite the similarities, the Roman client's position differed in that more emphasis was placed on the non-economic obligations owed his patron, especially the duty to accompany him to war in the days of single combat between knights of the Homeric type. Clients therefore had a position somewhere between retainers and helots. We can compare the captain (*senior*) in the Carolingian army, who advanced at the head of his men, and the Spartan or indeed any Greek hoplite, who was served by helots or slaves. Those are sharp extremes, and in the middle would be the squire [*Knappe*] of a mediaeval knight. The Roman client of early days seems to have fulfilled a military function very similar to that of the squire; at least that is the somewhat vague impression which one receives. Certainly the client was closer to the squire in status than to the Homeric charioteer, who was a true comrade of his lord.

As long as military tactics centred on single combat between knights, the Roman patrician advanced to battle at the head of his clients, and so did the Etruscan and Sabine; the highest honour was to have defeated an enemy commander in single combat and win his armour (*spolia opima*). Not only that; on occasion a clan (*gens*) even conducted hostilities on its own, as when the Fabii with their clients mobilized and marched on Veii.

The reason why the Roman client was entirely dependent as compared to the mediaeval vassal is that he was equipped by his patron, just as the mediaeval squire was equipped by his knight. This relationship continued to exist as late as the Gracchan period, at least as far as commanders were concerned; for example, Scipio offered his clients for the campaign against Numantia (134 B.C.). In the period of the civil wars (*c.* 50–27 B.C.) the *coloni* played a similar role.

However, when warfare came to depend upon the *classis*, the hoplite army, then clientage lost its military importance. At the same time it also lost its economic importance because of the increased use of purchased slaves and the letting of small plots on written lease. Then free clientage grew in political importance.

Free clientage may have existed from the first alongside the other, serf-like form. It was not feudal in character, but rather derived its forms from the ancient clientage and undoubtedly emerged because of the need to have the protection of influential men in courts. Nor was it limited to patricians or men who freed their slaves. At all times there were examples of families in comfortable circumstances who attached themselves to clans of the office aristocracy (*nobiles*), whether patrician or plebeian; they did this not merely to gain rights to the table of a wealthy man, but also to gain the benefit of his support in and out of court. Since the relationship was hereditary the families maintained it even when they became wealthy, and this was ended only when and if a member gained a curule magistracy, since that counted as a reason for ending a clientage. In the second and first centuries B.C. the position of clientage did not cast discredit on the client. This was partly due to the fact that as Rome became a major power foreign aristocrats, princes, and allied communities entered into relationships with Roman aristocratic families to gain protection in court, and this relationship took the form of clientage.

At the same time a new economic form of clientage was developed on the basis of the relationship between manumitted slaves and their patrons. We see this most clearly in the senatorial edict on Fecenia Hispala, which granted her (1) the right to wear the dress of a Roman matron, (2) the right to marry outside the clan of her patron (*gentis enuptio*), (3) the right to marry a free man without injury to his status. Contrary to the clientage of free persons, aristocratic feeling did not frown on the use of this new form of clientage for economic profit, and as we know it was so used by many.

There were then various types of personal dependence: the free clientage of foreigners and natives, the clientage of freedmen, and finally slavery. Together they formed in the Later Republic the basis for the special position held by the Roman aristocracy of office, a position which has no parallel in history. The position of the Greek aristocracy was not comparable, because politics was on a smaller scale and it was more dependent upon the citizenry and its good will; consider the examples of Lysander and Alcibiades. Even English aristocrats in the eighteenth century could not equal Roman aristocrats in power, although their position was structurally similar since it was based upon the high office of peer. For English law and custom never acknowledged as official institutions the completely personal patronage exercised by families over entire states. For example, the Claudian family was voluntarily accepted as patron by Sparta and Pergamum, and the patronage of victorious generals was imposed upon subjected cities and peoples.

It was because of these relationships of personal dependence that Roman politics always remained semi-feudal in character, for the foundations of the power of the great aristocratic clans could not be shaken by the 'democratic' decisions of the popular assemblies. The situation created by the political importance of clientage for the dominant position of the aristocracy in the period of the great class struggles of the second and first centuries

B.C. has been projected by the tradition back to the early period of Rome and to the struggle between patricians and plebeians. This resulted in two separate and in fact contradictory ideas: (1) that the plebeians were all clients of the ancient city aristocracy, so that client and plebeian were originally the same; (2) that, on the contrary, the power of the patricians over the plebeians rested upon the votes of their clients in the assemblies. It may be that neither of these traditions is accurate, and certainly the second must be false. There may be some element of truth in the first, but we cannot know what period it concerns for we are ignorant of how and when the clients were accepted into the voting units of the citizenry.

Apart from all the difficulties discussed above there remain more basic objections to the equation of plebeian and client. Consider the clients who followed Atta Clausus to Rome in 495 and were settled by him with 2 *iugera* of land apiece on his estate: was it these same clients who soon afterwards joined with other clients in a similar position to force the establishment of the tribunate with its revolutionary powers? Were these clients, whose lands were subject to reversion, the same who nevertheless had sufficient resources to arm themselves for the army's hoplite force (*classis*)? Clearly the answer to both questions must be no. It is possible that in the Later Republic some of the plebeian clans had names similar to those of patrician clans owing to ancient clientage relationships. But there is no reason whatever to think that for all the many plebeian clans of Roman origin there were patrician clans of the same name.

Furthermore, since it is clear that the events of the fifth century B.C. are reported in the tradition in such a manner as to indicate the existence even then of a plebs free from clientage, desperate attempts have been made to explain this away by positing the end of clientage for a part of the plebs. One factor responsible for this, supposedly, was the extinction of certain patrician clans and with them their patronage, but the main factor is supposed to have been the end of the monarchy and hence patronage over the royal clientage – as if a real such clientage, a king's military retinue, would have been allowed to remain in the city after their king had been expelled! Yet the royal clientage theory may contain an element of truth, for it is clear that the plebs consisted in part of artisans and in the early days of the city they were no doubt settled in Rome by the king, owed him labour services, and lived under his protection. It is also quite possible that the king, in the course of his struggles with the aristocrats, on occasion turned to the peasants for help against them, much as did the Greek tyrants.

It is also possible that the tribunate, a kind of negative tyranny, was instituted as a concession, a compromise by which the city aristocracy gained the support of the peasants and petty bourgeoisie not long after the end of the monarchy, in order to secure the continuance of the Republic and to prevent the return of 'tyranny'. It has often been noticed that the protection exercised by the tribunes on behalf of politically powerless citizens constituted a form of institutionalized patronage, and that it amounted to a surrogate for the protection extended by aristocratic clans to their members and clients. In this respect the tribunes may have inherited the royal clientage; but if so their patronage would then have been absolutely different from a feudal or manorial authority exercised over royal 'serfs'. Yet all of this is in the realm of hypothesis.

What must be insisted upon is this: plebs and clientage, plebeian and serf, feudal city-state and manor, are concepts which must not be considered identical. In the conflict of orders in the early Republic the patricians were supported generally by their clients against the plebs; here the tradition is correct. The urban plebeian's existence is securely attested by the fact that the four urban tribes were the oldest tribes, and it is absolutely sure that he cannot have been a serf. In the rural areas the serfdom of clients is possible, but not attested. As for the country peasants (*pagani*), later survivals make it most unlikely that they were serfs, and in the ancient hoplite army (which was older than the tribunate) they could not have been; the role of the clients in the Roman army corresponds to that of the helots, the role of the plebs to that of the perioeci in the Spartan system.

It is also clear that the structure of the ancient city-state of Rome was feudal because of the presence of clientage and because the plebs was excluded from a share in political power. Nevertheless, 'feudalism' is not synonymous with 'manorialism'. The lands of the patricians were worked, as elsewhere, by debt bondsmen and by the sons of peasants rented or held as collateral (*personae in mancipio*), and along with them there were prisoners of war (growing in number with time) and purchased slaves. It is possible that in early times clients holding land by grace (*precaria*) also rendered labour service at times of need.

Rome exercised a great attraction on lords of castles like Atta Clausus who moved to the city and joined the community. Certainly in early times this was not due to a desire to share in its public lands, at that time relatively small in extent. In fact the later eminence of the Claudian clan did not spring from the original grant of land it received. Rather, both phenomena – the assimilation of the Claudii and their later eminence – had a common origin in the character of Rome as a centre of transit trade, a town where one could gain wealth through the exploitation of slaves, lending on interest, participation in trading ventures, and the like. It was continental expansion, which went hand in hand with the victory of the plebs, which put an end to this. The facts reported concerning Atta Clausus serve only to show clearly how small the 'manors' of the ancient Roman patricians were imagined to have been, but in fact the ancient tradition may very well be correct.

According to the tradition the 16 rustic tribes with clan names were established *c*. 450 B.C. If this is true, and if we accept the traditions's figures for the extent of Rome's territory and reckon it at about 50,000–60,000 hectares in extent, then each rustic tribe had a territory of *c*. 3,200–3,500 hectares. These figures seem quite reasonable.

Now the agricultural territory subject to Rome probably included at most 30,000 hectares. From this we deduce that each of the 300 senatorial clans, using the figure given by the ancient tradition, had possessions somewhat in excess of 100 hectares, assuming that they owned all the land, and also the right to use the commons. If we compare this with conditions in the German East, then the size of a patrician holding seems to do no more than approach what we would consider a large estate. However one should remember the size of the estates held by Attic aristocrats: the highest class was defined as having at least *c*. 50 hectares; Alcibiades inherited 30 hectares.

Of course the figures here are only hypothetical examples for discussion. I do not mean to imply that the Roman patricians must have owned all the land, for their income – like that of every ancient city aristocracy – was derived partly from specifically urban sources (trade), and partly from ownership of cattle, for which they had the use of about half the lands in the ancient *pagi*, which were set aside as grazing commons (*compascua*). Furthermore, as a result of the increasing money power of the aristocracy, two tendencies we have encountered before set in at Rome as well: ownership of land became concentrated, and more and more free peasants in the *pagi* were reduced to debt bondage. The presence of these debt bondsmen was regarded as a serious threat to internal stability, as we can see from the provision of the Twelve Tables specifying that debtors who were personally liable and had failed to make their scheduled payments had to be killed or else sold abroad (*trans Tiberim*); Greek creditors, on the contrary, were allowed to keep them as slaves.

To sum up: it is out of the question that the ancient patrician estates (as pictured in the tradition) were larger or even as large as the estates cultivated by slaves in Cato's time, which were about 60 hectares. We must rather imagine them as about 30 hectares on the average, and an establishment of that size in the Campagna probably could support 60 adults or about 20 nuclear families. This calculation is based on several assumptions: that the land would be planted in spelt, that it would be cultivated well, and that the figures for the daily ration of soldiers and slaves (converted from wheat into spelt) given by Polybius and Cato constitute a valid basis for reckoning. Besides the 30 hectares one must also include (a) common grazing rights, for the production of milk, cheese, and wool, and (b) forest rights to get wood for heating, building, and tools. These factors together give a quantitative picture of the rural establishment of a Roman clan (*gens*) as presented in the tradition. What remains unknown is the relationship within the clan between free men, clients, and slaves.

There were about 300 patrician clans (*gentes*), and if our figures are correct they must have occupied altogether close to a third of the arable land in the Roman state. The remaining two-thirds would have supported between 3,000 and 5,000 peasant families, depending on the average size of farm which is used for calculations. These are maximum figures, based on agrarian data without regard to other factors; but if we suppose that Rome's citizenry had to be supported by food grown entirely on Rome's own territory (*ager*), then it is obvious that the figures given must be reduced. My estimate is that there would then have been 2,000 plebeian peasant families of 6–8 members each, and of these at most a half would have had the wealth to support a hoplite (equivalent to the *zeugitai* of Attica). As to the patricians, there were probably a little more than 100 clans with an average of 30 members each, varying of course significantly in lands and numbers among themselves. Each clan had perhaps 8 client families, giving a total of 800 client families with 4–5 members each; the basis of this estimate is in part the fact that in Attica the highest census rating of 500 bushels was equal to 8 or 9 times the minimum needs of a family.

All these estimates together give a total of about 22,000 persons to be supported by Rome's own produce. The figure cannot have been much more, for then we would have to assume that a very large portion of Roman territory (*ager Romanus*) was cultivated, so large in fact as to be quite improbable. Although much more of the Campagna could be cultivated than was the case with Attica, because of the latter's mountains, still the arable land cannot have been more than 15 per cent of the total, or about 15,000–18,000 hectares used to grow grain with fallow fields planted with grass; the rest of the land would have been used for gardens, pasture, and forest.

Since, however, throughout the history of Rome as a city-state it was never necessary for the community to live on its own produce, nor indeed was it ever in a position to do so, we must more than double our estimate of the number of people who could have been supported on Roman territory in its city and country. This applies even to the period of stagnation which preceded the wars of conquest. Furthermore, the possibility of producing market crops means that we must increase our estimate of peasant numbers.

All the above is of course entirely hypothetical, and its only justification is that it allows us to use the traditional accounts to reconstruct past conditions and translate them into figures. Yet it must be emphasized that our estimates are tentative, and that everything in them is uncertain. Indeed, we do not even know to what degree the ancient territory of Rome (*ager Romanus*) was ever identical with the area controlled by the Roman state.

From the first the Roman plebs did not consist entirely of peasants. There can be no doubt that some plebeians were, by contemporary standards, wealthy persons with property in both city and land, and in fact it was they who provided the leadership of the plebs. Essentially the plebs was that part of the citizen body which was excluded from offices, priesthoods, judgeships, and army commands – the people who did not belong to clan groupings and were peasants, artisans, and merchants, some of whom became rich while others remained poor. Hence it can be seen that the conflict of orders in the Early Republic was a social struggle only in so far as it concerned debt law (though this was, according to the tradition, less important at Rome than it had been in Greece); othewise it was a political struggle.

To understand this we must remember that from the first plebeians were entirely outside the clan structure, for at Rome just as in Greece the clan (*gens*) arose out of the artificial preservation of the community of goods among people living in the same house. The actual chain of causation was the same at Rome as elsewhere: it was not because they were plebeians that they had no clan, but rather it was because in earliest times they had not entered the circle of wealthy and powerful clans that they became plebeians. Then later, when a compromise settlement was reached between the orders, the plebeians gained the right to form clans and thereby entrance to the clan federation (*curiae*), to establish their own clientages, and to other clan institutions. Yet there continued to exist the ancient distinction, resting on feudal law, between two kinds of inheritance. The patrician inherited according to his clan rights (*gente*), the plebeian according to family rights (*stirpe*), and even in the Late Republic this opposition figured in the conflict between the patrician and the plebeian Claudians over the estate of a freedman.

According to tradition the aristocracy was broadened to include a new group of rich families in the regal period, and in fact this must have occurred at some time. This new aristocracy, the so-called 'lesser clans' (*gentes minores*), counted as patrician, and the reason for their incorporation was undoubtedly to double the army. Thus the lesser clans manned the 'later companies' (*centuriae posteriores*).

The feudal character of the Roman state was so pronounced that all free citizens were compelled to take clan names, and eventually this brought them into a clan federation (*curia*). Note the difference here between Rome and Attica: there the associations (*orgeōnes*) of non-noble phratry members were characterized by the absence of clan names.

In any case the political incorporation of the mass of plebeians into the body of full citizens did not take place by way of the *curiae*, but was rather the result of military developments, as elsewhere. Of course these developments were to a large extent possible only because of certain economic factors, just as in Greece. The city's prosperity increased very early as a result of the trade treaty made with Carthage and the commerce which this treaty allowed Rome to monopolize. This prosperity explains why a city with such a small territory suddenly acquired an unusually large fortification, the so-called Servian Wall. It is of course clear that this wall dates from the fourth century, but even the older part, which excludes the Capitol and Aventine, encloses a very large urban area, unquestionably as large as that of Athens. The commercial significance of Rome by the early fourth century, when Rome was sometimes called a Greek city, is indicated by the fact that the Greek world had accurate information about the city's sack by the Gauls, and also (more eloquently) by the aid Massilia and other Greek cities sent to Rome to help pay the ransom demanded by the Gauls.

But it was Rome's exposed position and the advance of mountain peoples such as Volscians and Samnites which forced the introduction of disciplined infantry tactics. Hence, too, the decisive role of the hoplite phalanx in Rome's wars. Nowhere else was this innovation adopted with such thoroughness as at Rome. It was, in fact, the needs of hoplite discipline that led to the extraordinary power of Roman magistrates, a phenomenon which astonished the Greeks and which they regarded – quite rightly – as specifically Roman. A legendary story tells how a knight fought and won a battle in single combat and then, because he had broken ranks, paid for his breach of discipline with his life even though he was the son of an honoured consul.

Now the decline of the ancient military significance of clientage is connected with the disappearance of knightly combat. The army was transformed into a hoplite phalanx (*classis*); mobilization of the economic resources of all citizens became the key to survival. As in the Draconian constitution of early Athens, Rome's citizenry was divided between those who had the economic means to equip themselves for the phalanx (*classis*), and those who did not, the latter being categorized as 'below the phalanx' (*infra classem*).

(It should be noted here that we cannot be sure when the division of the entire population into classes according to voting groups (as in Athens) occurred. Nor do we know whether the conditions for self-equipment were ever the basis of this class division, as reported by the tradition. In any case the centuriate assembly, which was organized according to these classes, was certainly not older than the third century B.C., and there is no reason to think that landownership was ever the basis of its divisions.)

Then the Roman phalanx of fully armed hoplites exacted a concession of decisive importance: the citizen army gained the right to participate in selecting the commanders (*praetores*) of the two legions into which the army was, it seems, originally divided. The hoplite army also had to be consulted when existing laws were amended. When the army exercised these political functions in assembly (*comitia*) the men were divided into military units – *centuriae* – by corporals, and proceedings were conducted under military discipline. Above all, the men were not allowed to discuss or question while proposals were read to them by the commanding officer, and then they were allowed only to reject or accept the proposals *in toto*. In all these characteristics the Roman centuriate *comitia* was strikingly different from a Greek *ekklēsia*. Its limited powers represented a first step towards participation in public decisions by a part of the plebeians, the propertied and, for the most part, urban families. Then the peasantry gained power in the epoch of Rome's great inland expansion during 450–300 B.C., and as elsewhere their rise was at once both condition and result of this expansion. The conclusion came in 287; after seceding to the Janiculan, the plebs gained the right to pass laws with binding force equal to those passed by the centuriate assembly. Thus the peasant army which had waged the Samnite Wars now won mastery of the state, in theory at any rate, and full eligibility for office for all its members.

The stages in this political struggle need not be traced here, for only the aspects which concern agrarian history are our concern. The aspect which was politically decisive was the growing and finally dominant role of the plebeian assembly (*comitia tributa*). Those laws most important for social development were generally plebiscites, laws proposed by tribunes and passed by the plebeian assembly. Later the centuriate assembly was reformed so that it became based upon the tribal divisions of the people, including both patricians and plebeians. The particulars of this reform have not yet been clarified, not even by Mommsen, but it is clear that henceforth the only differences between centuriate and tribal assemblies were that the patricians participated in the former while in the latter only tribunes could put motions to a vote (*agere cum plebe*). The number of patricians was relatively small, and indeed seems to have declined absolutely; at the end of the Republic there were less than 20 patrician clans (divided into many branches – *stirpes*), although just the lists of office-holders and the annalistic tradition preserve the names of about 60 clans. The number of recorded names of Attic clans had been even larger.

In any case, there can be no doubt that participation in the tribal assembly was based upon the tribes. These were actually local districts, or rather local groups of landowners, corresponding to the principles of peasant democracy. The four urban tribes, the original ones, included owners of property within the ancient walls. The group of 16 rural tribes which were the first to be added included owners of property in the ancient communities which had been incorporated. Each of these 16 was named for the castle clan which had its seat within the borders, but this does not mean that they were of clan origin – that is, had emerged as a result of the dissolution of all manors. Were this so, then only 16 out of the 300 clans (to use the traditional figure) would have been manorial lords, and among these 16 some of the most famous patricians names are missing. Furthermore we know that in later times the patrician Claudii did not belong to 'their' tribe, the one named for them. The explanation may be that there were villages situated near the clan castles of incorporated clans and bearing their names, and that when new tribes were formed they took their names from them.

As the boundary of Roman private property was pushed outward new tribes were added at first, until there were 35 in all; then the old ones were enlarged. The principle remained that every privately owned plot had to belong to a tribe.

Those citizens who owned land had the right to vote and were subject to conscription. In the Twelve Tables they are called *adsidui,* the equivalent of what in later Latin would have been *locupletes,* 'the rich'. Those who owned no land are called *proletarii,* which of course does not mean 'producers of children' but rather people who belong to the offspring (*proles*) of a full citizen and only because of this lineage count as citizens. One can compare with this a similar association of ideas in Hebrew usage: those members of the city population who did not belong to the old clans were called 'sons of odious women' – that is, they were born of concubines rather than of the legitimate wives of full citizens.

After the introduction of the tribal system the opposition of *adsidui–proletarii* gave way to a new one: *tribules–aerarii.* The *tribules* were the tribe members who were subject to conscription, while *aerarii* were those who had wealth but not land, and did not render military service but did pay taxes. These two pairs are not equivalents. A *proletarius* was a citizen who for the moment did not have wealth, in particular landed wealth, equal to the hoplite census, but might acquire it at any time. An *aerarius* was a citizen who, regardless of how much wealth he might have, was not accorded hoplite status; this was mainly, but not entirely, because he belonged to the resident classes which were excluded from landownership. One such class was undoubtedly made up of freedmen, who were excluded from landownership by city-state law.

The basic principle in these matters is known to us: just as only citizens – *proletarii* as much as *adsidui* – could acquire landed property, so also (as originally in all mediaeval towns) only landowners could be *tribules.* This however does not mean that membership in the hoplite *classis* and therefore – originally – full citizenship depended entirely upon landed property, or rather upon the amount of landed property possessed. At one time I too inclined to this view, but it is mistaken. The earliest census ranking of Romans was evidently not based on landed wealth alone, for as in the Greek commercial cities here too a development occurred because of the need to mobilize all available forces for military service. Hence the conscription of those who were not *adsidui,* a group growing in numbers and wealth. In Athens during emergencies even the metics were conscripted. Of course, making persons subject to conscription necessarily meant according them the status of full citizens. Clearly, whether a prosperous merchant rented his dwelling or owned it was often a matter of chance and could not remain a permanent criterion of whether or not he was subject to conscription.

However, it should be noted that in the manner in which non-property owners were incorporated, and generally in the manner in which the citizen body was divided into local units, the Roman state differed fundamentally from the Athenian state as shaped by Cleisthenes, with which it should always be compared. The differences arose out of basic and formative peculiarities of Rome's political structure.

Cleisthenes divided the population of Attica into demes, and the individual remained tied to his deme, without regard to where he lived or whether he owned land or what occupation he pursued. The deme was the intermediary by which the citizen was called upon to bear state burdens or to assume office on election by lot. In Rome the later tribal system was very different. Thus, according to Gellius, Scipio complained that frequently a son voted in a tribe other than his father's; which meant that he had sold the land inherited from his father (at least that is the way I interpret this passage). The matter was determined (a) by the location of one's farm (*fundus*), or (for the landless living in the city) (b) by the location of one's residence in the city, or (for people in the country who did not own land) (c) by the decision of the censor.

Originally, however, matters were different. Servius describes the situation as it existed (supposedly) at the time of the original four urban tribes – these, of course, did not cover the territory within the so-called Servian Wall, but rather the ancient city, which was smaller and in particular did not include the Aventine and the ancient citadel. There the individual citizen was inscribed on the census and had his official residence according to where his house stood. Once established, this residence could not be changed. This does not mean that he was limited in his freedom of movement, but rather that for the law he remained always a member of a particular tribe. This was the same as in Athens, where members of the demes Kydathen [in the city] and Paiania [in the country] so remained no matter where they might choose to dwell. In that period the urban plebeians of Rome were entered in the census lists 'as if they lived in villages' (*hōsper kōmētas*), to use Dionysius of Halicarnassus' striking and accurate phrase. His statement implies that the rural population living in *pagi* was handled in the same manner, which means that the original four urban tribes represented a transfer of the deme principle from the country to the city, just as in Cleisthenes' reform. Such is at least a possible version of early Roman organization. Whatever its character, it was evidently not extended to keep pace with Rome's territorial expansion, for nothing similar is recorded for the rural tribes.

It is, however, possible (though not attested) that during the Roman Middle Ages – a period for which we have virtually no sources, and which is characterized by compromise between the city aristocracy and the hoplite army – there were limitations on the alienation of property in order to maintain the number of independent farms, just as there were in the Greek Middle Ages. The concept of *fundus* (farm, estate) includes the idea of communal law; thus in the language of Italic treaties of alliance the phrase *fundus fieri* signifies 'to form a community sharing the same law'. This fits very well with the ancient type of action at law to determine ownership, corresponding to the Greek *diadikasia*, and *fundus* would then correspond to the older Greek concept of *klēros* (allotment). Down to a later period Roman cadasters use the *fundus* as a unit, bearing the name of its original owner even when it had in fact been divided up among several proprietors. Such limitations on alienation would not have been derived from ancient clan law and the ancient clan manors of the city aristocracy; rather, the reverse would have been the case, just as in Greece where measures were taken to prevent the sale of warriors' farms to the *astoi*, as the Greeks would say. This would be proven if it could be shown that the tribe in Rome, with which permanent legal domicile was connected, goes back to the Servian reforms.

Be that as it may, it is certain that in later times there were no limitations whatever on the alienation of property. A citizen could change his tribe when he changed his landed property or, if he had no property, when he changed his residence in the city, and it could be changed by the censor if that official decided that a citizen had failed to fulfil his political or moral duties and should therefore be struck from the list of *tribules*, that is, taken out of the army and put among the *aerarii*. The censor could also assign at will a citizen owning properties in several tribes or an old citizen without property or a new citizen (e.g. freedman). The manner in which these assignments were made sometimes gave rise to vigorous political struggles – we need not consider the historicity of their particulars here – since the assignments determined the political power held by landless citizens. Most of them were businessmen in Rome, where of course these were becoming more numerous, but were officially domiciled in tribes outside the city.

Now in Athens the principle introduced by Cleisthenes, that one's official domicile never changed no matter where the actual residence (later called *idia*) was, had led to the domination of the masses (*ochlos*) because they were present in the city and could take part in the popular assembly (*ekklēsia*). This result, certainly one not desired by Cleisthenes, was the foundation of the power of the 'demagogues', the leaders of the masses, among them Pericles. It was this same result at which Appius Claudius the Censor aimed, according to tradition, when he assigned citizens resident in Rome to all the tribes [rural as well as urban]. In later times similar conflicts arose over the assignment of freedmen.

It is also of great interest to note that the problem of what rights to assign the lower classes of citizens in all tribes arose first in Rome when the navy became important, as it did everywhere in Antiquity. This concerned the *proletarii, capite censi*, and *manumissi* in the time of Appius Claudius, later only the last group. The fact that Rome had no fleet at the beginning of the Punic Wars (264 B.C.), may indeed have been caused in part by internal politics.

For the career of Appius Claudius marks the time (in our tradition) when the development of Rome towards a democratic *polis* was arrested, partly because of the resistance of the Senate and partly because of that of the rural *tribules*, who had been privileged until then. An alliance was formed between the hoplite army (still dominated by rural property-owners), the senatorial clans, and the landed peasantry, and together they forced through a law limiting the landless permanently to the four urban tribes. This meant that henceforth the landless were powerless in the assemblies, and Rome continued to be a hoplite *polis*. In theory this meant that what Cleisthenes had aimed at (but not achieved) was henceforth secure: the domination of the assemblies by the peasantry. In reality, however, it meant that Roman politics continued to be dominated by a class of landowners living in the city on their rents, in particular those whose wealth was sufficient to allow them to be present in Rome at the elections. Above all, it meant the continued domination of the senatorial clans, the nobility. Then the nobility also arranged that certain old tribes (Arnensis, Fabia, Horatia, Lemonia, Menenia, Pupinia, Romulia, Voltinia) were not enlarged and so created a group of 'rotten boroughs'.

Furthermore the practice of holding an election in a camp outside the city (*sevocare populum*) was tried once and then forbidden by law. Thereafter those citizens of the rural tribes who owned no house in Rome lost influence in the assemblies, and this became more and more pronounced as the tribes were extended to cover all of Italy. Only when there were sharp struggles, such as those connected with the Gracchi, did large numbers of the rural middle class come to Rome for elections.

Eduard Meyer was right when he stressed the peasant character of the plebs in ancient times and pointed out that at the same time when the Lex Hortensiu (287 B.C.) made votes of the tribal assembly binding, it was also enacted that trials would be held on market days (when the peasants came to town). That corresponds in purpose (though not in means) to the village courts in Attica. For the assemblies, however, the political effect of this was to reduce the power of the urban population – artisans as well as capitalists. Generally the assemblies of Rome's first great period of expansion were dominated by landowners living off their rents. Their only concern was to make sure that the peasants did not use their legal voting rights to take power. The domination of the landed interest in the Senate was secured by a law which prohibited senators from engaging in maritime trade.

The first trade treaty between Rome and Carthage, assuming that the traditional date is correct, indicates that Rome at the end of the regal period was dominated by commercial interests, like all *poleis* of early Antiquity. The economic predominance of the ancient city aristocracy in Rome as among the Etruscans was clearly based on maritime trade and on the accumulation of property such trade made possible. But then came inland expansion and the growing power of the peasantry, and the dominant concern of the aristocracy became the acquisition of land.

So strong was this tendency that at the start of the First Punic War no fleet whatever was possessed by Rome (legend may have exaggerated somewhat), while at the same time it had pursued a programme of colonization such as no other state, certainly no other city-state of similarly small size, ever did in history. This colonization was connected in the first instance with Rome's geographical position, for unlike Greek cities it had a vast hinterland; it was also connected with the need to check the relentless invasions of the Sabellian mountain people.

The general tendency of Rome's subsequent evolution is to be seen in the social and political developments sketched above, and also in the legal and economic structure of land law as it developed during the period of the hoplite *polis'* great expansion. At the beginning of this development there is the work of the Decemviri, a board of ten lawgivers quite comparable to the *aisymnētoi* found in Greek history. But we must think of their legislation as only a stage in the transformation of Rome's structure, not the one and only transformation.

The basic importance of the work of the Decemviri was to provide a written, permanent, and rational code of law to take the place of simple dependence upon tradition and its interpretation by priestly aristocrats. Furthermore strict rules were established to expedite trials.

The specific provisions of the code, in so far as they are recorded and of importance for social history, do not form a logical unity. They represent, rather, a compromise, as so often in such matters. Certain provisions signified a reduction in the unlimited power of the master: the poor citizen (*civis proletarius*) was allowed to pick his guarantors in a trial freely, even outside the ranks of the *adsidui*; the patron who broke faith with a client was cursed; the son of a non-legitimate marriage became free after his father had sold him three times; and informal marriage (*sine manu*), similar to the Egyptian 'unwritten marriage' (*agraphos gamos*), was explicitly acknowledged.

(Regarding the grant of free choice of guarantors by the *civis proletarius*, it should be noted that this concession removed, in the manner of Solon, an important motive for assuming the position of client. Clientage, however, continued to exist as an institution. This fact is another reason to doubt that all plebeians were clients.)

On the other hand according to Cicero the Decemviri introduced the prohibition of marriage between plebeians and patricians (but at the same time Cicero cites what must certainly be a legendary tradition about the Decemviri of the second year). It is certain that the ancient debt law remained in force with all its severity. Indeed the law was reinforced which banned a creditor from keeping debt bondsmen within the state's borders, supposedly in order to avoid the danger of debt slaves' insurrections. Perhaps as a result of this, debt bondage assumed the form of *nexum*, which was a contract by which the debtor evaded that prohibition (as Mitteis has demonstrated) by putting himself into the power of the creditor as his *nexus* and then by rendering labour services.

Perhaps as a result of the development of the *nexum* a special law was passed prohibiting the bondage of debtors who could swear to have sufficient property to cover their obligations. In other words, the bondage of the propertied only was ended. This and a number of other laws regarding debt were counted as triumphs of the plebeians, another sign that they entered class conflicts not as serfs but as debtors. This of course does not exclude the possibility that the plebeians were politically interested in weakening and ending the institution of clientage.

For agrarian history the most important part of the work of the Decemviri, the Twelve Tables, as well as of the related legislation of the later years, was the establishment of complete freedom of trade in landed property. According to tradition the Twelve Tables expressly sanctioned absolute freedom of testament, and also made binding all agreements concluded according to the *mancipatio* formula and all conditions attached by the *nuncupatio* formula.

According to tradition the principle was maintained that land could be transferred only on full payment in cash. That was a survival from an earlier period of social law, and as such has Near Eastern analogies. But, looked at from another perspective, the meaning of this provision is simply that the buyer had to accept express responsibility for a debt equal to the full price as condition for full transfer of the land. In other words, this assured clarity in the legal situation, especially as regards ownership, and it did away with the practice of selling land with a mortgage to cover part of the purchase price.

(This dislike of purchase mortgages may of course have been partly due to economic factors: the great fluctuations in the price of land and in the value of money. Already in Sumerian inscriptions we see how concerned the ruler was that the little man selling land should receive his 'good money' immediately. Once officially stamped money came into use the danger of buying on credit was increased by the possibility of monetary depreciation. Solon was apparently accused in Antiquity of manipulations of this sort. Before the advent of official money this danger did not exist, of course, but even then fluctuations in imports of gold, silver, and copper had a similar effect if prices were fixed in specie.)

Furthermore one cannot exclude the possibility that another reason for prohibiting mortgages was the desire to prevent as far as possible the purchase of full citizenship rights on credit. As an analogy there is a provision in the Freiburg *Rodel* (par. 70) specifically forbidding that. (The effects of Roman land law are discussed in section b.)

Mortgages themselves do not seem to have been excluded by the Twelve Tables. The word for mortgage was *hypotheca*, from the Greek, a sure sign that it was borrowed late. However, even the *fiducia* only became subject to legal action at a late stage of development. This was the agreement that a formal purchase would be made retroactive after payment of a debt, and originally keeping such an agreement was an aspect of a person's honour (*fides*). It came under the jurisdiction of the censor's court of morals, once that official had usurped their control. Later, because of this, breaking a *fiducia* counted as a cause of legal disgrace (*infamia*) like other similar infractions of faith and trust in trade. As a result, purchase price mortgages came into use.

However, it seems to me most unlikely, considering analogies from the economic life of a trading centre, that purchase price mortgages had not existed in the period of the Twelve Tables. On the contrary, the non-acknowledgment of them may well have amounted in reality to abolishing them, just as was done with the bondage of debtors.

Debt bondage and land mortgages: these were the major social problems of all early Antiquity, and the Decemviri aimed to make them disappear. The land and the free citizens who owned it were now the foundations of the state's military power, and also of the state's financial power, for they provided (in the form of forced loans) the taxes (*tributus*). The first census was evidently a cadaster of the people (free plebeians, clients, slaves) and cattle available to the state for labour services, and the category of goods which needed mancipation (*res mancipi*) for conveyance was always limited by the criteria of such a census.

The transfer of responsibility for labour services to all plebeians was of special benefit to the four urban tribes; hence the permanence of a citizen's residence (*idia*). Land was now not the only basis for taxing citizens in a commercial centre like Rome, but it remained the most important. It became part of the *res mancipi*, and was the basis of the tribal divisions. The principle was that the landed property of each citizen must at all times be evident, and it must not be burdened by obligations and conditions of any sort; hence the limitations on mortgages. In Athens a citizen's statement of wealth was so formulated as to exclude mortgaged property from the determination of his class. This category of 'unburdened land' (*ousia eleutherio*) in Athens corresponds to that of 'non-obligated property' (*proprium non obligatum*) used in mediaeval Constance.

Furthermore every property had to be entirely available for use by its owner, just as available as urban and suburban gardens. This explains why, as all our sources agree, the Twelve Tables very clearly defined rights of way as well as road maintenance duties. In order to secure unconditional access to all properties and at the same time provide definite demarcations, the code also prescribed that there be five-foot pathways between properties (corresponding to Hellenistic *chalasma*) and that they should not be subject to usucaption.

These regulations represent to some extent the transfer of urban or garden land rules to arable land, but this transfer occurs most fully in the type of land division imposed on private property in this period, perhaps by the Twelve Tables themselves. Its principles were aimed at: (a) developing a network of public roads; (b) assigning each *fundus* to a definite owner, so that there would be separate farms, not village commons; (c) clarifying ownership by making official maps and by tying all owners' land rights to these maps. Together this meant the complete destruction of the old village and district structures and the establishment of a strictly individualistic type of land law and land use.

Land was made available for census and for conveyance by mancipation by a particular surveying procedure, and such land was then defined as 'land divided and assigned by boundaries into units of 100 *heredia* (i.e. centuriae)': *ager divisus et assignatus per limites in centuriis*. In later times this was used in Italy mainly, though not exclusively, for colonies of Roman citizens and also for the large areas granted to veterans' colonies. The surveying procedure, as it was used for every grant (*assignatio*), developed from Etruscan and perhaps also Greek models.

First the land area was divided by means of simple dioptric tools into rectangular sections, using coordinates (*limites*), usually so as to produce squares of 200 *iugera* each. Since 2 *iugera* constituted the ancient plebeian land allotment 200 *iugera* was the equivalent of 100 *heredia*; hence the name *centuria*, 100 (*heredia*), for this unit. Like the coordinates used in Greek cities, the coordinates used by the Roman surveys were oriented to the four cardinal points. A North–South line (*limes*) was a *cardo*, and East–West a *decumanus*.

The individual squares (*centuriae*) so formed were numbered according to the number of lines (*limites*) from the centre of the grid, with official boundary stones at the four corners. Every fifth surveyor's line remained a public path of prescribed width, but the others (*linearii*) were not necessarily public, at least in later times, and often disappeared. In general the *limites* were not meant to be property boundaries, and in fact allotted farms often cut through *centuria* lines.

By means of this surveying procedure a field map was produced showing the *limites* and *centuriae*. Within each *centuria* the names of those allotted land and the number of *iugera* in the *centuria* were entered, and this constituted the legal record of grant (*assignatio*). The field map did not show the boundaries of individual properties, as we can see from the extant *forma* of Arausio (modern Orange). It is true that this is a cadaster map rather than a field map, as Schulten has rightly emphasized, but it was obviously derived from a field map and it shows the old system still alive in the Early Empire.

Furthermore the bounds of private properties were not marked by official boundary stones, so that public authority concerned itself only with the area of land within each *centuria* – the 'measure of land' *(modus agri)*. This explains why the procedure of mancipation sufficed to convey land even though there was no record of previous ownership. It is also behind the type of legal action called 'a suit concerning the measure' *(controversia de modo)* which is discussed in extant Roman surveying manuals. In this type of suit the plaintiff asked for restitution of a certain area of land *(modus)* which had been assigned him (or a person whose rights he has inherited or purchased) by an official field map. Now the point here is that the plaintiff does not ask for a definite lot with defined boundaries but rather for a stated quota of land. In this it resembles the Reebning procedure in Germany.

Roman surveying manuals also mention a 'suit concerning the place' *(controversia de loco)*, calling it a supplementary form. In this ownership was determined, and it was also used to register prohibition of ownership.

Later the *controversia de modo* fell out of use because of the great increase in the practice of assigning ownership on the basis of long occupancy-usucaption. As a result the use of area *(modus)* as an official measure ceased.

Now since the development of usucaption as a means of acquiring land was rather late, it is very probable that in earlier times there were at first only three legal ways to gain title to land: (a) by laying claim to an entire *fundus (vindicatio fundi)*, the *fundus* being perhaps originally indivisible; (b) by reference to the official land survey and a legally defined area *(modus agri)*; (c) by gaining legal acknowledgment of the amount of land actually cultivated *(locus)* in the previous year and thereby protection against expropriation and theft.

If this hypothesis is true, then originally Roman citizens did not own land with legally defined boundaries; rather, their landed possessions were juristically defined only in terms of quantity of arable land in the area surveyed by the state. Properties with defined boundaries would then have fallen under the juristic concept of occupied land *(possessio)*. Ownership [*dominium*] and occupation *(possessio)* were therefore two distinct juristic forms of property, and this explains the sharp distinction which continued in later law; since property had by then become by definition a piece of real estate of a certain appraised value, this distinction is otherwise inexplicable.

This casts some light on the ancient system of Roman land use, but it does not allow further deductions. Later this ancient system was progressively abandoned as usucaption prevailed, and then it became only a survival as more and more non-surveyed land was added to the area of private ownership (the *ager privatus*). The largest such addition was made by the agrarian law of 111 B.C. Then the final blow to the old system came when foreign communities were incorporated into the Roman state as *municipia* at the end of the Social War (88 B.C.) without any new survey being made. These measures meant fundamental changes in the social and constitutional structures of the Roman state, and they probably also affected private law in important ways, especially in the legal forms used for suits involving property. Eventually, for instance, the formula used for making a counterclaim disappeared.

Lands surveyed in the manner described had certain economic characteristics, two of them especially important: (a) a network of roads was established and guaranteed by state authority; (b) land was assigned to settlers in unbroken units (*continuae possessiones*). Together these features made the land available for individual development.

It should be noted here that our sources distinguish between land allotments to colonies and to individuals, according to whether they were made to establish a community or simply to divide land among veterans or other recipients. In the case of individual allotments the land was first divided into equal allotments, so many *centuriae* in each, and these were then assigned to the individuals entitled to them. When colonial grants were made, however, it was important that the colonists receive equal treatment, and this could be achieved only – as I believe, despite Mommsen's doubts – by making an appraisal of the soil, however simple, and then by making unequal allocations (perhaps based on multiples of 2 *iugera*) which were assigned by lot.

In the Greek colonies of the Crimea a unit corresponding to the *centuria*, though of different size, was used – the 'hundred fathom' (*hekatorygoi*: cf. B. Keil, *Hermes* 38 (1903), pp. 140–4). If this was used from the first, as Bruno Keil assumes, then it indicates a different quality of soil.

A procedure similar to that used for new colonies was adopted when there was a new division and allotment of a tract, either partly or entirely among the former owners. This fact is securely attested in our sources. In such cases land was assigned 'measure per measure according to improvements' (*modus pro modo secundum bonitatem*). At the same time it was not necessary to incorporate the land into a colony with Roman law (*colonia civium Romanorum*), but in fact this was later done formally, reflecting the original idea linking this type of *assignatio* with colonies.

Much of the foregoing is hypothetical. Nevertheless, it must be emphasized that there is evidence indicating a difference as late as Hadrian's reign between private law in Roman citizen colonies and in *municipia*, which must have arisen from contrasted land laws. In this contrast the group of *municipia* includes the former Latin colonies which were inhabited by Latins rather than Romans, were not surveyed in the Roman manner, and like other *municipia* obeyed 'their own laws' (*suis legibus*).

Related to this is a problem we cannot consider here, the relation between the later concept of Italic law (*ius Italicum*) and the various distinctions of Republican times, when the state was interested in making land available for appraisal and taxation (*censui censendo esse*). Such land could also then be used as collateral in assuming state contracts, as was expressly stated in the laws defining land held in full ownership (*optimo iure privatus esto*). This may have been necessary because the censors' cadasters and also later subdivisions were based upon the original distributions and maps of Rome's arable land. But of course this is only a hypothesis.

Besides the procedures used for surveying Roman land in private ownership there were other procedures used for land of inferior legal status. These lands included the commons (*ager publicus populi Romani*), or rather that part of it which was not meant for private occupation (*possessio*) but rather for lease, and as such was subject to the censor's administrative competence. These lands were supposed to be mapped, and often were, just as were lands let on hereditary lease or in return for labour services (especially road maintenance). Provincial lands subject to taxes and divided were also normally recorded on field maps, and if state burdens were apportioned among the separate parcels the maps had to show their location and outlines.

For these types of land the Romans used a surveying procedure based on 'breadths and lengths' (*per scamna et strigas*). The sources definitely indicate – this is a point my critics ignore – that this procedure differed substantially from centuration. Not only did it result in oblong rather than square plots, a superficial differerence, but also it served to show the boundaries of private holdings (*per proximos possessorum rigores*). Mommsen's interpretation is unsupported, for Balbus (p. 68) is speaking of centuriation, and *rigor* is defined by Hyginus (p. 3) as a boundary of private property, which *limes* is not; cf. Th. Mommsen, 'Zum romischen Bodenrecht', p. 82 of *Hermes* 27 (1892), pp. 79–111 [=*Gesammelte Schriften*, vol. 5 (Berlin, 1908), pp. 85–122]. This means that the surveys and maps made with this procedure showed private property boundaries. This was demanded for land subject to taxation when the state had to be able to identify individual holdings; in other words, it was used for land on which taxes fell on individual properties. It was not necessary (a) if the land was not taxed, or (b) if, as in later times (from Caius Gracchus onwards), the land was held as colonists' possessions and state taxes were levied on areas (*modus agri*) rather than individual holdings.

For example, in the case of Arausio (modern Orange), where a tax of ½ denarius per *iugerum* was levelled on the *centuria* for which a document is extant, it was of course sufficient to note on the map the number of tax-paying and of tax-exempt *iugera* in each *centuria*, and that is what was done. Then the tax-rate was entered. The oldest such areas known to us are the *trientabula* and *ager quaestorius*, and these lands were entrusted to lenders as collateral by the state when unable to pay its bills or when it needed ready cash. In these cases *centuriae* were not at first used, but instead another surveying procedure by which squares of another size were formed. Here we have a parallel between legal and surveying forms. In the case of the *ager privatus vectigalisque* the normal form of centuriation was used.

But the very different type of procedure using breadths and lengths (*scamnatio*) had to be used when taxes were to be levied on individual properties. The distinction between *centuriatio* and *scamnatio* is the same as that between the two forms of tenancy on cash rent known to us from the papyri: in one the tenant pays a fixed sum for the entire parcel, in the other he pays so much per *aroura*.

The use of these two forms of surveying became somewhat lax in later times, and it is also true that the one or the other was employed then for purely technical reasons. The reason for these developments was that legal acknowledgment was extended to properties taken by usucaption (*possessiones*) from the private lands of the community (*ager privatus*), and later all Italian land was incorporated into the Roman tribal community; as a result the ancient land use system was completely undermined. Nevertheless the original and genuine significance of the difference between *centuriatio* and *scamnatio* still seems to me to be undoubtedly established.

There was still a third method of surveying and mapping land; in this only the outer boundaries of the area concerned were determined and recorded (*ager per extremitatem mensura comprehensus*). This procedure was developed in later times when large areas were being annexed, and it was used when non-private land was involved and the state had no interest in recording the bounds of each plot but needed information only on the size of land involved. These considerations applied to temple properties and to lands which had been granted to stipendiary communities or manorial lords (or left in their possession) in return for tribute (*stipendium*, as opposed to *tributum*, tax).

Finally, some land was left entirely unsurveyed (*ager arcifinius*). From very early times this was the case with those lands which belonged to acknowledged foreign cities. The oldest example known to us is the territory of Gabii (*ager Gabinus*).

These territories too, although never surveyed, were also included in the Roman community's lands at the end of the Republic. Small wonder, then, that by the time the extant surveying manuals started to be written [*c.* A.D. 100] the ancient connections between a property's legal status and the manner in which it was surveyed had become very confused.

(b) *Rome's Period of Expansion*

As the citizen yeoman army developed, Rome conquered Italy; the two developments were parallel and indeed conditioned each other. Latium had been threatened by the Sabellian mountain peoples and the Celts as well; hence Rome was forced to counter-attack to secure its own existence. In fact Rome's disciplined hoplite forces proved superior to both the feudal armies of the Etruscans and the peasant armies of the Sabellian mountain peoples and the barbarian Celts.

By the beginning of the fourth century B.C. South Etruria had been conquered. Then in 338 B.C. the Latin League was changed into a federal state under Rome's hegemony, and thereafter took up the struggle against the Sabellians. In the third century the Celts of the Po Valley were subjected and the attempt of the Greeks to dominate South Italy was thwarted. All these triumphs were accompanied by a colossal programme of colonization.

When an enemy state was defeated at least a third of its land was confiscated, sometimes all of it, and this was then divided among Rome and its allies. Part was distributed to the army, so much per soldier (*viritim*), and thereby became tribal territory. It was at this time, in fact, that the tribes grew in number to 35; then, their number having been fixed, the tribes' territories increased enormously in size, so that from being *c.* 3,000 hectares each they grew to the dimension of states.

Another part of confiscated land was sold, the state reserving the right of repurchase. This land (*ager quaestorius*) was evidently sold in order to replenish the treasury, and possibly also to make unnecessary the levying of direct taxes (*tributus*), for the latter were regarded as forced loans. The rest of the confiscated lands were added to the domains [*ager publicus*].

Along with this went the systematic foundation of new cities in conquered areas. In the inland areas the first colonies were founded by the Latin League; these colonies were entitled to Latin rights, with local self-government and their own land law. Romans sent to these as colonists lost their citizenship, being tied to the colony instead.

On the other hand Rome, as the trading centre of the league, took over the protection of the coast. Citizen colonies were set up there, and were allowed only limited autonomy. Indeed the later Roman colonies were essentially not colonies at all; they were administered from Rome, their land was Roman land, their inhabitants were Roman citizens, and they were really garrisons. Colonists in these places were exempt from conscription but undoubtedly had to remain there.

Then after 300 B.C. Rome's predominance became more and more pronounced, and as a result the system of Latin colonization gradually fell into disuse while at the same time Roman colonies were systematically founded in the interior as well as on the coast. During *c.* 270–240 B.C. the Latin colonies began to be at a disadvantage and their legal status worsened; it is possible that their citizens were limited in their rights of movement. Then after the Second Punic War (217–201 B.C.) the Roman citizen colonies flourished more than ever. This relative worsening of the position of the league's colonies and colonists, along with changes in league law (see above), corresponds to the developments which took place within the Athenian League: increasingly dominant position of the capital, oppression of the allies, and progressive subordination of the cleruchies to the capital (especially after Pericles).

It was through these distributions of land and colonial foundations that Rome provided for her landless citizens (*cives proletarii*), the peasantry's offspring. That is what the hoplite army fought for, and here too we see similarities with the Athenian cleruchies. These similarities are especially apparent in the case of the colonization of Brea, which by popular decree was available only to Athenian yeomen (*zeugitai*) and landless peasants (*thetes*). There was, however, also a difference due to geography, just as in modern times English and American colonization differ: whereas Athens could only build up a collection of scattered holdings, Rome was able to colonize a compact continental area.

Rome's steady territorial expansion was followed by massive increases in population. (This, incidentally, is of course the invariable causal relationship, never the reverse.) As large areas were incorporated into the Roman state, the inevitable result was the disappearance of the old pattern of land use as it had developed at the time of the Twelve Tables (*c.* 450 B.C.). The ancient rural districts (*pagi*) were fragmented by the centuriation procedure. Where their autonomy survived, as in local cults, their regulations were regarded as a kind of land tax. The ancient common lands (*ager compascuus*) were attached to individual estates (*fundi*), and villages were either ignored by the administrative system or else used as a temporary stop-gap. Jointly held properties were transferred to individual ownership by attribution (*assignatio*) in official surveys. Everywhere what had once been characteristic of aristocratic ownership only, the private farm (*villa*), becomes the dominant form of property.

For example, after the peasants of the Samnite mountains lost their struggle to maintain the ancient autonomy of their villages in the league wars, a survey was carried out under Sulla and large parts of their common lands were attributed to private ownership. Then under the Triumvirate there were massive confiscations and land distributions to veterans. Centuriation destroyed the old land use patterns. Everywhere the city and the city's land law triumphed.

Contrast this with Athens. Cleisthenes mitigated the class struggle there by forcing all aristocrats to join village communities. Rome took the opposite path: it destroyed the village communities and made all peasants 'manor-owners' (in theory, at least), which until then only aristocrats had been. Although it was said of Cleisthenes that 'he made all Athenians aristocrats', the truth is that this statement does not apply to his reforms, which in fact made all aristocrats into peasants; but it applies perfectly to the land system developed in Rome's period of expansion. This Roman land use system has many formal similarities with that used in Greek colonies, but in its purpose and effects it is virtually unique, for it aimed at destroying all obstacles to the free exploitation of the land and – more important – to the unlimited use of the slaves then available.

(Incidentally, not only the land use system but also the tribal system could be said 'to have made all Romans aristocrats'. Thus in Rome plebeian and patrician clans of the same name continued to exist side by side, whereas in Athens the most ancient aristocratic clan changed its name because as a result of Cleisthenes' reforms a deme carried the same name. The Athenian clan's action was a protest against forced democratization; in Rome there was no reason for such an action, since the agrarian reforms had in fact strengthened the position of the aristocracy rather than weakened it.)

The intentional, purposeful character of the changes in Rome's land use system can be seen in the ruthless destruction of all communal elements of the agrarian economy, in the extension of unlimited private ownership (*dominium*) over all the land, and in the provision for the easy transfer of such ownership by a special procedure (*mancipatio*) which did not in fact demand actual conveyance of the land. It is also apparent in the fact that labour services were abolished except for those which were absolutely indispensable (maintenance of roads and waterways), in the concession of complete freedom of testament and in the establishment of landed property – now easily bought and sold – as the basis of tribal membership. The extent of a citizen's property – as determined by periodic censuses – now became the key to his political and military rights and duties.

In Greece the agrarian policies of the democracies made the village the basic unit of society. In Rome agrarian policies had precisely the opposite effect. Indeed, to make a bold comparison, they had something like an American character. The American farmer lives on his single family farm, outside any village. His property is defined by 'section lines', surveyors' boundaries which run at right angles over mountains, valleys, forests, and hills. Just so – in theory, anyway – his Roman counterpart lived on his *villa*.

Another clear sign of the direction Roman development took is the sharp division made by the Roman state: land was either *ager privatus* or *ager publicus*. The communal forms of property ownership were deliberately put at a disadvantage, as the legal form of the private condominium shows. The ancient common lands (*ager compascuus*) were condemned to extinction, and the agrarian law of 111 B.C. (preserved by an inscription) prevented the creation of new commons.

The same purpose is even more apparent in the contrast between the status of land assigned as *ager privatus* and land that remained public. The former category was subject to the unlimited jurisdiction of the state, whereas with public land the civil law was only concerned with acts of violence or theft or with interference with the rights of a possessor by the person granted use of the land by the state. Hence the rule that the harvest belonged to him who cultivated the land; this is the original significance of the annual terms set by the interdicts.

Serious arguments have been advanced denying that the property interdicts were originally issued with reference to public lands occupied (*possessiones*). However it certainly cannot be proven that the interdicts did not apply to lands held from the public domain, least of all by reference to the fact that Italians held *possessiones*, for after all they enjoyed the right to conduct business (*commercium*) at Rome. The non-Roman was excluded only from the *ius Quiritium* and the formal procedures at law (*legis actiones*). I also think that the manner in which reference is made to the interdicts in the agrarian law of 111 B.C. indicates that they applied to the public lands (which were transferred to the *ager privatus* soon after).

Other property questions were left unregulated by the civil law in so far as the domains were concerned; they were left to mere administration. Now the domains (*ager publicus*) included all those lands which were neither private nor part of an allied state (e.g. *ager Gabinus*), nor acknowledged as part of tolerated communities by popular or senatorial act. All these domains were appropriated for private benefit as *possessiones*, and were either (1) subject only to administrative regulation or else (2) allowed to be completely unregulated.

(1) The regulated properties were partly held as grants in return for services to the state, especially road maintenance service (*viasii vicanii*); other properties were held on lease (or hereditary lease) and were considered 'revenue lands' (*ager vectigalis*). This continued as long as Rome was expanding within the bounds of Italy.

Hereditary lease and land grants were certainly not unknown to Roman law, but they were foreign to Roman private law as it was shaped by the Twelve Tables. Leases and grants fell within the sovereign rights of the state, and therefore no form for legal action regarding such state acts could exist. Hence civil law did not protect property rights arising from these acts, and it was necessary to have recourse to interdicts and administrative orders.

Then, when the allied communities ceased to be sovereign and became *municipia*, the praetors developed a set of standing rules for the municipal and state revenue lands (*ager vectigalis*).

The absence of any sort of legal private lease functioned to prevent the establishment of private manors. In this Roman practice resembled Greek and was opposed to Near Eastern. Also in mediaeval cities the land law, which was the basis of citizen rights, was limited to certain legal forms which excluded personal dependence; and here too this limitation was not a coincidence. Rather, it arose from the essential character of citizenship. In Constance (and certainly elsewhere) the transfer of a citizen's property to tax-paying land needed the consent of the authorities, just as in Freiburg the purchase of citizen land on credit was forbidden. It was only when the purchase of land for income became accepted that it became possible to develop within mediaeval cities a form of taxation which did not transform [property-owning] citizens into tenants.

(2) Unregulated properties on the public domains is our term for the lands held by squatter's right (*occupationes*). Every Roman had this right, and so did every citizen of the communities incorporated after the Social War (88 B.C.).

Originally this meant that uncultivated land could be occupied and improved, in return for which a part of the harvest was due the state. The payment seems not to have been collected, and the occupants were allowed to keep the land indefinitely, the state reserving only a theoretical right to repossess the land if needed. Later, it is true, official permission was needed before occupation took place.

It was this type of squatter's right that led to the formation of those enormous landed estates against which Gracchan legislation was later directed. As to the Licinian-Sextian law [of 367 limiting *occupationes*], despite Soltau's defence, it seems more and more doubtful that it is an historical reality. Most scholars agree that it projects back into the fourth century the conflicts of the Gracchan period, and most conclude that the limitation (supposedly mentioned by Cato the Elder) was enacted in the early years of the second century. However, it is not correct to say that this limitation could not have been passed in the fourth century simply because it sets a maximum of 500 *iugera* and the entire Roman territory available for agriculture amounted then to 'merely two square miles'. 500 *iugera* would be about 125 hectares, and since the Roman agricultural territory amounted to 50,000–60,000 hectares, holdings of that size in the hands of important individuals are by no means impossible (though they are, it is true, quite unlikely). Furthermore, Roman possessions in the fourth century already extended far beyond the boundaries of the *ager Romanus*.

Despite these reservations, it is nevertheless true that the traditional account of the Licinian–Sextian legislation limiting *occupationes* is highly suspect. It is probably an invention, and the most recent arguments against this view have been decisively refuted by Maschke.

Apart from this problem, however, the fact remains that the institution of *occupatio* had a certain brutal simplicity which has no precedent. One can, perhaps, compare the treatment of reclaimed lands on royal domains in Egypt, though even here the legal and operational aspects differ significantly.

Essentially *occupatio* grew out of an ancient institution used to put waste lands under cultivation. This was applied to the lands, generally already cultivated, which fell to the Roman state in the course of its great expansion. Hence the significance of *occupatio* was entirely altered. Since cattle and slave owners could 'occupy' land with much greater success than free peasants, the result was that once commercial slavery penetrated Roman society there developed an agrarian capitalism of unequalled dimensions. The peasantry reacted to this with demands that conquered lands be divided equably among all citizens and assigned as private property (*ager privatus*).

What actually happened was that after most successful wars the conquered land was distributed to the victorious army. Along with this went the use of testamentary freedom to disinherit all children except the one designated as heir. This was a very effective way to keep land in a family, and made sense as long as the probability existed that there would be conquered land available for the disinherited. Freedom of testament, therefore, like the other institutions of Roman land law, must be seen as closely related to the policies of agrarian expansion clearly pursued by the Roman state after the rise of the hoplite army.

The cattle and slave owners, on the other hand, were interested rather in the extension of the public domain (*ager publicus*), for this meant more lands available for occupation or state lease. Throughout the period when Rome was expanding within Italy, the masses frequently pressed for division of the *ager publicus*, and the propertied classes regularly responded with suggestions for conquering new lands to be divided or for sending out colonies. We find this mentioned many times in extant sources, and there is no reason to doubt the authenticity of these reports. Indeed, the interplay of class interests could hardly have been any different during the period when Rome waged its wars of conquest.

For example, expansion was accompanied by similar man-oeuvres in Elis, the essential point being that the aristocracy allowed the masses to have a share of the plunder. Of course in the long run the peasants got the worst in this partnership, and that aspect became more pronounced with time. Only when acute danger from abroad threatened, did the Roman aristocracy reconcile itself to support the foundation of a new colony. Hence the series of citizen colonies were established during the period c. 170–80 b.c.; first there was danger from the Celts and Carthaginians, then the need to repopulate areas devastated in war. Even so the large landowners often opposed colonization stubbornly, even in the period of the Gallic and Punic Wars. Thus the confiscation of the Senones' lands led to sharp struggle between the classes, and it was not divided among citizen colonies until C. Flaminius passed a law as tribune of the plebs against the express opposition of the Senate in 232 b.c.

Behind these conflicts was the struggle between free and unfree labour, a conflict which later led to revolution in the Gracchan period. In Greece and in the Hellenistic Near East the economic importance of slavery for the countryside remained somewhat limited. There were many small centres for trade in Greece, and they did not have large hinterlands suited for slave plantations. In the Near East the land was thickly settled and expensive. Furthermore the Hellenistic states were essentially monarchical and bureaucratic in character, and the large royal domains were farmed by tenants on small holdings; together these factors set narrow limits to the development of large-scale slave-run enter-prises. One sign of this is the rarity of slave uprisings in the Greek world. Except for the Spartan feudal state and Chios we know of virtually no slave uprisings in Greece and in the whole of the Near East, and the later the period the fewer they are.

But the insurrection led by Spartacus in South Italy and Sicily was one of the most frightful social struggles in Antiquity. It occurred because it was in the Roman state that servile masses were accumulated and exploited on a hitherto unprecedented scale. Several factors determined this: (a) the steady growth of liquid wealth; (b) the geographical limitations on expansion in the hinterland of Italy; (c) the capitalistic character of the exploitation of overseas conquests; (d) the great influx of slaves for sale on the market.

Large-scale slave imports are dated by our sources, as Ferrero has pointed out, at the time when plantations raising olives and grapes became critical factors in the economy, and this was also about the time of the Gracchan movement. However it is evident from Cato the Elder's work on agriculture that slavery and plantations must have appeared earlier. The plantation run by slaves as described by Cato could only have been possible after the pacification of Italy which followed Hannibal's defeat. Thereafter no enemy set foot on the land for 600 years, and so there started the decline of the hoplite yeomanry.

The further expansion proceeded, the less could conquered land be used for colonization by free peasants. During the period of overseas expansion such colonization ended completely. Between 177 B.C. and the colonial foundations of the Gracchi, over half a century, only a single citizen colony was established. The aristocracies of office and of money were on good terms – hence the tribunes of the plebs really functioned as tools of the Senate until the Gracchi appeared – and their aim was to preserve existing property relations and maintain the military strength of Italy along with that of the federated communities. Schulten has rightly drawn attention to the fact that the end of the old citizen colonization in 177 B.C. coincides with the passage of the *lex Claudia* which excluded Latins, while the still sharper law on the rights of foreigners (*lex Junia de peregrinis*) was enacted after the fall of Tiberius Gracchus and before Caius Gracchus' election. These restrictions on the freedom of movement of the allies were intended partly to exclude democratic and illegitimate elements from political assemblies (in which Latins owning Roman land may originally have had the right to vote), partly also to keep the yeoman hoplites on the land so that they would continue to form part of the local communities' tax base. Indeed, the yeomen supported these restrictions, and the *lex Claudia* was passed in response to their wishes.

However these measures also served the conservative interests of the aristocracy of office (the *nobilitas*). Thus legend reports that a typical representative of this aristocracy, Scipio Aemilianus, on one occasion refused to recite the traditional prayer for expansion of the state, and instead prayed for its 'preservation'. Such aristocrats were in fact as much concerned about preservation of the *status quo* in internal as in external affairs. Their control of the magistracies and the officers' corps would necessarily be undermined if Rome annexed territories outside Italy, for then armies would have to be maintained there and such armies could not possibly continue to be manned with conscripted citizens. Indeed, difficulties arose in replacing and posting non-commissioned officers as soon as overseas operations started.

Expansion overseas was capitalist in origin. The aristocracy of office preferred to maintain a cautious foreign policy and avoided interventions. It was the merchants, tax farmers, and domain leaseholders who prevailed and used Roman power to destroy the ancient trading centres of Carthage, Corinth, and Rhodes – all to serve their own capitalist interests. It was they who championed the policy of overseas annexations, which provided opportunities for capital investments rather than for colonization by free peasants.

Nor did either the aristocrats or the capitalists have any idea of handing these annexations over to the peasants. In any case, emigration overseas could not appeal to peasants except in times of extreme distress. One symptom of change is that as conquests ceased to be used as a source of settlement land for young peasants, so freedom of testament also began to be limited. Finally, in the last decades of the Republic it was effectively ended by a new type of legal action (*querela inofficioso testamenti*) by which wills might be invalidated. Freedom of testament no longer suited the new realities.

At the same time developments increasingly tended towards the advantage of slave-plantation owners. More and more they took possession of lands (as *occupationes*) from the public domain (*ager publicus*), which now covered a good part of Italy. Some of these lands were used as ranches, and indeed Cato the Elder had already pointed out that this was the most profitable way to invest capital because it involved the least expense and the least use of labour. From the first these ranches must have been large enterprises, for leaseholds on the state domains tended to go to wealthy capitalists. This was partly because they had better business contacts, partly because the peasants who kept their holdings on conquered land subject to the payment of tribute could be intimidated by pressure to which wealthy Romans were of course immune.

As a result the state leasing system of the Roman Republic was much more 'capitalist' in character than had been that of the Greek cities. Companies were formed to farm taxes and lease domains, and these companies (*societates publicanorum*) were essentially unregulated, a sharp contrast with conditions in the Hellenistic Near East. It was also contrary to the normal practice of the Greek republics, but here the controlling factor was that Rome had no permanent financial bureaucracy, nor could it have had one while it remained a republic and a city-state, but at the same time it had a vast territory to administer. This, then, explains why the tax farmers, for example, hired the entire fiscal bureaucracy themselves.

The Roman companies of publicans were the largest capitalist enterprises in Antiquity. Participation in these enterprises was limited to men with vast capital holdings in slaves and cash. They also needed to have extensive landed possessions, preferably with Italic status (which was privileged and therefore at an economic advantage), since they had to offer land as security when bidding for contracts.

This last condition, by which only land enjoying full privileges under Roman land law could be offered as security, had the effect of giving the capitalist class in the Roman state a distinctively national character. It was much more so than had any similar class been in the Near East. Under the Ptolemies, for example, the publicans seem to have been mainly foreigners, and in Greece the smaller states actually encouraged foreign capitalists to make bids in order to have more competition. As a result of its dissimilar policies the ancient aristocratic features of Rome's society and economy were greatly strengthened.

Hence a contrast with the Greek democracies. There again and again in their periods of prosperity a collectivist and petty bourgeois tendency manifested itself in policies stressing the provision of food supplies. At Rome, however, policies were much more thoroughly capitalist in character. Along with this went the development of close ties with the wealthy classes of the allied cities; note that all Italians, not just Romans, profited from the right to occupy lands in the public domain, and Italians also profited from the business enterprises which accompanied Roman expansion, from the settlement of conquered territories, and from the establishment of 'provinces'.

It is of course true that Roman expansion was accompanied by a sharp struggle of interests. There were the ancient class conflicts between peasants and estate owners (*possessores*) with large cattle and slave properties, and then in addition there was a struggle within the propertied classes. On one side was the aristocracy of office, primarily concerned about the political aspects of empire, centred on the Senate (which represented its interests), and excluded both by law and custom from industry and finance. Exclusion of aristocrats from direct involvement in industry was common throughout Antiquity, but Rome was unusual in that this exclusion was extended to include tax farming and shipping; a senator might possess ships only of a capacity just sufficient to transport the products of his own estates. As a result senators could gain wealth only from political office, from the rents paid by their tenants, from mortgages assumed through the agency of freedmen (though this was forbidden, it was commonly done as early as Cato the Elder), and from indirect investment in commerce and shipping.

On the other side was the class of capitalists, the men who participated directly in capitalist enterprise. They were excluded from the Senate, and therefore their political base was the group of voting units (*centuriae*) reserved for those with the highest census – the knights – in the centuriate assembly. From the time of Caius Gracchus they formed a legally constituted order.

The fact that as tax farmers the knights worked closely with officials [of senatorial rank] in the provinces to plunder the locals and share the booty did not lead to an alliance between the two groups. Quite the contrary: the senatorial clans showed themselves to be determined to keep the 'bourgeoisie' – the knights – under control, and in particular to reserve for senatorials membership of the judicial panels which ruled on acts of extortion and embezzlement by officials. Nevertheless the result of Rome's conquests was to increase steadily the opportunities for profit, and this meant that the economic power of capitalists constantly increased, for they were essential to the state treasury because they could advance cash and because they had the business training needed to manage public revenues.

As early as the time of the Second Punic War (217–201 B.C.) the capitalists constituted a political force, and indeed they saved the state's finances then, but in return gained the power to dictate policies. Starting from the time of the Gracchi (133–122 B.C.) the tax farmers controlled direct as well as indirect taxes, at least in the province of Asia Minor, and the Roman bourgeoisie enjoyed a golden age. One aspect of this was the development of commerce in slaves and the exploitation of slaves on a colossal scale, a scale such as Greece had never known.

Private plantations worked by slaves seem to have been first developed from pharaonic domains in Egypt worked by peasants rendering labour services. This model was then spread throughout the ancient world, especially the Western Mediterranean, by the Phoenicians (especially the Carthaginians), the first people interested in purely commercial colonization. Their slaves were kept under military discipline, and they were unrelentingly exploited since warfare made them easily replaceable. The slave plantation was always especially connected with the Roman province of Africa (modern Tunisia) and with Sicily. The first systematic treatment of plantation management seems to have been the 28-volume work by Mago of Carthage.

There were two forms of production which could be used to raise products of relatively high value that were worth transportting for market sale: (1) share-cropping, and (2) slave plantations. Since the lands of the Western Mediterranean were thinly settled, capitalists preferred to use slave labour as long as it was economically feasible to wage war for new lands and – especially – more slaves. One may say that from Cato the Elder until Augustus enterprises based on slave labour grew steadily larger and in fact became the dominant form of economic activity.

Roman writers on agriculture take it for granted that slaves would do most of the work, free labourers being used only for the harvest (as Mago had recommended earlier). The economic and social importance of both yeomanry and peasantry were declining as that of the wealthy rose, and as a result the expansive tendencies of these rural classes [*Ackerbürger- und Bauernstand*] progressively weakened. The landless sons of the peasantry flocked to the capital and no longer could be sent out to colonies, since they were no longer interested in owning land and so gaining full political rights. Instead they became in increasing numbers dependent on the city's system of grain doles. This in turn reduced the demand for Italian grain and so gave a further impulse to the displacement of free peasants from the countryside to the capital.

Another factor in this situation was the ruinous burdens borne by the yeoman conscripted for military service in overseas campaigns [during 200–146 B.C.], campaigns which were waged for others' interests rather than their own. It had already become apparent that lengthy wars could not be waged with a self-equipped citizen army, and now this became even more difficult because the increasing intensity of cultivation meant, as always, that the yeoman could not leave his farm without suffering serious economic losses.

L. M. Hartmann observed that in Antiquity slavery was necessary because of the burden of army service which was borne by citizens. That is in part correct, as I hope my discussion has demonstrated. However, it is also true that such a generalization cannot explain that which is characteristic in Roman society, the development of large plantations worked by slaves, nor indeed can one deduce from it the necessity of slavery. The situation demanded that yeoman citizens be able to leave their lands to serve the state in politics and war, and this need could have been met by other forms of unfree labour: serfdom, share-cropping, helotry, and so on. In any situation there are a variety of possible adaptations, generally very different in character. When one has determined which of these possibilities a society has chosen, then one has generally discovered the key to that society's historical individuality.

The decisive struggle between free and unfree forms of labour and land use was fought over the demands of the Gracchan movement, centred on the ancient question of division of the public domains (*ager publicus*). The Gracchi, or at least Tiberius, were personally interested mainly in political reforms. Their aim was to restore the ancient foundations of Rome's military system, and they assumed that it was a condition of this that the peasants should be able to buy land cheaply for themselves and their children. However, the only way to make available large areas for settlement was to limit the public lands available for occupation and also to confiscate some occupied lands. Such confiscations affected families which had enjoyed the use of properties for generations, and (as Eduard Meyer has emphasized) these families were not only Roman but also from the allied states, which had received rights equal to Rome's in the exploitation of the domains.

The Gracchan movement thus unleashed a struggle of classes at Rome, and also it gave rise to a conflict between the Roman citizenry and the allies. Therefore the allies, in order to protect their economic rights and in particular their rights to a share in distributed lands (*assignatio*), were driven to demand full Roman citizenship. Before this they had taken an opposite position, protesting against the emigration of their wealthier citizens to Rome.

The Gracchi led a movement which was ideologically motivated. Even with the peasantry's support they had no chance of success against the overwhelmingly superior strength of the opposition. Their only hope lay in dividing the opposition, and in fact they did win over what the English call 'the commercial interest': the class which owned slaves and capital but did not belong to the aristocracy of office, the bourgeoisie solely concerned with making money, in short the so-called equestrians. The Gracchi won their support by handing over the province of Asia Minor to equestrian collectors and by giving them control of the judicial panels. As a result the equestrians reached the height of their power, which they enjoyed until Sulla returned control of the panels to the senatorial clans.

Thus ancient capitalism reached the high point of its development, in forms which were quite individual to it. Because this capitalism was closely connected with the power of the equestrian capitalist class its triumph was achieved at the cost of the provincials, who were surrendered to ruthless plundering. Furthermore this triumph of ancient capitalism did not work to the permanent benefit of the Gracchan movement, for the Senate succeeded in winning back the equestrians once their thirst for gain had been satisfied. The Gracchan proposal to give citizenship to the allies and so win them over could not prevail in Rome; [limited] citizenship not only conferred a claim to distributed land, it also gave the popular assemblies their power and the opportunities for sharing wealth.

Hence the citizenry of Rome began to take a path very similar to that which the *dēmos* of Athens took before and under Pericles. Eventually, because of the military and political purposes behind his agrarian laws, Caius Gracchus found himself confronted with rivals for the favour of the masses, demagogues from the ranks of the large landowners. The Gracchi and their successors not only distributed lands but also tried to make sure that these lands would not be used for speculation and loans; the owners were to be working farmers only. Therefore they supported the preparation of inventories, and also enacted decisive legal limitations such as prohibition on sale and, as a sign of state ownership, payment of title fees. (When Sulla and Caesar distributed lands to their veterans they enacted prohibitions of sale and dower on the one hand, while on the other they granted tax exemptions.)

It was, then, precisely those limitations on ownership which were motivated by their social and political policies which caused the downfall of the Gracchi. The prohibition on sale and the introduction of title fees were used against Caius Gracchus. His enemies 'outbid' him, and so triumphed. This victory of 'the landed interest' and the violent suppression of the Gracchan movement signified the victory of unfree labour and thereby the destruction of the ancient foundations of the Roman state. The occupied lands on the public domains (*ager publicus*) were declared private properties (*ager privatus*) by the agrarian law of 111 B.C. which is extant in inscriptions; in other words, the occupied lands were definitively appropriated for private benefit, and the public domains of Italy were in effect liquidated.

Then followed the military reform of Marius in 104 B.C., by which the old self-equipped citizen army was replaced by an army equipped by the state and recruited from the proletariat, the men listed in the census as having no property (*capite censi*). This change came about because it was necessary to implement the reorganization of the army and to meet the pressing danger of the German invasions.

Later the Social War forced concession of Roman citizenship with all its benefits to the peasants and petty bourgeoisie of Italy. By that time, however, the political importance of the Roman peasantry was over; it ceased to be a factor in the political assemblies, public administration, and the exercise of imperial power. As for the army, after Marius' reform it had become a welfare agency for the poor; now it was the veteran, not the citizen, who had a claim on land distributed. Along with this went an increase in the size of allotments. These increased to 30 *iugera* under the Gracchi, to 50 under the Triumvirate; and significantly larger allotments were made in the provinces. Then, too, another class's role altered: the wealthy ceased to man the army's cavalry units, as in the past. Together these changes created the political basis for Caesarism.

Along with the above went a great increase in the numbers and importance of unfree rural labour, as the great slave uprisings testify. The large-scale confiscations and land distributions under the Triumvirate had a negative, not positive effect. The existing economic structures remained intact, and this involved the social degradation of the peasantry; while the veterans, despite the legal limitations on sale of allotments, did not in fact remain on their lands. To sum up: after the full ownership of occupied land was confirmed, the whole of Italy was to a very large extent in the hands of estate owners.

How much of these properties was purchased from peasants we cannot know; the estates (*massae*) mentioned in extant documents give only incidental and later information. One must also remember that the yeomanry did not cease to exist. Throughout the period of Roman rule there were always farmers working their own land, especially in areas where the land could not be let. Similarly there exist in our own times many independent craftsmen, and they will no doubt continue to be found. Schulten's thorough study of the geographical extent of Sabellian names indicates that yeomen kept their stability especially in mountainous areas, a fact which certainly was not due to the limitations on emigration imposed by Rome. Quantitatively, then, the yeoman remained in large numbers.

But qualitatively – taking into account his social and economic importance – the yeoman counted for nothing as compared to the slaveowner. To the agricultural writers he is – with some exaggeration – merely a poor fellow who works his land with the labour of his children (*pauperculus cum sua progenie*), his land being whatever was not suited for organized, rational production [with slave labour]. Caesar's law that at least one-third of all shepherds must be free shows the stage reached by this development, as does the speech of Tiberius [Gracchus] in the Senate on the consequences of the reliance on slave labour in agriculture.

The technology of Roman plantations was more or less on the same level as that of the Greeks. Manure was used as a fertilizer to some extent in Cato's time, as was stall feeding, but agricultural implements remained quite primitive. The smoothing board was not used until the Empire (and then rarely), the sickle was employed for harvesting and grain was threshed by cattle. Later the threshing cart was adopted from Carthage. Grain agriculture was not very profitable, especially in inland areas, and its technology was established early.

Generally only valuable products such as olive oil, wine, fattened cattle, and gourmet foods could be profitably produced in inland areas for sale on the market. This determined the kind of organization which developed on Roman estates. Large ranches with transmigratory herds were dominant in Apulia and along the passes in mountainous areas; elsewhere they were unusual. Everywhere capitalist enterprise turned away from raising grain.

The farmer's calender published by G. Wissowa as *Apophoreton* (Berlin, 1903) is interesting but does not indicate, as he thinks, anything precise about the type of farming on an estate. True, the calendar indicates times for the farmer's various activities – sowing, weeding, harvesting – in raising barley, wheat, spelt, peas, vetch, hay, fruit, olives, nutwood, reeds, wine, and cattle. This, however, does not mean, as Wissowa seems to assume, that all these products were raised on a single farm, nor even which ones would have been.

Enterprises needing relatively high capital investment were run with slave labour under direct supervision. This type included olive plantations, vineyards, and large-scale cash-crop production. Grain land may have been cultivated in Cato's time by piece-work labour, but increasingly this was entrusted to peasants working leased parcels, *coloni*, who paid a part of their crop or else a fixed sum in money. The latter system was increasingly preferred, and it figures nearly exclusively in our legal sources.

Slave plantations spread greatly in the period from Cato the Elder (234–149 B.C.) to Varro (116–27 B.C.). So long as the slave market received a steady supply the slaves were kept in barracks, living without wife or property and subject to strict military discipline. Female slaves were little used then for production. Generally only the overseer (*vilicus*) enjoyed the right to marry (*contubernium*) and to own property (*peculium*), whereas the slaves who worked in the vineyards in Cato's time were often chained and given increased rations for doing heavy labour under compulsion. In Late Republican times these slaves slept in barracks on the estates, arose at morning, fell into formation in regular groups of 10 (*decuriae*), and were then taken to work by their overseers. Thus unfree labour was fully exploited, much in the same manner as were the slaves in Egypt under the New Empire. Their better clothing was kept in storerooms for which the overseer was responsible, and this clothing was worn only on holidays or on special occasions at roll call. Hospitals were provided for sick slaves and prisons for those unwilling to work.

As the plantations grew larger more slaves were needed, and owners tried to buy them as cheaply as possible. Enslaved criminals were judged to be very useful: 'the wicked are more clever' (*velocior est animus improborum*). Still supply was a problem, for although bonuses were given to slaves for procreating and rearing children, still the fact that general promiscuity prevailed (affection for a slave girl would increase the propensity to malingering and the like, as Varro noted) meant that there could not possibly be a birth rate among the slaves sufficient to maintain their numbers, nor indeed sufficient to replace even a substantial part of the slave population. Hence the great necessity for constant purchase of slaves for the barracks; a cheap supply was critical, for slave production consumes the work force very quickly.

Rational exploitation of slave labour was one of the basic problems of Roman plantations, because their need for labour fluctuated. Just as today we say that idle machines 'eat up' profits, so in Antiquity slave capital (*instrumentum vocale*) literally ate up a plantation's profits (cf. Cato, *On Agriculture* 39.2). Plantations were originally of moderate size, a few hundred acres being the area Cato assumes as normal. Hence there could be little craft work on estates for internal use, and besides, as long as slaves were cheap there was no incentive to train them in crafts. The result was that while estates used their own workers for making woven goods and doing carpentry and repair work, most other needs were met with goods purchased on the market:

metal goods, evidently all slave clothing (Athens, for example, imported its slave clothing from Megara), fish and salt for slaves' food, pitch for vats, and so forth. Besides, nearly all crops, even wool, were sold as raw products.

Furthermore in addition to slaves free workers were used in harvest season for stoop labour, and they were also hired by the day for work in unhealthy land in order to spare the slaves (who represented a capital investment). These free workers were at first essential, especially at harvest time, but they declined steadily in relative importance. Partly this was because it seemed dangerous to use them alongside large masses of slaves, partly too because of the general psychological effects of unfree labour. Varro recommends that free workers should be kept only for a day at a time if possible, and this tells us much about these psychological effects. (Glaser and Gummerus interpret the text otherwise, but Pernice seems to me to have disproved their arguments.)

In Varro's time another group was available for day labour – the peasants who had to work off debts (*nexi*, *obaerati*). In ancient times still another group was available as extra help in harvest time – the peasants who held land by favour (*precarium*). The legal status of holders of *precaria* was much like that of the so-called free labourers in East Germany today, who are given a piece of land on which to raise potatoes to tie them to the estate during the harvest season; they have no title to the land or any other contractual guarantee, in contrast to estate workers [*Inst-leute*] and others on contract (cf. M. Weber, 'Die Lage der Landarbeiter im ostelbischen Deutschland', *Schriften des Vereins für Sozialpolitik* 50 (1893), pp. 773 ff.)

However as early as Cato's time a great deal of harvest work was entrusted to contractors who had crews of free workers. An even more simple device was to sell the crop as it stood, and it seems to have been very common. Teams of cattle were also rented out for harvesting. All these types of agreement are mentioned by Cato, and they indicate a low level of capital investment.

As a result of the type of solution adopted for the problem of seasonal labour, the ideal estate of the second century B.C. as described by Cato the Elder was very closely involved with the market as a centre of production and consumption and also, to a relatively high degree, as a centre of employment. Of course people believed in the old principle that one should not buy what one could produce, but this could only be followed to a very limited extent because of the structure of the estate economy. As Gummerus has elegantly demonstrated, the money economy was expanding in the time of Cato.

However, as more and more land came into the hands of large landowners, and as estates increased in average size – the two tendencies were of course separate, but in practice coincided – more and more estates as early as the time of Varro not only made bricks and pottery for the market but also had their own craftsmen producing goods for internal consumption. In addition female slaves were used to make slave clothing, a practice unknown to Cato and indeed to the Greeks. (Varro mentions male weavers, but I agree with Gummerus that they probably produced for the market. This was a capital investment out of business profits.) Female slaves were also used to make olive presses for estate use, involving a substantial outlay which only owners with plenty of capital could afford. On the other hand we find that a characteristic feature of agriculture in the Later Republic is renting out small parcels of land to tenant peasants, *coloni*.

Craftsmen working on estates for internal consumption are to be found, as one might expect, mostly where large plantations were established in areas with little urban or commercial development. As Varro expressly states, even in his day the average size of estates was such that putting capital into skilled slave craftsmen was quite risky. But the larger the estate and the further inland its site, the greater the role played on it by estate craftsmen and also by *coloni*.

Renting parcels of land on the basis of a mutual bona fide contract (the *locatio-conductio* form) developed at a time which we cannot determine, but it took the place (as in Egypt) of the ancient cession by favour, the feudal *precarium*. We can imagine the social position of the *colonus* in Republican times from the fact that not only were his property rights not protected against the landlord, in which his position resembled the holder of a *precarium*, but they were also not protected against third parties, a disability not shared by either the holder of a *precarium* or a tenant on public lands. Instead the *colonus'* contract only entitled him to an indemnity payment if the landlord chose not to allow him to remain on his rented parcel.

Already under the Republic there were *coloni* in all areas, and their number multiplied as the large estates or *latifundia* increased in size. Some of these estates were made up of scattered holdings, others were single, continuous tracts. Naturally *coloni* were more common on the former, but they were also to be found on the latter. After hopes for agrarian reform were thwarted it became clear that Italian peasants would have to find their place as tenants on the expanding estates. In the provinces the imperial government took possession of great areas, partly confiscated and partly acquired otherwise from rulers or aristocratic houses, and on these lands the government settled *coloni* or peasants with rights similar to those of a *precarium* holder.

As early as *c.* 100 B.C. scholarly discussion started as to whether it was more advantageous to work an estate oneself (that is, use slaves) or else rent it out to tenants. In practice the decision continued to be in favour of slave labour as long as slaves were cheap (as they were in Republican times), but even then they could only be used for those products which were produced on labour extensive plantations. Many acres of grain land and in particular isolated fields (*agri longinquiores*) of the growing estates were probably let to tenants even in Varro's day (although he does not mention it), as we know was done later. The less a large estate concentrated on a few cash crops the stronger would be the tendency to divide the land among tenant peasants, *coloni*. It is perfectly clear that even before Varro's time *coloni* were a familiar element of agricultural society. Caesar (*Civil Wars* 1.34.2) speaks of them as dependents of a landlord, along with his slaves and freedmen. Already in the Late Republic, therefore, *coloni* were essentially copyhold tenants on large estates [*Gutsinsassen*], generally owning no property except some cattle, paying rent for their lands and its improvements, and working these lands as the landlord directed. Sometimes a general directive (*lex*) for all *coloni* on an estate was issued, similar in character to our German 'work regulations' [*Arbeitsordnungen*]. Often *coloni* borrowed from their landlord and put up their movables as collateral, thus becoming even more dependent.

To what extent did tenants become share-croppers? First, it

should be noted that in Western provinces there is no documentary evidence for the existence of share-cropping on private land until late in the imperial period. In any case, however, the deciding factor must have always been whether the tenant was regarded primarily as having assumed the duty of working his land to produce as much as possible, and so pay the landlord as much as possible in the form of a part of the crops; or, alternatively, whether the tenant was regarded as a tenant who paid rent and in return received the right to use the land as agreed. But even in the last case, when money rent was paid, if the landlord supplied the equipment the former attitude must have prevailed from the first. In the language of the day it was the landlord who 'makes use of' (*exercet*) his land 'by means of his tenants' (*per colonos*).

It is also logically quite likely that the *coloni* were obliged by their tenancy agreements to render labour services at times of need on their estates. This can be said even though it is not attested in extant sources nor is it mentioned by Varro. At a later time, we know, tenants working for their estate were treated as were most free labourers in Antiquity, receiving food from the landlord and working under direction of an inspector (but this is based upon a disputed interpretation of a text).

Thus as more and more land passed into the hands of large estate owners, the great mass of yeomen ended up on land which they held only as tenants under revocable agreements, for part of the land occupied by the *coloni* had originally been worked by freeholders. Similarly the army, which had originally been recruited from self-equipped yeomen (as in every *polis*), first took in the landless (*capite censi*) and then became a state-equipped force in which the *coloni* increasingly replaced the yeomen.

Estates were poorly managed in Republican times, mainly because landlords lived in the city, were involved in the political life of the city, and therefore were necessarily absentee. Generally the landlord appeared only occasionally to receive reports from his overseer, and how little he knew of estate management – and each generation it grew less – is indicated by the simple rules of thumb suggested by the agrarian handbooks. Careful accounts were usually kept only for valuable cash crops, oil and wine in particular. Monetary income was what the owner wanted, nothing else; this explains the lack of interest in any extensive improvements, for which in fact no credit was available.

This explains, too, why often grape and olive crops were sold on the stem. The cultivation of these crops was labour extensive and was not characterized by much care. Grain cultivation, on the other hand, remained labour intensive in technology; the crop was used mainly for the consumption needs of the manorial estates. Probably the limited needs of the local markets were met by *coloni*. As for Rome, it was supplied with grain imported from overseas under state control. Even these imports were not procured on the open market; the largest part, which was destined for distribution to the urban masses, was increasingly collected as tribute from subject peoples.

Wherever the Roman aristocracy controlled the administration it furthered the formation of large landed estates. Partly this was because the Roman government generally favoured oligarchical regimes in the overseas areas under its control and indeed depended on the oligarchies for political support. That was an indirect stimulus to large holdings, but a direct stimulus was the manner in which the Romans disposed of the land and land law. This subject will be discussed in the article on the colonate, but a few points deserve attention here.

Lands not in full private ownership differed greatly in legal status. As stated above, lands held from the public domain – the *ager publicus populi Romani* (the public lands of the Roman people) – were all originally classed as *possessiones* in private law. But the Italian *ager publicus* was distributed and disappeared, partly as a result of the conversion of pre-empted lands (*occupationes*) into private property, partly as a result of the massive land allotments (*assignationes*) of Caesar in Campania and of the Triumvirate. The little that remained (*subseciva*) was given to squatters by Domitian. The situation, then, was that after Caesar's distributions no domain land suitable for cultivation was left in Italy, except for the domains of the municipalities; thus henceforth the domains of the Roman state were all in the provinces.

Persons who were allowed to hold lands from the public domain on written lease were always such as enjoyed the right to engage in business with Romans – the right of *commercium*. Now there is a problem: did these tenants receive full legal protection of their rights against third parties, even when their lease was of limited duration? Mitteis thinks not, but I am sure that they did and that this is attested by Hyginus.

Of course it is true that *coloni* on private land did not have the right to institute legal proceedings, but this was because of their social position. Everywhere the people who leased public lands were of a different status, both in law and in fact.

Transfer of a lease on public land to a substitute (*vicarius*) could be done if the authorities gave approval. But the legal recourse to Roman courts was available only to persons who were part of the Roman legal community – Roman citizens and their allies, not their subjects. When subjects did settle on Roman domains, whether by virtue of written lease or payment of customary tributes, their tenures were *precaria*, subject to tribute levies and cancellation. Such *precaria* holders were generally the former owners of land which had been conquered and confiscated, and they remained there until they were replaced by the arbitrary power of the censors or by a general disposition of lands for foundation of a colony.

The leasing out of whole domains was essentially no more than a revision of the normal conditions set by domain leases for specified periods. Tax farming, however, was very different, because it involved among other things the collection of dues from tenants on the domains, and the contract for this collection was sold to a publican at auction. Now the two types of enterprise – domain leasing and tax farming – could be combined in the activities of an individual. This happened when a large-scale operator leased a domain and at the same time took the contract to collect taxes from the peasants on the domain, the *coloni*, or when he sub-leased domain land. As a result, alongside the old forms of ownership [of public land] subject to legal census periods and the conditions of *precarium* tenure, there developed new relationships based on hereditary lease, especially in the case of lands needing improvement.

As early as 111 B.C. an agrarian law set the amount of tax to be raised on African domains let on hereditary lease, and gradually it became the rule that domain lands were let on contract for 100 years or more in return for rent and fees for transfer to heirs. The contractors (*mancipes*) then either sub-let the land or farmed it themselves as a large enterprise.

Despite the objections of Mitteis, I still believe that the system of large-scale leases without time limits, combined with sub-leases to *coloni* – a system clearly present in Constantine's law of A.D. 319 (*Code of Justinian* 11.63.1) – was already known in essentials to Hyginus (*De condicionibus agrorum*, in *Die Schriften der romischen Feldmesser*, ed. K. Lachmann *et al.*, 2 vols., Berlin, 1848–52, vol. 1, p. 116) in *c.* A.D. 100. Here be it noted that it is not true, as Mitteis and Schulten assume, that a lease for 100 years is equivalent to a permanent lease; consider usage in England! But the contractor in Hyginus (*mancipes*) is obviously the precursor of the contractor (*emphyteuticarius*) in Constantine's law, unless one wants to consider the former an entrepreneur whose business it was to settle the land with hereditary tenants – something which seems to me most unlikely.

Mitteis' arguments on this matter are mainly based on deductions, and cannot be supported by texts. They do not convince me. When Hyginus speaks of 'all the adjoining landowners' (*proximi quique possessores*) he does not necessarily mean peasants any more than references to *katoikoi* in Egypt mean peasants. Small tenants holding hereditary lease are mentioned in Roman as in Greek law, even though less frequently in Roman because the economic structure of Roman rule differed from the Greek, which was based on small-town policies. Also this group is not attested for lands paying quit-rent to the state (*ager vectigalis*). However, the characteristic feature of Roman economic development is clearly the steady increase of the amount of land held as private or semi-private property. Mitteis agrees with this as far as the Later Empire is concerned. Yet it seems unlikely that this did not begin in the Later Republic; since its administration then already made use of large contractors (*mancipes*), why presume that it avoided leasing land in large blocks to these contractors?

Very early, at some unknown date, public lands were occupied on terms which left the time-limits unspecified. Such occupations were authorized by senatorial decree, as in the case of the lease of the lands set aside for public ways (*viasii vicani*), and were then subject to administrative regulation and guarantee; or else they were authorized by a law passed by an assembly, as in the case of the land let on hereditary lease (*ager privatus vectigalisque*) in Africa.

As a result of this only a small part of Roman territory was affected by the regular land law of the state, with its particular tendencies; the great mass of landowners held their property on a variety of terms, most involving revocability of tenure so that their properties were really *precaria*. Along with them there were also those who owned land outside the Roman state – land in the 'foreign territories' (*ager peregrinus*).

Within the Latin League the legal status of land and the right to commerce with Romans were regulated by treaty; each of the two partners – Roman and Latin – had a certain share, varying from period to period, in the national land rights of the other. Then in the overseas possessions of Rome full legal autonomy was guaranteed by treaty to some of the allied city-states (*civitates foederatae*), and this meant that their citizens held their land under their own land laws and possessed irrevocable title. However, much of the land in the overseas possessions was made public (*ager publicus*) and thereby placed under direct control of the central authorities in Rome. These lands had been confiscated or had been domains of conquered regimes, and a part – perhaps a large part – of them seems to have been provisionally ceded to the local city-states in return for payment of tribute. Such lands were surveyed in the simple manner used when only boundary lines were needed (*ager per extremitatem mensura comprehensus*), as described above. (It was the efforts of the state to reassert claim to these lands in the fourth century A.D. which caused such serious economic disturbances, at Mitteis has rightly argued.) This cession of land to city-states could arise for many reasons, in particular when they contracted to collect the state taxes due in their territories, at first for a defined period and then permanently; this practice had developed already in Syria under Ptolemaic rule.

Another part of overseas lands was provisionally defined as foreign (*ager peregrinus*), which meant that this status could be cancelled by law but not by administrative order. Such lands included the possessions of the *stipendiarii* in Africa – large landowners who owed tribute and who held their land under their own law rather than under Roman private law or as rented domain land. This meant that the provincial governor could intervene to modify their property rights, as was possible in the case of all property held by subjects.

Finally, part of the land in overseas territories was in communities which owed tribute, hence called specifically *civitates stipendiariae*, and here ownership was in the nature of *precarium*: a revocable privilege conceded by senatorial decree for an undefined period with the formula 'we order that they hold and enjoy', *habere uti frui liceat*, translated as *hemon heneken echein exeinai* in the *Senatusconsultum de Thisbaeis* of 170 B.C. (cf. C. Bruns, *Fontes Iuris Romani Antiqui*, 7th ed., Tübingen, 1909, p. 167). Such lands were always subject to the obligation to pay tribute (*stipendium* was a regular payment for military expenses), and never assimilated to the Roman public domain.

The Senate's power to dispose of public lands and alter property law in the provinces changed with time. We cannot go into particulars here, but in general one can say that this power increased steadily, and with it there was a steady increase in the Roman oligarchy's power over the lands of their great empire. Possibilities for acquisitions were quite numerous, as the sketch just given should indicate. Let me merely emphasize the fact that in the last period of the Republic most of the population settled on the lands in Rome's vast possessions were not protected by any treaty. Whatever rights to the land they had were revocable; their holdings were *precaria*. This applied especially to the peasants who actually worked the soil. Those living on confiscated lands, or on the domains of conquered regimes, or on the estates of owners or city-states owing tribute (*stipendiarii*), were all in the same position as the *ethnē* of the Hellenistic states and in particular the *laoi* of Ptolemaic Egypt.

In other words, the peasants were subject to the arbitrary power of the provincial governors and, in so far as he did not intervene, to the power of the tax farmers. Their personal status and their rights to the soil they worked were no protection. Their only recourse was to institute proceedings at Rome, as in the case of Verres. Such proceedings, of course, were only possible if the plaintiffs had powerful protectors and plenty of money, conditions which the peasants themselves could hardly achieve (even though they figure so large in Cicero's charges).

From all this, then, we may conclude that under the Roman Republic every provincial governor – not just those like Verres, but 'normal' ones as well – tended to reduce the land available to peasant cultivation and to increase the great estates worked by slaves. The figure given by Cicero for the land distribution of the territories of Leontini are simply an especially striking example of this.

Similarly the complicated and hierarchical system of grades of political and economic rights worked in the same direction, and it was upon this hierarchical system that the Roman Republic based its power. For example: only the Roman citizen with full rights enjoyed complete freedom of movement; citizens with Latin rights were expelled from Rome when their communities so requested, in order that they might assume their political obligations. Exactly the same treatment was accorded citizens of all the communities which entered the empire, whatever their form of allied or subject status. Of course in practice many non-Roman citizens moved about quite freely, but legally they could always be sent or recalled home.

This had consequences for the structure of agrarian society, consequences which were not fully realized until the Later Empire. No less significant were the restrictions placed on subjects' right to trade (*commercium*) and their right to marry (*connubium*). The latter, for example, involved the right to transmit property by inheritance and therefore affected the property titles of the citizens of every single allied or subject community. This matter was regulated by treaty or – more frequently – by the decisions and favour of individual governors.

Furthermore, the other aspect of the situation was that the Roman nobles used the praetorian edicts to create a system of land appraisal which in effect gave them exactly the kind of law they wanted to regulate the ownership, inheritance, and sale of land – often at the cost of the traditional rights of Roman commoners. This development can be compared to the way the English aristocracy used the old court of chancery to develop a law of equity.

The result was that in this as in every other respect the Roman bourgeoisie formed a privileged order in the provinces, and its profit-making opportunities were thereby greatly enhanced, as was the economic dependence of the non-privileged provincials.

Indebtedness increased enormously, especially in those areas where tax collecting was farmed out to equestrian publicans.

This is the essential background to the 'Sicilian Vespers' of 88 B.C., when Mithridates had 100,000 Romans massacred on a single day. As Ferrero and others have rightly stressed, Mithridates' success was due above all to his revolutionary call for a cancellation of all debts, a new *seisachtheia* like that of Solon. This was the last time in Antiquity that this call was heard (Catiline really represented a small group of the indebted, the landowners of the old aristocracy). Because of Mithridates' promise he gathered the support of the middle classes of the Near East against Roman rule, just as at this very same time the middle classes of Italy were fighting Roman rule in the Social War in order to gain for themselves the right to participate in the privileges of Roman citizenship. This demand was opposed by the Roman equestrians because they wanted to keep for themselves monopoly rights to the plunder of the provinces, especially the plundering of provincial land.

This great struggle was concluded with the triumph of the Roman nobles. They made peace with the Italian middle classes on the basis of concessions which cost them nothing. Instead, the political and economic cost of these concessions was charged to the equestrian middle classes of Rome by Sulla's restoration regime: politically, they lost that control of the courts which Caius Gracchus had given them; economically, they lost the chance to profit from the tax farming of Asia Minor's tribute which was also due to Gracchus.

But the result of these changes was that the equestrians were driven to support Caesarism, which thus was able to rely on economic as well as military interests in its conquest of power.

7
Roman Empire

Under the Roman Empire the *polis* continued its triumphant expansion throughout the ancient world. Just as the Macedonians brought the *polis* to the Far East with the founding of Alexandreschata on the borders of Turkestan, so the Romans reached the Far West with their unification of the Lusitanians; with their colonies and policies of urbanization they extended the sway of the *polis* throughout Britain, Gaul, Mauretania, and the lands bordering on the Rhine and Danube.

In the West, too, large areas were 'attributed' to the cities, larger in fact than had been the practice in the Hellenistic states. Partly by transferring local administration to urban centres, partly by creating a privileged order of hereditary councillors (*decuriones*) from those paying the highest taxes, the Romans succeeded – using both direct and indirect pressure – in inducing all or at least part of the large landowners to move into the cities.

Thus when Strabo describes the capital of the Allobroges, Vienne, his words might apply as well to Athens after it became the capital of Attica: just as the large landowners, the Eupatrids, lived in Athens itself, so the 'most distinguished' (*epiphanestatoi*) of the Allobroges lived in Vienne (*auto to asty oikountes*), while the peasants (*geōrgountes*) lived in the villages (*kōmai*) and formed the rural plebs. Roman rule based itself on the support of the first class, the urbanized landowners; it was they who were given the opportunity of gradually gaining Roman citizenship.

As with the state, so with the church: the main contingent of Christians was from the first urban petty bourgeois (this lasted until the era of forced conversions). Thus the word for countryman, *paganus*, which had acquired a connotation of contempt in the usage of town dwellers, was applied under the military monarchy to civilian, and was then used by the church for heathen. When the church began to organize itself as a state within the state, the principle was introduced and then more and more strictly enforced that a bishop had to reside in a city.

Roman synoecisms, like Greek, were often accompanied by clashes between political and economic interests. In Greece the dissolution of Mantineia and Patras reflected the wishes of their landowners to live on their estates, and similar attitudes gave rise to resistance to urbanization through synoecism in the Roman Empire. This resistance increased as urbanization progressed inland, for there less opportunity existed for capital investment in sea trade. In any case it is clear that the establishment of cities, especially those with large dependent hinterlands, inevitably meant that the landowners became absentee and their estates were worked by slaves or *coloni*.

Beginning with the third century the expansion of urbanization met increasingly serious difficulties. Before examining the reasons for this development let us consider again the essential characteristics of the ancient *polis*, keeping in mind above all this problem: In what respects were the *polis* and the mediaeval city similar, and in what were they different?

Among the similarities were: the combination of land ownership and participation in the market as characteristic of the bourgeoisie, the gradual accumulation of land with the profits of trade, the treatment of the landless as 'guests' (metics), the civic liturgies rendered to the city government, the military organization of the citizen body, in particular those citizens in trades of military importance, and the social distance separating cavalry from infantry. All these elements were present in the early stages of mediaeval cities just as they were in those of the ancient *polis*.

Otherwise, however, the differences are striking. To begin with, one must remember how greatly mediaeval cities varied in social structure. Take one basic element, the situation of the knightly aristocracy: in Antiquity it was everywhere and always the nucleus of urban development, but the mediaeval examples differed. The early development of Genoa resembled that of an ancient city, but in Florence the citizen body forced the landed aristocracy to move into the city (the *incasamento*), and there were even moments in Florentine history when people

were ennobled as a kind of punishment. Then there were many
cities which by direct or indirect means obliged aristocrats to
join the guilds, whereas other cities such as Freiburg im Breisgau
excluded aristocrats entirely. Finally, there were many cities,
among them the majority of the large ones, in which a knightly
class of patricians arose out of the bourgeoisie.

Thus there were obviously many differences among mediaeval
cities, and yet one can make this generalization: the Mediterranean coastal cities, in which commercial interests and commercial
wealth were dominant, were the closest in type to the great cities
of Antiquity, while the secondary agricultural cities were most
similar to the small cities of Antiquity; but the industrial cities of
the Middle Ages were very different in type from the ancient
polis.

These distinctions are necessarily approximate, as is always the
case when dealing with large economic complexes. Nevertheless
they lend support to the thesis of Lastig, that the distinctively
original developments in the institutions of business capital
occurred mainly in industrial cities such as Florence, and disprove the objections of Goldschmidt. It is clear, for example, that
it was in these industrial cities that a new kind of labour structure developed, based on the social power of the guilds and the
guild organization of production. This was the first time free
labour was organized on a large scale, for in Antiquity the first
steps towards this had been taken, but nothing reached comple-
tion.

A slave market existed in the Carolingian Empire and was
regulated. In the hinterland of East Europe the slave trade
continued just as it did in Mediterranean port cities such as
Genoa, but on the other hand it disappeared in the industrial
cities of the interior. This does not mean that serfdom, for
example, was from the first unknown in these cities. On the
contrary, the craftsmen and merchants who moved to a newly
organized city were to a great extent serfs themselves, men whose
masters allowed them to move to the city in order to profit from
their tributes and from what they left behind, just as in Antiquity
slaveowners profited from slaves 'living outside' (*chōris oikountes*).
Only gradually, sometimes only after centuries, did these serfs
in mediaeval cities gain full personal freedom. Like the slaves in
Antiquity who paid their masters a share (*apophora*) of their

earnings, these serfs pursued their various trades alongside their fellow craftsmen.

There was, however, one basic difference. The mass of free and unfree workers in mediaeval cities formed functional associations which transcended existing class contrasts in their memberships and which were the seed from which sprang autonomous communities with clearly defined liberties. So it came about that those who actually paid taxes from the proceeds of their work or their land constituted the mediaeval city, whereas in Antiquity it was the rich alone. At least such was the situation in that type we call the industrial inland city, and in particular in all those cities where the guilds gained dominant influence.

'Inland city' does not mean a city in an area without any external trade; cities never develop in such areas. Rather, it means a city in which production and consumption centre round local markets. Similarly, 'industrial city' obviously does not mean a city which satisfies its needs for agricultural products entirely and only by the sale of its manufacturing products, but rather the type of city in which a concentration of free industry forms the basis of economic activity and differentiates the city from the surrounding countryside.

Cities which had economies based on income from slaves and from estates in their hinterland, such as Moscow until this century, form one extreme type; an opposite extreme is represented by cities, such as Genoa, which had economies based on profits from maritime trade, overseas investments, and colonial plantations. Mediaeval cities of these extreme types were more similar to the ancient *polis* than cities of the intermediate type: the mediaeval industrial city as described above.

Of course it is true that the types were not always distinct; industrial cities and commercial cities often blended into one another, as was true of Venice, Flemish cities, and many towns on the Rhine and in North Germany. It is also true that in Antiquity industry could play an important role in the development of a *polis*. Nevertheless, the differences between the typical mediaeval city and the typical ancient *polis* remain fundamental. Above all, the crucial point is that in Antiquity the position of industry – social as well as economic – did not improve as wealth increased, nor did it ever reach the commanding importance which industry enjoyed in the mediaeval industrial cities.

Furthermore, the specific characteristic of modern capitalist development, industrial capitalism, is based on legal institutions which were created in the mediaeval industrial cities, institutions which did not exist in the ancient *polis*.

Indeed, the course of development in Antiquity was the reverse of that of the Middle Ages. The craftsmen of the early period of the ancient *polis* declined in status as time passed and as capital investment in slaves accumulated. In the Middle Ages, on the other hand, there was at first a mass of free and unfree people of low status, as despised as their counterparts in Antiquity were despised by merchants, and likewise excluded from offices. These people were the artisans, and as time passed they increased in economic and political importance.

Of course it is true that in Antiquity there existed corporate groups of craftsmen. The books of Liebenam and Ziebarth have demonstrated that. There is this difference, however, whereas, just as in the Middle Ages, the artisans who produced goods needed for military supply formed corporate groups for electoral and military functions in the archaic *polis*, the organizations of craftsmen in the 'classical' period of the ancient world had no importance whatever. It was only when the relative importance of commercial slavery declined that artisans' groups gained social importance. But even these lacked the legal rights typical of mediaeval guilds; only after the complete decline of capitalism in Antiquity did the artisans' groups start to acquire such legal rights, a development which L. M. Hartmann has rightly emphasized.

Hence two basic contrasts: (1) in the ancient *polis* the most characteristic feature of the mediaeval city was lacking, namely the guilds, along with their struggles against the urban patricians and their foundation of specifically guild-cities; (2) likewise, the mediaeval city lacked anything similar to the most characteristic feature of the free cities of Antiquity, namely the struggle of the peasants against the patricians and the formation of what has been described above as the hoplite *polis* – which meant, in essence, that political domination passed to the peasants eligible for military service. The typical mediaeval city began by excluding all peasants from sharing in citizens' rights, and later when the city began to extend its protection to them as 'outside citizens' (*Ausbürger*), this was opposed by nobles and princes.

The lands which were acquired by the wealthy citizens of mediaeval towns did not mean that these towns were thereby
extended.

It is true, of course, that transitional cases existed here as
always in history. It is evident even from the sketch given above
that the hoplite *polis* did not exist in pure form either in the
Athens of Cleisthenes and Ephialtes or in Rome after the Hor-
tensian Law (287 B.C.). Furthermore one must remember that the
hoplite citizenry was to a large extent made up of urban petty
bourgeois – especially house-owners. Craftsmen and their social
position in Antiquity have already been discussed, and there is
also the fact that in mediaeval cities the small peasant proprietors
were an important citizen group. One must also remember that
special communities (in mediaeval cities) had an important
administrative role, and rural areas were a significant part of
Italian city-states.

So one might take these anomalies and exceptions as yet another demonstration that 'there is nothing new under the sun',
and that all or nearly all distinctions are simply matters of degree.
The latter is true enough, of course; but the former notion annuls
any historical study. One must, instead, focus upon what is of
central importance in a society, despite all analogies, and use the
similarities of two societies to highlight the specific individuality
of each. This specificity is always discernible.

Thus we see that in the Middle Ages the guilds became dominant in cities and forced aristocrats, in order to exercise political
rights like everyone else, to enrol in guilds and submit to their
taxes and regulations, whereas in Antiquity it was the village (e.g.
the *dēmos* in the Athenian Empire) which exercised similar compulsion. Again: whereas in Antiquity graded responsibilities for
arming oneself were assigned to citizens according to the class
of their land rentals, in the Middle Ages this was done according
to guild membership. The difference is unusually striking, and
suffices to demonstrate that 'the mediaeval city' – that is, the type
of city characteristic of the age – was in fundamental economic
and social aspects constituted quite otherwise from the city of
Antiquity. Even before the appearance of any forms of capitalist
organization, the mediaeval city was much closer to the development of modern capitalism than was the ancient *polis*.

The difference becomes even more obvious if we compare

ancient with mediaeval social struggles. In the typical class conflict of Antiquity the line was drawn according to simple contrasts of property – landlords versus yeomen. Struggles centred round the issues of political equality and allocation of public burdens. When economic issues were also involved, then – apart from the question of the public lands – the class struggle resolved itself into (1) creditors versus debtors, leading to another stage marked by the opposition of (2) landowners versus those who had lost their land and, therefore, their social standing. Debtors were mainly, though not exclusively, peasants in the countryside. Now the urban conflicts of the High Middle Ages (thirteenth and fourteenth centuries), centring round the opposition between guilds and great clans, can be compared to the struggles within the *polis* in the 'Middle Ages' of Antiquity; the great issues in both were deprivation of political rights, oppression by fiscal authorities, and unfair disposition of common lands. But there is this great difference: the core of the opposition in Europe's Middle Ages was not recruited from country peasants, as in Antiquity, but from urban artisans. Then, once the effects of nascent capitalism were felt, the ensuing conflicts were not simply between richer and poorer or creditors and debtors as in Antiquity. Rather, the further conflicts of economic interest developed, the sharper was the opposition between merchant and artisan, an opposition which in Antiquity had been of little significance.

In Antiquity the peasant did not want to become a debt bondsman, which meant working the land for an urban rentier. In late mediaeval cities the artisan did not want to become a cottage industry worker, which meant producing goods for a capitalist entrepreneur. Then, after the triumph of the guilds, a new social contrast appeared, one unknown to Antiquity, that between master and journeyman. In the Ancient Near East serfs went on strike with the demand 'Give us our bread', meaning the amount set by tradition. The ancient slave in the country revolted in order to regain his freedom. (Note that we never hear about insurrections of industrial slaves; industrial work was advantageous from the ancient slave's point of view, for it gave him the chance to buy his freedom, a chance the agricultural slave did not have.) But in Antiquity there are absolutely no social demands from journeymen craftsmen, and the reason is that journeymen either did not exist or, if they did, did not form a socially relevant class.

(It is possible that journeymen existed in Antiquity, as for example the assistants of Attic vase painters who later appeared as independent masters. But we do not know the rules under which they worked; were they paid wages or were they given a share of the profits?)

Indeed, one can say that nearly all social struggles in Antiquity were essentially for the ownership and use of land – and this applies in particular to struggles in the city-states. This was a type of struggle which simply did not exist in the Middle Ages, at least in this form as a distinctly urban struggle, for mediaeval struggles for land were between rural classes: the peasants and their masters, sometimes landlords and sometimes political lords, but always non-urban. We see this in the various, generally unsuccessful, peasant rebellions in England, France, and Germany. It is, of course, true that the cities often took sides in these struggles, and that they ended feudalism in Italy and fought it (though in the end in vain) in Germany. But only in a few larger city-states in Italy was this struggle waged within the urban community or within its territory, and in those cases it was a struggle between bourgeoisie and aristocrats, not between peasants and aristocrats. The struggles of the hoplite yeomanry against city aristocrats in the Western part of the ancient world therefore have no mediaeval parallels except for the struggles of the Swiss cantons against the feudal chivalry and territorial princes. The struggles of the Swiss most resemble the struggles of the Israelites against the Philistine city aristocracy (see above), or those of Sabellian mountain peoples against Rome. But in the latter case there was a difference, for the hoplite yeomanry of Rome was fighting for possession of their land against the invading mountain people, and through their disciplined and therefore superior military technology they drove the Samnites back and finally conquered them, whereas in the Later Middle Ages the Swiss were (like the Spartans) the masters of infantry combat, and indeed their agricultural system was adjusted to complement their activities as mercenaries. Anyway it is known how important a role was played by the citizens of the cities in the Swiss wars of independence.

These differences point to a basic distinction between ancient and mediaeval urban development: the difference in residence and character of the aristocracy and princes. Whereas the ancient *polis* started its development as a city kingdom and then passed into the stage when the monarchy was ended by the city aristocracy, followed by the political emancipation of the countryside and its domination over the city, mediaeval society was characterized by a rural landed aristocracy and kings and princes of a specifically agrarian type. Mediaeval urban development therefore consisted in the emancipation of urban citizens from manorial and legal dependence on these non-urban authorities.

Here too, of course, one must not make the distinctions absolute. The large commercial cities on the southern border of mediaeval urban development, such as Pisa, Venice, and Genoa, as well as many large French and Spanish towns, were to a considerable extent centres of aristocratic life – indeed actually became so in that period. Similarly some cities in Italy were so aristocratic that in eighteenth-century Tuscany a *città* was distinguished from a *borgo* or *castello* partly by virtue of being an episcopal seat, but partly too according to the rank of aristocrats among its residents. The leagues which were formed in these cities and usurped local autonomy, such as the *compagna communis* in Genoa, were – despite differences in their social composition – very similar to the synoecisms of Antiquity. At least one can make the comparison, for in these Italian cities of the Early Middle Ages the aristocracy was present too, and indeed held a dominant position. So too, the economic basis of the urban patriciates that emerged in these cities was not dissimilar to that of the great clans of the ancient *polis*: overseas trade, conducted with non-permanent organizational forms such as the *commenda* as in the Ancient Near East, combined with landed possessions which were steadily enlarged with trading profits. In general the patriciates of mediaeval cities shared this similarity in economic structure with the patriciates of the *poleis* of early Antiquity.

On the other hand there was a great difference between the free *poleis* of Antiquity and most mediaeval towns, especially North European and continental industrial cities, in their relation to properly feudal authorities, both in their origins as well as in their later stages of development. This difference was due to the fact that mediaeval cities emerged in a loose but nevertheless significant relationship with the large mediaeval states of which they were a part, and hence they received privileges from princes and lords and were surrounded by their territories. Even when the cities' dependence was very attenuated they were still conditioned by these authorities in the extent and character of their development, because they were constantly forced to seek compromises with them. It was precisely this which gave North European mediaeval cities a much more pronouncedly bourgeois character, based as they were much more on profits gained from industrial monopolies and retail trade, than the Mediterranean cities with their sea-trading patricians. Furthermore, they were from the first very different from the ancient *polis* of the classical period because of their much more definitely economic character, whereas the Hellenistic cities and those of Late Antiquity were in this more similar to them.

The great majority of mediaeval cities developed from settlements on the land of a prince or feudal lord, who then expected to receive rent, market dues and court fees, all directly derived from the simple market concession (which served the same purpose). Speculation sometimes failed in these urban foundations, as it did in establishing markets. If success followed, then the land made available by the lord was settled by a mass of free and unfree immigrants, who received land for a house, garden, use of the commons, and right to trade in the city's market. Soon after they typically received further commercial privileges, such as the right to participate in the city's staple and to trade in the suburbs.

Such settlements either immediately or in a short time became fortresses, and gradually they established – though in varying degree – a certain independence from their founders. Sometimes there was a complete alienation. Sometimes a mere economic and police autonomy. But as a rule the large cities gained only full internal autonomy, whereas they continued externally to pay rent to a lord and acknowledged the authority of his court. The lords therefore continued to be interested in mediaeval cities, partly for political reasons but mainly for economic ones, since cities were a source of fees and rents.

This points to a further contrast: mediaeval cities steadily expanded their autonomy within the larger states of which they were part until well on in the fifteenth century, whereas Hellenistic and Roman cities steadily lost autonomy within their monarchical states. The reason for this difference is the contrasting structures of the states within which ancient and mediaeval cities developed. The monarchical state of Antiquity was or became a bureaucratic state. In Egypt, as we saw, as early as the second millennium B.C. the royal clientele had grown into a universally dominant bureaucracy. This bureaucracy, along with theocracy, throttled the free *polis* in the Ancient Near East, and the same happened in the Later Roman Empire. In the mediaeval West the transformation of the ministeriales into a bureaucracy and the expansion of the power of territorial princes started in the thirteenth century and was completed in the sixteenth, after which the autonomy of the cities was steadily reduced and then eliminated (the process began in the fifteenth century), and the cities were incorporated into the dynastic bureaucratic state But before that, during all of the Early and High Middle Ages, towns had political space in which to develop their characteristic features, and in this period cities were not only centres of a money economy but also of administration, because of their official responsibilities. They were surrounded by the hierarchy of authorities based on feudal and service relationships, but in general their own citizens did not participate in these relationships.

From this flowed important consequences. The citizens of the ancient *polis* were divided into tribes, phratries, and military classes ranked by wealth. Militarism affected all aspects of the *polis*, and indeed military service and citizenship were inextricably joined. Trade monopolies, mortgage rates, and – above all – land ownership depended on military victories. Each city was in a state of war with all other states. The *polis* of the classical period was the most fully developed military organization produced by Antiquity. It was essentially founded for military purposes, whereas the great majority of mediaeval cities were founded for economic purposes. The militarism of the ancient *polis* and its ruthless aggressiveness have their analogies in the port cities of mediaeval Italy: consider the merciless destruction of Amalfi by Pisa, the crippling of Pisa by Genoa, the wars of Genoa with Venice – they all spring from policies familiar to students of the ancient *polis*. There are also analogies in inland cities: the destruction of Fiesole, the subjection of Arezzo, and the crippling of Siena by Florence, also the policies of the Hanse League – all are similar.

Nevertheless it is true that a policy of military expansion and plunder was from the first not a real possibility for most mediaeval cities, especially those in continental France and Germany and in England. The mediaeval city was not, as was the *polis* of early Antiquity, the most developed military organization of its time. Thus during the period of feudal wars the continental cities were merely able to maintain their independence and assert their merchants' right to safe conduct, and they could do this only through city leagues. In the time of the condottieri and mercenary armies they gained an advantage because of the power of money; yet this was only true, even in Italy, in those areas where capitalism was sufficiently developed to supply the necessary funds. Thus even the revolutionary war of the Dutch cities was waged entirely with mercenaries in so far as land operations (except for the defence of walls) were concerned. The expansion of Florence was similar. The inland city of the Middle Ages was, despite all its emphasis on the military duties of citizens, from the first of bourgeois character and was more and more shaped by the peaceful pursuit of profit in the market. The mediaeval burgher was from the first much more motivated by material interests than his ancient counterpart could have been or wanted to be. The most striking difference is that the mediaeval bourgeoisie was generally not interested in conquering lands for colonization, the most basic reason being that there were no recruits ready to go out to such colonies; there never existed in mediaeval cities that great mass of peasants who had lost their land to creditors or who sought new lands for their children, the group which shaped the policies of the ancient *polis*. Hence the mediaeval cities did not strive to expand, even though mediaeval patricians, like ancient patricians, preferred to invest their money in country estates.

Even the mediaeval expansion of the peasants in the East and in the virgin forests was of a distinctive character. In Antiquity land was conquered and then settled, but this was impossible in the Middle Ages because the peasants were part of a feudal system, and their expansion was managed by the manorial lords and the territorial princes. For the average mediaeval city to have aimed at establishing colonies similar to the Athenian cleruchies would have as much a military as an an economic impossibility, whereas it was the normal thing for the ancient *polis*. For the citizens of a mediaeval town – apart from the few large cities which exploited overseas trade and colonies – the major aim of policy was and remained peaceful expansion of the local and inter-local markets for the sale of their products.

It is of course true that in the latter half of the Middle Ages capitalism did find great opportunities for profit (as Sombart rightly emphasizes) in such activities as farming state taxes and domains (as in Genoa and Florence) and, above all, in supplying the financial needs of kings. Nevertheless: these developments, and all the figures connected with them – the Acciajuoli, Bardi, Peruzzi, Medici, Fugger, and the like – were no different from the activity of the financiers of Antiquity, a type well known from Hammurabi to Crassus. It is not here, nor in the manner in which the first great accumulations of money were collected, that we can find the answer to the basic problem: what is the origin of the later mediaeval and modern economic system – in a word, of modern capitalism?

Instead, we must examine the development of the market: how did consumer demand develop in mediaeval times for the industries later organized on capitalist lines? We must also consider the organization of production: how did the endeavour to exploit capital lead to the creation of organizations of free labour such as never existed in Antiquity?

These problems cannot be solved here, but a few further remarks can be made regarding the differences between mediaeval and ancient developments in so far as agrarian conditions are involved.

There was a slow but steady improvement in the economic position of the mediaeval peasantry, and it ended only when the internal colonization in the forests and Eastern lands came to an end. But this mediaeval colonization meant the gradual expansion of the market for the cities, just as in turn the development of cities meant increased consumption of agricultural products. All of this, like the bourgeois development of mediaeval cities as opposed to ancient (see above), grew out of the living conditions which the feudal system of society afforded the continental peasantry – a system, be it noted, which was established outside the cities. A comparison of these features of mediaeval society with their counterparts in Antiquity is appropriate at this point. We have already discussed the great importance of feudal elements throughout the whole of Antiquity, for example, the dominant position held in Egypt by the patron–client relationship. Such relationships were sanctioned by religion, and considering the extraordinary power of religion in Antiquity, when even artificial and rational organizations such as newly created tribes quickly assumed a religious character, we should not underestimate even for the later periods of Antiquity the enduring strength of feudal relations of dependence. Furthermore the origins of feudalism in Antiquity and the Middle Ages were similar.

In both periods feudalism developed from the personal retinues of tribal chiefs, e.g. the Frankish *trustis*. These then reappear in expanded form as royal retinues, and in ancient as well as mediaeval times their members were often regarded as foreign or, at least, as standing outside the regular law of the land and subject only to the royal ban. In both periods steps are taken to establish a royal storehouse system and to supply the army with it and also prevent price increases. In both periods, too, the royal retinue was the institution from which a knightly aristocracy developed (other institutions played a role too), and this became so powerful and indispensable as to make kings dependent, sometime even reducing them to elective status and so dominating the state completely. But just as the mediaeval king was not an urban ruler so the mediaeval aristocracy was not an urban aristocracy, nor did it become so in the Middle Ages – at least in continental areas, the situation being somewhat different in Mediterranean lands.

The same contrast between Antiquity and Middle Ages applies to manorial institutions. In Antiquity manors remained the economic basis of an urban rentier class down into the period of the Roman Empire. The basic reason for this was as follows: what we mean by Antiquity really refers to the civilization of the coastal areas; as soon as one goes inland to Thessaly, for example, one finds a type of manorial regime much closer to that of the Middle Ages. We hear little of conditions in the hinterland until Hellenistic and especially Roman imperial times. In the Middle Ages, on the other hand, there is a great change: throughout the great area linked by a continuous historical tradition stretching from pharaonic to modern times there was a great shift in the centre of gravity from the coastal to the inland areas. Most of the

manors were not suburban but rural institutions, and they supported an agrarian ruling class – princes, free vassals, and their
knightly ministeriales.

Furthermore, the manors supported the mediaeval ruling class
only in part with payments in kind, the large manors not even
mainly with such payments. Indeed, kings, princes, and great
vassals all wanted to use manor payments to gain profits from
commerce. Thus the establishment of markets and cities was due
to the desire of princes and barons to increase their income from
fees and rents. Even so, aristocrats and manorial lords were not,
as in Antiquity, citizens of cities as such; on the contrary, they
tried to keep their feudal estates from being incorporated in the
free communities of the cities, and they also sought to associate
themselves with the cities as 'external citizens' [Ausbürger]. In
short, rural and urban interest groups sought to keep themselves
separate. They did not, of course, succeed in doing this completely, but even so they remained apart to a degree never
possible in the ancient *polis*, which was the military training
ground and encampment of a social order.

It is also true that the internal social structure of the feudal
classes in the Middle Ages differed from that of Antiquity. The
vassals of the princes of the Ancient Near East, and the helots,
slaves, clients, cotters and *coloni* of Mediterranean manorial lords
existed in the time of ancient chivalry, and they were people of
low status, as discussed above. In wartime feudal lords rode to
battle in chariots and fought in single combat, and members of
these classes attended them as servants and light infantrymen. In
the period of hoplite armies the heavy-armed hoplite needed only
one or two attendants (helots or slaves) as bearers and servants.
Henceforth cavalry was less important in Antiquity; indeed the
stirrup did not exist in the classical period, and in general cavalry
techniques remained quite elementary until Parthian times. In
contrast to this the feudal army of the Middle Ages was from the
first primarily a cavalry army, and it remained so throughout its
existence, with steadily improved armour, equipment, and discipline. Consequently the small peasant allotments (*klēroi*) given
to the hereditary warriors (*machimoi*) of the Ancient Near East
or (perhaps!) to clients in Rome, and above all the low social
position such as was held by vassals in the ancient patron–client
relationship – these were not feasible in the Middle Ages even for

the ministeriales, the lowest group of feudal vassals, if they were to be able to go into battle fully armed as cavalrymen. It was always necessary that they could maintain a knightly style. Everything pertaining to the peasant way of life was necessarily beneath their dignity. For the vassals of feudal times were essentially a rentier class (I simplify here what is in fact a very complicated matter.)

Now this is the key to the way in which the continental peasantry developed during the Early Middle Ages: the very lowest group of vassals was superior in status to the peasantry, and was a rentier class with interests of a non-economic character, while at the same time the peasantry was an increasingly unwarlike class. True, this peasantry won territorial conquests as great as any won by an ancient hoplite army, but – just like the mediaeval city – the peasantry did this mainly in a peaceful fashion and, above all, under the command of feudal rentiers. The virgin forests were cleared and the Eastern lands were colonized by the peasants, but these achievements were shaped by the landowning interests of the ruling class.

This great 'internal colonization' of the Middle Ages was conditioned by three factors: (1) few slaves were available; (2) food for slaves was expensive and became more so, (3) slave labour could not be used profitably to put forest land under cultivation or to work the sandy lands of the East. Hence the internal colonization was the work of free peasants – that is, peasants bound to render essentially fixed payments. The individualistic squatters' rights to virgin land in Germanic tribal law had exactly the opposite effect to that of Roman *occupatio* on conquered territories (which helped create the great plantations), or that of the reclamation of new lands by canals – necessarily under bureaucratic direction – in the early periods of the Ancient Near Eastern states. The mediaeval peasantry remained an expanding and ascending class as long as the ruling class of the pure feudal state remained in command and continued to seek feudal rents and not market profits. The limitations imposed by a barter economy were such that within the large area of continental Europe (large from the point of view of the transport technology of the time) the growth of distant markets for agricultural products was arrested, and this gave the peasantry enough time to expand over Central Europe.

At the end of the Middle Ages the average farmer was a peasant on a manor, normally subject only to traditional feudal dues, generally selling his goods in the nearby city, and himself the normal and assured consumer of the city's industrial products (since the city monopolized industry as much as possible and did all it could to suppress rural industries). The feudal army and the feudal state helped create the mediaeval peasantry and mediaeval city – both interested only in economic expansion.

These conditions provide the context in which modern capitalism transformed industry and agriculture, by a process of gradual dissolution. But one should not underestimate the importance of many mediaeval institutions in establishing the commerce which was the basis of capitalist development, institutions such as the system of liberties and rights, cooperatives, labour services, and staple and market privileges. Above all there were the price regulations based on tradition or policy, which limited capital's drive for profits but nevertheless provided a basis for long range calculation such as the bargaining of the Near East could not provide. It is clear that mediaeval trade organization, as it developed within the theocratic and feudal world of the time, was one of the elements which made possible a commodity system amenable to planned calculation, just as the classes of free peasants and petty bourgeoisie which were shaped by feudal organization provided that large, relatively stable consumer market which modern capitalism needs for its products.

There was then a great difference between the development of the bourgeoisie and the peasant economy in mediaeval Western Europe and analogous developments in Antiquity. This was due in the first place to a shift in geographical setting, secondly to a great change in the military organization of the Middle Ages, caused by a great number of factors. The mediaeval army of knights made feudal social organization inevitable; then its displacement by mercenary armies and later (beginning with Maurice of Orange) by disciplined troops led to the establishment of the modern state. Antiquity experienced two great revolutions in military technology: (1) the introduction of the horse from the East (either from Persia or Turkestan), which led to the creation of the citadel (as in the Middle Ages), the Near

Eastern conquest state, and the Mediterranean knightly society;
(2) the use of iron for thrusting weapons (iron had of course been
known since prehistoric times, but iron weapons became of
decisive importance only in post-Homeric times) and the training
of disciplined infantrymen to fight at close quarters in hoplite
armour, which led to the establishment of armies recruited from
large peasants and petty bourgeois and, therefore, the ancient
'citizen *polis*'.

Everything else then followed from the geographical setting in
which these developments took place. The ancient *polis* remained
warlike and expansionist, pursuing trade monopolies and tribute-
paying subjects, but also seeking to win land for the sons of its
hoplites or opportunities for its bourgeoisie to increase their rents.
The only factor that held a *polis* back from these ends was the
presence of a stronger political power. Economic organization
and techniques, on the other hand, made relatively little progress
in the period between the Ramessids and Assurbanipal, the only
exception being the invention of coinage. How many – or how
few – technological advances were made in the ages of Antiquity
known to history will only be known when scholars use the extant
evidence to write a history of industry in Egypt and Mesopotamia, with special attention to the development of technology
in Egypt.

So much originated in the Ancient Near East! From Babylonia
came the forms of trade which remained dominant until the end
of Europe's Middle Ages; from Egypt came the estate worked by
serfs; from Egypt too came the use of unfree domestic labour,
the liturgy system, and the bureaucratic state; from Egypt and
the Hebrews came the monastery and other forms of ecclesiastical
organization. It is, therefore, entirely possible that the Ancient
Near East was also the area in which originated the great
majority of the technological innovations which were made in
industrial production down to the end of the Middle Ages.

In the field of agricultural technology a number of ancient
innovations deserve notice because they increased the productivity of labour. These include better tools for threshing, ploughing, and harvesting – but the last two advances were made,
significantly, only after the end of the classical period and in the
northern hinterland.

As to industrial technology, apart from military machines and related devices for hoisting (mainly used on public works), whatever progress we can see served mainly to improve the specialized labour of individual workers rather than to facilitate the joint labour of groups of workers. The same is true of the economic organization of industry. Both aspects, given the nature of the internal structure of ancient industry and profit interests of slaveowners, need cause no surprise.

Modern capitalism emerged on the basis prepared by the mediaeval organization of commerce and industry, using its material and legal forms. Capitalism developed partly outside this organization, partly within it, and partly in opposition to it – in particular the guilds – but still a necessary connection was there. For example: the *commenda*, a prevalent form of commerce from the time of Hammurabi down to the thirteenth century, was the origin of the limited liability company (only the first steps towards this were taken in Antiquity, and those were – characteristically – in connection with companies formed to assume state farming contracts). Again: in Antiquity the only enterprises based on joint liability were simple artisans' groups resembling the Russian artel, but in later mediaeval law this has developed into sophisticated forms of trading and manufacturing companies. It was also in the Later Middle Ages that the legal institutions were created for permanent capitalist enterprises in commerce and industry, whereas in Antiquity the law regulating private business continued to be fashioned for temporary enterprises in which capital was invested to exploit a particular opportunity and then withdrawn. (This does not mean, of course, that only temporary enterprises existed in ancient times, but they were the characteristic form in which capital was put to use.)

As soon as capitalism became established in industrial production in the Middle Ages it started the process of merging the small workshops of artisans. First it organized sales and then purchase of raw materials. Next it inexorably moved towards the production process itself, gradually developing a more rationalized technology and establishing increasingly larger productive units which were increasingly more separated from the family. These large units were more and more created to further the concentration of workers and the division of labour. Nothing

similar is known to us from Antiquity, at least as regards purely
private industry.

Let it be noted here that this difference is what one would
expect; the achievements of ancient capitalism were in other
fields. Of course, this does not mean that there was no division
of labour in Antiquity, for without it a significant part of ancient
industry simply could not have existed.

Merging small enterprises was also something new. It was
pointed out above that simply bringing together several dozen
slaves – or, for that matter, several thousand – and using them
for the same type of production did not signify the establishment
of a factory in the economic sense, just as today the man who
buys the stock of several breweries has not thereby established a
new brewery. Another example: some Attic vases have a mark
put there by the potter, stating that he 'has made this vase, and
X.Y. [his competitor] cannot make its equal'. I leave it to the
reader's judgment – the less trained in economics the better –
to deduce for himself the fundamental difference between this
statement and comparable messages on modern objects – and
yet both belong to the genre of advertising. Bringing together
many slaves was simply a particular disposition of property; the
organization and technology of production were not affected,
and the slaves remained what they had been before, small-scale
artisans who were used by a wealthy man as a source of rent or
by an importer as processers of his raw materials. An example of
the latter type was Demosthenes, and this kind of slave production was the closest approach in Antiquity to large-scale capitalist
production.

We discussed above how impermanent were such enterprises,
how small was the importance of fixed capital, and how completely the existence of such enterprises depended on the owner's
personal situation. Here another point deserves notice. When we
come upon examples in Antiquity of men such as Timarchus
[cf. Aeschines, *Against Timarchus*, delivered 345 B.C.] who own
slaves trained in a great variety of different crafts, that is no more
the result of chance than is the case of a modern investor who
owns stocks in different firms with different earning potential.
We all know that to spread one's investments is the cautious
thing to do, and the same was true in Antiquity with respect to
investments in slaves. The only exceptions were the use of slaves

for stable enterprises such as gold and silver mines (e.g. Nicias) or the use of slaves to capitalize one's own stock of merchandise (e.g. Demosthenes). Otherwise it was the counsel of caution to buy slaves with varied skills, a form of insurance against loss. One can compare with this the practice we discussed of a man owning a share of many different rented houses.

From this follows an important conclusion: ancient capitalism was used to produce rents, and when this capitalism affected industry it did not act to create large enterprises specializing in the manufacture of a particular product. This was because the sale of industrial products, especially the sale of these products abroad, had much too much the character of intermittent trade which was spurred by special chances for profit but was also subject to innumerable political changes and, above all, to shifts in the price of grain. The latter factor in particular was rarely as significant after the Later Middle Ages.

Furthermore the masses in Antiquity had so little disposable income left after having purchased the necessities of life, that they provided little demand for industrial products; while supply for the consumer demands of the masses is always characteristic of modern capitalism. So small was consumer demand in Antiquity that no socially powerful enterprises, large home industries and certainly no factories, could come into existence.

The foregoing discussion concerns differences between ancient and mediaeval conditions which are unquestionably real. True, these differences have necessarily been emphasized here for purposes of argument. It is also undeniable that occasionally in Antiquity there were approaches towards rationalized, large-scale production; indeed, these instances deserve close study. Nevertheless it is clear that what was typical of Antiquity was a development quite the opposite of what is characteristic of modern capitalism. It is a basic fact that profitable valorization of capital in Antiquity was blocked by the existence of slave labour. In the Middle Ages the situation was otherwise, a major cause being the change in the geographical setting of capitalist development. Climate meant that consumption differed; one need merely contrast what an Egyptian field worker needs with the minimum physiological necessities of someone in Northern Europe's climate who does only sedentary work. Northern Europe's climate also keeps people indoors a good part of the year, whereas in the ancient world the population lived out of doors and frequented public places (cf. Greek *agorazein*), much as modern Spaniards and Italians frequent cafés.

These climactic contrasts explain differences in temperament. There is no need to rely on any of the current racial theories, which are anyway unsupported by science, and should be excluded from serious discussion. These contrasts also explain new features of mediaeval society: the many centres of commerce in the hinterland, and in these centres the constant expansion of consumption and production. These new phenomena interacted with the technological traditions inherited from Antiquity and the renewed impulse to put capital to profitable use.

Another difference was that the use of slave labour was not practicable in the Middle Ages. This was due to several factors: (1) feeding, clothing, and housing slaves was more costly in Northern Europe; (2) mediaeval military structure meant that the cities, where industry was centred, could not embark on wars to gain slaves, as the ancient *poleis* did; (3) the struggles between the aristocrats of the hinterland were concluded with the transfer of peasants (with their tributes) from one lord to another and with the extension of one lord's territorial suzerainty at the expense of another, but not with the appropriation of slaves, as was done by the plundering expeditions sent over the seas by the coastal societies of Antiquity. Thus as cultivation of inland areas became more intense slavery declined, at least relatively, while the development of free labour benefited from the factors just discussed (ulterior analysis cannot be given here).

There was a further basic difference: in Antiquity the wars of the *poleis* down to the end of the Roman Republic generally meant that the losing state's property system would be annihilated and its territory would be subjected to massive confiscations and colonization, the *polis* in this respect acting like the German tribes of the *Völkerwanderung*; in the Middle Ages, on the other hand, despite knightly love of battle, and even more so in Early Modern times, an international community existed which can be called 'pacified' in comparison with Antiquity. This is not to say that there was a quantitative decline in warlike activity; there was, rather, an increasing pacification of the elements engaged in private business and industry, in particular the cities and the bourgeoisie.

It is of course true that modern capitalism gained its largest profits from military contracts in mediaeval and modern times. But there was still something new: the capitalist organization of industrial production was based on the 'pacification' mentioned above, and so despite all the vicissitudes of war and politics it maintained the continuity of economic development, a development in which the large feudal states and – even more – the international Church had their share. In Antiquity, on the contrary, everything about a *polis* from its foundation onwards was motivated by political and military considerations; the development of every *polis* depended on military events, and so ancient capitalism was shaped by political forces. It was, one might say, only indirectly economic in character, for the critical factors were the political fortunes of the *polis* and the opportunities it provided for profit through contracts for tax farming and wars for human and (especially in Rome) territorial booty.

When the Mediterranean world was unified and pacified in the Hellenistic period and then under the Roman Empire, the ancient city became the centre of exclusively economic interests. As a result the trade associations of merchants and artisans, previously present only in elementary form, now began to develop and flourish. They were used by the Roman Empire for its own purposes, and we can follow their further development down to the beginnings of the mediaeval guilds. But the death-knell of ancient capitalism had sounded long before; the new peace and the monarchical state, the shift of society's centre from the coasts to the hinterland – all these changes throttled ancient capitalism instead of causing it to flourish (as one might *a priori* expect). It was the Roman Empire which established this peace and brought about the rise of the hinterland.

Peace was provisionally established under Tiberius, definitively under Hadrian. This meant the end of wars for human and territorial booty. At the same time large inland areas were added to the Empire: Gaul, the lands along the Rhine and Danube, Illyria, and (as an addition to the old province of Macedonia) the entire interior of the Balkan peninsula.

Peace also meant the gradual disappearance of slave imports. Now slaves were used up at such a rate by the plantations (see the principles Varro suggests) and the mines, that the speculative rearing of slaves and peaceful slave trade were not adequate to meet the demand. At first slave prices increased rapidly, because the market's supply was insufficient, but then in the Later Roman Empire slave prices were very low, because by then economic organization had altered and demand declined sharply. At one time I overestimated the importance of this change; now I would say that it should not be underestimated.

The disappearance of slave barracks, the establishment of family life among the slaves, and also the decline of capitalist, large-scale agricultural enterprises – these are all historical realities, and they were connected with the changes discussed above (hence the sources stress 'the shortage of workers'). The great estates in the huge hinterland to the North, an area with little commerce, simply could not be worked according to rules derived from the plantations of Carthage and Rome. As early as Tacitus (or his informant) notice was taken of another system, under which estates were worked by peasants paying rent in kind. This may have been observed on the estates of the Ubii, a German tribe on the Rhenish frontier, and it was dominant in the Merovingian period. It is the opposite of the Roman system based on slaves kept in barracks and subjected to military discipline.

Roman villas slowly penetrated the Northern lands, bringing with them methods of cultivation which were, despite all difficulties, unquestionably more advanced than the indigenous traditions. Eventually villas were established as far north as the Scottish border.

As the sources indicate, these villas were increasingly larger in size, the reason being that more and more land was needed to support a lordly style of life. The expansion of country estates had already set in under the Republic, and it continued steadily under the Empire; the result was that country estates gradually became independent of markets, since they could satisfy their consumption needs themselves. This development will be discussed in the article on the 'Colonate'.

Coercive political synoecism of the estates was the aim of the Roman monarchy, as the sources relate, against the increasing resistance of the great landowners (*possessores*). However, the flight from the towns triumphed. Thus the aristocracy became to a great degree settled on the land, and with this shift went a decline in the social and economic importance of the towns; the Middle Ages had begun.

During the three and a half centuries between the Gracchi and Caracalla trade increased greatly in absolute terms in the vast area encompassed by the Roman Empire. Relatively, however, this was not true, if one considers the amount of regions and populations, citizen or subject, of a characteristically ancient character that were now integrated into it. Ancient society expanded enormously with the enlargement of the Roman Empire, but since it was a coastal civilization its transformation into a hinterland civilization necessarily meant a relative decline in the intensity of trade, due to the means of transportation then available.

In coastal areas the food and clothing needed for slaves in the large households (*oikoi*) were entirely or partly purchased on the market. In inland regions, on the other hand, the slaves or *coloni* of landowners assured their necessities by a subsistence economy (as one would expect). Only members of the small class of wealthy landowners had needs which caused them to make purchases, and these were paid for by sale of their estates' surplus products. This trade was, therefore, a minor supplement; the foundation of society was a natural economy.

This was reinforced by urban developments, for in the major cities the masses were not supplied by private trade but rather by state procurements (*annona*). This situation did not of course prevent an increase of the absolute numbers settled in the cities in the interior and in the cultivation of lands in the interior; indeed, it is perfectly clear that both population and cultivation did increase. However, this too enhanced the effect of the shift to a continental society. We see this most clearly in two phenomena: (1) in the disarming of the cities, and their definitive loss of any sphere in which they might develop independent policies, which meant the loss of all those opportunities for profit which had depended on the cities and which had promoted capitalism; (2) in the new prominence of the large landowners of the interior and their interests in the policies of the Later Roman Empire.

The latter phenomenon had important consequences in the political as well as the economic sphere. It was at least partly responsible for the decline in the Roman army's offensive power, made evident by the dispersion of military units over the entire northern frontier, for the great landowners of the provinces who now lived on their estates demanded that their possessions be protected and so imposed on the army a defensive mission. Along with this went the monarchical character of the state, which brought with it all the consequences associated with ancient monarchy.

The federation of Italian cities led by Rome had been able to defeat the Celts, and it had relied solely on an army levied from its own citizens. The Celts had been just as numerous as the tribes, about 15,000 to 20,000 each, of Goths and Vandals who defeated Roman armies of the Later Empire. The Italian federation had also put into the field against Hannibal a mighty army which could have easily conquered the German tribes of the so-called *Völkerwanderung*.

But there was this difference: the citizen armies of the Italian federation were recruited for specific campaigns, and they were not suited to maintaining constant guard over the length of a frontier traversing the whole of Europe. That this was done was due to the demands of the landowners of the interior and the men who leased the domains. Such a task demanded a standing army, and ancient conditions meant that this must be a professional army. (Of course there is also the question – not considered here – whether the social structure of the Empire made it possible any longer to base the military system on a levy of self-equipped citizen soldiers, which in the ancient *polis* meant self-equipped peasants.)

Furthermore, in the Roman Empire the class interests of the great landowners of the interior coincided with the dynastic interests of monarchs, as indeed they always do. A dynastic professional army along with a dynastic bureaucracy took the place once occupied by the *polis* administrations, establishing a system modelled on that of the Ptolemaic monarchy, for *polis* institutions were completely inadequate for the problems of an empire. It was simply the inevitable conclusion of this development when the monarchical state transferred its capital to Constantinople in the East and proclaimed itself the heir of Hellenistic traditions.

It is of course also true that Augustus and his abler successors during the first two centuries of the Empire were all essentially Roman in their policies; in particular, they awarded citizenship sparingly, especially to Near Eastern peoples, and took care to preserve the privileged position of the Roman nation. Yet in order to maintain their own rule over the dominant nation these same emperors were forced to disarm the Romans gradually. We can see this clearly from the provenance of veterans recorded in the military diplomas. This explains why it was possible for a *coup d'état* to be carried out under the Severi, in which without conflict or resistance the dominance of the Romans was ended. Henceforth control of the Empire was shared in turn by men from the Near East and by Illyrians, the latter a people entirely outside the civilizations of Antiquity.

As a result the Roman peoples ceased to man the officer corps and the bureaucracy, and the ancient governing traditions of the Roman aristocracy disappeared. This, and not 'racial influences' (for which no tangible evidence exists), meant that the foundations of the state were undermined, and in fact there followed a series of donatives to the troops of the all-powerful armies, which were wildly extravagant (as Von Domaszewski has shown) and caused a bankruptcy of the state and a collapse of the money economy which lasted a generation. Later laws concerning the state's 'treasure fund' indicate where precious metals were hoarded in this as in similar cases. The Empire then entered upon a decline, was reorganized on an entirely new basis, and was transformed into a liturgy state on the lines of Ptolemaic Egypt. The first steps towards this transformation go back to the second century A.D.

Imperial society was stratified, the upper levels extending from the highly privileged senatorial order down to the small-town freedman bourgeoisie organized as *Augustales* for the service of the imperial cult, with specific levels for members of the town councillor class (*decuriones*) and those who profited from the extra-urban domains and manors. It was on these privileged groups that Caracalla bestowed a general grant of citizenship in A.D. 212; they formed the social basis of the imperial regime, as opposed to the lower strata who continued to pay a poll tax: the peasantry of the countryside and the proletariat of the cities (*laoi, plebs, coloni, tributarii*). Then there were the great landowners (*possessores*) who were exempt from the 'obligations of the base-

born' (*munera sordida*), and they formed an officially acknowledged order similar to the immediate [*reichsunmittelbaren*]
vassals of the Holy Roman Empire.

Thus the institutions of the Republic which governed the status
of subjects were perfected, in itself an indication of the Hellenistic character of the Empire. We do not know how much was
borrowed directly from the practices of Hellenistic states, but
the demands of ancient monarchy made new institutions inevitable. The manner in which military supplies were procured was
undoubtedly borrowed from the Near East, especially Egypt, and
so was the allotment of lands to the legions, which were now
manned by what became in fact a hereditary class of soldier-
farmers settled on the frontiers. We must ascribe to the same
source also the monopolies, state workshops, compulsory guild
organization, joint responsibility of the councillor class (*decuriones*) for taxes, and all the other liturgies which bound the
individual in a net of obligations and kept him at his post in
society.

With this net of obligations the ancient state throttled capitalism slowly but surely. For otherwise how can we explain the fact
that capitalism did not flourish either in the first two centuries of
the Empire nor in the fourth century, both periods of relative
peace and order without parallel in the whole classical age of
Antiquity? True, the money economy continued to expand at
least down to the time of Marcus Aurelius (A.D. 161–80), but a
money economy is not the same as capitalism. Large manors
emerged and expanded, while at the same time the small merchants and the small artisans of the Near East emigrated to the
Western provinces in great numbers throughout the imperial
period, including its last phase. Indeed it was they who spread
Christianity there. But we never hear of the development of
capitalist economic organization either in commerce or in agriculture or, above all, in industry.

On the contrary: the great merchants of the Early Empire,
whose trading ventures extended to Scandinavia, disappeared,
their place was taken by shopkeepers, and the sales taxes dwindled so completely in the great troubles of the third century that,
as Von Domaszewski has shown, even the officials responsible for
collecting it vanished. However, even as early as the reign of
Marcus Aurelius, the economy had become stagnant and the tax

burden on the lower classes was very heavy, as the papyri indicate. As to the troubles of the third century, there had been periods of harsher warfare and greater losses in Antiquity. Why was it, then, precisely these troubles from which there was no recovery?

The answer is that ancient capitalism was based on politics, on the exploitation for private profit of the political conquests of the imperialist city-state, and when this source of profit disappeared capital formation ceased. The very first achievement of the Roman emperors had been the regulation of the tax system, when the arbitary power of the tax farmers was curbed. Like the Ptolemies, the Roman emperors could not at first dispense with the capital resources and the business experience of the tax farmers, but it was quite natural that the more their bureaucracy mastered the situation the less reason they saw for letting private individuals use the state's revenues for their own profit. Therefore they gradually 'nationalized' the tax-collecting system, and eventually (as Von Domaszewski and Rostovtzeff have shown) the tax farmer was transformed into a state official.

Thus by protecting subjects and by establishing peace the Roman Empire condemned ancient capitalism to death. The supply of slaves dwindled, and gone were all those opportunities for profit which the wars of *polis* with *polis* had created; gone too were the trade monopolies held by individual city-states, and above all, gone were the profits from plundering the public domains and the subject peoples. These changes together meant that ancient capitalism lost the sources from which it had drawn nourishment.

In the liturgy state created by Diocletian capitalism found no anchorage for itself, no chance for profit. Bureaucracy destroyed economic as well as political initiative, for the opportunities for gain were gone. Whereas capitalism always strives to transform the 'wealth' of the possessing classes into investment 'capital', the tendency under the Empire was to exclude capital and to conserve wealth, as in the Ptolemaic state. In earlier days the possessing classes had served the state with spear and shield; now they served with their property, to guarantee State revenues and procurements. Thus, whereas in the mercantilist state of Early Modern times an alliance was established between monarch and capital, under the Roman Empire the state employed its wealthier subjects to perform liturgies. Mercantilism involved a shift from a direct to an indirect relation between state and capital, and this shift could not occur before industrial capitalism had developed and examples of private capitalistic wealth were provided by the Netherlands and England.

Bureaucracy stifled private enterprise in Antiquity. There is nothing unusual in this, nothing peculiar to Antiquity. Every bureaucracy tends to intervene in economic matters with the same result. This applies to the bureaucracy of modern Germany too. Whereas in Antiquity the policies of the *polis* necessarily set the pace for capitalism, today capitalism itself sets the pace for bureaucratization of the economy.

To have a true image of the Later Roman Empire in modern terms, one must imagine a society in which the state owns or controls and regulates the iron, coal, and mining industries, all foundries, all production of liquor, sugar, tobacco, matches, and all the mass consumption products now produced by cartels. In addition the state would have enormous domains, would run workshops to produce military supplies as well as goods for bureaucrats, would own all ships and railways, and would conclude state treaties to regulate wool imports. One must imagine the whole complex managed according to the rules of bureaucratic organization, and along with it a system of guilds and a plethora of documents, academic or otherwise, needed for every activity. If we imagine all this, under a militaristic and dynastic regime, then we have summoned up the state of things under the Later Roman Empire, the only difference being that the technological basis was not then so far advanced.

Today the average German bourgeois is as little like his mediaeval ancestor as was Athenian of the Lower Roman Empire like the man who fought at Marathon. The German bourgeois now strives above all for 'order', usually even if he is a 'social-democrat'. Thus in all probability some day the bureaucratization of German society will encompass capitalism too, just as it did in Antiquity. We too will then enjoy the benefits of bureaucratic 'order' instead of the 'anarchy' of free enterprise, and this order will be essentially the same as that which characterized the Roman Empire and – even more – the New Empire in Egypt and the Ptolemaic state.

Furthermore, let no one think that the conscription of citizens will provide a 'countervailing force', for these citizens serve in a bureaucratic army which the state equips, uniforms, feeds, drills, commands, and houses in barracks. Conscription in modern dynastic states is a form of labour service. It has no inner relationship with the militia service rendered by citizens to their cities in a time now long past.

This is not the place, however, to pursue such reflections. I shall only add that the long and continuous history of Mediterranean-European civilization does not show either closed cycles or linear progress. Sometimes phenomena of ancient civilization have disappeared entirely and then come to light again in an entirely new context. In other respects, however, the cities of Late Antiquity, especially of the Hellenistic Near East, were the precursors of mediaeval industrial organization, just as the manors of Late Antiquity were precursors of the estates of mediaeval agriculture.

The character, extent, and significance of this influence of Antiquity are, however, topics which will have to be explored elsewhere.

III. Bibliography

Bibliography

1. General

The *Jahresberichte der Geschichtswissenschaft* regularly lists studies and sources pertaining to all Antiquity, and the same service is performed for Greece and Rome by the *Jahresberichte der klassischen Altertumswissenschaften*. The latter is more thorough, a model of its kind, though the rubrics under which separate areas are handled, especially those concerned with economic matters – generally treated as part of political history – are rather broad and variable. In general, economic matters receive rather slight attention.

Two journals which give valuable bibliographic information are the *Historische Zeitschrift* and the *Zeitschrift für Sozial– und Wirtschaftsgeschichte*. Most of the other German and foreign journals of social science occasionally print articles and reviews of importance, and so do journals of anthropology, archaeology (e.g. *Revue Archéologique*), and comparative law (e.g. *Kohlers Zeitschrift*).

All Antiquity is covered by the journal *Klio: Beiträge zür alten Geschichte*. Its volumes and supplements include a number of very valuable articles on ancient social history, many of which have been used for this essay.

Among surveys, the most important for ancient social history is the great work of Eduard Meyer, *Geschichte des Altertums*, in five volumes. So far it goes down to the end of Greece's independent history (404 B.C.), furnishing more of interest for the social historian with each successive volume. The first part of the second edition of this work appeared after the present essay was sent to the printer; it contains much that is very valuable, but also a number of general reflections which seem disputable. In dealing with the prehistory of the state and the transformations of politics in the course of history, Meyer's judgment is marked by lucid realism whenever he has facts to work with. Nevertheless his paper in the Transactions of 1907 of the Berlin Academy[1] indicates that at times his penetrating historical analysis may be hampered by too much trust in Stammler's legal theories, an influence as dangerous for the historian as rigid theories from natural science or economics.

Regarding the discussion of general matters in the Introduction, compare the views of Eduard Meyer in two papers: 'Die Wirtschaftliche Entwicklung des Altertums' and 'Die Sklaverei im Altertum'.[2] See also for this polemic, the works of Karl Bücher, especially *Die Entstehung der Volkswirtschaft* and his papers on Greek economic history in the Schäffle Festschrift, on Diocletian's Edict on Prices in volume 50 of the *Zeitschrift für Staatswissenschaft*, and (more briefly), on 'Gewerbe' in the *Handwörterbuch der Staatswissenschaften*.

On slavery see in particular Ciccotti's *Tramonto della Schiavitd nel Mondo Antico*, which applies to ancient conditions the conclusions of Cairnes' *Slave Power*, and despite a certain lack of precision is undoubtedly a valuable work. Note also the paper by A. Loria in volume 4 of the *Zeitschrift für Wirtschafts– und Sozialgeschichte*. The important works of Wilcken, Rostovtzeff, and others are given below under Hellenistic Age. Further bibliography will be found in the works there listed.

Rodbertus' writings were published in volumes 4, 5 and 8 of the *Jahrbücher fur National-Oekonomie*.

It is worth noting here that the advances in historical knowledge achieved by Eduard Meyer and his students have been achieved partly in the course of disputes with Bücher and other economists, and that in these disputes they have fortunately made use of the work of the economic theorists whom they once despised, and so have achieved clear concepts. So far, however, their ideas on the factory in Antiquity have not benefited from this.

For the social aspect of ancient political thought see Fustel de

1. 'Ueber die Anfänge des Staats und sein Verhältnis zu den Geschlechtsverbänden und zum Volksthum,' *Sitzungsberichte der k. Preussischen Akademie der Wissenschaften*, 1907 (no. 27), pp. 508–38.
2. Reprinted in E. Meyer, *Kleine Schriften* [I] (Halle, 1910), pp. 79–212

Coulange's penetrating works, especially *La Cité Antique* (well worth reading, but with caution). For the political achievements of the *polis* the works of Kuhn are still fundamental, especially *Die Städte der Alten: Synoikismos und Komenverfassung*. See also the works of Eduard Meyer listed under no. 4, and the early chapters of Kaerst, *Geschichte des Hellenismus*, especially pp. 62 ff. and his bibliographies for each section.

At this point I want to note that the editors and publishers [of the *Handwörterbuch der Staatswissenschaften*] have been extraordinarily generous to me, but that I have nevertheless felt obliged to rewrite the version of this essay published in the previous edition of *Handbuch*, the reason being that recent research has made it quite out of date. Because of the *Handwörterbuch*'s production schedule I have not had sufficient time to review the enormous mass of evidence, and indeed I only saw a number of important primary sources while correcting the second proofs; some sources I never succeeded in procuring. However it is only natural that anyone who is not engaged in constant study of the sources (especially the inscriptions) must inevitably make mistakes,[3] and so it is natural that the final decision on the problems discussed must be left to the historians, philologists, and archaeologists. My aim has been to use my own particular knowledge and experience to develop heuristic aids, to suggest the questions which need to be answered.

The gravest error to which most historians (though not all) still fall prey is to assume that the complexity and flux of historical phenomena rule out the use of definite and precise concepts. Now it is obviously true that if, for example, we speak of craftsmen there exists a wide variety of possible uses of this term, an infinite series of gradations, ranging from the artisan working on a small scale who intermittently or regularly employs a slave to work alongside him, to the man who has learned the craft but devotes himself mainly to supervising his slaves, to the man who occasionally or often or always leaves the supervision

---

3. Let me correct three facts here: (1) a friendly suggestion from Professor V. Duhn has convinced me that Attic vase inscriptions do not give an eponym but always the producer (no other change in my discussion is needed); (2) the *epikrisis* of Roman Egypt cannot be regarded as a cadaster, and on this Wessely is correct; (3) in discussing property distribution I should not have used the term *ager Romanus* – a religious term! – but rather 'territory'.

to a slave, to the businessman who knows little or nothing of the craft but instead manages the plant, to the merchant who has his slaves process only a part of his raw material, to the business-man or private individual who occasionally invests his money in one or several skilled slaves, finally to the princely household in which slaves produce goods for the market or for the house-hold's own use or for both. Nevertheless this unordered variety of facts does not prove that we must make use of imprecise terms, but rather the contrary: we must create precise concepts and use them properly, concepts which I prefer to call 'ideal types': cf. *Archiv für Sozialwissenschaft*, vol. 19.1. Such types should not be used as rigid schemata to which historical truth is made to conform, but as tools with which to determine the economic character of a phenomenon, by asking to what degree does that phenomenon resemble this or another ideal type. Of course a brief essay such as the present one cannot entirely avoid having a somewhat summary, schematic character.

2. *Mesopotamia*

The documentary source material in translation are still to be found most conveniently in the older collections of Oppert and Menant, *Documents juridiques de l'Assyrie*: see also the *Keilin-schriftliche Bibliothek*, and Meissner's *Urkunden und Texten* and *Beiträge zum altbabylonischen Privatrecht*. Of the many German editions of Hammurabi's Code see that of Kohler and Peiser, with a juristic commentary.

For the Sumerian laws see Haupt, *Die sumerischen Familien-gesetze*. Further primary material will be found in: Moldenke, *Babylonian Contract Tablets;* Hilprecht's report on excavations by the University of Pennsylvania; the building inscriptions of Sennacherib, edited by Meissner and Rost; *Babylonische Verträge des Berliner Museums* by Peiser, with an excursus by Kohler on pre-emptive purchase.

The social divisions of the Babylonians are discussed by Oppert in the *Journal Asiatique*, ser.7, vol. 15, pp. 543 ff.; but this is out of date now. Very important for the early period is Thureau-Dangin's edition of the Sumerian and Akkadian royal inscriptions, volume I of the *Vörderasiatische Bibliothek*. One must also consult the valuable studies in C. Bezold's *Zeitschrift für Assyriologie*, which also contains reviews and a continuous bibliography. See also Delitzsch's *Beiträge zur Assyriologie und semitische Sprachwissenschaft*, and (more valuable) *Travaux relatives à la philologie et archéologie egyptienne et assyriologique*, edited by Maspero. Useful work is also published occasionally in: *Journal Asiatique*, *Proceedings of Biblical Archaeology*, and *Zeitschrift der deutschen morgenländischen Gesellschaft*. *Babylonian and Oriental Records* is of special importance.

For a general introduction see: Winckler's *Altorientalische Forschungen*, *his Völker des alten Orients*, vol. 3, and his brief but well-written survey in Helmholt's *Weltgeschichte*. Maspero's *Histoire ancienne des peuples de l'Orient classique* only gives short sketches of social conditions but is nevertheless worth reading.

We still do not have a work devoted to the economic development of Mesopotamia, and probably the time is not yet ripe for such a work. First the enormous mass of documentary material must be analyzed, not only to cast light on the basic questions of chronology and genealogy, but also to give us information on the development of technology and the economy, on price movements, and on how the economy put capital to work and met consumption needs.

3. *Egypt*

Translations of the long temple and royal inscriptions are generally most easily consulted in the older English collections. Recently the assumption is again increasingly being made [in Germany], as in the important studies of Steindorf, that every educated person interested in Egypt reads hieroglyphics!

For information on the most recent excavations see the publications of the Egyptian Exploration Fund.

E. Revillout's work continually gives translations of the same documents. This is tiresome, and his translations, especially of demotic texts, are often doubtful. Reliable translations are to be found in the works of W. Spiegelberg, *Rechnungen aus der Zeit Setis I*, and *Demotische Papyri der Strasburger Bibliothek*; also in the works of Griffiths, especially *The Petrie Papyri*.

Documents with commentary are published in the *Recueil* (mentioned above), and most of the articles cited in the text came from there. See also the *Bibliothèque Egyptologique, Zeitschrift fur ägyptische Sprache und Altertumskunde, Sphinx,* and *Proceedings of Biblical Archaeology.* The commentaries in the *Revue égyptologique* are edited by E. Revillout (earlier by V. Revillout). They are often written nearly entirely by the former, and they suffer from the same faults as E. Revillout's books: *Cours de droit égyptien* (readable), and *Precis de droit égyptien* (a monstrous compilation, in which a few good ideas – already used – are mixed with useless 'analogies'). The documents published in the *Corpus Papyrorum Aegypti* by Revillout and Eisenlohr have been characterized by Spiegelberg as 'best regarded as first attempts'.

For an introduction there is still much of value in Brugsch, *Aegyptologie*, though much is also out of date. More popular in character are works of Ebers, among them *Aegyptische Studien.* Comprehensive, but generally out-of-date, information is given by Gardner Wilkinson, *Manners and Customs of the Ancient Egyptians.* The best work, though lacking clear economic concepts, is Erman, *Aegypten und agyptisches Leben im Altertum.* Steindorf, *Die Blütezeit des Pharaoreichs* is an attractive work of popularization.

A short sketch of Egypt's social history is given by Thurnwald in *Zeitschrift für Sozialwissenschaft*, vol. 4 (1901). For land distribution under the Ramessides see the important study by Erman, 'Zur Erklärung des Pap. Harris', *SPAW* 1903. For Maspero the remarks in section 2 apply. Useful material is to be found in Wiedemann's works, especially his commentary on Book Two of Herodotus.

For a general historical survey there is the important work of Sethe, *Untersuchung zur Geschichte und Altertumskunde Aegyptens* (unavailable to me for this work). See also the works of E. Meyer, *Geschichte des alten Aegyptens* and volume I of his *Geschichte des Altertums*; also the works of Petrie, including *History of Egypt* and *Koptos.* For Bocchoris we now have the Paris dissertation of A. Moret, *De Bocchori rege* (1903).

As long as twenty years ago Eduard Meyer said that we needed a new history of Egyptian industry to replace the outdated work of Gardner Wilkinson. Since excavated objects and illustrations allow us to trace the very early states of technology, what is essential here is an exact description of the development of tools, raw materials, and products – a description that, for example, would show the effect of the introduction of iron. Probably the help of technologists would be necessary for this. One could then construct a synthesis to show how these developments influenced the division of labour within the sphere of large households and within the sphere of industry run with free labour, and how the two spheres influenced each other. One would also want to determine the precise economic meaning of industrial work in each case.

The careful investigations of terminology which are cited in the text are of course part of the preliminary work necessary for a programme such as that just sketched, and indeed for any real attempt to describe agrarian history.

4. Israel

The basic works are J. Wellhausen's *Prolegomena* and *Israelitische und jüdische Geschichte*, but they furnish little material for social history. For that one must consult E. Meyer, *Die Entstehung des Judentums* for post-Exilic times; for the pre-Exilic period see the works (often somewhat daring) of Winckler, especially his history of Israel in the *Altorientalische Forschungen* (unfortunately inaccessible to me while writing this work). See also Jeremias, *Das Alte Testament im Lichte des alten Orients* and the somewhat uneven literature on the Bible-Babel problem, which has been usefully summarized by C. Bezold.

For legal and agrarian history see, among older works: Nowack, *Judische Archäologie*; Buhl, *Die sozialen Verhältnisse der Israeliten*. More recent, and very valuable: A. Merx, *Die Bücher Moses und Josua*, published in *Religionsgeschichtliche Volksbibliothek*; despite the use of 'Volksbibliothek' these works are by no means 'popular'. A useful sketch of Hebrew history is given by Guthe, 'Geschichte des Volkes Israel', in *Grundriss der Theologie*, vols. 2 and 3, with good bibliography.

A great mass of primary source material is published in all the journals dealing with the Old Testament and the Semitic languages, including those cited above. See also the modern commentaries on the *Old Testament* and the many good articles in the *Jewish Encyclopedia* and the *Realenzyklopädie für Protestantische Theologie und Kirche* (with useful bibliographies). A modern and scholarly translation of the *Talmud* has been published by Goldschmidt. For studies on Hebrew law see the journals devoted to Jewish studies.

5. Greek and Roman Antiquity

The *Realenzyclopädie* edited by Pauly and Wissowa (now as far as the letter E, inclusive) covers Classical Antiquity, and most of its articles are excellent. As to periodicals, there is the *Jahresberichte* mentioned above, and then a great number of historical and archaeological journals, among them the two main German ones being *Hermes* and *Philologus*. The latter publishes a monographic series; neither publish reviews or give attention to bibliography.

Also deserving note are: *Neue Jahrbücher für das klassische Altertum*, the *Mitteilungen* of the German and Austrian archaeological institutes in Athens and Rome, and the *Mélanges d'Archéologie* of the French school in Rome.

For Greek and Hellenistic studies see the *Journal of Hellenic Studies*, *Bulletin de correspondence hellénique* (important for information on new source material), and *Revue des Etudes grecques*. Social history is given attention mainly in the first two. The Romanistic section of the *Zeitschrift für Rechtsgeschichte* has recently begun publishing articles on Greek law.

The work on Greco-Italic legal history by B. W. Leist was an attempt at comparative study, but like the author's other works (*Altarisches jus gentium, Altarisches jus civile*), it suffered from an exaggerated emphasis on tribal influences. For the current views of scholarship see the fundamental works of Mitteis, which are thoroughly based upon comparative method and papyrological sources.

J. Beloch has been criticized by many, sometimes with justice, but he deserves credit for laying the foundations of knowledge about the demography of Antiquity; cf. *Die Bevölkerung der griechischen-romischen Welt* and many articles. He has also published studies on ancient economy, and these are more open to criticism; see, e.g., Conrad's *Jahrbuch für National-Oekonomic*, ser. 3, vol. 18, p. 626.

J. Burckhardt's posthumously published lecture series, *Griechische Kulturgeschichte*, ignores all modern scholarship and the non-literary sources. Therefore its views, though they reveal the thought of a cultivated mind, should be used with great caution. In any event it gives little attention to specifically economic matters. On the importance of this work, in opposition to Von Wilamowitz, see the essay of C. Neumann in *Historische Zeitschrift* and Kaerst's preface to his *Hellenismus*.

Blümner's well-known and valuable work *Gewerbe und Kunst* needs revision (partly supplied in several valuable articles by him in Pauly–Wissowa, such as those on *Ackerbau* and *Eisen*), but even more important is the fact that it has nothing about economic theory. It is unfortunate that for many matters we must still rely on the book of Büchsenschütz, *Besitz und Erwerb im griechischen Altertum*, an accurate work but completely devoid of economic categories.

In the text I have discussed the work of Francotte published as volumes 7 and 8 of the *Bibliothèque de la Faculté de Philosophie et Lettres de Liège*. This is an important study; the only thing it lacks is attention to the ways in which capital was invested. Francotte fails to ask constantly what were the relationships between market, origin, and type of raw materials, and what were the chances for profit which arose from these conditions and the structure of the economy. Of course the existence of these relationships is itself unsure. But without hypotheses there can be no advance in this field.

Francotte's avenue of research should be continued and applied to Hellenistic and Roman times. Further work has been done towards this by Guiraud, in the *Bibliothèque de la faculté de lettres* of Paris, vol. 12 (1900).

H. Delbrück's works on military history, especially *Geschichte der Kriegskunst*, have been criticized sharply by specialists, just as he (though not a specialist!) has criticized the works of W. Sombart. Some of the criticisms directed against Delbrück may have more basis than his criticisms of Sombart, but some are also very unjust. For despite many obvious mistakes in his economic ideas, his works are nevertheless not only very stimulating but also often of fundamental value. This applies especially to his work *Die Perserkriege und die Burgunderkriege* and to those parts of his *Kriegskunst* which are shaped by his special talent for giving a realistic analysis of the causes of political and military events.

Eduard Meyer's *Forschungen zur alten Geschichte* includes essays on several matters of fundamental importance for social history, including the number of slaves at Athens, the relation between population density and land use, Lycurgus, and the concept of the city-state. It is hardly necessary to mention the larger works of Von Wilamowitz, such as *Aus Kydathen* and *Aristoteles und Athen*, but it should be noted that much of value is also to be found in works of his where one would not expect social history to be treated, such as the introduction to his edition of the *Heracles* [of Euripides]. He ingeniously develops the idea of a Dorian culture which was the antithesis of the genuinely Hellenic culture as represented by Athens; I find this construction unconvincing. Wilamowitz uses social and economic data for many particular aspects of his argument, although as a matter of principle he would reject reliance on such evidence as 'materialistic'.

Nor need much space be used here to describe the major works of Eduard Meyer (see above), Busolt (who in vol. 1 of his Greek history gives a valuable account of barter trade in the Mycenaean Age on the basis of the archaeological material), and Beloch (his works are notable for thorough attention to economic factors, but sometimes lack clear concepts).

Valuable material is given in Hermann's manual, *Lehrbuch der griechischen Antiquitäten*, newly edited by Blümner and Dittenberger; vol. 2 on legal antiquities by Thalheim and vol. 4 on private antiquities by Blümner are very useful but generally fail to class the material by economic categories. Marquardt's *Römische Privataltertümer* is indispensable, but it is out of date and also lacks organization. The same is true of the various works of Pöhlmann, especially his article in the *Historische Zeitschrift*, new ser. vol. 44, pp. 193 ff., 385 ff., also *Neue Jahrbücher fur das klassische Altertum*, vol. 1, pp. 205 ff., and his well-known *Geschichte des antiken Sozialismus und Kommunismus*. In all his works, especially in this major one, Pöhlmann presents interpretations of permanent value along with untenable theories which lack above all precision in economic matters. For his views concerning the origins of Christianity see the conclusion of the section in my text on the Hellenistic Age, as well as Troeltsch, *Archiv fur Sozialwissenschaft*, vol. 26.1.

For Greek legal history there is Guiraud, *Histoire de la propriété foncière en Grece*, and the more recent work of Beauchet, *Droit privé de la Republique Athenienne* (a work which is inclusive rather than analytic). For Roman law there is the useful but completely unoriginal work of Karlowa, and now the *Römische Privatrecht bis auf Diokletian* by Mitteis (so far only volume I published). Agrarian history is often illuminated by Pernice's 'Parerga' in the *Zeitschrift für Rechtsgeschichte*.

The non-literary material pertaining to Greek legal history can be most easily consulted in Dittenberger's *Sylloge*, and in the *Recueil des Inscriptions juridiques*, edited by Dareste, Haussouillier, and Reinach. For that pertaining to Roman legal history see Bruns' *Fontes*.

6. Greece

This section will note only those works which make an important contribution to problems and controversies mentioned in the text.

The theory that there are survivals of communal lands in Homer was exploded by Pöhlmann in volume I of the *Zeitschrift für Soz. und Geschichte*. The definitive work on the Greek tribes is the monograph of Szanto, *Sitzungsberichte der Wiener Akademie*, vol. 144 (1902), no. 5. On the phratries see the book by Schäfer and the article by Rudolf Schöll on the Cleisthenic tribes, *Sitzungsberichte der Bayerischen Akademie* 1889, vol. 2.1 (not entirely convincing), and especially the excellent article by Szanto, 'Demotionidai', in Pauly–Wissowa. In my discussion of the clan I agree in all essentials with the views of Eduard Meyer (in part *contra* Von Wilamowitz), and I also follow Meyer on the much discussed question of the Mycenaean culture.

The problem as to whether the limitations on the sale of land which survived into historical times were due to clan interests or political policies cannot be easily determined for each separate case, and could not be settled in the text. There are, however, good reasons for believing that by far the most cases were due to political policies designed to maintain military strength. The theory that they were due to a tradition of clan ownership has most recently been argued by Wilbrandt, *Politische und soziale Bedeutung der attischen Geschlechter vor Solon*, supplement 7 to *Philologus*.

For the early stages of the *polis* see Toepffer, *Attische Genealogie*, and Fr. Cauer, *Parteien und Politiker in Megara und Athen* (but his work suffers from a basic misconception; he believes that nearly always it is economically oppressed classes which turn to revolution. History teaches the opposite), and Bruno Keil, *Die Solonische Verfassung*. On the character of tyranny see R. Nordin, 'Aisymnetie und Tyrannis' in *Klio*, vol. 3, and also Ed. Meyer in *Geschichte des Altertums*.

For the history of imprisonment of debtors, mortgages, and mortgage law we now have Szanto's monograph in the *Sitzungs-berichte* of the Vienna Academy, Hitzig's *Griechisches Pfand-recht*, and Swoboda's *Beiträge zur griechischen Rechtsgeschichte*, all important (see text). On Cretan law see Bücheler and Zitel-mann, *Das Recht von Gortyn*, published as a supplement to *Rheinisches Museum fur Philologie*, new ser., vol. 40.

On Sparta see the works of Busolt, Niese, and Ed. Meyer. The latter's paper in his *Forschungen* errs (I think) in exaggerating the antiquity of Spartan institutions. Greek military colonies are considered by Gomperz, *Mitteilungen des Archäologischen Instituts*, *Athen* 13 (1888), to which add the remarks of Meyer, *Geschichte des Altertums*, vol. 4, sections 393 ff.; Gomperz gives the relevant bibliography.

The land law of the classical period is discussed in the cited works of Guiraud and Beauchet; one should also still turn to Leist, *Der attische Prozess und die Diadikasien*. The demes and social divisions of Athens have been recently studied by Sundwall in supplement I to *Klio*.

Regarding the question of 'capitalism' and 'factories' in Antiquity, see the works mentioned in the general section, especially Bücher's article in the *Festgabe für Schäffle*, in which he discusses the so-called 'shield factory' of Lysias and Attic factories in general, as well as the character of ancient commerce. Recent studies of what Demosthenes' guardians did with his estate were in part inaccessible to me while writing this essay. Of the older studies see volume I of Schäfer, *Demosthenes und seine Zeit*.

Loans made within fraternal associations (*eranoi*) are discussed by Ziebarth, *Griechische Vereinswesen* (*Jablonowskische Preis-schrift*, no. 34), which also gives a thorough survey of Greek craft associations; a similar study of Roman craft associations is given by the older work of Liebenam.

For the economic conditions of ancient Greece the great work of Boeckh is still fundamental. Indeed, the fact that for the second time an unrevised edition of this work has been published indicates how little study there has been in the field recently. The municipal sale of grain in Samos is discussed by Thalheim in *Hermes* 39 (1904).

7. Hellenistic Age

For the Hebrews see above under section 4. Not much of value for social history is to be found in the general works of Droysen, Niese, and Kaerst, but see Kaerst, pp. 62 ff., and the concluding chapter of his first volume. Economic factors are given thorough treatment by Beloch in the third volume of his *Griechische Geschichte*, a feature for which that work deserves particular credit.

Of works on Hellenistic Egypt, those of Lombroso were once standard: *Recherches sur l'économie politique sous les Lagides*, and *Egitto dei Greci e Romani*. However they have been rendered out of date on many points by subsequent papyri finds. Mahaffy, *The Empire of the Ptolemies*, does not provide much for social history. Papyrology has come to dominate research in this field, and it has been supplied with admirable bibliographic tools by Ulrich Wilcken, who in the first volume of his *Archiv für Papyruskunde* gave a general register of extant papyri arranged according to subject, and has since kept it up to date with each successive volume. This is supplemented by the well-organized and exhaustive bibliographies by Viereck in the *Jahresberichte der klassischen Altertumswissenschaft*.

The bibliography on papyri and the related field of ostraca is increasing very rapidly. See the introduction to juristic papyrology by Gradenwitz and the article 'Papyrus und Papyrologie' by Deissmann in the *Realenzyklopädi für protestantische Theologie und Kirche*. Here we can only mention a few sources and studies which are of particular importance for agrarian history.

Fundamental for our knowledge of the Hellenistic Age, especially the economy of Egypt under Ptolemaic and the Early Roman Empire, is the work of U. Wilcken on *Griechische Ostraka*. The same is true of Mitteis' *Reichsrecht und Volksrecht* for constitutional development under the Later Roman Empire, together with Mitteis' many works on comparative law.

Among papyri publications the most useful both for method (translation and commentary are printed alongside the text) and contents are: the *Flinders Petrie Papyri*, ed. Mahaffy; *Revenue Laws of Ptolemy Philadelphus*, ed. Grenfell and Hunt (basic for the state's monopolies, leases, and tax farming system in the early Ptolemaic period); *Tebtunis Papyri* and *Oxyrhynchos Papyri*, both giving important information on land use, especially in the Fayyum, also edited by Grenfell and Hunt; and the publications edited by Kenyon, Brunet de Presle, Egger (*Papyri du Musée du Louvre*), and Wessely (*Corpus papyrorum Raineri*). The publications of the Berlin administration in *Aegyptische Urkunden aus dem Koeniglichem Museum* include very few documents from the Ptolemaic period.

Of Wessely's many works the following deserve special attention: *Karanis und Soknopaiu Nesos, Denkschrift der Wiener Akademie* 47 (1902), important for land use; *Studien über das Verhaltnis des griechischen zum ägyptischen Recht im Lagidenreich, Sitzungsberichte der Wiener Akademie, Philosophisch-historische Klasse* 124 (1891); and his analysis of the population of Arsinoe, in the last publication, vol. 145 (1902). Important works for determining the general economic character of the Ptolemaic state are: Rostovtzeff, *Geschichte der Staatspacht in der römischen Kaiserzeit, Philologus*, supp. 9 (1902), extremely important for the light it casts on the economic development of ancient capitalism in general, as noted in the text; Otto, *Priester und Tempel im hellenistischen Aegypten* 1, vol. 1 (vol. 2 is now in press; see discussion in the text); P. M. Meyer, *Heerwesen der Ptolemäer und Römer* (but this has been recently much criticized; cf. Schubart, *Archiv fur Papyrus-Forschung* 2 [1902], pp. 147 ff.).

On the problem of the *epikrisis* see Wessely, *Sitzungsberichte der Wiener Akademie* 142 (1900), and his *Studien zur Paläographie und Papyrus-Kunde*, no. 1; also the incomplete monograph of Wachsmuth, *Wirtschaftliche Zustande in Aegypten während der Ptolemäerzeit*, based on household account books. Land leases are treated by Waszynski, *Bodenpacht*; vol. 1 is on private leases, vol. 2 is to cover state leases. Domain leases are examined by Rostovtzeff and P. M. Meyer in *Klio* 1 (1902), and Rostovtzeff describes grain collection and transport in *Archiv für Papyrusforschung* 3 (1904), pp. 201 ff. In general the systematic bibliographies cited above in section I should be consulted.

8. *Roman Republic*

See the bibliography above at the beginning of section 5.

A great part of the tradition in our sources has been rejected as spurious by Ettore Pais in his *Storia di Roma* (vols. 1 and 2 published so far), but few have accepted his radical criticism. Nevertheless a number of his conjectures seem very convincing. At present scholarly opinion on the earliest period of Rome is in flux due to the excavations in the Forum; however, data relevant to social history will probably appear only as an indirect result of this.

On the rural communities see the article, with good bibliography, by Schulten in *Philologus*, vol. 53 (but note: the table of contents of that volume does not include it!). K. J. Neumann's *Die Grundherrlichkeit der römischen Republic (Strasburger Rektoratsrede*, 1900) contains a number of arguments against my *Römische Agrargeschichte*; most of these arguments seem to me unconvincing (see the text), but otherwise the work is admirable for its subtle reasoning. For clientage the fundamental study is still that of M. Voigt, *Verhandlungen der Königlichen Sächsischen Gesellschaft der Wissenschaften, Philosophisch-historische Klasse* 30 (1878); very good, but in part to be rejected, is Premerstein's 'Clientes' in Pauly–Wissowa.

On the Roman plebs see Ed. Meyer, '*Der Ursprung des Tribunats und die Gemeinde der vier Tribus*', *Hermes* 30 (1895), a brief summary of which is given in the article 'Plebs' in the second edition of this *Handwörterbuch* [*der Staatswissenschaften*]. Debt bondage is discussed by Mitteis, 'Ueber das Nexum', *Zeitschrift für Rechtsgeschichte, romanistische Abteilung* 22 (1901), and by F. Kleineidam, *Die Personalexekution der Zwölftafeln* (Breslau, 1904).

For the distinctive economic aspect of Roman surveying see: Beaudouin, *La limitation des fonds de terre*; Brugi, *Le dottrine giuridiche degli agrimensori Romani* (especially valuable); and Schulten, 'Vom römischen Kataster', *Hermes* 41 (1906). For Roman colonies and *municipia* see Toutain in *Mélanges archéologiques* 16 (1898), 18 (1898). Otherwise I refer the reader to the introduction by Rudorff to the *Schriften römischen Feldmesser*, edited by Lachmann, and to the work based on this, my own *Römische Agrargeschichte*. In the text I could do no more, because of considerations of space, than hint at the degree to which I still stand by this work, even though it has many of the errors young scholars make; e.g. for the origin of the colonate see now Rostovtzeff's article 'Kolonat' in this *Handwörterbuch*. However, it is clear that my book was basically wrong on some matters because it relied too heavily on the theories of Meitzen, exaggerating them and applying them to heterogeneous conditions. Of course, on many matters it is now out of date. Beaudouin, a scholar who is himself neither particularly creative nor original, though when he can use others' research he does competent work, declares that my book is overestimated. I certainly have no objection to his opinion, especially in view of the present level of scholarship in the field, but on the other hand I do not feel responsible for this overestimate. Mommsen's criticisms of my book, published in *Hermes* 27, seem to me only partly valid. On the *hekatorygos* see B. Keil, *Hermes* 38 (1903).

G. Ferrero's well-written and original work begins with the period of conquests; he says much on the Republican period which is very provocative, but some of his views arouse distrust because they seem to be inspired by modern conceptions, much as are many sections of Mommsen's *Römische Geschichte*. Soltau has defended the authenticity of the Sexto-Licinian agrarian laws in *Hermes* 30, pp. 624 ff., against Niese in *Hermes* 23 and Pais in his *Storia di Roma*, vol. 2, pp. 141 ff. A penetrating analysis of the religious and legal aspects of the problems of agrarian history is presented by Maschke, *Zur Theorie und Geschichte der römischen Agrargesetze* (1906); he too concludes that the extant sources retroject events.

On hereditary leases, see Mitteis in the *Abhandlungen der königlichen Sächsischen Gesellschaft der Wissenschaften, Philosophisch-historische Klasse* 20 (1903), and Rostovtzeff's article

'Kolonat' in this *Handworterbuch*. For the organization of estate production see the account in my *Römische Agrargeschichte*, to be supplemented now with the excellent work of Gummerus, *Der römische Gutsbetrieb als wirtschaftlicher Organismus nach Cato, Varro und Columella, Klio* supp. 1, no. 5. The Gracchan period is analysed in Eduard Meyer's paper in the *Festschrift zum 200 jähr. Jubiläum der Universitat Halle* (1894), also by Kornemann in *Klio*, supp. 1, and by Maschke in the work just cited. The interpretation of the agrarian law of 111 B.C. must still start with Mommsen's commentary in the *Corpus Inscriptionum Latinarum*. For further studies see general histories of Rome and Liebenam's bibliographic reviews in the *Jahresberichte der Geschichtswissenschaft*.

9. *Roman Empire*

For general bibliography see Rostovtzeff's article 'Kolonat' in this *Handwörterbuch*. Regarding my lecture, 'Die sozialen Grunde des Untergangs der antiken Kultur', published in *Die Wahrheit* of May 1896, see the remarks in the text.

[*Concluding Note on Method*]

A genuinely analytic study comparing the stages of development of the ancient *polis* with those of the mediaeval city would be welcome and productive. See the remarks on this subject by E. Gothein in *Wirtschaftsgeschichte des Schwarzwalds*, pp. 61 ff.

Of course I say this on the assumption that such a comparative study would not aim at finding 'analogies' and 'parallels', as is done by those engrossed in the currently fashionable enterprise of constructing general schemes of development. The aim should, rather, be precisely the opposite: to identify and define the individuality of each development, the characteristics which made the one conclude in a manner so different from that of the other. This done, one can then determine the causes which led to these differences.

It is also my assumption that an indispensable preliminary to such a comparative study would be the isolation and abstraction of the individual elements in each development, the study of these elements in the light of general rules drawn from experience, and finally, the formulation of clear concepts, as discussed above in the first section. Without these preliminary steps no causal relationships whatever can be established.

These rules of method apply especially to the study of economic history, for in this field insufficiently precise concepts can lead the scholar to conclusions which are completely absurd.

IV. The Social Causes of the Decline of Ancient Civilization

The Social Causes of the Decline of
Ancient Civilization

The fall of the Roman Empire was not due to external factors such as the numerical superiority of its enemies or the incapacity of its leaders. Indeed, in its last century the Empire was served by great statesmen, heroic figures like Stilicho who combined Germanic courage with sophisticated diplomacy. Yet whereas illiterate Merovingians, Carolingians, and Saxons could mobilize great forces and resist the onslaughts of Saracens and Huns, such feats were impossible even for Stilicho. The Empire had ceased to be what it once was, and the barbarian invasions simply concluded a development which had begun long before.

First, however, one basic point must be stressed: the civilization of Antiquity did not decline because the Empire fell, for the Roman Empire as a political structure existed for centuries after ancient civilization had passed its prime. In fact, this civilization had been in eclipse for a long time. By the early third century Roman literature was played out, and Roman jurisprudence deteriorated together with its schools. Greek and Latin poetry were moribund, historiography faded away, and even inscriptions started to fall silent. Latin itself soon gave way to dialects.

When, after one and a half centuries of decline, the Western Empire finally disappeared, barbarism had already conquered the Empire from within. Nor were the barbarian invasions followed by the establishment of new institutions to replace those of the Empire. Thus the Merovingian state, at least in Gaul, was for some time essentially a continuation of Roman provincial organization.

Hence the question we must answer is this: what caused the decline of civilization in the ancient world?

Many replies have been advanced, some quite mistaken, others making bad use of good ideas. For example, it is argued that despotism stunted the minds of ancient men and their political life. Yet it is clear that the despotism of Frederick the Great was a force for healthy growth. Others have claimed that the alleged luxury and actual amorality of the upper classes called down upon them the condemnation of history. But luxury and amorality are only symptoms, not causes, and the decline of ancient civilization was due to forces far more significant than the vices of individuals.

Still another explanation focuses on the emancipated Roman woman, the dissolution of marriage ties among the ruling classes, which allegedly weakened the foundations of ancient society. The fables of a biased reactionary, Tacitus, about the German woman, in reality a wretched slave of a fighting peasant, are still repeated by reactionaries of our own day. The truth is that the idealized 'German woman' did as little to assure the triumph of the Germans as did the well-known 'Prussian schoolmaster' the victory of Königgratz. In fact, as we shall see, the decline of ancient civilization was connected with the re-establishment of family ties among the lower classes of society.

From an ancient witness comes another explanation: Pliny the Elder's statement, 'The large estates ruined Italy.' 'There you are,' says a contemporary commentator, 'it was the Roman Junkers who destroyed the Empire.' 'Perhaps so,' says an opponent, 'but only because the estates themselves were ruined by imports of foreign grain; had agriculture been protected by high tariffs, the Empire would exist to this day.' Yet we shall see that the fall of ancient civilization marked the start of the rehabilitation of the peasant class.

Nor are Darwinian theories absent, for recently it has been argued that the process of natural selection was adversely affected by recruitment for the army, which condemned the strongest to celibacy, with the result that the Roman race degenerated in late Antiquity. Yet we shall see that in fact the army was increasingly recruited from soldiers' sons, and that this development proceeded apace with the decline of the Empire.

But let this suffice to show what answers others give. First I shall make some preliminary remarks on method, and then I shall give my own.

A storyteller can always count on heightened interest if his listeners believe that the story applies to their own lives too.

Then he can end with a moral exhortation. My story, however, is not of that sort. There is little or nothing which ancient history can teach us about our own social problems. A proletarian of today and a slave of Antiquity would have as little in common as do a European and a Chinese. Our problems and those of Antiquity are entirely different. Therefore the story I tell has only historical interest. Yet it is one of the most absorbing man knows, for it describes the internal disintegration of an ancient civilization.

Our first task must be to define clearly the characteristics of the social structure of Antiquity. We shall see that these characteristics determined the cycle of development of ancient civilization.

First: the civilization of Antiquity was essentially urban in character. The city was the centre of political life, of art, and of literature. The economy too, at least in the early period of Antiquity, was shaped by what we usually now call 'urban economics'.

In Hellenic times the city was not essentially different from the mediaeval city. Whatever differences existed were due to contrasts in climate and race between the Mediterranean region and Central Europe, just as today there are differences between English and Italian workers and between German and Italian artisans.

Economically the ancient city was based on the exchange of its industrial products for the agricultural products of its rural hinterland, an exchange centred in the city's own market. The trade involved was directly effected between producer and consumer, and essentially covered all needs; no imports from outside were needed, and so Aristotle's ideal of urban self-sufficiency (*autarkia*) was in fact realized by most Greek cities.

Now it is also true that upon the foundation of this local trade an international trade developed in very early times, which covered a large territory and included many items. Much of ancient history centres round those cities whose ships were engaged in international trade, but because we hear of these cities we easily forget how insignificant this trade was in quantity. The civilization of ancient Europe was a coastal civilization, and its history was above all a history of the coastal cities. However, alongside the highly developed commercial economy of these towns there existed – exactly opposite in character – the natural economy of the primitive peasants of the interior, living in tribal communities or under the domination of feudal patriarchs. A truly regular and stable international trade was maintained only via sea routes or on the large rivers. There was no trade with the interior in Antiquity, not even such as could be compared with that of the Middle Ages. The much-praised Roman roads were not used for anything resembling modern trade, nor was the Roman postal system. Hence the enormous difference between the rent derived from lands in the interior and that from lands on water routes. To be near a Roman road was considered a misfortune rather than an advantage, for it brought billeting and vermin. In short: Roman roads served the army, not commerce.

The natural economy therefore remained largely unaffected, and so commerce could not develop very far. Such trade as existed was mainly in a small number of expensive articles: precious metals, amber, fine textiles, some ironware and pottery, and the like. These were generally luxury items which, because of their high price, could be traded profitably despite the high cost of transport. Such trade cannot be compared in any way with modern commerce. It would be as if today only champagne, silk, and the like were traded, whereas all statistics indicate that the bulk of commerce is now in mass consumer goods.

It is of course true that certain cities such as Athens and Rome became dependent upon imports for their grain supplies. However, such instances were always historically abnormal, and the collection of these supplies was entrusted to public authority. The ancient city neither could nor would leave them to unregulated private trade.

Therefore it was not the masses and their everyday needs with which international trade was concerned, but rather a small stratum of the wealthy classes. Expansion of trade in Antiquity was only possible if there was an increasing differentiation in wealth. Furthermore – and here we encounter a third characteristic feature of ancient civilization – this differentiation took a particular form and direction: the civilization of Antiquity was based upon slavery.

From the first, free labour in the cities coexisted with unfree labour in the country; there was free division of labour producing goods for exchange on the urban market, and there was also unfree labour organized to produce goods on and for rural estates, as in the Middle Ages. Again, in ancient as in mediaeval society, a natural antagonism sprang up between these two forms of organized human labour.

In general, economic progress is achieved by increased division of labour. When free labour prevails, progress at first demands expansion of the market, extensively by drawing new geographical areas into the exchange economy, and intensively by drawing more persons into it; hence the townsmen of Antiquity sought to break up manors and incorporate their serfs into the free market. When unfree labour prevails, economic progress is achieved by a steady accumulation of workers, for the more slaves or serfs are assembled the more specialization of unfree occupations is possible.

Now whereas in the Middle Ages the victory was won by free labour and free exchange of goods, in Antiquity the outcome of the struggle was just the opposite. Why was this? For the same reason that technological development in Antiquity was limited: human beings could be bought cheaply, because of the character of the chronic warfare of ancient civilization. Ancient wars were also slave hunts; they constantly supplied the slave markets and so promoted to an extraordinary degree the unfree labour sector of the economy and the accumulation of labour-power. The result of this was that the free sector ceased to expand; the crafts could not advance beyond the stage in which production was wage work done for customers by non-propertied artisans. No competition could arise between free entrepreneurs and free wage labourers in production for the market, which would have set a premium on labour-saving inventions such as those induced by competition in modern times.

In Antiquity, on the contrary, it was the economic importance of unfree labour in autarkic households which increased steadily. Only slaveowners could develop production based on a division of labour, and only they could improve their standard of living. More and more it was slave enterprises which could produce for the market after meeting their own needs.

This determined the deviation of economic development in Antiquity from that of the Middle Ages. In mediaeval society, free division of labour developed its market intensively within the local economic territory of the city on the basis of production for both the individual orders of customers and the local market. Then as trade with non-local markets increased there was a division of production between local centres. First the putting-out system was used, then manufactures, creating new forms of production designed to supply external markets and employing free labour. The development of the modern economy was then inextricably connected with the tendency for the masses to satisfy their needs more and more through interlocal and then international trade.

In Antiquity, on the contrary, the development of international trade was connected with the consolidation of unfree labour in large slave households. Therefore the exchange economy was a sort of superstructure; beneath it was a constantly expanding infrastructure of natural economy in which needs were met without exchange, the economy of the slave establishments which perpetually absorbed human material and satisfied their consumption needs mainly out of their own production rather than from the market. The more the consumption of the upper class of slaveowners increased, the more trade expanded extensively, but the greater the extensive expansion of trade, the more it lost in intensity. Thus trade in Antiquity more and more became a thin net spread over a large natural economy, and as time passed the meshes of this net became finer and its threads became more tenuous.

In the Middle Ages there was a transition from production for individual local orders to production for an interlocal market. This transition was made possible by the slow ascent of capitalist free enterprise and the principle of competition, and their penetration into the centre of local economic structures. In Antiquity, on the contrary, international trade increased the growth of *oikoi*, autarkic establishments based on unfree labour, and these *oikoi* decreased the basis of the local exchange economies.

This development occurred in most pronounced form under Roman rule. After the victory of the plebs [in 287 B.C.] Rome was a conquering peasant state – or, rather, a conquering state of town-organized yeomen. Every war meant the annexation of more land for settlement. The Roman army was recruited from the younger sons of Roman yeomen; having no hope of an inheritance, they fought to win land for themselves and so gain the status of a full citizen. This was the secret of Rome's conquering power. However, the situation changed once Roman expansion was extended to overseas territories, for the peasants had no wish to settle there; now the driving force was the aristocracy's quest for plunder from overseas provinces. Wars served as slave hunts and were followed by confiscation of lands; the lands were formed into domains, and leased for exploitation to wealthy contractors.

Then the peasantry of Italy was decimated by the Second Punic War; the consequences of its downfall may be called Hannibal's belated revenge. The Gracchan movement to restore small peasant agriculture was followed by a reaction which marked the decisive triumph of slave labour on the land. Henceforth the slaveowners alone benefited from a rising standard of living, contributed to increased consumer demand and developed production for the market. This does not mean that free labour disappeared entirely, but rather that slave-labour enterprises were now the sole dynamic element in the economy. Roman writers on agriculture take it for granted that the organization of work will be based on slave labour.

Finally, the importance of slave labour in ancient civilization was enormously increased when the Empire incorporated vast continental areas into the Roman world: Spain, Gaul, Illyria, and the lands along the Danube. The demographic centre of the Empire shifted inland, and an attempt was made to move ancient civilization to a different arena, to transform it from a coastal into a continental civilization. Ancient society now spread its economic system over an enormous area, one so large that even centuries would not have sufficed for the task of assimilating it to the commercial system and the money economy which had developed on the shores of the Mediterranean. For even on those shores, as we noted before, interlocal commerce was no more than a thin net, and when it was stretched out over inland areas it became still thinner. Indeed, the development of civilization in these hinterland regions on the basis of free labour and the development of intensive commerce was simply not possible. If these areas were to be gradually incorporated into Mediterranean civilization, it would have to be done through the establishment of a landed aristocracy, based on the ownership of slaves and of autarkic estates worked by unfree labour. In inland areas transport was much more expensive than on the coasts, and so inland commerce was at first exclusively concerned with supplying luxuries for a small group, the wealthy slaveowners. Similarly the possibility of producing goods for sale on the market was available only to a small number of large slave enterprises.

Thus the slaveowner became the dominant figure in the economy of Antiquity, and a slave-labour system became the indispensable foundation of Roman society. We must, therefore, direct our attention to the peculiarities of this system.

Because of the sources available to us, we know most about the use of slave labour on the large landed estates of the Late Republic and the Early Empire. In any case the large estate was the basic form of wealth, for even money used for speculation was derived from it and usually a large-scale speculator was also a large-scale landowner. This was necessarily so, for land was needed as collateral by anyone wishing to engage in the most lucrative forms of speculation: tax farming, leasing domains, and public works contracts.

As a rule the Roman landowner did not manage his estates personally. He was, rather, a city dweller, active in politics, and interested above all in cash rents. The management of his estates he left to unfree overseers (*villici*). The main features of the resulting agricultural system were as follows.

Grain production for sale on the market was generally unprofitable. The city of Rome was not a possible market, since a state agency supervised the capital's grain supply, while the price paid for grain could not cover the costs of transportation from inland areas. Furthermore slave labour was not suited for raising grain, especially because the Roman technique of row cultivation needed very careful labour and therefore depended upon the self-interest of the worker. Because of these factors cereal culture was generally practised at least in part by leasing land in small parcels to *coloni* – descendants of the yeomen who had lost their farms. From the first *coloni* were not independent tenants managing their own affairs; the landlord provided seed and tools, and his overseer supervised cultivation. Furthermore, *coloni* from the outset often had to render labour services, especially at harvest time. Leasing land to *coloni* was considered one of the ways a landlord could manage his estate, as the language shows: the owner cultivated his land 'by means of tenants' (*per colonos*).

The alternative type of estate management was for the landlord to exploit his land directly for the production of cash crops, mainly high-value products such as olive oil and wine, supplemented by garden vegetables, fodder, poultry, and luxury items for the discriminating palates of the very wealthy, who were the only ones with money for such things. Such products took up the more fertile lands, the remainder being left to *coloni* on which to raise grain. The directly managed estate was essentially a plantation, and its work force was made up of slaves who were considered part of the owner's extended household, his *familia*. Slaves and *coloni* worked the great estates side by side under the Late Republic and also under the Empire.

Let us first turn to the slave population. What was its situation?

If we look at the ideal plantation as described by the Roman manuals of agriculture we find that the slaves ('the speaking tools': *instrumentum vocale*) were housed next to the cattle ('semi-speaking tools': *instrumentum semivocale*), and that the slave quarters included dormitories, an infirmary (*valetudinarium*), a prison (*carcer*), and a workshop for the estate's craftsmen (*ergastulum*). Now anyone who has worn a uniform will instantly see something very familiar here. This was a barracks. In actual fact, a slave's life was generally very much like a soldier's. Slaves ate and slept in common rooms under an overseer's supervision. Their better clothes were stored away in charge of the overseer's wife (*villica*), who functioned as a quartermaster, and every month clothing was inspected at a special roll-call. Slaves worked under strict military discipline. They formed squads (*decuriae*) every morning and were then marched off under command of slave drivers (*monitores*). Nor was any other system possible, for it has never been feasible to use unfree labourers for market production unless they fear the whip.

Now one factor in this situation is especially important for the present argument: the slave who lived in a barrack was not only without property, he was also without a family. Only the overseer (*villicus*) lived in his own cell with his own woman, to whom he was bound in slave marriage (*contubernium*); his position thus resembled that of a married NCO in a barracks today. The overseer, in fact, was supposed to be married, according to the agricultural manuals, in the interests of the landlord.

Then, just as always, private property and nuclear family went hand in hand: slave marriage was accompanied by slave property. The overseer, and according to the manuals only the overseer, could own private property, his *peculium*; as the word [from *pecus*, cattle] indicates, this was originally used for the overseer's cattle, which he grazed on the landlord's pasture, just as the estate worker does today in Eastern Germany. But the great mass of slaves had no *peculium*, just as they had no monogamous relationship. Their sex life was a kind of supervised prostitution, with bonuses for the slave girls who reared children, some receiving their freedom if they reared three.

Now this custom in itself suffices to indicate the situation that resulted from the lack of monogamous family life. Man thrives only in families, and so slaves condemned to live in barracks did not reproduce themselves. The barracks demanded constant replenishment; hence new slaves had to be continually purchased. Indeed this was assumed to be a recurrent expenditure in the agricultural manuals. The ancient plantation consumed slaves the way a modern blast furnace consumes coal. Hence a slave market regularly and amply supplied with human material was the indispensable precondition for a barracks slave system engaged in market production.

Slave-buyers spent little. Varro recommends the purchase of malefactors and such low-priced material; his reasoning is characteristic: 'criminals are more ingenious' (*velocior est animus hominum improborum*). This meant that the Roman plantations depended on a slave market which received regular supplies of human material. But what if the market failed to find these supplies? This would inevitably affect the slave barracks, just as today closing the coal mines would affect the blast furnaces.

In fact that is just what happened; which brings us to the turning point in the development of ancient civilization.

If we are asked to name the date at which the decline of Roman power and civilization began, then every German immediately thinks of the day when the Empire suffered its great defeat in the

Teutoburg Forest. There is in fact a kernel of truth in that popular idea, even though it is contradicted by the fact that it was later, under Trajan, that the Empire achieved the zenith of its power. The battle was not, of course, decisive in itself, for it was the sort of setback every nation expanding into barbarian territory experiences. It was the sequel which was decisive: the resolution by Tiberius to abandon the wars of conquest on the Rhine, a resolution later repeated on the Danube by Hadrian's evacuation of Dacia. These imperial policies meant that the Roman Empire ceased to expand. The entire area of ancient civilization was now pacified internally and (to a large extent) externally; but therewith the regular supply of human material for the slave markets ceased. As early as the reign of Tiberius the consequence seems to have become apparent: an acute shortage of labour. We are told that Tiberius was compelled to order an inspection of estate workshops, because the large landowners were seizing people. Like mediaeval robber barons they lay in wait on the roads, it seems; but whereas the barons wanted gold and goods, the landowners wanted workers to cultivate their deserted fields.

Even more important was the gradually increasing difficulty of maintaining a system of production based upon the slave barracks, for the barracks demanded constant replenishment and this was no longer possible. When the supply of slaves stagnated, the slave barracks were doomed to disappear.

At first, to judge by the later agricultural manuals, the increase in slave prices caused an improvement in technique as the slaves were given better training. But after the final offensive wars of the second century, which were in fact little more than slave raids, it became impossible to maintain the great plantations worked by slaves without family and without property.

To confirm and comprehend how the change occurred, we can compare conditions on large Roman plantations as described in the manuals with those on landed estates in Carolingian times as described in Charlemagne's instructions to the bailiffs of his domains (*capitulare de villis imperialibus*) and in the monastic records of the period. In both periods we find that slaves were used as agricultural labourers, that they were without legal rights, and that in particular they were subject to unlimited exploitation by their masters. There was no change, then, in these respects. Likewise many aspects of the Roman manor [*Grundherrschaft*] were still alive in Carolingian times; they extended even to terminology: for example, the women's house of Antiquity was called *gynaikeion*, and this survived in the form *genitium*.

However, one aspect of the Roman manor changed radically: whereas Roman slaves lived in a collectivist barracks, the slave of Carolingian times had his own cottage (*mansus servilis*) on the land which he held from his lord in return for labour services. The Carolingian slave was really a 'small peasant'. In particular, he had his own family and his own property.

To sum up, then, we can say that the slave was now separated from the *oikos*. This change occurred under the Later Empire, because slaves in barracks simply did not reproduce themselves. When slaveowners allowed their slaves to have their own families and made them hereditary dependants, they thereby assured themselves young slaves to take their parents' place and work the fields. This was now essential, since workers could not be purchased on the slave market, which indeed disappeared completely in Carolingian times. Furthermore, whereas the plantation owner had to invest capital in maintaining his slaves, this burden was now shifted to the slaves themselves.

This transformation was slow but irreversible, and its effects were profound. It constituted a great alteration of the institutions which shaped the lowest classes of society; they once again had a right to family life and private property. I can only note briefly here how closely this transformation was connected with the triumph of Christianity: in the slave barracks of earlier times Christianity would have made little headway, but in the age of St Augustine the free peasants of Africa were actually fervent supporters of a local heresy.

Thus the slave rose in social status to become an unfree serf. At the same time the *colonus* fell in status and became a serf too. This happened because the *colonus'* relation to his landlord became more and more closely tied to labour services. Originally the landlord was mainly interested in payment of money rent, although as mentioned labour on the estate was also exacted from the first. However, even under the Early Roman Empire the agricultural manuals stressed the labour services rendered by the *colonus*, and the scarcer slave labour became the more this tendency increased. African inscriptions from the reign of Commodus (A.D. 161–92) show us that the *colonus* there was already a serf who held land from a lord in return for specified labour services. Thus an economic transformation of the position of the *colonus* had occurred, and then there followed a change in his legal position, formally codifying his role as the basis of an estate's labour force: he was bound to the soil. To explain the origins of this rule we must review briefly certain matters connected with public administration.

At the end of the Republic and at the beginning of the Empire the basis of Roman public administration was the city (*municipium*), just as the economic basis of ancient civilization was also the city. As new areas were incorporated into the Empire they were systematically organized into urban units, in a wide variety of gradations of political dependence. Thus the administrative form of the *municipium* was spread throughout the Roman Empire, and the city was everywhere the lowest unit of administration. The city's magistrates were responsible to the state for raising taxes and supplying recruits.

However, this system was gradually modified as social conditions evolved under the Empire. The great estates successfully sought to escape incorporation into the urban system, and the more the demographic centre of the Empire moved inland the more it was the agrarian population that supplied military recruits. Therewith, more and more influence on state policies was exercised by the 'Junkers' of Antiquity, the great estate owners. Today Junkers resist official incorporation of their Prussian estates into the administration of local communities. In the Roman Empire the reverse process occurred: estates were removed from urban jurisdiction and the government offered very little resistance. Great numbers of rural properties (*saltus, territoria*) started to appear alongside the cities as administrative units, and in these the landowners were the source of local authority, just as the German owners of baronial estates are today in the manorial districts of Prussia. The Roman state depended on the landowner and gave him authority because it was he who collected the taxes levied on his *territorium* (sometimes advancing the money due from his tenants, then collecting from them), and it was also he who supplied the contingent of recruits from his manor. Supply of recruits therefore came to be regarded as another public assessment levied on an estate – an assessment, be it noted, which decimated its labour force.

These developments in Roman public administration prepared the way for the legal provisions which bound the *colonus* to the land.

Here it should be remembered that no general freedom of movement guaranteed by law ever existed under the Roman Empire. Let it suffice to recall the Gospel of St Luke, in which it is taken for granted that for purposes of taking a census everyone could be ordered to return to his home community, his *origo*. That is why the family of Jesus had to return to the town of Bethlehem. In the country, however, the *origo* of a *colonus* was the manorial district of his lord.

Very early [under the Empire] we find in existence a legal process by which a person might be ordered to return to his home community to fulfil public duties. If a senator neglected to attend meetings of the Senate over a period of time he was merely fined; but if a member of a town council in the provinces, a *decurio*, neglected his duties, he was treated more summarily, and would be brought back to his town on request. That was frequently necessary, since the position of decurion in Antiquity involved liability for the town's tax levy, and was therefore a burdensome honour. Later, when juristic formulas fell into decay and confusion, a town's request for the return of a *decurio* took the form of the ancient claim to ownership of property (*vindicatio*), so that in effect towns pursued their errant councillors the way a village pursued a runaway bull from the common herd.

If this could be done to a *decurio*, the *colonus* could not expect any milder treatment. The labour services which he owed his lord were not distinguished from his public duties, since the lord was both estate owner and local authority, and so the *colonus* who fled his duties was returned to fulfil them. What this meant was that administrative practice demanded that the *colonus* remain in his home district and so made him subject to the manorial authority of the estate owner whom he served. The *colonus* had thus become a serf, bound to his land.

Between the state and the *colonus* there was now interposed an intermediate authority, the landowner. The landowners themselves, the *possessores*, formed a class of magnates who obeyed no local or provincial authority, only the emperor himself. We find this class in the Later Roman Empire, in Ostrogothic Italy, and in Merovingian Gaul. In short, the old simple distinction between free and unfree had been replaced by a division of society into orders [ständische Gliederung]. A series of changes, each in itself quite gradual, together constituted a development towards this new social structure, which economic conditions had made inevitable. Feudal society had already started to emerge in the Later Roman Empire.

Thus the manor of the Later Empire had two types of peasants owing labour services: unfree peasants (servi) with unlimited obligations, and personally free peasants (coloni, tributarii) who owed precisely defined payments in money, produce, and then – increasingly – a share of their crops, as well as (usually, though not always) specified labour services. Once this is understood, it is obvious that the landed estate of the Later Empire has all the characteristics of a mediaeval manor.

Now it was impossible to maintain market production on the estates of the Later Empire with labour services of tenants, given ancient transportation. The disciplined slave labour of the barracks was indispensable for market production. Thus as soon as slave barracks gave way to peasant cottages, especially in the interior, production for the market disappeared and the thin net of commerce, which had covered the natural economy of Antiquity, frayed and then snapped. We can see this clearly in Palladius, the last important writer on agriculture; he recommends that the estate owner should arrange things so that his workers will supply all the estate's needs themselves, and so make purchases unnecessary. From ancient times the women of an estate had done the spinning, weaving, milling, and baking, but now craftsmen rendering labour service also did the work of smiths, cabinet-makers, masons, and carpenters. Finally the estates became self-sufficient, and as a result the small class of free craftsmen in the cities, most of whom worked for wages and food, now lost even their relative importance in society. The economically dominant establishments of the landed magnates were able to supply their own needs.

Thus the large estate became an oikos; more and more its main economic function was to supply its own needs with its own specialized labour. The great estates broke away from the city markets. Most of the medium and small towns lost their economic foundation – the exchange of labour and goods with their hinterlands. Thus the legal sources of the Later Empire reveal to us the decay of the cities. The emperors now constantly inveigh against flight from the cities, and complain that the *possessores* are giving up and tearing down their town houses, taking off wainscoting and furniture to their country mansions.

The decline of the cities was hastened by the state's financial policies. The state too increasingly met its own increasing needs on a natural economy basis; the fiscus was run like an *oikos*, producing as much as possible what it needed and buying as little as possible on the market. The result was that it impeded the formation of monetary fortunes. Tax farming, a major form of speculation, was abolished; the state itself collected the taxes. A more rational method of transporting the public grain supply was found, using ships whose makers were rewarded with lands. A number of lucrative trades were made state monopolies, and the mines were also taken over, bringing great profit to the treasury. All these measures were beneficial from the subjects' point of view, but their effect was to arrest private capital formation and check every tendency towards the emergence of a class corresponding to the bourgeoisie of modern times. This financial system based on natural economy policies developed steadily as the Empire ceased to be an agglomeration of cities exploiting rural regions, with its economic activities centred on the coast and sea trade, and became instead a unified state aiming at the political integration and organization of large continental areas with a subsistence economy. The consequence was an enormous increase in state expenditure, that could not be met from monetary income because the exchange system was far too tenuous. Necessity therefore dictated the growth of the natural economy within the state's own financial system.

From the first the provinces had paid tribute to the state mainly in kind, especially grain; this was the grain with which the public storehouses were supplied. Under the Empire manufactured products were also collected as tax payments; deliveries were assessed on urban crafts; the craftsmen were often mobilized for this purpose into compulsory guilds. The state now increasingly satisfied its needs for goods in this way, rather than by purchase on the market or public contracts. Meanwhile the poor free craftsmen were forced into a position where they were in practice hereditary guild serfs.

What the treasury received from tax payments in kind, it used to cover expenditures in kind. This was the way it sought to maintain the two largest items in its budget: the bureaucracy and the army. Here alone, however, the natural economy revealed its limits.

A large continental state cannot be governed permanently without a salaried bureaucracy, something with which the city-states of Antiquity had been able to dispense. Under the monarchy established by Diocletian, the officials of the Roman state were paid largely in kind; their salaries were much like those now paid to day labourers on a Mecklenburg estate, only much larger: a few thousand bushels of grain, so many head of cattle, and proportionate quantities of salt, oil, and the other things needed for sustenance – all drawn from the imperial storehouses. To supplement this there was a rather modest sum paid in cash for pocket money.

Nevertheless, in spite of the manifest tendency towards provisioning in kind, the maintenance of a powerful and hierarchical bureaucracy demanded considerable money expenditures. Nor was this the only drain on the government's money supply, for even higher cash outlays were needed for the imperial army.

A continental state with hostile neighbours must have a standing army. Rome's ancient army was recruited from citizen landowners who supplied their own equipment, but by the end of the Republic this had given way to an army equipped by the state and recruited from the proletariat – the army on which the Caesars relied. Under the Empire the standing army became in theory as well as in fact a professional body. Now in order to maintain a professional army two things are essential: men and money. Thus it was their recruitment needs which led mercantilist rulers in the age of enlightened despotism, such as Frederick II and Maria Theresa, to discourage large-scale agricultural enterprises and to forbid the enclosure of common lands. These policies were not motivated by humanitarian concern for the peasants, nor were the rights of the individual peasant protected, for his landlord could send him away without hindrance if he found another peasant to cultivate his land. The reason is rather to be found in a remark of Frederick William I, that his army would be recruited from 'surplus peasant lads'. But that meant that there had to be a surplus, and so enclosure of peasant lands was prevented, for that would have reduced the peasant population, depopulated the rural areas, and so made recruitment much more difficult.

For very similar reasons the Roman emperors intervened to regulate the conditions affecting *coloni*, for example forbidding any increase in the burdens imposed on them. Other policies, however, unknown to Rome, were followed by Europe's mercantilist rulers. In particular, they fostered large-scale manufacturing because it would increase the population and draw money into the country. Frederick the Great issued warrants for the arrest of workers and manufacturers leaving the country just as he did for deserting soldiers. This policy could not be followed by the Roman emperors, for large-scale industry producing for the market with free labour did not exist in the Empire, and could not exist.

In fact what happened in the Empire was that as commerce and cities declined, and as society relapsed into a natural economy, rural districts were more and more unable to raise the steadily increasing sums of money demanded by the tax system. At the same time there was a shortage of labour, caused by the closure of the slave market, and so army recruitment among the *coloni* became a ruinous burden on the estates, whose owners tried to help their peasants evade the recruitment officers. Men eligible for the draft therefore fled from the decaying cities to the countryside and the safety of serfdom, for the great landowner (*possessor*) needed workers and would aid them to escape conscription. The later emperors struggled to stem the flight of townsmen to the countryside, just as the later Hohenstaufen struggled to stop serfs fleeing into the city.

Recruitment for the army therefore became more and more difficult, with effects that were soon readily apparent. From the reign of Vespasian onwards, Italy was exempted from conscription; from Hadrian on army units ceased to be mixed, each one being recruited as much as possible from the district where it was stationed in order to save money – the earliest sign of the Empire's disintegration. Furthermore, if we look at the place of birth given on veterans' discharge documents over the centuries, we discover that a steadily increasing number of soldiers are identified as 'children of the camps' (*castrenses*); under the Empire this group increased from a few per cent of the total to

nearly half. In other words: the Roman army increasingly repro-
duced itself. Just as the slave living in a barracks without a wife
was replaced by a peasant living in the home of his own family,
so in the army the celibate soldier in the barracks gave way – at
least in part – to the married soldier who was really a hereditary
and professional mercenary.

Similarly the increased recruitment of barbarians was designed
mainly to husband the labour force of the rural areas, especially
the large estates. Barbarians were also given lands in return for
military duty on the borders, a measure entirely in the tradition
of a natural economy and also noteworthy as a distant precursor
of the fief. This form of land grant became increasingly common.

As a result of these developments the army which controlled
the Empire became a host of barbarians with increasingly fewer
ties to the native population. When the victorious barbarians
from outside the Empire crossed its borders their invasions at first
meant little more to the provincials than a change in the troops
billeted on them, and actually the Roman system of billeting
continued to be used. Indeed, in Gaul the invading barbarians do
not seem to have been generally feared as conquerors, for many
welcomed them as liberators from the oppression of the imperial
administration. That was certainly understandable.

For it was not just recruits which the decaying Empire had
difficulty finding in its own population. As the Empire relapsed
more and more into a natural economy, cash taxes became a
heavier and heavier burden on the population. But money is
absolutely essential for maintaining a mercenary army. In consequence the state's efforts were increasingly concentrated on the
problem of mustering ready money, while at the same time it
became ever more apparent that the estate owners, who produced
only for their own needs, were now economically unable to pay
adequate money taxes.

Of course, the problem would have been solved if the emperor
had said to the estate owners: 'Very well: have your *coloni* make
weapons for yourselves, then get on your horses, and together we
shall defend our country.' That would have been feasible for the
estate owners. But such a programme would have meant creating
a feudal army. The Middle Ages would have started.

In reality, a feudal social structure and a feudal military system
were the natural conclusion towards which developments under

the Later Roman Empire tended. During the period of barbarian invasions this trend was interrupted briefly by the local appearance of Germanic peasant armies fighting for land on which to settle, but then previous tendencies reasserted themselves and by Carolingian times a feudal order had been established.

Now a feudal army can overthrow kingdoms and defend a march, but no feudal army has ever been able to maintain the unity of a great empire or stand guard against land-hungry invaders on frontiers stretching hundreds of miles. This explains why the Roman Empire could not shift to a feudal military system, of a type that would have corresponded to the Empire's natural economy.

Therefore, in order to maintain the Empire, Diocletian found it necessary to try to reorganize public finances on the basis of uniform taxes in money, and the city was kept to the last as the official basis of the state administrative system. But the economic foundations of most cities were by now crumbling away; their main function was to obtain money for the state bureaucracy, while about them the land was transformed into a network of manorial estates.

It is clear, therefore, that the disintegration of the Roman Empire was the inevitable political consequence of a basic economic development: the gradual disappearance of commerce and the expansion of a barter economy. Essentially this disintegration simply meant that the monetarized administrative system and political superstructure of the Empire disappeared, for they were no longer adapted to the infrastructure of a natural economy.

It was on the basis of institutions which were adapted to a natural economy that the political unity of the West was re-established. This was accomplished by Charlemagne, who carried out Diocletian's will half a millennium later. The natural economy basis of his system is apparent to anyone who reads the instruction he sent to the bailiffs (*villici*) of his domains. These instructions, the celebrated *Capitulare de villis*, remind us by their homely knowledge and plain style of the edicts of Frederick William I.

Note that in the *Capitulare* the queen figures alongside the king, for as mistress of the royal household she was the king's

minister of finance. Nor should this cause surprise, for Charlemagne's fiscal administration was mainly concerned with collecting
food for his table and supplies for his household; the royal household's income and expenditures constituted the state's revenue
system. Hence the bailiffs were instructed what to provide for
the court: grain, meat, textiles, rather large quantities of soap,
in other words, what the king needed for himself, for his
courtiers, and for his servants, for example horses and transport
vehicles for warfare.

From the *Capitulare* it is clear what has disappeared: the standing army, the salaried bureaucracy, and therefore the taxes
(even the concept is gone) of the Roman Empire. The king feeds
his officials at his own table or gives them land. An army recruited
from men who supply their own arms, is about to become an army
of cavalrymen, and thereby a military order of manor-owning
knights.

Interlocal commerce has also disappeared; the commercial
ties connecting the self-sufficient cells of economic life have been
cut, trade has relapsed to the level of peddling left to foreigners
– Greeks and Jews. Above all else, the city has disappeared;
indeed, the Carolingian age does not know this word as a term of
administrative law. The manors are the centres of civilization,
and they also provide the support needed by monasteries.
Manorial lords run the political system, and the greatest manorial
lord is the king himself, a rural illiterate in his way of life. The
king has his castles in the country, and he has no capital; he is a
monarch who travels about for sustenance, even more than do
the monarchs of today. He travels so much because he goes from
castle to castle to consume what has been stored up there for
himself.

In a word, then: the civilization of Western Europe has become
completely rural. The economic development of the ancient world
has come full circle.

Looking back at the Carolingian Age, one might imagine the
cultural achievements of Antiquity to have been entirely lost. Just
as the commerce and the marble pomp of the ancient cities have
disappeared, so too all the intellectual achievements and values of
these cities seem sunk in darkness: their art, their literature, their

science, and their sophisticated commercial law. Meanwhile, on the manors of the *possessores* and seigneurs the songs of the troubadours were not yet heard.

It is impossible not to feel a certain sadness as we view this spectacle – a great civilization apparently approaches the heights of perfection, then loses its economic basis and crumbles away. Yet what did this mighty process really involve?

What we have described was a transformation of the fundamental structures of society, a transformation which was necessary and which must be interpreted as a tremendous process of recovery. For the great masses of unfree people regained family life and private property, and they themselves were elevated from the status of 'speaking tools' to the plane of humanity. Ascendant Christianity now surrounded their family life with firm moral guarantees; indeed even the laws of the Later Empire for the protection of peasants' rights acknowledged the unity of the unfree family to an unprecedented degree.

It is of course also true that at the same time a part of the free population sank to a position equivalent to serfdom, and the civilized aristocracy of Antiquity was barbarized. Furthermore, the natural economy now became dominant. It had always formed the infrastructure of ancient civilization, but the expansion of unfree labour had for a time relegated it to a subordinate position, although the more slave property caused differentiation in wealth the more it in turn grew. However, when the political centre of the Empire shifted from the coastal areas to the interior, and slave supplies dried up, then the natural economy imposed its pressures towards feudalism on the once commercialized superstructure of the ancient world.

Thus the framework of ancient civilization weakened and then collapsed, and the intellectual life of Western Europe sank into a long darkness. Yet its fall was like that of Antaeus, who drew new strength from Mother Earth each time he returned to it. Certainly, if one of the classic authors could have awoken from a manuscript in a monastery and looked out at the world of Carolingian times, he would have found it strange indeed. An odour of dung from the courtyard would have assailed his nostrils.

But of course no Greek or Roman authors appeared. They slept in hibernation, as did all civilization, in an economic world that had once again become rural in character. Nor were the classics remembered when the troubadours and tournaments of feudal society appeared. It was only when the mediaeval city developed out of free division of labour and commercial exchange, when the transition to a natural economy made possible the development of burgher freedoms, and when the bonds imposed by outer and inner feudal authorities were cast off, that – like Antaeus – the classical giants regained a new power, and the cultural heritage of Antiquity revived in the light of modern bourgeois civilization.

Index of Names

Index of Authorities